THE ECONOMICS OF WAR IN ANCIENT GREECE

Also available from Bloomsbury

Authority and History: Ancient Models, Modern Questions edited by Juliana Bastos Marques and Federico Santangelo

Demagogues, Power, and Friendship in Classical Athens: Leaders as Friends in Aristophanes, Euripides, and Xenophon by Robert Holschuh Simmons

Military Departures, Homecomings and Death in Classical Athens: Hoplite Transitions by Owen Rees

Money, Warfare and Power in the Ancient World: Studies in Honour of Matthew Freeman Trundle edited by Jeremy Armstrong, Arthur J. Pomeroy and David Rosenbloom

THE ECONOMICS OF WAR IN ANCIENT GREECE

Edited by Roel Konijnendijk and Manu Dal Borgo

BLOOMSBURY ACADEMIC
LONDON • NEW YORK • OXFORD • NEW DELHI • SYDNEY

BLOOMSBURY ACADEMIC
Bloomsbury Publishing Plc
50 Bedford Square, London, WC1B 3DP, UK
1385 Broadway, New York, NY 10018, USA
29 Earlsfort Terrace, Dublin 2, Ireland

BLOOMSBURY, BLOOMSBURY ACADEMIC and the Diana logo are trademarks of Bloomsbury Publishing Plc

First published in Great Britain 2025

Cover image: Boeotian Shield (obverse), 379–338 BC. Greek, minted at Thebes (Boiotia). Silver; diameter: 2 cm (13/16 in.)
© CCMA/BOT/Alamy Stock Photo

A catalogue record for this book is available from the British Library.

Library of Congress Control Number: 2024942336

ISBN: HB: 978-1-3504-7178-8
ePDF: 978-1-3504-7179-5
eBook: 978-1-3504-7180-1

Typeset by RefineCatch Ltd, Bungay, Suffolk

To find out more about our authors and books, visit www.bloomsbury.com and sign up for our newsletters.

To

Chris Carey, Hans van Wees

and

Matthew Trundle

CONTENTS

ILLUSTRATIONS

Matrices

Figures

Tables

CONTRIBUTORS

Manu Dal Borgo is a Lecturer in Game Theory and Computer Science at University College London (UCL). Prior to this, they held a British Academy postdoctoral fellowship at the University of Cambridge, focusing on ancient economic history and network theory. Dal Borgo earned their doctorate in Philology and Economics from UCL. Their scholarly contributions include articles on the ancient Greek economy and strategic behaviour in Thucydidean narrative. They are also the author of the forthcoming monograph titled *Thucydides, Father of Game Theory*. In addition to their academic work, Dal Borgo is a Senior Data Scientist for an economics consultancy in London.

John Davies FBA was Rathbone Professor of Ancient History and Classical Archaeology at the University of Liverpool and is now Emeritus. His publications have mostly concerned the social and economic history of Classical Greece and the wider Mediterranean from the Archaic to the Hellenistic period, with especial emphasis on Athens and more recently on Greek historiography, but his time is now particularly devoted to joint-editing a volume on the history of business in the pre-Islamic Mediterranean and its hinterlands.

Annabel Florence is Lecturer in Classics & Ancient History at the University of Queensland, AUS. She is a Classicist and Social Historian of the Classical Greek world whose research interests include the public finance, warfare, foreign policy, democracy and economy of Classical Athens, Greek and Latin epigraphy, and the material culture of the ancient world. Her current research focuses on the public financing of Athenian military campaigns during the fourth century BC.

Edward M. Harris is Emeritus Professor of Ancient History at Durham University. He is the author of *Aeschines and Athenian Politics* (1995), *Democracy and the Rule of Law in Classical Athens* (2010) and *The Rule of Law in Action in Democratic Athens* (2013). He has co-edited with David Lewis and Mark Woolmer, *The Ancient Greek Economy: Markets, Households and City-States* (2015), with Edmund Stewart and David Lewis, *Skilled Labour and Professionalism in Ancient Greece and Rome* (2020) and with Sylvian Fachard, *The Destruction of Cities in the Ancient Greek World* (2021).

Roel Konijnendijk is Darby Fellow in Ancient History at Lincoln College, University of Oxford. He works on Classical Greek warfare, its place in society and culture, and its scholarly tradition. He is the author of *Classical Greek Tactics: A Cultural History* (2018) and *Between Miltiades and Moltke: Early German Studies in Greek Military History* (2023). He is also co-editor of *Brill's Companion to Greek Land Warfare Beyond the Phalanx* (2021).

Jennifer Martinez Morales is Honorary Fellow at the University of Liverpool. She is also a History Department faculty member at Holderness School, NH, and the school's Archivist. Her main research areas include ancient warfare, classical archaeology and, more recently, the rationalization of atrocities. Recent publications include women in siege warfare and their wartime contributions off the battlefield.

Stephen O'Connor is Professor of History at California State University, Fullerton. His research focuses on the economics and logistics of Classical Greek warfare. He has published articles on the diet and pay of Greek sailors and soldiers and, especially, the markets they participated in while on campaign. He is currently preparing a monograph entitled *Feeding the Rulers of the Sea: Grain Markets and Athenian Naval Power in the 5th Century* BC.

Robin Osborne is Emeritus Professor of Ancient History at the University of Cambridge and a Fellow of King's College, Cambridge, and of the British Academy. His work ranges across archaic and Classical Greek history, Greek archaeology and the history of Greek art. His most recent publications are *The Transformation of Athens: Painted Pottery and the Creation of Classical Greece* (2018) and *Athens and Attica: Oxford History of the Archaic Greek World* Vol. 2 (2023).

Mark Pyzyk is Data Analyst and Facilitator at the Getty Research Institute, Los Angeles, CA. His work focuses on Greek history, numismatics and the digital humanities. Recent publications include 'Digitizing the Coin Finds of Ukraine' (*Ukrainian Numismatic Annual*, 7:2023) and 'A hoard of Pontic coins from the time of Mithridates VI Eupator from the chora of Olbia' (*Revista Arheologica* 19.1:2023).

Matthew Trundle († 2019) was Professor of Classics and Ancient History at the University of Auckland, New Zealand. He wrote *Greek Mercenaries: From the Late Archaic Period to Alexander* (2004), edited *New Perspectives on Ancient Warfare* (2010), *Beyond the Gates of Fire: New Perspectives on the Battle of Thermopylae* (2013) and *Brill's Companion to Sieges in the Ancient Mediterranean* (2019), and published numerous articles and book chapters on aspects of Greek warfare, the Greek economy, and the links between the two.

Christopher J. Tuplin is Gladstone Professor of Greek at the University of Liverpool. He is author of *Failings of Empire* (1993), *Achaemenid Studies* (1997) and nearly 150 research essays on Greek, Roman and Achaemenid topics, editor of *Pontus and the Outside World* (2004), *Xenophon and his World* (2004) and *Persian Responses: Cultural Interaction (with) in the Achaemenid Empire* (2007), co-editor of *Science and Mathematics in Ancient Greek Culture* (2002), *Xenophon: Ethical Principles and Historical Enquiry* (2012) and *Aršāma and his World: The Bodleian Letters in Context* (2020), and a series-editor of *Xenophon Studies*.

INTRODUCTION

Manu Dal Borgo and Roel Konijnendijk

In recent decades, the study of both the ancient Greek economy and Greek warfare has been transformed by ground-breaking new studies. Old paradigms are questioned and superseded; new evidence is produced in great quantities and new questions are constantly being asked. However, surprisingly few publications have brought these two vibrant fields together: only a handful of studies focus on the effects that economic and military developments could have on each other.[1] Our volume is intended to foster, and inspire, more of them. Its chapters explore the variety of historical connections between warfare and the economy across the Greek states and their most important neighbours. They show how much experts in the study of both fields may learn from each other. This book is meant for economic historians of antiquity who recognize the military sphere as a test case and pool of evidence, and for military historians who are conscious of the importance of economic factors in shaping the realities of war.

Ancient thinkers already knew that war is inextricably tied to economics. The course of wars is determined by the abundance or scarcity of capital and labour, levels of supply and demand for certain goods and services, monetary and fiscal policy, and human capital. Conflict is triggered, shaped and then transformed by these economic factors, as the evolution of war transforms these factors in turn. But the long-term trend toward specialization in modern scholarship means that this interconnected whole is rarely studied in tandem. Economics and warfare are distinct subfields in the present-day study of ancient history; they may overlap substantially, but ancient historians cannot presuppose either have knowledge of each other. Historians working in one of these subfields rarely have the opportunity or incentive to stay up to date on developments in the other. Now that both subfields are changing rapidly, it is unfortunately likely that key ideas and perspectives that ought to inform the work of other scholars will be missed.

The transformation of both fields is indeed momentous. In the case of warfare, revitalized by new methodologies and new interpretations, the study of ancient military history has shaken its old image as an antiquarian and irrelevant pursuit. Much of this shift is thanks to an increased emphasis on the socio-political context of violent conflict. Works like J. Rich and G. Shipley's *War and Society in the Greek World* (1993) or V. D. Hanson's *The Other Greeks* (1995) were prominent initiators of the trend in English-language scholarship; works like H. van Wees' *Greek Warfare: Myths and Realities* (2004) and J. E. Lendon's *Soldiers and Ghosts* (2005) have codified views of ancient warfare that shift the focus from technical details to a socially and culturally embedded interpretation of the subject. Around the same time, E. L. Wheeler highlighted the glut of publications under the broad heading of 'war and society',[2] which continues to the present.[3] Standard works like the two-volume *Cambridge History of Greek and Roman Warfare* (2007) now duly feature chapters on 'War and Society' and 'Warfare and the State'.

Yet, in the case of economics, the *Cambridge History* has no chapter on 'War and the Economy', and such chapters are not always found in other surveys either. Even M. Sears' introductory *Understanding Greek Warfare* (2019) and S. Manning's encyclopaedic work *Armed Forces in the Teispid-Achaemenid Empire* (2021) contain few mentions of economics.[4] Groundbreaking studies into the logistics, pay and public costing of ancient armies, like M. Trundle's *Greek Mercenaries* (2004), J. W. I. Lee's *A Greek Army on the March* (2007) and H. van Wees' *Ships and Silver, Taxes and Tribute* (2013), as well as collections like F. Burrer and H. Müller's *Kriegskosten und Kriegsfinanzierung in der Antike* (2008) and D. M. Pritchard's *Athenian Democracy at War* (2019), have indicated how much Greek military historians may gain from a greater integration of economic factors. The chapters of this volume detail the specific impact of changes in warfare on the economy and the impact of changes in the economy on the fighting of wars. Economics should have a major role in discussions of ancient warfare, especially now that our understanding of the nature of the ancient economy is changing in fundamental ways in a mature post-Finley world.

The study of the ancient economy has, in fact, undergone a radical methodological transformation which has allowed scholars to talk about the economy as a distinct field from politics or society. The subfield has reached a provocative new stage which began with the publication of works like the *Cambridge Economic History of the Greco-Roman World* (2007), C. Flament's *Une économie monétarisée* (2007) and A. Bresson's two-volume *L'économie de la Grèce des cités* (2007–8), which was later translated into English (2016). These generalist overviews of the ancient economy were followed by specific analyses like J. Ober's *The Rise and Fall of Classical Greece* (2015) and C. Taylor's *Poverty, Wealth and Well-Being* (2017). Methods drawn from new institutional economics and other contemporary theories like game theory, development economics and the economics of conflict are gaining momentum. Our interpretation of economic behaviour in antiquity is changing with an increasing number of scholars borrowing concepts from contemporary economics to interpret ancient history. Therefore, our view of the way economic conditions shaped ancient warfare should change with it. The time is ripe for further integration of these two fields.

To do our part to make such integration happen, we organized the 'War in the Ancient World: The Economic Perspective' international conference at University College London in April 2016. With this conference, we sought to accommodate and consolidate the growing research on the role of economics in ancient warfare. The three-day programme was quickly filled with a selection of veteran scholars and early-career researchers, and the conference proved an immensely stimulating and fruitful experience. Encouraged by the response and result, we decided that elaborated versions of the papers we found most illuminating should be collected and presented as studies on a coherent theme. For the sake of that same coherence, we decided to consolidate the range of papers focused particularly on Greece and its neighbours.

Within that theme – the latest research on the interface between the economic and military history of the ancient Greek world, broadly defined – our chapters cover as wide a range of topics as we have been able to bring together. The chapters below explore how armed conflict affected markets and economic opportunities, and how ancient rulers and states struggled to mobilize resources and tackle fiscal challenges to wage war more efficiently. They show how the study of economic factors – too often neglected in works on ancient warfare – allows a deeper understanding of military cultures and events. They demonstrate how matters of war can be an invaluable source of information on the way ancient economies worked and developed.

The first two chapters examine aspects of the economic basis of Greek warfare and the ways it has been factored into ancient and modern accounts. Roel Konijnendijk and Robin Osborne explore the latter, suggesting some reasons why economics have never been very well integrated into the modern study of Greek warfare. They show that such integration may be more fruitful now than ever, in light of the recent paradigm shift in the way scholars characterize the Classical Greek economy. Turning to ancient narratives, Stephen O'Connor tackles the long-neglected question of the food supply of Classical Greek armies operating abroad. His chapter establishes more broadly by what means and procedures Greek communities might provide supplies through markets.

Four chapters follow with a focus on financing war. First, Manu Dal Borgo takes a broad view, examining the place of warfare in the economies of Archaic and Classical Greece through epic and historical case studies. Applying game theory and models from the emerging discipline called the 'economics of conflict', this chapter illuminates the dynamics of long-term economic strategies in a network of states. Next, Christopher Tuplin surveys the available evidence for the fiscal policy and military expenses of the Achaemenid Persian empire, revealing not just the many fragments of financial information that survive, but also the complex relationship of Persian power to Persian wealth. Annabel Florence then offers a treatment of the finances of Athens during the Corinthian War in unprecedented depth, reconstructing the expenses incurred by the war and arguing that Athens pursued a careful and informed policy to meet those expenses. Mark Pyzyk subsequently turns to what may be termed ancient fiscal theory; his chapter examines the interaction between the needs of war and the development of state finance in Classical Greece, with a particular focus on the emergence of expertise in matters of state revenue as a growing necessity for Greek states facing rapidly escalating military expenses.

Next, a pair of chapters looks at personnel and its costs. Matthew Trundle's addresses the labour market for Athenian naval crews, arguing that the Athenian fleet gradually came to rely more on foreign and mercenary rowers and less on citizens. In the process, it builds a further challenge to the old notion that naval service is bound up with democratic ideology. Jennifer Martinez Morales explores the role of women in armies of the same period from an economic perspective, arguing that their presence may have put a strain on provisions and military flexibility, but often came with enough tangible and intangible benefits to complicate the question of their supposed impact on military efficiency.

A final set of chapters examines the economic consequences of war, and especially of defeat. Edward Harris challenges the paradigm that war was one of the main sources –

and inhibitors – of economic growth in the ancient world, showing on the one hand that the profits derived from war tended to be limited, and on the other hand that cities, markets and trade networks tended to recover quickly from wartime damage. John Davies delves into the specific theme of reparations; he ventures into Roman Republican history and deploys comparative evidence from eras in which the phenomenon has been studied in more detail to make up for the lack of attention ancient historians have paid to it, and to work out how we might quantify the effect of these post-war punitive impositions on the economies of ancient states.

This volume has been a long time in the making. We owe a debt of gratitude to our contributors for their patience and continued faith in the project. None deserves our thanks more than Matthew Trundle, who heroically worked with us to complete his chapter from his hospital bed, never for a moment abandoning his kindness and cheer. It is our great regret that he could not see the result of his labours in print. This volume is dedicated to his memory.

Notes

1. For example, Van Wees 2013a; Scheidel 2017; O'Halloran 2019; Kallet and Kroll 2020.
2. Wheeler 2007, xi; 2011, 58–64.
3. See, for example, edited volumes like O'Brien and Boatright 2013; Brice 2020.
4. An exception is Heckel et al. 2021, which contains multiple chapters touching on economic aspects of warfare.

CHAPTER 1

WAR AND WEALTHY HELLAS: ECONOMICS AND THE HISTORIOGRAPHY OF GREEK WARFARE

Roel Konijnendijk and Robin Osborne

The Classical Greeks may not have shared the modern concept of economics, but they were well aware of the links between resources, money and war. Questions of the economics of warfare are frequently raised in our sources. By the fifth century there was a well-developed understanding that state finances made war possible: 'war is not a matter of arms', Thucydides made Archidamos say, 'but of money, which makes arms useful' (1.83.2). Mardonios' argument that Xerxes should attack the Greeks begins with a rhetorical question (Hdt. 7.9α.1): 'What do we have to fear? What gathered masses, what store of wealth?' Plato (*Rep.* 422a) applied the same reasoning to the other side when he made his character ask, 'How will our *polis* be able to wage war, given that it has no money?' Xenophon observed that Athens always filled its treasury in peacetime only to empty it in war (*Poroi* 5.12). He also pointed out repeatedly that armies could not function if they were not adequately supplied, stressing that markets and provisions should be a primary concern of the general (*Mem.* 3.1.6; *Kyr.* 1.6.14). Answering the call for expert knowledge in such matters, Aineias the Tactician devoted a treatise to the financial aspects of military preparation.[1]

Modern experts on Greek warfare have not always been so interested in war's economics. The attention they paid to the material conditions of Greek military practice has waxed and waned with changing interpretations of the scope of the subject and the origins of its peculiar features. Although Pritchett did not entirely neglect the economic side of warfare, thoroughgoing analysis of the economics of Greek warfare had to wait for the work of David Pritchard.[2] Nor have economic historians been much more interested in the finance and economics of war, despite the early engagement with the topic of August Böckh.[3]

But if the economics of warfare has been under-studied in modern scholarship, the economic context of warfare has been scrutinized even less, and it is that context in which we are interested in this paper. That is, our question is, what do we have to believe about the nature of the economy of ancient Greece to make the way in which Greeks fought wars make sense? The traditional picture of a ritualized and primitive form of warfare was once tied intimately to contemporary views on the Greek economy, but the late twentieth century saw an almost complete detachment of these spheres and the emergence of a model that explained the Greek way of war in purely moral and socio-political terms. This model, in turn, has become the target of criticism in recent decades, but without issues of economics figuring in the discussion. In this chapter, we offer a brief outline of some of these trends in the historiography; we also present some suggestions of what could be gained from greater communication between historians of warfare and the economy at a pivotal time in the development of scholarship on both subjects.

1. A brief historiography

Any reader of the first histories of Greek warfare will find that they had little to say on the economic conditions in which it existed.[4] The authors of these early academic handbooks did not write integrated military histories with due consideration for the material and financial background of military practice.[5] They wrote military history in a narrower sense, focusing primarily on technology and tactics; they linked emerging systems of organization and conscription to different socio-political institutions, but rarely considered them as the product of economic factors. They did have some interest in logistics, and they might remark on the absence of quartermasters and supply trains in Greek warfare and the limits it imposed on the length of campaigns,[6] or think about the social class of infantry soldiers and point in the direction of vaguely defined demographic and economic growth as the reason behind the spread of hoplite armour.[7] But these were brief remarks that received no elaboration. The examination of the economic conditions and institutions of Greek life was left to other scholars. It might inspire thought about some of the external realities of warfare,[8] but it was not taken up as a constituent element of military history. Broadly speaking, the early works took the foundations of Greek warfare for granted. Their authors were much more interested in tracing technological improvements, describing tactical forms and reconstructing land battles. Even naval and siege warfare were treated as strictly technical matters of secondary importance. The fruit of their labours was a picture of a way of war that was, for reasons that remained unexplored, limited to the ritualized encounter of hoplites in open ground. Even the end of this way of war came in the form of a purely tactical revolution set in motion by the military genius of Epameinondas and Philip.

Because of this technical focus, even though the first sixty years of serious scholarship on Greek warfare was written almost exclusively in German, the first effort to place the phenomenon in its economic context was made in a separate scholarly tradition by the Oxford scholar George Grundy. Apparently unprompted by any academic predecessor, but perhaps inspired by his experience of the contemporary army, the Boer Wars and the Greek countryside in his own day, he came to believe that the explanation for many peculiarities of Greek history lay in 'the economic conditions under which men lived' – that one had to consider Greeks 'moving in a material rather than an ideal world' to understand their culture and behaviour.[9] His companion to Thucydides shows that he took this perspective very seriously. The section on 'The Economic Background of Greek History' occupies more than 150 pages. He apologized in advance for the fact that he would be repeating many of the same points in the much shorter section on warfare.[10]

In Grundy's view, the simplistic ritual of hoplite battle described by his predecessors was the result of raw existential necessities. As he put it, 'there was hardly a single state in Greece except Thessaly which would not in the fifth century have been seriously embarrassed, or, in some cases, brought to the verge of starvation by the destruction of its annual crops'. Only a hoplite phalanx had the capacity to prevent such destruction by forming a physical obstacle to the invader, and '*that* fact is the factor which determined the composition of Greek armies in the fifth century'.[11] The priorities of a subsistence economy ruled out any alternative approaches until imperial naval power and resources allowed the Athenians to treat their farmland as expendable. States without such means had no choice: 'the fruit and cereal crops had to be saved at all costs, either by facing the enemy in the field or by prompt submission to his demands'.[12] Seen in this light, the material conditions of Greek life explained both the supposedly ritual form of hoplite warfare and its apparent lack of development over time.

Despite his ground-breaking approach, Grundy's theory ultimately validated the focus of earlier German scholars on battles and technology: after all, there could be little else of significance in Greek military history. As a result, while Grundy believed that material conditions were the key to understanding the Greeks, his theory inadvertently shut the door to further study of the economic context of warfare. From Grundy onward, surveys of Greek land warfare were built on the consensus that the material conditions of Greek life formed an essential factor in only one sense, and were otherwise largely irrelevant.[13] If all Greek military practice could be summed up as 'a walking tour ending in a combat',[14] there was little need for further investigation into its interactions with resources, markets, or state finance. As Finley put it, the ritual of hoplite battle meant that 'there was no occasion for deep strategy, little need for financial preparations, nothing that one could seriously call logistics'.[15]

When Yvon Garlan first suggested an adjustment to this consensus in 1974, it was to *diminish* the role of material conditions in shaping the Greek way of war even further. Garlan stressed how impressed he was with Grundy's theory, 'que je tiens pour fondamentalement juste'.[16] Even so, he believed some nuance was necessary. The evidence showed that communities did not immediately starve if they did not fight or submit. Therefore, crop devastation could not have been an existential threat. Instead, ravaging was to be understood as an attack on the social order and political will of the affected community, whose self-sufficiency was being undermined and whose inequalities of wealth were being laid bare. Fear of civic unrest and revolution prompted the defenders to march out and fight the invader. In other words, economic pressure only worked indirectly; the real factors that pushed Greeks to resolve conflicts in their peculiar way were socio-political.[17]

Several scholars took up this point in the years that followed. In his response to Garlan's work, Edouard Will criticized the notion that ravaging was intended to exploit social divisions, but not in order to reinstate the primacy of economic factors; in his view, the pressure exerted by agricultural devastation was religious and psychological. Communities simply could not bear to leave their land and sanctuaries at the mercy of the enemy.[18] Josiah Ober, despite his claim that a successful ravaging expedition could deal 'a shattering blow to the economic and financial stability of Athens', embraced Will's argument that the *real* damage was moral and religious, at least until the intensification of economic warfare in the fourth century.[19] The same belief lay at the foundation of Victor Hanson's doctoral thesis, which was to replace Grundy's theory as the consensus view on the relationship between warfare and its economic context. Hanson used his practical knowledge of farming to show that ravaging could not have done lasting damage to Greek crops and farming infrastructure. A single harvest may have been lost, but food production would soon have recovered, and starvation was unlikely to result. If Greek communities nevertheless tended to march out to defend their farmland, it was not out of fear of food shortages, but out of the moral indignation felt by the class of independent farmers at the violation of their property.[20] The invader counted on this indignation to bring these farmers to battle. Since the cycle of provocation and response was wholly predictable, Hanson concluded that 'ravaging was not so much economic warfare as part of the extensive rituals of Classical hoplite warfare'.[21] When Lin Foxhall took up the subject a decade later, it was only to reinforce the conclusion that 'attacks on crops would almost never actually threaten a city's food supply' and were therefore best understood as assaults on citizen unity with the intent of bringing the defenders out to fight.[22] The conclusion shared between these scholars was that ravaging could be no more than an indirect means to an end. By threatening the stability and dignity of the defending community, invaders could bring about a formulaic hoplite battle of the sort described so well by Prussian scholars a century earlier.

Writing in 1993, Foxhall noted that in the wake of Hanson's work, warfare and agriculture 'have become divorced and have gone off in separate directions'.[23] There were no further studies of the effect they had on each other. But Garlan and Will's reframing of Grundy's theory, transmitted to Anglophone scholarship by Hanson and Ober, seems to have given a deeper meaning to Foxhall's words. By detaching the supposed imperative to open battle from the looming threat of crop devastation and famine, the new consensus removed the need to frame Archaic and fifth-century Greek land warfare in economic terms. Unlike the warfare of other ancient peoples, Will argued, 'la guerre grecque traditionelle n'est pas affaire des moyens matériels (...) mais affrontement de communautés humaines, plus précisément de communautés civiques'.[24] In France, scholars continued to explore other aspects of economics and ancient warfare regardless; 'war and economy' remained a fixture of their general accounts of the subject.[25] But Anglophone ancient historians were persuaded to shift their focus entirely to the role and importance of cultural and political values in the peculiar Greek way of war. The authors cited in the previous paragraph had demonstrated that 'it is hard to find *economic* reasons for the Greeks to have thought' that they must march out to fight for their farmland; it stood to reason that 'the intense territorialism of Greek warfare was more symbolic than material'.[26] It was the symbolic, then, and not the material, that ought to take centre stage.

This is not to say that Anglo-American academics lost sight of the importance of wealth, finance and material needs. There are plenty of statements, for example, to the effect that poverty prevented the *poleis* from pursuing more intensive forms of military action. But these tended to shrink down to little more than offhand remarks. In some of the most influential works of modern scholarship in English, economic factors are downplayed in favour of moral ones: the Greeks did things the way they did because they thought it was *right*, not because of the economic conditions in which they lived.[27] Overseas campaigns and protracted sieges were rare, not just because of their cost, but because they were 'frowned upon' by the high-minded Greeks, who considered them 'unpalatable' and 'distasteful'.[28] The deployment of massed forces of heavy cavalry and professional light infantry was perhaps partially prevented by a lack of money, but also because there was 'no place' for them in hoplite warfare; they could not simply overrule 'over 200 years of hoplite supremacy'; these troops were 'ungriechisch' and to rely on them was ideologically impossible.[29] Hanson moved the centre of gravity from the farms to the farmers, arguing that the 'yeomen' of Archaic and Early Classical Greece formed a cohesive socio-economic class whose shared 'agrarian' ideology compelled them to monopolize warfare and restrict it in ways that suited them.[30] His view tied in with the older notion that Greek communities refused to raise standing forces, either out of a suspicion of the potential ambitions of a professional officer class or out of a moral refusal to pay taxes.[31] Their way of war, in short, was intended 'to maintain the long-term practical workability of the hoplite-dominated socio-military system'.[32] Any move towards a more professional army or a greater commitment of resources to war represented an attack on the identity and status of male citizens. To the sociologist Garry Runciman, this explanation was both necessary and sufficient: 'it is difficult to see how the persistence of hoplite warfare can be accounted for without reference to the distinctive set of norms, values, and beliefs which both encouraged and legitimated it.'[33] Satisfied with ideology and culture as the origin of Greek military practice, general works produced in this theoretical frame often had little or nothing to say about its economic background.[34]

The first challenges to the new consensus did not come from economic historians.[35] Instead, scholars like Peter Krentz cast doubt on the perceived singularity and single-mindedness of Greek warfare. The sources offered plenty of examples, even from early wars, in which Greek communities did not choose to fight ritualized battles between regular formations in the open.[36] To stress this was also to raise questions about the economic background of Greek warfare. If there were common and accepted alternatives to hoplite battle, the notion of ravaging as a mere ritual provocation was no longer tenable, and the limits imposed on strategy and tactics by material and financial resources and markets were much more relevant than previously thought. As military historians began to question traditional interpretations of the Greek way of war, the economic context offered fertile ground for alternative explanations.

The specific question of the impact of ravaging was taken up first by Christophe Chandezon, who suggested a shift towards ever more economically devastating methods,[37] and then by James Thorne, who concluded that agricultural devastation always had been as serious a threat to Greeks' livelihood as Grundy first suggested.[38] This rejection of the consensus of the latter half of the twentieth century may not have settled the issue entirely,[39] but it is a clear signal of a wider trend. Old controversies are being reopened, and material conditions are often the source of new insight. Since the early 2000s, several monographs have looked at aspects of Greek military history through the lens of logistics, wages, markets and fiscal policy,[40] and some volumes on ancient warfare have included discussions of economics and war,[41] but, as with Louis Rawlings' lengthy chapter titled 'War and Economy' in his introductory handbook on the subject, these have often essentially repeated the traditional model.[42] Only the work of Hans van Wees, with his insistence upon the wealth of the hoplite, which draws a distinction between the hoplite and the small farmer, has significantly challenged the basis of earlier discussions.[43] As Van Wees' work clearly indicates, the nature of war and the nature of the economy are better understood when they are discussed together, not separately. It is time that recent arguments from historians of the Greek economy are integrated into the way we understand warfare.

2. A new perspective

If the world of the history of warfare has seen significant changes in our understanding, the world of economic history has seen no fewer changes. No small element of the persistence of the model of warfare offered by Grundy has been the continued prevalence of the claim that the Greek world was fundamentally one of subsistence economy. This is the view famously insisted upon by Finley in *The Ancient Economy* and has been displaced only over the past two decades.[44] In the world of the subsistence economy, the economics of war did not seem hard to understand. Land was not just the major economic asset, but the resource without access to which the great majority of the population could not survive; it was the site of most of the free labour, and the generator of most respectable wealth. No surprise, then, that in such a world land should also be fought over, and fought over primarily by soldiers who more or less exactly, depending on how one etymologized *zeugitai*, corresponded with the landowning farmers (whom Greek historians often bizarrely referred to as 'yeomen' or 'peasants', despite both terms belonging to quite different social situations). The point was that since farming was at the heart of individual and city wealth, agricultural land was the prized possession, the place where a city's pride could be most easily damaged, her economic interests compromised, and social relations within the citizen body most easily disrupted. Put another way, warfare in the Greek world saw those who had the strongest personal interest in the damage that war might do, band together to protect their interests.

The problems with this picture were largely brushed under the carpet. So the challenging fact that war rarely led actually to the annexation of territory – that is, that agricultural land was rarely itself the prize of war – was admitted but passed over. So was the fact that the one clear instance where an invasion leads to a local pressure group forming is the first invasion of the Peloponnesian War: the pressure group in question was made up of the Archarnians, whose economy is characterized by Aristophanes as based on commercial charcoal-burning, not agriculture, let alone subsistence agriculture.[45] What is more, as part of a larger reluctance to acknowledge the role of non-citizens in warfare that also encompasses the suppression of slave involvement, scholars also passed over the willingness of cities to substitute mercenaries, who had no stake at all in the land (but a significant stake in a city's on-going prosperity), for citizen hoplites.[46]

As we have noted above, warfare's symbolic role has been acknowledged, even stressed; Pierre Vidal-Naquet, in particular, encouraged appreciation of this aspect in his analysis of the aitiological myth for the coming-of-age festival celebrated by Athenian phratries, the Apatouria, with its exploration of hoplite warfare by reversal in its single symbolic conflict between Xanthos (Mr. Fair) and Melanthos (Mr. Dark) located at the border between Attica and Boiotia, not in the agricultural heartlands in which hoplite battles took place, and involving deception, and other scholars have developed this insight.[47] But through a structuralist reading that stressed the exploration of values through their inversion, this symbolic aspect made no difference to the model; indeed it simply reinforced it. Equally, the debate about the extent of rural devastation caused by hoplite warfare has been conducted without consideration of how it might affect the model either way, and the prominence in discussions of the economy played by arguments regarding the comparative evidence that subsistence farmers regularly keep at least a year's supplies in store has not undermined the claim that it was the importance of protecting the city's most vital economic asset that underpinned hoplite warfare.

Even more remarkably, the centrality of naval warfare has simply been dismissed from view. Why would anyone build and man extremely expensive ships, useless for anything except fighting, if they all essentially lived off their agricultural land? Marathon had shown that trying to mount a campaign of conquest with amphibious forces was always going to be problematic, even if one had significant numerical superiority, and in its very much smaller way the ability of Demosthenes' troops at Pylos to resist Spartan attack from the sea reinforced this lesson (Thuc. 4.9–13). And how could a subsistence economy ever afford to build such ships in the first place? In a serious subsistence economy, navies would be unnecessary, impossible and impractical, and yet scholars continued to assert that Classical Greece had such a subsistence economy while never challenging the evidence for naval warfare becoming at least as important as land warfare in Classical Greece – in strong contrast to the Hellenistic and Roman worlds. Explaining that Athens could afford a navy because of silver mines and tribute, as Finley did,[48] was never going to be sufficient, since one had to explain why Athens' possession of a navy worried anyone else, and why and how others manned navies to fight against the Athenians.

While not denying the existence of 'self-consumption' (i.e. eating what you grow), recent scholarship has challenged the old picture of the subsistence economy; as Bresson has pointed out, 'if Greek farms had really operated on the basis of self-consumption, they would have been unaffected by economic fluctuations'.[49] The economy of Greek cities is increasingly being described in terms very different from those describing a subsistence economy. So Bresson: 'Thanks to the flexibility of its institutional system, in the Classical and Hellenistic periods Greece established an exceptionally dynamic and prosperous economy that exploited to the maximum the possibilities offered by its environment. By keeping its internal and external markets separate, it managed to maintain for several centuries an equilibrium that began to break down only in the late Hellenistic period.'[50] Bresson goes on: '"economic actors" retained control over most of what they produced, and this encouraged them to improve its quality and increase its quantity. Initiative, inventiveness, the quest for the most profitable institutional solution, and at the same time the limitless exploitation of slaves: such were the driving forces in the economy of the Greek city-states.'[51]

That this impinges heavily on our sense of the place of the countryside has been seen by Josiah Ober, to whom we owe the 'Wealthy Hellas' of our title. 'Highly specialized, relatively urbanized, trade-intensive Classical Greece certainly remained much more oriented around agricultural production than is the case in any developed-world modern economy. But what I take to be the ordinary connotations of the phrase "massively and unalterably rural" will need to be adjusted if we hope even to describe, much more to explain, the efflorescence of classical Hellas.'[52]

While we may dispute the details of Bresson's and Ober's pictures, there can be no real doubt that, with due recognition of the varying and sometimes high levels of 'self-consumption' across different sectors of society in different *poleis*, the view that the Classical Greek economy as a whole can be described as a subsistence economy must be dead. Indeed, it is not simply the Classical Greek economy that should no longer be thought of as a subsistence economy. The same is true of the economy of the Archaic period. The distribution of Athenian pottery shows that already by the end of the seventh century, there was an intense network of exchange across the Mediterranean, enabling goods to be targeted to particular markets.[53] It is arguable indeed that the whole phenomenon of Greek settlement abroad, once its nature is properly understood, was enabled only by pre-existing networks of exchange. It is, for instance, very hard to account for the phenomenon that is the Greek settlement on Pithekousai in other circumstances.[54] We are dealing with 'wealthy Hellas' as far back as we are dealing with the warrior type we identify as 'hoplite'. But can this new understanding of 'wealthy Hellas' make better sense of the nature of Greek warfare than the old model of the subsistence economy did? It makes sense to start with the features that the old explanation could not cope with.

The model of 'wealthy Hellas' certainly helps explain the prominence of naval warfare.[55] Wealthy Hellas not only can afford to build and man triremes, it needs to do so in order to protect its sea routes, since it is 'trade-intensive'. We can go back to believing that Athens did indeed, as Herodotus (7.144) relates, create her navy in order to fight Aigina; in a world where Athens and Aigina (and Corinth) were alternative hubs and in a world where maritime trade was essential to the economic life of the city, investing in a fleet that could protect shipping servicing one's own ports, and keep away hostile warships that might seek to deflect shipping elsewhere, became a high priority. No city that prided itself on its independence, bar the exceptional case and very different economy of Sparta (cf. Thuc. 1.120.2), could afford to be incapable of preventing others controlling the sea. It was vital to minimize disruption to merchant shipping from pirates, or from maverick cities or their rulers. Permanently patrolling great swathes of sea was impractical; what was required was to be able to make speedy intervention whenever any local dispute threatened to interrupt the route from place of production to the place of market or from the place of market to the place of consumption. The trireme was the designer-weapon for these conditions – a designer-weapon which itself indicates a world where manpower is available and can be spared from directly productive activities, and where the high cost of intervention indicates its importance.[56]

As to the problems with fitting the traditional view to the realities of warfare on land, the model of wealthy Hellas again reveals its advantages. The issue of just how devastating invasion was, and could be, really does become secondary when we are dealing with a world in which the minority, rather than the majority, are reliant on self-consumption and live at 'subsistence level', and in which the minority, rather than the majority, are innocent of the market. Whereas one can imagine the Acharnians as a group foreseeing their stores of charcoal almost literally going up in smoke, in an ancient equivalent of setting fire to oil wells, no rural community dependent upon arable agriculture would face such an existential threat – individuals might indeed suffer, but the impact across a community would be variegated according to the particular economic strategy each household was pursuing and the particular resources they commanded.

Similarly, the infrequency with which cities actually annexed territory becomes more comprehensible once additional hectares of agricultural land were not the only way to feed a growing population. Having borders that were uncontested, in a way that newly conquered territory was unlikely to be, and that could be relatively easily defended, was much more important than acquiring some more agricultural land – particularly if that additional land would not easily contribute to the overall local economic strategy. Even when the *polis* in question was not a democracy, the effects of incorporating other communities into an existing citizen body were unlikely to cause no political instability and disturbance, and all political disturbance was economically threatening.

But how does the model of wealthy Hellas fit with the practice of warfare on land? Let us start with the urban centre. Why did cities fortify themselves? We have become used to explaining in terms of military technology how the nature of the fortifications built at different periods changes – from the fifth- and early fourth-century priority given to very long circuits, hard to circumvallate, to the priority from the middle of the fourth century on given to short, strong walls that could withstand the attacks of the new artillery and siege-engines.[57] But why did cities have fortifications at all? If destroying isolated farmhouses and crops is not easy, nor is destroying urban buildings. In the absence of explosives, tanks and bulldozers, fire is the only option, and mud-brick structures burn no better in urban than in rural environments. Disastrous urban fires are not a major feature of the ancient Mediterranean.

If total destruction of the urban fabric is an unlikely consequence of being attacked in war – and one that fortification would not prevent once a city was defeated (think Corinth in 146) – plundering was even more of a problem than it was in a rural setting. Walls made plundering difficult. But they served another purpose too: preventing the splintering of the urban residents. Aineias the Tactician's deep-seated fears of treachery within the city give us a strong sense of the depth of distrust within many civic communities. Walls did not just keep the enemy out, they kept urban residents in, kept them together, and enabled them to keep each other under surveillance. Politically, keeping citizens together was crucial; in economic terms, what mattered was keeping slaves together. Cities had great concentrations of unfree labourers, particularly in certain sorts of workshops, and the infiltration of such slave bodies by the enemy represented a very significant threat: slaves were in a position to undermine their masters, or indeed to destroy them. Slaves kept in place only by fear of their masters had that fear removed when an enemy offered them a quick getaway. As Sara Forsdyke has emphasized, the truth of this is very clearly demonstrated in a number of episodes of Chian history where actual or possible slave revolt determines Chios' fate in war.[58]

Slaves were one form in which wealth was concentrated primarily in towns (Athens' silver mines should be considered a subterranean town from that point of view), but towns were also places where other types of wealth were concentrated – in the treasures in urban sanctuaries, for instance, but also in the workshops, storehouses and houses of individuals (as becomes clear from Lysias 12.10–11 where, even if one is sceptical that there was quite as much money in the chest seized from his house by the Thirty as Lysias claims, his claim needed to be perfectly plausible to the jury), and indeed in such communal facilities as the mint. The greater the degree of specialization, the more the chances that a targeted enemy raid could seriously reduce a city's supply in a potential crucial area, or lead to local impoverishment. Again, we might take the 700 shields taken from Lysias' family's shield factory as our example (Lysias 12.19).

Concentrating attacks on the town can be understood in any circumstances – the town was the political centre, and identity was bound up in the urban form. It is concentrating *defence* upon the town that takes more explanation. As behaviour in the Persian wars demonstrates, when the Athenians were not alone in simply abandoning their city, political existence in the end depended on the *politai*, not the physical urban form (that this truism goes back to Alkaios and is repeated by the Athenian Nikias in Thucydides shows how independent it was of the particular form the town took). What depended on the urban form, and required the people to be clustered in a particular place, was economic existence. For most Greek communities, the city was the sole significant cluster throughout their history. Where Athens was different was that its very large territory, and its the distance from the sea, meant that there were other significant clusters. And here the Athenian world changed between 480 and 432: in 480, the infrastructure that made Athens the essential economic centre was only incipient; the Peiraieus was only then developing, and so too the networks of roads rutted across Attica that linked deme communities to Athens were only then becoming the major arteries that tied the demes into a single economic network, rather than leaving them as hubs of independent networks.[59] By 432, Athens could survive without the demes better than the demes could survive without Athens. Hence the futility of the Spartan invasion and even of the occupation of Deceleia.

And what about war in the countryside? If the crucial economic resources to defend are the infrastructure of markets, the craft workshops found predominantly in the town, the institutions of lending and borrowing, and the wealth stored up, one way or another, in urban areas, why did the hoplite battle continue to be so important? One answer is that it continued to be important precisely because the unprocessed crops in the fields are *not* at the centre of the economy – even in parts of Greece where agriculture was undoubtedly important, it was processed crops (wine and bread for human nutrition, oil for nutrition but also for lighting and cosmetic uses) that were where wealth resided. As is clear from the comments passed by Thucydides and the *Hellenika Oxyrhynchia* about the effects of the Spartan occupation of Dekeleia, the wealth of the countryside was very considerable, and a significant amount of that wealth was in processed agricultural products. Invaders could not only live off the land, but stood to carry off a great deal of wealth with relative ease. And while the city as a whole might, in the short term at least, be relatively unaffected by these losses, individual families would be devastated. If the aim of war was not to destroy a city but to make it change its mind on a particular issue, or to adopt a different attitude, then being able to fight it out in an arena where the psychological effects of enemy presence were enormous but little or no lasting damage was done was ideal. Farmers – and particularly the relatively prosperous landowners who qualified as *zeugitai* – were dispensable in a way that urban residents were not, and in any case could relatively easily make their escape. And the countryside too, or at least the rather small part of it that any invading army would ever occupy, was, at least temporarily, dispensable; however much any particular part of it gets trampled, the economic interests of the city as a whole are not threatened. The larger the agricultural plains involved, the harder it was for an army even to seem to make an impression – in Boiotia or Thessaly even large armies manifestly occupied only a tiny part of the agricultural land.

Another way of making this point is to turn to basic game theory. For Greek city-states war is a game that they play with each other, in which each party tries to guess the move of the other party. Changing one's military habits is rational only if the opponent also changes their military habits, if the change comes without serious risk, or if the change enables one better to do what one is already doing. So siege-warfare techniques change in part because experimentation has a very low cost – failing to take a city that one besieges is not like losing a battle – and potentially a very high reward. Developing light-armed troops or cavalry happens only in the context of using light-armed troops or cavalry against hoplites – none of the cities of southern Greece was prepared to change the whole way they fought to make battles entirely cavalry battles or entirely battles among light troops. It only took one or two major powers to have their own reasons for retaining hoplite armies (and Sparta, with its peculiar economy, had strong reasons to do so), to ensure that the other cities which engaged with that city retained their hoplite armies too.

The ends of war are always political, and in that sense the expectation that priorities in warfare mirror economic priorities is unreasonable. By contrast, the ways wars are fought are what are always going to be governed by economics. It is no small support for the 'wealthy Hellas' reconstructed by Ober and Bresson that it makes much better sense of the ways Greeks fought wars.

Notes

1. He refers the reader to this treatise – now lost – in his *Poliorcetics* 14.2.
2. Pritchett 1971–91; Pritchard 2012; 2015a; 2015b; 2019, 138–79; and cf. Kallet 1993, Gabrielsen 1994 and O'Halloran 2019 for naval warfare.
3. Böckh 1842, Book 2, chapters 19–24; and see Florence, this volume. Bresson 2016, by contrast, has no index entry for 'war'.
4. We refer primarily to Rüstow and Köchly 1852; Droysen 1889; Bauer 1893; Delbrück 1900; and Kromayer's survey in Kromayer and Veith 1928. On this scholarly tradition, see Konijnendijk 2023.
5. The sole exception is the work of Hugo Liers (1895), which contains a section on military finance (129–36) as well as a lengthy discussion of supply and logistics (200–27). Though cited and praised by Delbrück (1900, 3), the book has fallen into obscurity.
6. Rüstow and Köchly 1852, 103.
7. Kromayer and Veith 1928, 22.
8. Delbrück (1900, x–xi) cites the demographic studies of Julius Beloch as the bedrock of his controversial views on the size of ancient armies. Beloch himself devoted an unusual amount of space to economic history in his general history of Archaic and Classical Greece (1893, chapters 8 and 12; the unique focus is noted by Meyer 1901, 294).
9. Grundy 1911, v – unprompted because, unlike Delbrück, he did not cite any earlier scholars as inspiration.
10. Grundy 1911, 240.
11. Grundy 1911, 247 (emphasis in the original).
12. Grundy 1911, 248.
13. See for example Gomme 1945, 10–12; Adcock 1957, 6–7; Anderson 1970, 2.
14. Adcock 1957, 82.
15. Finley 1963, 61; similarly, Feyel 1999, 210.
16. Garlan 1974, 41–2: 'which I hold to be fundamentally correct.'
17. Garlan 1974, 42–4; 1989, 103–7.
18. Will 1975, 302–4. He did, however, reaffirm Garlan's points that Greek states depended on their own farmland for sustenance (302, 314) and that their offensive and defensive siege techniques were limited by a lack of financial resources (307–8, 311).
19. Ober 1985, 30–5.
20. Hanson 1983, 147–9; 1995, 254, 280–9. The point was first made by Garlan (1974, 20); it was wholly accepted by Harvey 1986. Cf. also Osborne 1987, 138–45.
21. This line occurs only in the revised second edition of the work: Hanson 1998, 180.
22. Foxhall 1993, 141–3; similarly, Chandezon 1999, 206–7.
23. Foxhall 1993, 134.
24. Will 1975, 299: 'traditional Greek warfare is not a matter of material means, but a confrontation between human communities, more precisely between civic communities.'
25. Note, for example, the proceedings of a colloquium held in Paris on ancient armies and fiscal policy (1977); Brun 1983; Ducrey 1985; Garlan 1989; Brun and Bielman 1999; Prost 1999.
26. Dawson 1996, 50–1 (emphasis in the original).

27. Garlan (1989, 33–4) lamented the parallel tendency of narrative histories to dismiss economic causes of war in favour of purely political ones.
28. Hanson 1995, 251, 259; Mitchell 1996, 97, 101.
29. Lazenby 1989, 71–7; Spence 1993, 229; Hanson 1998, 7–8; Toalster 2011, 9: 'un-Greek.'
30. Hanson 1991; 1995.
31. Gomme 1950, 14–15; Anderson 1970, 5; Hanson 1983, 74; 1995, 301–16.
32. Ober 1994, 17; see also Connor 1988; Hanson 1995, 238, 251, 255; Mitchell 1996, 101; Kagan and Viggiano 2013, 10–11.
33. Runciman 1998, 733.
34. For instance, Sage 1996 covers only provisions and pay in a handful of pages (55–60). Other examples include Warry 1980; Mitchell 1996; Hanson 1999; Sabin, Van Wees and Whitby 2007. For a rare French work in this mould, which follows Garlan entirely, see Debidour 2002.
35. Arguably, there was an early response to the demise of economic factors in Rich and Shipley 1993, which contains multiple chapters with an economic focus. Shipley stresses the importance of economics in warfare in his introduction (1993, 14–18). However, as noted above, Foxhall's contribution reinforced the status quo; Millett's chapter was more concerned with the internal dynamics of democracy than its title would suggest.
36. Krentz 1997; 2000; 2002.
37. Chandezon 1999.
38. Thorne 2001; his argument was anticipated by Bryant 1990, 511 n.7, and later reconfirmed for the Hellenistic period by Chaniotis 2005a, 121–9.
39. Note the questions raised in response by Wheeler 2007, xli–xlii.
40. For example Trundle 2004; Lee 2007; Bettalli 2013; Pritchard 2019; O'Halloran 2019.
41. For example Fagan and Trundle 2010; Armstrong 2016.
42. Rawlings 2007, 144–76; Campbell and Tritle 2013 contains chapters on mercenaries and provisions only.
43. Van Wees 2004, 235–9; 2013b.
44. Finley 1973. For an attempt to understand the Greek world, including the world of war, on this assumption can be seen in Osborne 1987 (for reservations about which see Osborne 1996a). The most significant contributions to rewriting the history of the ancient economy have been Scheidel, Morris and Saller 2007 and Bresson 2016.
45. On Acharnai, see Kellogg 2013.
46. On mercenaries, Péré-Noguès 2000; Trundle 2004; Luraghi 2006; Bettali 2013; Gômez-Castro 2018; Sänger and Scheuble-Reiter 2022; on slaves see Hunt 1998.
47. Vidal-Naquet 1968 (reprinted in Vidal-Naquet 1986); see also Connor 1988.
48. Finley 1973, 131–9.
49. Bresson 2016, 202–3.
50. Bresson 2016, 221–2.
51. Bresson 2016, 222.
52. Ober 2015a, 102. For 'Wealthy Hellas', see also Ober 2011a.
53. Osborne 1996b.
54. On the nature of early Greek settlement, see Osborne 1998; 2009, 98–123. For the consequences for Pithekousai, see in particular Osborne 2004, ch.3.

55. cf. Van Wees 2013a; O'Halloran 2019.

56. We have been helped in our understanding of the importance of the trireme as a designer weapon by discussion with Callum Farnden.

57. So Osborne 1987, 153–64; cf. Frederiksen 2011; Hülden 2020.

58. Forsdyke 2012, 86–7, citing Thuc. 8. 39–40, Polyainos 3.9.23, Poseidonios, *FGrHist* 87 F 38, and Nic. Dam., *FrGrHist* 90 F 1, 33 and the contrary case at Plut. *Mor*. 245b.

59. cf. Osborne 2023.

CHAPTER 2

ARMIES, NAVIES AND ECONOMIES IN THE CLASSICAL GREEK WORLD: THE RECEPTION OF MILITARY FORCES BY *POLEIS*

Stephen O'Connor

1. Introduction

In 1962, Moses Finley, in a typically trenchant and brilliant article, exposed the theoretical poverty of then current approaches to Classical Greek economic history and suggested several 'lines of investigation' that could wrench the subject out of the conceptual crisis it was undergoing.[1] The fifth line of investigation suggested by Finley reads as follows:

> The army and war deserve a full study in themselves, as feeders into the trade network by seizing mines, by providing slaves and other booty, and as consumers of arms and food.

This chapter will not be the full study recommended by Finley but will instead focus on one specific part of the research project he outlined:[2] Greek military forces as consumers of food in the markets of *poleis*. To be more precise, I will be discussing the markets provided to Classical Greek armies and navies by city-states as part of the set of customary diplomatic protocols governing the reception of foreign military forces in the Greek world.

The practice of *poleis* granting permission to military forces marching or sailing through their territories to purchase provisions for their onward march or voyage by admitting them into their marketplaces or by establishing temporary markets for them outside their city walls is a well-known one: it is described (sometimes more, sometimes less accurately) in most modern treatments of Classical Greek military logistics and general treatments of Greek warfare.[3] But these descriptions have always been cursory, never amounting to much more than a brief summary of the convention accompanied (or not, as the case may be) by some illustrative examples. The same applies to the few discussions of the subject in work on international relations in the Greek world.[4] Even more strikingly, given Finley's urgent call for action on the subject half a century ago, the provision of markets by Greek cities to foreign military forces is hardly mentioned at all in scholarship on the economies of Classical Greece.[5]

This chapter, in contrast, represents the first attempt to integrate the provision of these markets into the wider economic history of the Classical Greek world. The decision whether or not to receive a foreign army or navy – and so, whether or not to provide a market as part of the reception of that army or navy – was always at the discretion of the *polis* whose territory the military force was passing through.[6] This chapter will focus first on the factors that motivated Greek city-states to grant markets – or not – to the military forces marching or sailing through their territory. It will begin by employing a detailed analysis of Xenophon's narrative in the *Anabasis* of the experiences of the Ten Thousand during their march along the coasts of the southern Black Sea and the Propontis to show that the capacity of *poleis* in these regions to provide sufficient amounts of food for sale to passing armies was never a determining factor in their decisions whether or not to receive, and thus provide markets for, passing military forces. Next, an examination of some other ancient military narratives will build on this first section to demonstrate that Greek armies and navies on the move could rely on the provision of markets by cities for their food supply (almost) everywhere in the Greek world. A fourth section will then analyse the economic structures within the Greek world that enabled Greek military forces and their generals to presume that the *poleis* on their way to and from theatres of operations would usually have the capability to provide markets sufficient to provision them for their onward journeys. In doing this work, this chapter will show that investigation of a seemingly minor diplomatic protocol can help us to gain important insights into the performance of grain markets throughout the Classical Greek Mediterranean and Black Sea.

2. The reception of the Ten Thousand by *poleis* on the southern Black Sea coast and the Propontis

Xenophon's narrative of the march of the Cyreans along the southern coast of the Black Sea mentions provisioning only in exceptional circumstances. This is not unusual: markets provided by *poleis* to military forces and other logistical realia are mentioned only rarely in ancient accounts of Greek warfare. But the Ten Thousand were an extraordinary military force: as a stateless entity, their relations with the *poleis* whose territory they passed through were often and unusually controversial. Disputes over the reception of the Ten Thousand and their behaviour towards the Greek communities they encountered as they marched (or sailed) along the Pontic coast (and Xenophon's wish to defend himself and the men against charges of uncivilized and violent behaviour in their dealings with Greek cities)[7] mean that the diplomatic convention of the granting of markets by Greek *poleis* to passing armies is sometimes explicitly discussed in speeches of Xenophon's found in this part of the *Anabasis*. One speech in particular, given by Xenophon during the army's halt at the *polis* of Cotyora, tells us much about the expected, customary procedures of the protocol of reception by Greek cities of military forces as well as the factors motivating cities to provide markets (or not) to such forces.

In describing the halt at Cotyora, Xenophon narrates that the men stayed outside the city for forty-five days, and that they initially got their provisions there by foraging, partly from Paphlagonian territory and partly from the estates of the Cotyorites, since the Cotyorites did not provide them with a market (οὐ γὰρ παρεῖχον ἀγοράν, Xen. *An.*

5.5.6).[8] The foraging from Cotyorite territory brought Sinopean ambassadors to the city, to complain to the mercenaries on behalf of the Cotyorites, who were their colonists, that it was not proper for the mercenaries to house their sick inside the city and take whatever they needed from the Cotyorites without the latter's permission. Hecatonymus, who spoke on behalf of the Sinopeans, emphasized the common Greek ethnicity of the Ten Thousand and the Sinopeans, and thus the Sinopeans' shock at the (allegedly) hostile actions of the mercenaries, before concluding with the threat that, if the soldiers continued to do these things, the Sinopeans would make an alliance with Corylas, ruler of Paphlagonia, against the mercenaries (Xen. *An.* 5.5.7–12).

Xenophon responded to Hecatonymus with a speech generalizing about the obligations and relationships the Cyreans expected to exist between communities and passing armies – and especially, in light of the Cotyorites' refusal to provide a market, the expectation the Cyreans had that a friendly community would provide a market to them. Xenophon first used the example of Trapezus to illustrate the point that when the mercenaries on their march had received a market from a community, they had regarded this community as friendly. After the men had reached again the world of Greek city-states, they had obtained their provisions by purchase in Trapezus, for the Trapezuntians had provided a market (καὶ νῦν ἐπεὶ εἰς τὰς Ἑλληνίδας πόλεις ἤλθομεν, ἐν Τραπεζοῦντι μέν, παρεῖχον γὰρ ἡμῖν ἀγοράν, ὠνούμενοι εἴχομεν τὰ ἐπιτήδεια, Xen. *An.* 5.5.14) and other signs of friendship to them; in return, the army had behaved as friends towards the Trapezuntians (Xen. *An.* 5.5.14–15). Importantly, the only consideration Xenophon mentions here influencing the Trapezuntians' provision of a market to the Cyreans is their friendliness towards the Ten Thousand.

Xenophon then continued in order to contrast the actions of the Ten Thousand when a community did *not* receive them as friends and provide a market to them: if this happened, the mercenaries foraged or plundered the community's territory for their supplies, but only because they had not been provided a market in which they could acquire provisions (*An.* 5.5.16–18). This explained the taking of provisions from the Cotyorites' lands: Κοτυωρίτας δέ, οὓς ὑμετέρους φατὲ εἶναι, εἴ τι αὐτῶν εἰλήφαμεν, αὐτοὶ αἴτιοί εἰσιν· οὐ γὰρ ὡς φίλοι προσεφέροντο ἡμῖν, ἀλλὰ κλείσαντες τὰς πύλας οὔτε εἴσω ἐδέχοντο οὔτε ἔξω ἀγορὰν ἔπεμπον ('As for the Cotyorites, whom you claim as yours, if we have taken anything that belonged to them, they are themselves to blame; for they did not behave toward us as friends, but did not receive us within their city walls and would neither admit us within or send a market without': Xen. *An.* 5.5.19).[9]

So, just as the only consideration Xenophon mentions in his speech to the Sinopean ambassadors as influencing the Trapezuntians' provision of a market to the Cyreans was their attitude (friendliness) towards the army,[10] the capacity of the Cotyorites to provide a market is also taken for granted, and their failure to provide one for the army is explained by their attitude towards the mercenaries. And this ability of the Cotyorites to provide a market is confirmed by events after Xenophon's speech, which persuaded the Sinopean ambassadors to treat the men as friends and to direct the Cotyorites to behave similarly (*An.* 5.5.24): friendly relations were established between the mercenaries and the Cotyorites by the latter's granting of *xenia* to the army (*An.* 5.5.25)[11] – and the Cotyorites, accordingly, provided a market to the men (*An.* 6.1.1).

The point that the mercenaries presumed that Greek *poleis* had the capability to receive and provide *agorai* to the army is confirmed in a second speech Xenophon made to the men at Cotyora (the day after his speech to the Sinopeans). The speech's subject was the growing lawlessness in the army, as demonstrated by the murder of some Colchian ambassadors to the army and the stoning of *agoranomoi* chosen by the men. Xenophon ended the speech by asking a series of rhetorical questions to bring out the potential dangers for the army if they continued their outrageous behaviour: What gods would they be able to pray to? What praise could they expect to receive from other Greek communities? What traders would provide a market to accompany the army as it marched? And significantly: πόλις δὲ φιλία τίς ἡμᾶς δέξεται, ἥτις ἂν ὁρᾷ τοσαύτην ἀνομίαν ἐν ἡμῖν; ('And what friendly city will receive us when it sees so great lawlessness amongst us?' *An.* 5.7.33).[12] In a speech to 8,500 men, drawn from all over the Greek world (and beyond),[13] then, Xenophon could presume it as a given that the assembled soldiers would share his belief that the decision of a Greek city to receive the army and provide a market to it was not based on its capability to do so, but on whether or not that city wished to be friendly to the passing military force in question.

In other rhetorical settings, too, as when Cleander, the Spartan harmost of Byzantium, and Xenophon addressed the army at Calpe Harbour, the reception of the Ten Thousand by *poleis* is presented as being determined by friendliness or hostility; in this case, of the Spartans, who (in Xenophon's formulation) ruled all the Greeks at this time, towards the army.[14] But, importantly, when we move from rhetoric to the mercenaries' actual planning and practice, the capacity of the markets provided by the inhabitants of the Greek cities on the southern coast of the Black Sea, as well as the northern coast of the Bosporus and the Propontis, to meet the army's demand for food is also taken for granted. As there was no ruler or state agent providing pay or access to supplies to the Cyreans as they travelled along these coasts, the subject of pay is continually raised in the army's strategic deliberations, and always with the idea that the men would be able to use this pay to buy sufficient provisions for the next part of their journey in the markets given to them by *poleis*. Thus, the day after friendship between the mercenaries and the Cotyorites was established, Timasion the Dardanian and Thorax the Boeotian began a scheme to extort money from the Heracleots and the Sinopeans in order that the Greeks would have provisions for the voyage from Cotyora (Xen. *An.* 5.6.19). At Heraclea, Lycon the Achaean told the army to demand 3,000 Cyzicene staters from the Heracleots so that the men might be able to purchase supplies for their onward journey (Xen. *An.* 6.2.4–5). When the Cyreans reached Byzantium, the Spartan *nauarchos*, Anaxibius, refused to give them the pay he had promised them and demanded that they leave the city – at which the soldiers became angry because they had no money with which to procure provisions for the journey onwards (Xen. *An.* 7.1.7). At Perinthus, Xenophon advised the men in assembly that, since they had no money to buy provisions in a market and the Perinthians would not let them take provisions without paying for them, they ought to proceed to some villages from which the Aristarchus the Spartan and the Perinthians would allow them to seize provisions and then decide their course of action, with provisions in hand (*An.* 7.3.5). In all of these schemes, disputes and deliberations, then, all of the actors concerned simply presumed in the respective *poleis* the existence of a market in which the mercenaries would be able (if they had the money) to buy sufficient provisions for an onward march or voyage.

Markets provided by *poleis*, however, are mentioned in Xenophon's description of the army's journey along the Pontic and Propontic coasts only when they impinge on the army's strategic deliberations (as when the men were unable to provision in markets at Trapezus (*An.* 5.1.6) and Perinthus (*An.* 7.3.13, 7.6.24)) or help to explain the army's strategic situation (Cotyora: *An.* 6.1.1); or when something extraordinary happens in connection with them, as when Xenophon mentions the market at Heraclea only at the point when the Heracleots decided to move it within their city walls as part of their defensive response to the demands and threats of the mercenaries (*An.* 6.2.8). Otherwise, when the mercenaries were in the territory of a friendly Greek city on the southern Black Sea coast, the Bosporus or the Propontis, a market provided by that city is simply presumed by Xenophon as the men's default mode of provisioning, and foraging for provisions a measure only turned to when a *polis* fails to provide a market or when the men do not have the means to use the market.[15]

3. The reception of military forces by *poleis* throughout the Greek world

In Xenophon's other historical works, too, markets provided by *poleis* to passing armies – and the capacity of those *polis* markets to meet the provisioning demands of passing military forces – are presumed in descriptions of the movements of armies in mainland Greece and Anatolia (and so are mentioned only when something unusual occurs in connection with them). Thus, Xenophon narrates in the *Hellenica* and the *Agesilaos* that Agesilaos, in order to trick Tissaphernes into believing that he would be attacking Caria in 396, sent instructions to all the cities on the route from Ephesus to Caria that they should make a market available for his army.[16] Xenophon also mentions in the *Hellenica* that Agesilaos used the same trick again in 377 so that his army could make its way safely into Boeotia. This time he planned to advance by the route to Erythrae, so made it look to the Thebans as if he were going to Thespiae by sending messengers ahead to that *polis* to demand that a market be prepared for his men there.[17] These two stratagems show again that Greek armies could rely on *agorai* provided by friendly *poleis* to supply themselves during their marches to theatres of operations: both ruses could have worked only if all the actors involved believed that the markets in both Thespiae and the *poleis* on the route from Ephesus to Caria had the capability to feed Agesilaos' armies.

The presumption that Greek armies operating throughout the Classical Greek world could supply themselves through markets provided by friendly *poleis* is found outside Xenophon, too, most importantly in pseudo-Xenophon's *Constitution of the Athenians*. Pseudo-Xenophon contrasts in this work the strategic flexibility of naval forces with those of land forces (*Ath. Pol.* 2.4–5). In contrast to naval campaigns, journeys on land were slow and it was not possible for armies to bring many days' provisions with them.[18] Because of this, he states, it was necessary 'for an army traveling on foot either to pass through friendly territory or fight and conquer [in hostile territory]' (καὶ τὸν μὲν πεζῇ ἰόντα δεῖ διὰ φιλίας ἰέναι ἢ νικᾶν μαχόμενον, *Ath. Pol.* 2.5). That is, this late fifth-century author thought that it was necessary for armies travelling overland to supply themselves by either passing through the territory of friendly *poleis* and purchasing in the markets provided to them,[19] or to gain tactical superiority (and the ability to forage) in hostile territory by military success. In this generalizing passage on the practices of contemporary Greek land warfare,[20] then, pseudo-Xenophon simply took it granted that armies could rely for their provisioning in friendly territory on markets provided by cities.

Contemporary authors also presumed that navies on the move to and from theatres of operations could supply themselves through markets provided by friendly cities. So Xenophon, for example, mentions in the *Hellenica*, in his account of the events leading up to the battle of Aegospotamoi, the buying of provisions from an allied *polis* only because it was the fact that the Athenian crews had had to walk some distance from their triremes to purchase provisions in Sestos that had led directly to their lack of readiness for the battle (and thus their subsequent and decisive defeat).[21] But this casual and incidental mention of the convention of the provision of an *agora* by a friendly *polis* to a fleet halting in its territory – without any prior mention or explication of this convention here or previously in the *Hellenica* – is significant in that it demonstrates that Xenophon (and his audience) took it for granted that *agorai* were the usual means of provisioning for naval detachments and fleets on the move to and between theatres of operations in the Aegean and surrounding waters. When the provisioning of transient navies by other Greek cities within the Aegean bursts exceptionally to the surface of other ancient narratives, it, too, always takes place through the institution of the *agora*. Thus, in Thucydides, the provision of an *agora* by the Eretrians to the crews of thirty-six Athenian triremes (which had sailed to Euboea in order to guard the island from attack by the Peloponnesians (8.95.2)) is mentioned only because the location of this *agora* played an integral part in a ruse executed by the Eretrians which led to the destruction of the Athenian fleet (8.95.4–7). Similarly, the purchase of food and drink some time in the fourth century by sailors of an unknown fleet of triremes in the *agora* of Lampsacus is mentioned in the pseudo-Aristotelian *Oeconomica* because, exceptionally, the city authorities of Lampsacus used the approach of the fleet to benefit their treasury by raising prices in the *agora* in which the sailors bought their barley groats, wine, oil and other foods.[22]

Contemporaries presumed that markets provided by *poleis* could provision naval forces on the move along the coasts of southern Italy and Sicily, too. This can be seen clearly in a speech attributed to Hermocrates by Thucydides before the coming of the Athenians to the west in 415. Hermocrates proposes in the first part of this speech a series of measures for the medium term to prepare the Syracusans for the eventuality of an Athenian invading force arriving in Sicily.[23] In the first of these measures, Hermocrates advises the Syracusans to send envoys to the rest of the Greek cities in Sicily, and Italy, too, in order to make them allies, or else prevent their receiving the Athenians (ὅπως ...

μὴ δέχωνται Ἀθηναίους, Thuc. 6.34.1). Hermocrates presumes here that it will be the *poleis*' attitudes towards the Athenians that will determine whether they will receive them or not. In other words, he simply takes it for granted that the Sicilian and Italian *poleis* will all have the capability to provide markets to passing trireme fleets. The correctness of Hermocrates' reasoning and presumptions is seen later in Thucydides' narrative when the Athenians were provided markets in the friendly or neutral *poleis* of Rhegium (6.44.3), Messana (6.50.1) and Naxos (6.50.3), but not in unfriendly *poleis* such as Himera (6.62.2) or the *poleis* of the southern Italian coast (6.44.2).[24]

The leaders and members of Classical Greek land and naval forces, then, both presumed the existence of – and actually purchased their food supplies in – *agorai* in cities all across the Greek world, from as far west as Sicily to as far east as the southern Black Sea coast. This is not to say that there were not interstitial regions in the Greek world where there were no *poleis* and thus no markets in which military forces could purchase food for their onward marches or sails to war zones. But these regions were few and marginal. On the eastern fringes of Greek settlement, on the southern Black Sea coast, the Greek *poleis* whose markets the Cyreans provisioned themselves in were separated by extensive areas inhabited by indigenous, non-Greek peoples.[25] On the other side of the world, so to speak, the western Peloponnesian coast was notoriously desolate.[26] The south-eastern coast of Italy was another deserted region, as emerges from a later passage in Hermocrates' speech to the Syracusans about the coming Athenian expedition. In this later part of his speech, Hermocrates moves from medium-term to short-term measures to deter the Athenians from attacking Sicily.[27] Hermocrates first advises the Sicilian *poleis* to send a fleet to Tarentum and the Iapygian promontory in order to deter the Athenians from sailing across the Ionian Sea. If the Athenians sailed across without their supply ships to the area around Cape Iapygium, Hermocrates reasons, the Sicilians could retire to the friendly city of Tarentum, which would leave the Athenians at a loss for food in uninhabited regions, a situation which would only get worse if they remained there.

But it is important to note the other scenario Hermocrates envisioned for the Athenians: if they attempted to sail from Iapygium along the Italian coast, they would definitively abandon their supply ships 'and uncertain as to the attitude of the cities, whether they would receive them or not, they would become disheartened' (καὶ τὰ τῶν πόλεων οὐκ ἂν βέβαια ἔχοντες, εἰ ὑποδέξοιντο, ἀθυμοῖεν, Thuc. 6.34.5).[28] Immediately after sailing past the uninhabited regions around Cape Iapygium, then, the Athenians would be back in a Greek world where the attitudes of *poleis* would determine their reception – and thus where the capability of *polis* markets to provision them could be taken for granted, just as it was in Thucydides' account of the actual operations of the Athenian expedition to Sicily. The continuing taken-for-grantedness, so to speak, of the provision of markets by cities in the Greek west to passing military forces is also reinforced by the fact that the only other mention in our extant sources of the practice in this region occurs in exceptional circumstances when, in 391, Dionysius I deceitfully manufactured a diplomatic controversy over the provision of an *agora* to his force by either Rhegium (so Diodorus and Frontinus) or Himera (so Polyaenus) in order to declare war on the 'offending' *polis*.[29]

4. *Polis* markets: meeting the demand of passing armies and navies

So far, then, this discussion has established that the capacity of friendly, allied and neutral *poleis* to provide markets sufficient to feed armies and navies on the move to and from war zones could be presumed throughout (almost) the entire Classical Greek world. To put this another way, the leaders and members of Greek military forces (and the contemporary authors describing their movements) presumed that markets provided by *poleis* had the ability to cope with their demand for grain – that *polis* markets, in other words, were able to perform well enough to deal with the demand shocks that the arrival of these military forces caused.[30] This section of the chapter will investigate the factors that enabled this market performance.

The first step to answering this question is to ascertain the scale of Greek military forces' demand for food – the scale of the demand shocks that had to be absorbed by markets provided by *poleis*. First, sailors and soldiers needed to purchase provisions to subsist during their halts at friendly, allied and neutral *poleis*. The duration of these halts is not usually indicated by ancient authors, although Xenophon's *Anabasis* again proves an exception: there is a pattern throughout the Cyreans' march from Sardis to Cunaxa of a series of multi-day marches followed by a three-day halt;[31] in fact, this pattern recurs after Cunaxa and throughout the march to Trapezus, too.[32] But the distance between halts on the Cyreans' march to and from Cunaxa was much greater than for marches by armies operating in the Classical Greek world of micro-states closely packed together; the normal five to eight kilometres' distance between *poleis* could have been easily covered by Greek armies in a day's march.[33] Naval forces, too, would normally have taken no more than one or two days to sail between the island and coastal *poleis* on the way to their theatres of operations. Thus, the Cyreans needed prolonged halts to rest and refit, as well as reprovision, after lengthy marches of many days between settlements, on a campaign that brought them many months away from their homes; in contrast, typical Greek armies and navies, on much shorter marches or voyages during much briefer journeys to campaign theatres, would not have needed to refit or as much rest, and therefore would usually have needed a stay of no more than one, or at most two, days at *poleis* before resuming their journeys.[34]

Second, sailors and soldiers needed to purchase provisions for their onward marches or voyages. Although, as just discussed, the opportunity to purchase at other friendly *poleis* (or to forage in enemy territory, or to purchase from accompanying traders on overseas campaigns)[35] would usually be available within a day or two of leaving a friendly city, three days' provisions were the usual amount purchased by the members of Classical Greek military forces in the *agorai* of friendly *poleis* before they departed for the next part of their march or voyage:[36] the 'extra' days' provisions were probably meant to constitute a safe margin of supplies in case of unforeseen circumstances causing delays in the onward march or sail.

Third, sailors and soldiers needed sufficient money to purchase provisions in the markets established for them by cities for their halts at those cities and for their onward journeys. While the failure of their employers to (properly) pay military forces on campaign is a common theme in contemporary accounts of Greek warfare (at least from the late fifth and early fourth centuries onwards),[37] the men who made up Greek armies and navies generally would have had sufficient purchasing power to meet their demand for food in *polis*-provided markets on their way to campaign theatres. We can say this for four reasons. First, Classical Greek soldiers and sailors received pay before setting out on campaigns.[38] Second, rowers and especially members of the *hyperesiai* of triremes often received bonuses and advance payments as part of their recruitment for upcoming expeditions.[39] Third, it was standard for Greek mercenaries at the turn of the fifth century (at least) to receive recruitment bonuses paid out before campaigns.[40] Finally, it was common practice for Classical Greek sailors and soldiers to bring money in addition to their state pay to spend during campaigns, both long and short.[41]

As for their return journey from campaign theatres, given the usually brief nature of overland campaigns in the Greek world, soldiers usually would have had sufficient money still on hand on their way home to satisfy their demand for food in markets provided for them by *poleis*. Difficulties with payments are associated in our sources, rather, with extended overseas campaigns when navies could spend months or years away from home. These difficulties should not be exaggerated, however. First, even at the height of the mid-fourth century financial crisis at Athens, it was still the expectation and the practice that trireme crews received at least subsistence payments (*siteresion*) in order to buy food as they sailed to, around, and back from theatres of war.[42] Second, if circumstances were desperate, Greek military leaders were usually able to cook up ingenious schemes to obtain pay for their men.[43] Even on their voyages around or home from overseas war zones, then, Classical Greek sailors and soldiers usually had sufficient purchasing power to buy the provisions they needed during their halts at friendly *poleis* and for their onward voyages from those halts.

Classical Greek sailors and soldiers' demand for food in markets provided to them by *poleis* was, then, an effective one. To focus just on the demand for grain, the main component of Greek military diets,[44] the amounts of this food passing military forces had to acquire in the *agorai* of friendly *poleis* to meet their daily energy requirements were not usually great. The figures in Table 2.1 below are indicative of the scale. These figures can only be indicative, in the lack of complete certainty regarding some of the variables in the calculations, but they do serve to illustrate the orders of magnitude one should have in mind. The table shows that the amounts of grain bought in *agorai* provided by friendly Greek *poleis* to the exceptionally large Athenian forces of the Sicilian expedition and Aigospotamoi represented the yield of barley (or wheat) harvests of one to two hundred hectares,[45] or the cargoes of four or five trading ships;[46] while the demand of smaller, more commonly-sized naval or land forces could be satisfied by the grain harvest of a few dozen or so hectares (at most) or the cargo of one trading ship.

The demand of fifth- and fourth-century Greek armies and navies for grain from the friendly *poleis* they passed was limited not only in scale but also in frequency. As Christopher Tuplin has pointed out, Classical Greek armies 'did not commonly pass back and forth across the same areas often'.[62] The absence of regular marching routes in the Classical Greek world meant that there were no areas in the Greek world that experienced

Table 2.1 Estimates of grain-consumption requirements for selected military forces in markets of receiving *poleis*[47]

Military force	*Date*	*Size of force*	*Receiving* poleis	*Consumption requirements*[48]
Athenian expedition to Sicily	415	30,000–50,000[49]	Southern Italian and Sicilian cities	6,000–11,000 med. (100,000–170,000kg. w.e.)[50]
Detachment of Athenian expedition to Sicily	415	12,000	Naxos	2,500 med. (41,000kg. w.e.)[51]
36 Athenian triremes	411	7,200	Eretria	1,500 med. (25,000kg. w.e.)[52]
Athenian fleet before Aigospotamoi	405	30,600 or 36,000[53]	Sestos[54]	6,375 or 7,500 med. (105,000 or 123,000kg. w.e.)[55]
Agesilaos' force in Asia Minor	396	10,000–15,000[56]	Cities on way from Ephesus to Caria, Ephesus to Phyrgia[57]	2,000–3,000 med. (30,000–50,000kg. w.e.)[58]
Peloponnesian force led by Aristeus	432	3,600[59]	(Friendly or neutral) cities on land route from Peloponnese to Potidaea[60]	750 med. (12,000kg. w.e)[61]

the regular demand for food of passing armies, unlike in later pre-industrial European warfare.[63] Classical Greek armies were (almost) always invasion forces, too: that is, it was rare for two Greek armies to be operating against each other in areas outside their respective *polis* territories. This meant that the inhabitants of *poleis* receiving a Classical Greek army, having provided an *agora* to that passing army, did not normally have to be concerned by the prospect of having to provide an *agora* to another army within a short period of time thereafter (or of having their territory foraged or pillaged by enemy troops).[64]

Similar considerations hold for the operations of Classical Greek naval forces, too. These did not sail regularly back and forth through the same areas of the Aegean or the western Mediterranean; rather, naval campaigns, because of their expense, could only be undertaken by a handful of *poleis* and, even then, not very frequently.[65] Naval forces, too, typically sailed out to their target of operations, engaged in military (raiding, assault, and/or siege) and sometimes naval (a battle might be required to establish superiority at sea) actions solely at that target, and then sailed home again after some weeks, months, or perhaps years had elapsed.[66] Classical Greek naval forces were invasion forces, too, then, and it was accordingly rare for two Greek naval forces to be operating against each other in overseas operations. In addition, even navies that spent months or years away from home engaged in overseas operations passed most of that time in semi-permanent camps (rather than engaging in constant or even frequent naval movements around theatres of operations).[67] As a result, there was no regular demand from naval forces for food from cities anywhere in the Greek world. Usually, therefore, the demand of passing Greek armies and navies for grain and other foods in the *agorai* provided to them was not only not very onerous, but also very infrequent.

So, having established the parameters of the demand of military forces, we can return to the question of how *polis* markets were able to cope with this demand. Here, I will use the recent brief discussion by R. J. van der Spek, Bas van Leeuwen, and J. L. van Zanden[68] of the main determinants of market performance as the framework for my analysis. They identify the following factors as enabling markets to adapt to external (demand) shocks: trade, storage and technology; and, as underlying factors, geography and institutions.[69] The working of these factors to enable the capacity of markets to satisfy the provisioning requirements, limited in scale and frequency, of passing military forces will obviously have varied from *polis* to *polis* and from harvest to harvest. We can still employ them, however, to construct a basic model of how the structures of production, distribution and consumption of grain in the Aegean and 'mainland' Greece 'core'[70] of the Greek world enabled travelling military forces to satisfy their demand for food in markets provided by friendly, allied and neutral *poleis*.

To turn first to inland *poleis*, grain markets in inland areas in the Greek core were not closely integrated across space.[71] 'As far as the distribution of grain was concerned, inland regions in antiquity were truly isolated.'[72] This was primarily because of the high costs of the overland transport of grain common to all pre-industrial societies,[73] which meant that the 'long-distance transport over land of low value bulk goods such as grain was far too expensive for it to become a regular phenomenon'.[74] This point is best illustrated from an incident Xenophon reports concerning the Phliasians in 367. Having been cut off from their own land by the Argives and Sicyonians, the Phliasians obtained part of their provisions from Corinth by purchase (Xen. *Hell.* 7.2.17). But when the Athenian general Chares cleared the way from Corinth to Phlius and made it safe for transport (Xen. *Hell.* 7.2.22–3), the Corinthians officially ordered out all their wagons and pack-animals (κηρύξαντες τὰ ζεύγη καὶ τὰ ὑποζύγια πάντα), loaded them with grain, and sent them to Phlius (Xen. *Hell.* 7.2.23). The point is that, even in Corinth, with its *diolkos* and which served as an entrepôt for goods from the interior of the Peloponnese (Thuc. 1.120.2), the land transport (along a safe route)[75] of sufficient grain to fulfil the needs of a nearby *polis* required the official call-out of all available transport in the city. Land transport had to be requisitioned (even) at Corinth because the private 'organization of men and animals to trade and transport staples in bulk overland was simply not available'.[76] This organization was not available since, ordinarily, the costs of hauling grain by land to other *poleis* would make that grain more expensive than grain grown in those *poleis*; the usual absence of profit in overland trade in grain meant that private traders had no incentive to develop and continuously maintain the necessary marketing networks and commercial transport capabilities to collect, distribute and sell grain overland.[77] In the absence of market integration by trade, the inhabitants of inland *poleis* instead aimed, individually and collectively, at self-sufficiency in grain production.[78]

Geography and the absence or poor development of an institutional framework for trade worked together, too, to bring it about that many small and medium-sized maritime Classical Greek *poleis* within the Aegean core also were not regularly integrated into wider grain-trading networks. This comes out clearly from an analysis of the economic structures of the *poleis* found in Aeneas Tacticus. Aeneas, in his work on preparations for and defence against sieges, did not restrict his treatment of the subject to any particular part of the Greek world or to any particular type of *polis*; rather, he clearly meant his prescriptions to be applicable to as wide a range of *poleis* as possible.[79] Aeneas' 'Durchschnittpolis'[80] was a maritime one; it is assumed throughout his text that it possesses access to the sea.[81] But this generic *polis* did not usually depend on imports by sea for its grain. Instead, its own grain production was dominantly necessary for the survival of its citizens, as a passage detailing measures to be taken in case of the presence of enemy troops near the city demonstrates: 'At harvest-time, if the enemy are close at hand, it is probable that many of the citizens, in their anxiety to save their crops, will remain in the fields near the walls.'[82] Grain (and oil) imports to Aeneas' typical *polis* were only envisioned as emergency measures in case of a food shortage: 'When the city is running short of grain or oil or something else, incentives proportionate to the size of his cargo – and a crown in his honour – should be on offer to anyone who imports them; and the ship's *naukleros* should have beaching and re-launching facilities.'[83] Aeneas clearly thought, then, that the usual workings of the commercial networks of grain traders in his Greek world would not make up his average city's grain shortage. Rather and instead, large incentives would be necessary to draw traders in grain and other foods to his normal *polis* when, extraordinarily, it needed food from outside its territory.

Aeneas' typical coastal and insular cities were, then, 'poorly integrated' into broader grain-trading networks, and so 'had to rely on [their] output, the yearly harvest' to meet their grain consumption needs.[84] Because these cities were infrequently visited by grain traders, the latter did not usually have sound or recent information about their market conditions – and thus could not be confident of making a profit in them.[85] The usually relatively low levels of demand for foreign grain in these *poleis*, because of their reliance on their own agricultural production due to their not being a regular part of networks of grain distribution, further discouraged maritime traders from visiting them. Price levels for grain (and other goods) in the markets of smaller to medium-sized maritime *poleis* could collapse with the arrival of just one ship; traders could never be sure that they would not be anticipated by competitors before they arrived with their grain at these *poleis*.[86] Aeneas' *poleis*' poor market development and dependence on their own production thus produced a negative feedback loop that discouraged traders from investing the capital and time to sail to their *agorai*, and locked their inhabitants into the strategy of self-sufficiency in grain production.[87]

As Alain Bresson has recently discussed in his incisive and insightful discussion of grain markets in the Greek world,[88] there was one crucial additional factor that both shaped and further reinforced the strategies of self-sufficiency pursued by the inhabitants of inland *poleis* and smaller maritime *poleis* off main trading routes: the 'extreme variability and unpredictability' of the Mediterranean climatic regime.[89] As Bresson has noted, the vagaries of the Mediterranean climate led to random and massive variations year-on-year in the size of grain harvests and thus added to the risk and uncertainty of a strategy of relying on markets for achieving security in grain supply.[90] In response to these conditions of distribution and production, at the *polis* level the *astu* of each Classical Greek inland and smaller maritime micro-state, as centre of consumption and administrative control of distribution of grain and other goods produced in its territory, strictly controlled the export of grain from its territory.[91] At the individual level, (especially smaller) farmers living in poorly integrated *poleis* responded by overproducing grain and storing the surplus as security against the threat of crop failure in the following year.[92] The practice of overproduction and storage of surpluses to guard against crop failure is evidenced in the frequent references in Classical Greek sources to 'old' grain, the stored and still available grain from the last year's (or years') harvest, to be contrasted with the 'new' grain of the present year's harvest.[93] This production and storage strategy, too, is why Xenophon could note that the Spartan king Agesipolis learned in 385 that there was a lot of grain within the *astu* of Mantinea since the previous harvest had been good (Xen. *Hell.* 5.2.4): even in the case of abundant surpluses, grain did not leave the territories of inland *poleis* in the Classical Greek core, but stayed instead on the farms within these *poleis*.[94]

This strategy of storage enables us to explain why, as T. W. Gallant has already noted for inland *poleis*, the inhabitants of inland and smaller maritime *poleis* 'off the beaten track' usually had more than sufficient surpluses of grain to sell in *agorai* to meet the usually limited and unrepeated demands of passing military forces.[95] The question then becomes how did these surpluses make it from farms to *polis* markets? After all, although farmers in inland and smaller maritime *poleis* always needed to engage with their *polis* markets at some level in order to obtain items they could not produce themselves, it was, as Gallant has noted, precisely and paradoxically because they did not 'regularly mobilize their surplus production through the mechanism of the market'[96] that they had surpluses available for sale to passing military forces. This – that is, the small scale and irregularity of commercialization of the distribution of grain within these *poleis* – rather than the need for *polis* authorities to acquire grain[97] – is one reason why the leaders of Classical Greek armies alerted inland *poleis* along their lines of march in advance of their coming.[98] As J. K. Anderson put it, '[e]ven willing allies ... could not be expected to provide an adequate and convenient market for a large body of men without notice in advance, and a prudent commander would warn friends along his proposed line of march to have food ready.'[99]

Advance notice from armies gave inland *poleis* the chance to alert producers (i.e., farmers within their *poleis*) and traders to the opportunity to trade with passing armies. Although Classical Greek armies could be found fighting throughout the year, the great majority of campaigns took place just before or around harvest time, or in the late summer/early autumn.[100] In the first case, the call to producers to sell grain to a passing army would have come shortly before or right around the time of harvest. Farmers, then, would have received notification when the success of the new harvest would have been certain and its size predictable.[101] Consequently, they could mobilize their 'old' grain from the previous harvest(s) – grain that in the case of a successful harvest would have been usually wasted or underused as feed for animals or poor-quality seed grain[102] – to sell to passing soldiers, safe in the knowledge that they would be able to replenish their stores from the upcoming harvest. The certainty of the arrival of an approaching army and its demand for grain therefore gave farmers an exceptional opportunity to profit from surpluses that normally would have been 'lost' to trade.[103] In the case of armies arriving at a *polis* in the late summer or early autumn, farmers would also have been able to sell their 'old' grain, while using the overproduction of the current harvest to store sufficient reserves for the following year. In this case, too, then, the demand of the passing soldiers would have provided farmers with an extraordinary, and more or less risk-free, opportunity to profit from production that usually never moved from their farms.[104] The opportunity for profit presented by passing military forces will also have incentivized traders within *poleis* to join farmers in mobilizing grain and other food products to the markets provided by their *poleis* to soldiers.[105]

The practice of navies alerting *poleis* in advance to provide a market is not specifically attested, but it may have occurred, too;[106] in any case, news of the preparation and coming of fleets of triremes will usually have reached cities before those triremes.[107] Although triremes could sail in winter, naval activity in winter was an exception in Classical Greek warfare; trireme fleets, especially major expeditions, tried to operate as much as possible in summer.[108] Since navies would have arrived at *poleis* at or, more usually, after harvest time, then, the same incentives found in inland *poleis* – the extraordinary, risk-free opportunity for producers to monetize and profit from stored surpluses – would also have been at work in most small and medium-sized maritime *poleis* to mobilize grain for sale to passing armies and navies. In addition, there might have been other factors that contributed to these maritime cities' capacity to feed larger naval forces halting in their territories. News of the preparations and targets of major overseas expeditions, which could take several weeks to launch,[109] would have reached maritime traders, too. This recent and accurate news could have motivated traders to sail to cities about to receive or just having received a major fleet since these cities, which usually did not offer the hopes of profit because of their small size and lack of integration into information networks, now did.[110] Finally, in the case of the impending arrival of really big fleets, if *polis* authorities thought that there might not be enough grain in their cities or in the cargoes of outside traders to absorb the demand shock of these fleets, as inhabitants of maritime cities they always had the options of providing incentives for traders to come to their cities or sending out representatives to buy grain in foreign markets.[111]

The other reason why Greek generals sent ahead to friendly, allied or neutral *poleis* to ask them to prepare markets for their military forces was that the large numbers of men 'involved meant that... the authorities in the friendly states through which [armies] passed had to . . . provide places to buy and sell where their [producers'] safety would be guaranteed'.[112] *Poleis* facilitated the sale of food to passing armies and navies by providing the demarcated, physical space of an *agora* and an institutional framework (*agoranomoi*, weights and measures) for exchanges within it. This often meant that marketplaces for forces were established outside city walls. This does not mean that these markets were in any way institutionally different from the usual *agorai* of cities,[113] but shows only that cities were aware of the clear and obvious danger of admitting large numbers of armed men from other cities within their walls.[114] Besides, *poleis* often admitted men from passing armies and navies into their regular marketplace.[115]

There was, then, no difference in legal framework between the *agorai* in which passing military forces took part in the permanent central marketplaces of Greek *poleis* and the temporary marketplaces set up for them outside the city walls of *poleis*.[116] This legal framework of *polis* markets also contributed to their ability to cope with the demand shock of transient armies and navies.[117] The framework provided the legal protections necessary to protect sellers of grain (and other foods) against violent or arbitrary appropriations of their goods by sailors and soldiers; inversely, it also protected the members of military forces against cheating by sellers. In so doing, the institutional framework of these *polis* markets lowered transactions costs, and so further increased farmers' and traders' opportunities and incentives to mobilize their grain surpluses to sell to passing sailors and soldiers.

The physical and legal infrastructure of markets were provided to navies, too, by those maritime *poleis* within the Greek core, untypical as the evidence of Aeneas shows, that regularly depended on imports of grain in the fifth and fourth centuries – and would have enabled their markets, too, to absorb the demand shocks of passing navies. Some cities, such as the *polis* of Clazomenae in the early fourth century, regularly imported grain from neighbouring *poleis*.[118] In cases such as this, a combination of short distance and long-standing links would have made imports from nearby *poleis* a predictable source of supply to supplement 'home'-based production.[119] The traders who regularly imported and exported grain surpluses between neighbouring cities would have had rapid and accurate information about the trading conditions in each of the cities that formed part of the local network. Their certain knowledge of the (impending) arrival of a fleet at a *polis* in one of their local networks, then, would have provided these traders with a low-risk opportunity to profit, especially as fleets would be arriving in the summer, and thus would have incentivized them to sail to add their grain stocks to the home production of the *polis* at which the fleet was halting.

Other Aegean coastal cities depending on imports could do so because they were located near to or on commonly-sailed trading routes. The busiest were the trading routes to Athens, the major consumer of imported grain in the Greek world. As Procles the Phliasian put it in 369 when arguing for Athenian naval leadership of a Spartan and Athenian-led alliance, 'most *poleis* which are dependent on the sea are situated round your state, and they are all weaker than your state'.[120] These cities, and others on other shipping lanes in the Aegean,[121] were, by virtue of their location, frequently visited by traders. As a result, they developed as 'centres of networking and information', as providers of 'marketing infrastructure and facilities' to traders, and thus as 'stable markets' for imported grain.[122] The opportunities for profit their location and marketing infrastructure made possible enabled them to develop a structural dependence on imports of grain. For these *poleis*, the purchases of grain of navies were not a threat to their own supply since their proximity to frequently sailed trading routes and their proven purchasing power for imports meant that any deficits could be made up by trade, especially since trireme fleets usually sailed in summer, the time of year offering the best conditions for exchanges of information and the shipping of grain surpluses.[123] The geography of these cities enabled them to be fully integrated into wider grain-trading networks – and this integration enabled their markets to meet the demand shocks of passing navies, which again could be absorbed by the cargoes of just a few trading ships.

Outside the 'core', *poleis* in southern Italy and Sicily as well as on the southern Black Sea also provided the physical and legal infrastructures of markets to passing military forces. The reasons why the markets of these *poleis* were also able to sell sufficient supplies of food to passing armies and navies contrasted greatly by region, however. In Sicily, the territories and productive arable areas of *poleis* were, compared to other areas in the Greek world, vast,[124] which in turn allowed Greek city-states in Sicily to produce comparatively massive amounts of grain. There were also the structures in place in these *poleis* to bring at least some of this grain to market on a regular basis. Preventing the export of grain from some Sicilian *poleis* to the Peloponnese was, according to Thucydides, a major factor motivating the Athenians to send an expedition to Sicily in 427 (3.86.4). One *polis* alone, Catana, was able to export enough grain to feed the entire Athenian force encamped outside Syracuse in the summer of 413 (Thuc. 7.60.2).[125] In southern Italy, while the territories of Greek *poleis* were smaller on average than those in Sicily, they were still, at the low hundreds to over 1,000 square kilometres, much greater on average than those in the Greek core.[126] Just as in Sicily, there were also the commercial supply mechanisms in place in southern Italian *poleis* to market some of their greater surpluses of grain. Thus, in the summer of 414, the Athenian force, made up of tens of thousands of men, besieging Syracuse was able to rely for its food supply on imports of food from Italian *poleis* (Thuc. 6.103.2). Their production of comparatively enormous amounts of grain and the presence of commercial networks able to mobilize part of that grain for sale in markets meant, then, that the markets in *poleis* in Sicily and southern Italy had the capacity to receive forces even as great as the Athenian expedition in 415.

Things were very different on the further eastern stretches of the southern Black Sea coast. The further east one went from the Bosporus, the more isolated the *poleis* of this coast were.[127] As Gallo has pointed out, these city-states were not connected by (good) roads[128] nor were they centres of maritime trading.[129] There were no trading ships present during the Cyreans' halt at Cerasus[130] and at Cotyora, for example.[131] Cerasus and Cotyora were remote places without local networks of maritime traders. Because of their communities' lack of integration into larger networks of trade, farmers in these cities would have pursued the strategy of storage and overproduction described earlier. The arrival of the Cyreans in the late spring[132] would therefore also have presented an exceptional opportunity for the cities' residents to convert their stored surpluses of 'old' grain into money, which would have given their *agorai* the capacity to meet the demand of the mercenaries.

Nearer to the Bosporus, there were in Heraclea and (probably) Sinope – in contrast to cities further east – the marketing structures and facilities in place to mobilize large amounts of grain for sale in markets. There were trading vessels at Sinope (Xen. *An.* 5.6.2, 5) and many of them, too, at Heraclea (Xen. *An.* 5.6.10), so that each *polis* could send ships to Cotyora to transport the Cyreans from that city further along the coast (Xen. *An.* 5.6.31, 5.6.35, 6.1.14).[133] The Heracleots could also provide enough ships to transport by sea six thousand of the Cyreans from their city (Xen. *An.* 6.2.17, 19). Sinope and, especially, Heraclea had, then, sufficient trading capacity to transport any surpluses of food (to or) from their home territories.

In addition, there were marketing structures at Heraclea (certainly) and Sinope (perhaps) to enable maritime traders to accumulate substantial amounts of grain and other foods for sale. After their stay at Heraclea, the Cyreans were encamped at Calpe Harbour a little later in the summer of 400. After the mercenaries had established their ability to dominate the surrounding countryside and therefore plunder food from it (*An.* 6.6.1), Xenophon could also note that '. . . by this time there was a great abundance of everything, for market products came in [to Calpe] from the Greek cities on all sides . . .'[134] The fact that traders came to Calpe from the Greek cities on all sides, including (almost certainly) Heraclea, which had already provided substantial *xenia*[135] as well as a market to the Cyreans (Xen. *An.* 6.2.8), and perhaps Sinope, which also had already provided *xenia*[136] to the mercenaries, strongly suggests the capacity of the traders of these *poleis* to mobilize large surpluses of grain and other goods for trade.[137] This capacity is confirmed for Heraclea by another incident from the last decade of the fifth century, when the people of Heraclea did not have enough money to provide pay for a fleet of forty triremes for an upcoming expedition against Byzantium ([Arist.], *Oec.* 2.2.8, 1347b3–15). The Heracleots instead bought two months' food for the fleet on credit from the maritime traders present in their city. On this occasion, and without any advance warning or preparation, maritime traders at Heraclea had enough stocks of grain, olive oil, wine and other foods so as to be able to feed a fleet of 8,000 men for two months. The presence of substantial marketable surpluses of grain and other foods explains the capacity of the *agorai* of Heraclea (especially) and Sinope to provide a sufficient amount of provisions for sale to the passing Cyreans.[138]

All these considerations explain why it could be assumed by all actors in wars all over the Classical Greek world that *poleis* could meet the usually limited and irregular demand shocks of passing armies and navies, even ones as large as the Sicilian expedition. They also explain why the problems of supply we do sometimes find mentioned in our ancient literary sources in connection with markets provided by *poleis* were all products of extraordinary circumstances. Xenophon mentions scarcity of supply in markets supplied by the *poleis* of Trapezus (*An.* 5.1.6) and Perinthus (*An.* 7.6.24) to the Ten Thousand. This scarcity can be explained by two factors. First, in both the case of Trapezus and Perinthus, the mercenaries were staying outside these cities in midwinter,[139] months after the old harvest and months before the new harvest, when stored grain reserves had been drawn upon for some months and when there was no way of ascertaining the success of the next harvest. Farmers in Trapezus and Perinthus therefore had to be much more cautious about how much of their stored reserves they could sell to the mercenaries, especially since the winter effectively cut off their communities from any opportunity to resupply through maritime grain traders.[140] Second, the Cyreans, because of their stateless and leaderless status, were in an extraordinary position at both Trapezus and Perinthus; rather than halting briefly at these *poleis* on their way to a campaign theatre, they had to stay for extended periods at both cities as they attempted to figure out where they would go next. The extraordinary length of the mercenaries' stays near their cities,[141] combined with farmers' inability to be sure of the results of the next harvest or to resupply through trade, meant that, after a certain point, it simply became too risky for farmers to sell from their stores the amounts of grain necessary to meet the demand of the Cyreans. The same problems presented by an army's protracted winter stays at *poleis* probably explain, too, Xenophon's comment that Derkylidas, having taken nine cities in eight days in Asia Minor in 398, set about planning how he might avoid being a burden to his allies, as Thibron had been the previous winter, by wintering in a friendly country.[142] The pressures exerted by the continued and prolonged demand of Thibron's forces for grain in winter would have eventually placed an intolerably dangerous burden on the grain stores of farmers in these *poleis*.

Even outside of winter, *poleis* could not receive and provision a market for larger military forces in the event that those forces spent an unexpectedly long time at their *polis*. This factor explains the logic of Dionysius' ruse in 391 when he asked Rhegium (or Himera) to provide his large force with an *agora*.[143] He asked for the *agora* with the intention that if the Rhegians (or Himeraeans) did not provide one, he would have a pretext to attack their city; and that, if Rhegium (or Himera) did provide an *agora*, he could easily reduce the city by starvation after their supplies had been exhausted in provisioning his force (Diod. Sic. 14.108.1). In the event, the Rhegians (or Himeraeans) provided the market for several days but ceased doing so when they became suspicious after Dionysius' force continued to remain outside their city for a prolonged period; Dionysius used the refusal to continue providing an *agora* as a pretext to lay siege to the city. Again, the reasoning behind Dionysius' ruse was that a city was usually capable of absorbing the demand shock of a passing military force for a limited period; it was only an extended stay by a very large military force that could to lead to grain supply problems in an *agora* provided by a *polis* to such a force. Usually, however, in their summer campaigns within the Greek world, Classical Greek armies and navies could expect that the markets of *poleis* would be capable of providing a sufficient market supply of grain and other foods for their brief halts and onward marches and voyages.

5. Conclusion: the reception of Greek military forces and the performance of grain markets in the Classical Greek Mediterranean and Black Sea

The aim of this chapter has been to meet the challenge set out by Finley all those years ago. It has sought to demonstrate, in other words, that an investigation of the convention of reception of military forces by Greek *poleis* and its concomitant provision of an *agora* to those military forces can give us new information about, and new insights into, the Classical Greek economy. The focus of the chapter has been on the performance of Classical Greek *polis* markets.

The planning and prosecution of Classical Greek wars were predicated upon the capacity of *polis* markets to mobilize sufficient surpluses of grain and other foods to meet the demand shocks caused by passing military forces. Using the framework laid out by Van der Spek, Van Leeuwen and Van Zanden, this chapter has demonstrated how the factors of trade, storage, technology, geography and institutions worked together in different ways in different *poleis* in different parts of the Classical Greek world to enable the markets in those *poleis* to respond to the external demand shock of the arrival of thousands of sailors and soldiers wishing to purchase food for the duration of their halts and for their onward journeys. For inland cities, geography, combined with limited pre-industrial overland transport technologies and reinforced by political-institutional constraints, meant that there was within these cities sufficient private storage of surpluses of grain, wine and other foods to be organized and prepared for sale to cope with the usually relatively limited demand of passing armies. For most maritime cities in the Greek 'core', and for cities on the southern Black Sea coast east of Sinope, the absence or poor development of information technologies for disseminating news about market conditions, and resulting political-institutional constraints on movements of grain outside *polis* territories, meant that there was an adequate amount of privately stored surpluses in these *poleis*, too, to deal effectively with the demand of passing navies. In contrast, a minority of coastal or island cities in the Greek 'core' were on 'favorable trading routes' and thus part of 'well-organized trading systems',[144] made possible by the much cheaper transactions costs of sea transport, that enabled them to use trade to make up for any shortages in grain and other foods caused by the purchases of passing naval forces. Finally, for cities in southern Italy and Sicily, and for Heraclea and (perhaps) Sinope in the Black Sea, a combination of geography (their locations on coasts), political institutions (the size of their territories), and commercial institutions (commercial transport capacity and developed marketing structures) meant that they were capable of dealing easily with the external demand shock of transient military forces.

In addition to these interplays of factors varying by region and location of *polis*, there were also three institutional factors shared across Classical *poleis* that were crucial in making the markets within these *poleis* capable of mobilizing sufficient surpluses for sale to passing military forces. First, as part of the diplomatic protocol of the reception of military forces, armies provided notifications to the cities on their routes of march to war zones; navies probably attempted to do the same for the maritime cities that they wished to moor at on their way to theatres of operations. These notifications gave farmers and traders the time and opportunity to mobilize the necessary amounts of surplus grain and other foods for sale within *polis* markets to forces. Second, the legal framework of *polis* markets also facilitated their ability to cope with the demand shock of transient armies and navies. The markets provided to these armies and navies, even when they were established outside city walls, differed from 'regular' *agorai* only in the much greater than usual numbers of sellers and buyers present in them. They did not differ institutionally in any other way from 'regular' *agorai*. For inland and most small and middling maritime *poleis*, then, the institutions of *polis agorai*, which greatly reduced the cost and risk of participating in markets, enabled and incentivized agricultural producers and traders to invest the time, effort and capital to bring stored grain to market. In more integrated island and coastal *poleis*, these institutions, and the stable trading conditions they enabled, incentivized producers and maritime traders to use trade to make it possible to use imports to meet the demand shocks of passing armies and navies.

Third, low levels of state intervention in the distribution of food within Classical Greek city-states also encouraged the trade of grain and other food surpluses between sellers and sailors and soldiers; this was another factor improving the performance of markets provided to passing military forces. A brief comparison with another time and place in pre-industrial European history when military forces provisioned themselves through a market mechanism provided by communities whose territories they were passing through will serve to highlight this important institutional factor. In the late 1500s CE, Spanish forces using 'the Spanish Road' to move through friendly and neutral territory from northern Italy to their theatre of operations in the Low Countries requested *étapes* from local communities.[145] In the first stage of the development of the *étape*, the civil authorities of communities organized the collection from the inhabitants of those communities of a set amount of food supplies requested by the Spanish authorities; these supplies would be then organized and prepared for distribution to Spanish forces as and when they passed through the community's territory. After the Spanish army had passed through, special officials would assess the total amount of provisions contributed by the community's inhabitants. These food supplies would have been already assigned a 'just price' by the local civil authorities; the inhabitants either would be paid at this set price for the food they had provided or have the amount (i.e. food supplies × just price) deducted from their tax bill.

The contrast with the *agorai* provided by Classical Greek city-states as part of the convention of reception is striking. In the case of these markets, there was no state-controlled collection of grain (and other foods) from the private stores of citizens; rather, farmers and traders were free to manage their stores in whatever manner they saw fit on the arrival of a military force at their *polis*.[146] Unlike the order to give up grain at a fixed price – effectively a form of requisitioning – the only restriction on the prices that could be charged to passing sailors and soldiers in Classical Greek *agorai* would have been a limit on the maximum profits that could be made from retail transactions in basic foods.[147] Classical Greek farmers and traders, then, had much greater incentives than the inhabitants of communities along the Spanish Road to make available their food stores for trade with transient military forces.[148] Additionally, the absence of direct produce taxes on grain and other foods in Classical *poleis* also meant the absence of another constraint on farmers' decisions so that 'an unusually high proportion of [their] individual output could potentially be put on the market' to meet the demand of military forces.[149]

All of these factors contribute to explaining why in the Classical Greek world the capacity to provide sufficient grain for sale was never a factor in friendly, allied and neutral *poleis*' decisions whether or not to offer markets to passing armies and navies.

This is not to exaggerate the levels of performance of *polis* markets or to suggest, by any means, that there were no limits on the ability of *polis* markets to cope with the demand shocks of passing military forces. First, since military forces usually requested *agorai* from *poleis* only for the brief periods of their halts and on a once-off basis, the demand shocks these *agorai* had to cope with were (mostly) limited in extent. Second, the performance of *polis* markets was limited by season – they struggled to supply military forces in winter – and in duration – at least for larger forces, they struggled to provide supplies for more than several days. But again, usually, the markets of *poleis* all over the Greek world functioned well enough to absorb the demand shock of military forces halting in their territories.

To conclude by returning to the start of this chapter, what would Finley have thought of this response to his challenge? Finley was, in fact, generally happy to admit the presence of markets in the ancient Mediterranean world,[150] and even the presence in the Classical Greek world of price-setting markets in which considerable quantities of food could be sold.[151] But the typical local *polis* market in his *Ancient Economy* always remained exiguous, discontinuous and prone to failure.[152] There is some overlap there, then, with the paradox described in this chapter of how the usually irregular and small-scale participation of farmers in inland and smaller maritime *polis* markets meant that those farmers had underused surpluses that were crucial to the success of these markets in meeting sailors' and soldiers' demand for grain. But, and here this chapter parts from Finley, this success was also, and crucially, intrinsically linked to the institutional organization of *polis agorai* that enabled and incentivized farmers and traders to mobilize surpluses to supply these markets, and maritime traders to import grain to better-integrated coastal *poleis*. The investigation of Greek military forces as consumers of food in markets provided to them as part of the convention of their reception by friendly, allied and neutral *poleis* gives a very different picture, then, of the ancient Greek economy than the Finleyian orthodoxy.[153] It presents us, instead, with a picture of a world full of *polis* markets capable of moving and distributing tens of thousands, sometimes hundreds of thousands, of kilogrammes of food to deal effectively with the demand of thousands, sometimes tens of thousands, of sailors and soldiers on campaign.

Notes

1. Finley 1965 (publication of a paper given in 1962).
2. For recent work addressing other parts of Finley's suggested research plan, see e.g. O'Connor 2015 on armies as consumers of food in markets attached to their camps; Rawlings 2007, 157–8 for armies as purchasers of weapons and armour; O'Connor 2015, 198–203 and Rawlings 2007, 153–4 for armies as sellers of plunder.
3. More accurately: see e.g. the brief discussions at Lazenby 1994, 10; Casson 1995, 262–3; Van Wees 2004, 105; Rawlings 2007, 79. Less accurately: see e.g. Pritchett 1971, 45–6 (mixing up these markets with markets organized by *poleis* in their own territory for their own and allied forces); Trundle 2020, 18 (confusing the requisitioning of supplies from settlements with markets provided by cities and confusing markets organized within army camps with markets

provided by cities); and Dalby 1992, 25 (not realizing the existence of the convention and thus mistakenly likening the granting of markets to Greek armies to those granted to caravans in Asia).

4. See e.g. Mosley 1973, 167–8; Alonso Troncoso 1987, 99–101; Bauslaugh 1991, 73, 147–8. But see now O'Connor 2022 for discussion of the origins of this protocol in the late sixth century and the political and ideological reasons for its persistence through the Classical period.
5. Stanley 1976, 117–23 is, by far, the lengthiest discussion. Stanley's useful treatment is marred, however, by the mistaken idea that the Greeks had a specific concept of a 'military *agora*': see nn. 113, 115 below. Apart from Stanley, Austin and Vidal-Naquet (1980, 124) mention markets set up by *poleis* for foreign armies outside city walls in passing in a discussion of *poleis*' concern for law and order in their marketplaces. Even in the resurgence of work in the last decade or so on economic development in the Greek world, markets provided by *poleis* to passing military forces are mentioned (and then in passing) only by Harris and Lewis 2016, 11.
6. For this point, see Stanley 1976, 120; Alonso Troncoso 1997, 100. See Thuc. 6.44.2 for what the reception by a *polis* of a passing military force comprised: a market, water, and (in the case of navies) anchorage.
7. See e.g. Erbse 2010.
8. Nor did the Cotyorites accept the Cyrean ill inside their walls (Xen. *An.* 5.5.6).
9. Translation taken from the Loeb edition.
10. This part of Xenophon's speech coheres completely with the preceding narrative of the army's stay at Trapezus: when the men had arrived near the city (Xen. *An.* 4.8.22–3), the Trapezuntians demonstrated their friendliness by providing a market to the army, receiving it, and providing *xenia* of oxen, barley groats and wine (Xen. *An.* 4.8.23).
11. On the function of *xenia* as establishing a formal relationship of friendliness, see Herman 1987 (esp. 12 on the giving of *xenia* not limited to individuals, but practised by *poleis* and other communities, too).
12. See O'Connor 2016a, 94–6 for a recent full explication of this passage and esp. 95 n.30 for reception here (as always) including the provision of a market to the passing military force.
13. See Roy 1967, 302–9; Lee 2007, Table 2.
14. Xen. *An.* 6.6.9, 6.6.12–13, 6.6.36.
15. See again Xen. *An.* 5.1.6 (Trapezus), 5.5.14–19 (Cotyora), 6.2.4 (Heraclea), 7.3.5, 7.3.13, 7.6.24 (Perinthus).
16. Xen. *Hell.* 3.4.11–12, *Ages.* 1.14–17, esp. Xen. *Hell.* 3.4.11: ταῖς δὲ πόλεσιν εἰς ἃς ἀνάγκη ἦν ἀφικνεῖσθαι στρατευομένῳ ἐπὶ Καρίαν προεῖπεν ἀγορὰν παρασκευάζειν. Agesilaos invaded Phrygia instead of Caria.
17. And also that embassies should wait for him there: πάλιν προσεποιήσατο εἰς τὰς Θεσπιὰς πρῶτον ἰέναι, καὶ πέμπων ἀγοράν τε ἐκέλευε παρασκευάζειν καὶ τὰς πρεσβείας ἐκεῖ περιμένειν (5.4.48).
18. See O'Connor 2021a, 228–9 for contemporary sources confirming the point that Classical Greek armies departed for campaigns with very few provisions.
19. In the absence of any state institutions to feed armies operating at distance (O'Connor 2021a, 239–40), pseudo-Xenophon must be referring here to provisioning in markets in friendly territory.
20. On the general validity of pseudo-Xenophon's reasoning in this passage, see e.g. Gomme 1962, 50–1; De Ste. Croix 1972, 309; Mattingly 1997, 353.

21. See Xen. *Hell.* 2.1.27: the Athenian crews having to go a long way to buy their food (τά τε σιτία πόρρωθεν ὠνούμενοι) – at Sestos, as Xen. *Hell.* 2.1.25 makes clear.

22. [Arist.] *Oec.* 2.2.7, 1347a.32–1347b.2. See Brodersen 2008, 110–12 for the date (no date mentioned for the Lampsacenes' ruse but the vast majority of anecdotes in the *Oeconomica* able to be dated to the fourth century).

23. See Stahl 2003, 193–8.

24. I treat the provisioning of the Athenian expedition on its way to Sicily in detail in a monograph in progress.

25. See e.g. Barat 2012, 239; Gallo 2015 for references and discussion. See also Xen. *An.* 6.4.2 with Lee 2007, 38 on 'the *polis*-free zone between Heracleia and Byzantium'.

26. See e.g. Thuc. 4.27.1, Xen. *Hell.* 4.8.7.

27. See Thuc. 6.34.4–8, together with the excellent discussions at Stahl 2003, 194–8, and Morrison, Coates and Rankov 2000, 100–2, for what follows.

28. This translation is based on the Loeb and that found at Morrison, Coates and Rankov 2000, 101.

29. Diod. Sic. 14.108.1–2, Frontin. *Str.* 3.4.3; Polyaenus, *Strat.* 5.2.10. See Brodersen 2008, 111 for the dating of this episode. See p. 36 below for further discussion of this market.

30. See Van der Spek, Van Leeuwen, and Van Zanden 2015a for discussion of market performance. For specific definitions and the ideas and language in this paragraph, see especially Van der Spek, Van Leeuwen and Van Zanden 2015b, 3 (market performance defined as 'the capability of markets to adapt to exogenous shocks'); Foldvari and Van Leeuwen 2015, 19–20, 29; Van der Spek, Van Leeuwen and Van Zanden 2015c, 532.

31. Tuplin 1999, 346; Lee 2007, 174, 219.

32. Lee 2007, 219.

33. For Classical Greek micro-states and the short distances between them, see Hansen and Nielsen 2004, 71–2, and esp. Bintliff 2008, 19: '60 per cent of all Greek *poleis* [had] a territory of 5-6km radius, and 80 per cent [were] within an 8km radius.' See Krentz 2007, 161 for typical marching rates of Greek armies.

34. See O'Connor 2021a, 230 for Classical Greek soldiers typically not needing any re-equipment during their brief campaigns. Note also that Dionysius' ruse at Rhegium (or Himera) (see the discussion on p. 36) exploited the fact that *poleis* could typically expect military forces to halt in their territories for brief periods.

35. See e.g. O'Connor 2016b, 339–40.

36. See e.g. Pritchett 1971, 32–4.

37. See e.g. Thuc. 8.57.1, 8.78, 8.83.3; *Hell. Oxy.* 19.2; Dem. 4.23; [Dem.] 50.23, 50.53–6.

38. See e.g. Ar. *Ach.* 544–57; Thuc. 7.27.1–2 with Loomis 1998, 44; [Dem.] 50.14.

39. See e.g. Gabrielsen 1994, 121–2.

40. Roy 1967, 312 and n.98.

41. As so often, the evidence is from Athens: see Thuc. 6.31.5, Lys. 16.14, Dem. 19.84 with Cook 1990, 75–6. It is very unlikely that this phenomenon was limited to Athens, however, and Xenophon looks to be referring to the same practice among the Ten Thousand at *An.* 6.4.8 (see Lee 2007, 78, 105).

42. See e.g. Dem. 4.28–9; [Dem.] 50.8–9, 10.

43. See Van Wees 2004, 238 for some examples.

44. O'Connor 2013, 342. I also focus on grain here because demand for this food was much more inelastic than for other foods such as wine and oil (Erdkamp 2005, 167–70; Bresson 2016, 119–20). See Xen. *Cyr.* 6.2.26 for Cyrus assuming that water could be substituted for wine on a long march.

45. See Cahill 2002, 331 n.20 for a summary of the debate on the yields of barley and wheat per hectare in Classical Greece: the figures are essentially unrecoverable but modern estimates range between 400 kilograms and 900 kilograms per hectare (wheat yields being at the lower end of this range, barley yields at the higher end). See Erdkamp 2005, 34–45, esp. 35–8 for reasons not to accept the 650 kilogram/hectare grain yield 'ceiling' of Sallares 1991, 389 (and thus Moreno's 600 kilogram/hectare estimate (2007, 6–10, 26–8) for yields based on Sallares's figures). See O'Connor 2013, 331 n.25 for barley groats being the form of grain most commonly consumed by members of Classical Greek military forces.

46. See Bresson 2016, 86–7 on trading-ship capacities in the fifth and fourth centuries.

47. See O'Connor 2013: the typical daily grain consumption of Classical Greek sailors and soldiers was two *choinikes* of barley groats. See also O'Connor 2013, 338–9: one *medimnos* (48 *choinikes*) of barley groats = 16.482 kilograms of wheat equivalent. *Medimnoi* of barley groats are abbreviated in the table as med.; wheat equivalent of grain as w.e.

48. The estimates of grain consumption requirements here are for *each polis* at which the respective forces would have halted.

49. Estimate based on Hornblower's discussion of the size of the expedition (2008, 1061–6).

50. 30,000 x 2 *choinikes* of barley groats x 5 days (2 halt, 3 for onward voyage) = 6,250 *medimnoi* of barley groats. 50,000 x 2 *choinikes* of barley groats x 5 days = 10,416.67 *medimnoi* of barley groats.

51. See Thuc. 6.50.2–3. 60 triremes x 200 men (see e.g. Morrison 1984, 55 for 200 men being the usual crew of a trireme in the Classical period): 12,000 men. 12,000 x 2 *choinikes* of barley groats x 5 days (2 halt, 3 for onward voyage) = 2,500 *medimnoi* of barley groats (= 41,205kg. wheat equivalent of grain).

52. See again Thuc. 8.95.4–7. 36 triremes = 7,200 men. 7,200 x 2 *choinikes* of barley groats x 5 days (2 halt, 3 for onward voyage) = 1,500 *medimnoi* of barley groats (= 24,723kg. wheat equivalent of grain).

53. 180 Athenian triremes (= 36,000 men) before the battle of Aigospotamoi: Xen. *Hell.* 2.1.20; Diod. Sic. 13.105.1. on 153 triremes (= 30,600 men): Diod. Sic. 13.104.2 (20 left at Samos before battle).

54. See again Xen. *Hell.* 2.1.27 with 2.1.25.

55. The length of the Athenian fleet's halt at Aegospotamoi was five days (see Xen. *Hell.* 2.1.20–1, 27). 30,600 x 2 *choinikes* x 5 days = 6,375 *medimnoi* of barley groats (= 105,072.75kg. of wheat equivalent of grain). 36,000 x 2 *choinikes* x 5 days = 7,500 *medimnoi* of barley groats (= 123,615kg. of wheat equivalent of grain).

56. Agesilaos left for Asia Minor with thirty Spartiates, 2,000 *neodamodeis*, and 6,000 allied soldiers (Xen. *Hell.* 3.4.2–3). The *neodamodeis* will not have been accompanied by slave attendants; it is unclear how many of the allied soldiers were hoplites (accompanied by slave attendants). Agesilaos also had contingents from allied *poleis* in Asia Minor serving under him (Xen., *Hell.* 3.4.11, 3.4.12), but Xenophon does not specify how many men these contingents comprised. Diodorus has Agesilaos enlisting 4,000 troops at Ephesus to make a total of 10,000 infantry and 400 cavalry (14.79.2); the figures of Xenophon, who accompanied Agesilaos on this campaign, should be preferred. In the light of the vagueness of Xenophon's figures, however, I will adopt an estimate of 10,000 to 15,000 men.

57. See p. 23 above: although Agesilaos actually marched from Ephesus to Phrygia, it was presumed by all parties to the conflict that the cities on the way to Caria could provide sufficient markets to his force, too.

58. 10,000 x 2 *choinikes* of barley groats x 5 days (2 halt, 3 for onward march) = 2,083.33 *medimnoi* of barley groats (= 34,337.5kg. of wheat equivalent of grain); 15,000 x 2 *choinikes* of barley groats x 5 days (2 halt, 3 for onward march) = 3,125 *medimnoi* of barley groats (= 51,506.25kg. of w.e. of grain).

59. I include this force as an example of a typical smaller Classical Greek infantry force on the move to a war zone. Aristeus' force consisted of 1,600 hoplites (an unknown number of whom were mercenaries) and 400 light troops (Thuc. 1.60.1): although it is doubtful that each of the mercenary hoplites was accompanied by a slave attendant, I will proceed on the basis that they were (the light troops will not have been accompanied by slave attendants).

60. Although Thucydides does not explicitly say that the members of Aristeus' force provisioned itself in the markets of friendly *poleis* on their journeys to the north, the previous sections of this chapter have demonstrated that this must have been the case.

61. 3,600 x 2 *choinikes* of barley groats x 5 days (2 halt, 3 for onward march) = 750 *medimnoi* of barley groats (=12,631.5kg. of w.e. of grain).

62. Tuplin 1997, 373.

63. See Erdkamp 1998, 24 for discussion. For examples, see e.g. France 2006, 81; Pryor 2006b, 287 for Crusading forces experiencing supply problems when marching on routes along which other Crusading forces had passed and had received markets from the cities on those routes a few weeks previously (again, never an issue in Classical Greek warfare).

64. See Erdkamp 1998, 20 for examples and discussion.

65. Even the major naval operations of the Athenians in the fifth century were infrequent (see e.g. Krentz 2007, 180, Table 6.3) until the late 430s and early 420s when their increased frequency led to unprecedented financial problems at Athens (Blamire 2001, 109–12). See Rawlings 2007, 120 on financial limitations constraining Athenian naval operations in the fourth century.

66. Krentz 2007, 147–8, for this and the next point on invasion forces.

67. The Ionian War can give a good illustrative example: see e.g. the Athenian naval forces encamped at Samos from the summer of 412 to the summer of 411 (Thuc. 8.27.4, 8.76.3–4, 8.100.1) and from early 407 until the summer of 405 (407 (Xen. *Hell.* 1.4.23); 406 (Xen. *Hell.* 1.5.18, 20; Diod. Sic. 13.76.1, 13.100.6); 405 (Xen. *Hell.* 2.1.12, 2.1.16; Diod. Sic. 13.104.1)).

68. Van der Spek, Van Leeuwen and Van Zanden 2015b, 3–5.

69. See also the summary of the main determinants of market performance at Foldvari and Van Leeuwen 2015, 21. I omit here 'consumption diversification' as a factor enabling market performance since it is not pertinent to the markets discussed here. Trade is also referred to in some discussions as 'market integration'.

70. I use the term 'core' to denote the areas of 'mainland' Greece, the Aegean (including the coasts of northern Greece and western Anatolia), and the Propontis merely as a convenient shorthand to distinguish these areas from the southern Black Sea coast, southern Italy and Sicily (see pp. 34–5 below for discussion of these areas). The term is not meant to connote any greater importance or value for the Greek mainland, Aegean and Propontis, or to suggest in any way that other areas of the Greek world were peripheral.

71. I also owe much of the theoretical framework of the following discussion to Erdkamp's lucid discussion of market integration (2005, 175–205). Again, I am focusing on grain here but the following comments can be taken to apply for wine, which, as Bresson has recently illustrated

(2016, 122–7), was mostly consumed locally within the territories of the same *poleis* in which it was produced.

72. See Erdkamp 2005, 199, citing Xen. *Hell.* 4.7.1: the Acarnanians submitting to the Spartans after they learned that Agesilaos was about to invade their territory and destroy their grain which, because of the situation of their cities inland, would leave them without any means to acquire food.

73. See e.g. Pleket 2008, 182; Langton 1998, 387; Bresson 2016, 79–84.

74. Pleket 2008, 182. See also e.g. Temin 2001, 179–80; Erdkamp 2005, 141 (both discussing conditions in the Roman world, but their conclusions are equally valid for conditions in fifth and fourth century Greece).

75. As Cruickshank notes (1954, 72), it was only when the route was made safe that grain was transported to Phlius by both pack animal *and* wagon.

76. Hopkins 1983, 104–5; see also Hopkins' penetrating discussion of this topic at 1978, 46.

77. This is the reason why, after the loss of two harvests, the *polis* of Thebes had to make an extraordinary state intervention into the grain trade by sending representatives of the *polis* to buy grain at Pagasae in 377 (Xen. *Hell.* 5.4.56). One should also imagine that the transport of grain from Mantinea to Argos in the early fourth century mentioned at Xen. *Hell.* 5.2.2 was organized by the *polis* authorities at Mantinea, too, given that the Spartans raised this action among its charges of disloyalty against the *polis* of the Mantineans as a whole.

78. Osborne 1987, 104.

79. See e.g. Whitehead 1990, 40 and n.122; Winterling 1991, 206: Aeneas wanted his measures to have 'die möglichst universelle Anwendbarkeit'; Shipley 2017, 49, 64.

80. Winterling 1990, 205–6.

81. See e.g. Whitehead 1990, 114 for references; see also de Souza 2017, 217–22 on the 'The Maritime Context of the City under Attack'.

82. Aen. Tact. 7.1: Ὅταν δὲ ἡ χώρα ἐγκάρπως διακέηται μὴ πόρρω ὄντων πολεμίων, εἰκὸς πολλοὺς τῶν ἐν τῇ πόλει περὶ τοὺς ἐγγὺς χώρους διατελεῖν, γλιχομένους τοῦ καρποῦ. The translation is taken from the edition of Hunter and Handford 1927.

83. Aen. Tact. 10.12: καὶ ὧν ἂν σπανίζῃ ἡ πόλις, σίτου ἢ ἐλαίου ἢ ἄλλου τινός, τῷ εἰσάγοντι κατὰ πλῆθος τῶν εἰσαγομένων τόκους προκεῖσθαι καὶ στέφανον δίδοσθαι εἰς τιμήν, τῷ δὲ ναυκλήρῳ ἀνολκὴν καὶ καθολκήν. The translation is taken from Whitehead 1990. Whitehead (1990, 124) thinks the incentives described at 10.12 are to reward 'blockade-runners' bringing grain to a city under siege. But Aeneas' city is clearly not yet under siege in chapter 10; this chapter, rather, outlines measures to be taken in the face of a threat of siege: see e.g. Hunter and Handford 1927, 128, and Bettalli 1990, 234. Aen. Tact. 10.12 is thus describing actions to be taken in the case of a food shortage outside of actual wartime (as already realized by Bettalli 1990, 241–2).

84. Quotes from Persson 2015, 70.

85. See the discussions at Reger 1994, 79–80; Erdkamp 2005, 185–96; Pleket 2008, 183.

86. See again Pleket 2008, 183, and also Erdkamp 2005, 190–1; Bresson 2016, 385–6.

87. Compare Reger 1994, 79–80.

88. The structure and ideas of this paragraph owe much to Bresson 2016, 158–60, 393–5, 430–6.

89. Bresson 2016, 158. See Garnsey 1988, 9–10 for a classic discussion of the Mediterranean climatic regime.

90. Bresson 2016, 159–60, 430–6; see also Erdkamp 2005, 144.

91. Gauthier 1979; Bresson 2016, 393–5, 402–5, 431–3.
92. See Bresson 2016, 158–60, 393, 431, 434. See also Reger 1994, 90–3.
93. See Bresson 2016, 431 with the discussion and references at Gauthier 1987, 417.
94. See already Gallant 1991, 94–5 on the implications of this passage.
95. Gallant 1991, 95, 100–1. See again Tuplin 1997, 373 on Achaemenid armies operating in Asia and Greece: 'Our historical sources are, for the most part, sovereignly disdainful about such mundane matters as how easy it was to keep bodies of soldiers sufficiently well fed and watered for them to be effective (and how often their effectiveness was hampered by failings in this regard). To some extent this must be because the ordinary processes of the agricultural economy produced substantial stored surpluses of food in many regions and that armies did not commonly pass back and forth across the same areas often enough to exhaust the possibility of such surpluses for pillage or purchase – so major problems were rare.' Gallant and Tuplin make crucial points but it is still necessary here to discuss the different factors that produced stored surpluses, which were different between inland and maritime *poleis* and between regions in the Greek world (see the rest of this section for more on this point); and, also and more importantly, the incentive structures and institutions specific to the inhabitants of Classical Greek *poleis* that enabled trade to make available those stored surpluses to passing military forces (see the following discussion and esp. section 5 for this point).
96. Gallant 1991, 98. See also Bresson 2016, 393.
97. The authorities of *poleis* did not requisition the supplies available for sale in the markets they offered to armies. See again e.g. [Arist.] *Oec.* 2.2.7, 1347a 32–1347b 2: apart from the extraordinary order by the authorities at Lampsacus to those trading in the market to raise prices, there was no other control of those men trading in the market, or their stocks of food, in the face of the upcoming arrival of a fleet of triremes. Tänzer (1912, 22–3, 48–9) and Cruickshank (1954, 75, 79) are therefore incorrect to refer to the purchase of Classical Greek armies in the *agorai* provided to them by *poleis* as requisitioning.
98. See again Xen. *Hell.* 3.4.11; Xen. *Hell.* 5.4.48.
99. Anderson 1970, 53.
100. See e.g. Osborne 1987, 13–14; Rawlings 2007, 144–5; Krentz 2007, 155.
101. See Garnsey, Gallant and Rathbone 1984, 53 for the idea.
102. See the excellent discussion at Bresson 2016, 160 and 395 for the terms 'waste' and 'underuse'; see also Garnsey 1987, 54–5 on Theophr. *Hist. pl.* 8.11.5 for seed grain.
103. Persson 2015, 79; Bresson 2016, 160.
104. Bresson 2011, 81–2, 91 was especially useful in formulating these ideas.
105. See Pl. *Resp.* 371C for traders purchasing agricultural goods from farmers for resale in *agorai* in Greek cities. Compare here O'Connor 2015, 209, 211 for farmers and traders mobilizing grain and other foods to sell in camp markets to soldiers from their own and friendly *poleis* who were operating for protracted periods within their territories but at a distance from the urban centre and its marketplace. See also e.g. Erdkamp 1998, 62–6, and O'Connor 2015, 214 for the reasons for the abundance of 'low', intra-*polis* transport capacity that made this possible (as opposed to the absence of land transport capacity to trade grain overland between *poleis* discussed above).
106. The generals of the Sicilian expedition sent three triremes ahead of the main body of the expedition to find out which of the cities along the coasts of Italy and Sicily would receive them (Thuc. 6.42.3); this is not quite the same thing, however, as alerting *poleis* on the

expected route of a voyage of the need to prepare a market. Perhaps the practice of notification was less common for naval forces because the vagaries of weather, and triremes' limited ability to adapt to those vagaries, meant that there was no such thing as consistent or expected voyage routes to war zones (especially in the Aegean) (see e.g. Horden and Purcell 2000, 137–42). The *poleis* of southern Italy and Sicily were a special case in that a fleet of triremes wishing to sail to Sicily from 'mainland' Greece had to coast by these *poleis*.

107. See again [Arist.] *Oec.* 2.2.7, 1347a32–1347b2: the authorities at Lampsacus apparently hearing by chance about the fleet of triremes sailing to their *polis* rather than having been instructed of their coming.
108. See e.g. Casson 1971, 270–2; Krentz 2007, 155; Beresford 2013, 134–47.
109. Van Wees 2004, 215–18.
110. Compare Erdkamp 2019, 4.
111. See again Aen. Tact. 10.12 with Erdkamp 2005, 186; Erdkamp 2019, 11; Bresson 2016, 384–93.
112. Murray's description of the actions of the military leaders of the First Crusade and the friendly communities whose territories they passed through (2006, 241) can be used (with the slight amendments in brackets) for the practices of Greek armies and friendly/neutral communities.
113. See O'Connor 2021b, 527–8 with Descat 1993, 151–5 and esp. Descat 1995, 106: the concept of a separate 'military *agora*' did not exist in the Greek world; rather, these external *agorai* were extensions of the city's usual *agora*. It is therefore imprecise to refer to markets provided by *poleis* to military forces as 'special' (as at e.g. de Ste. Croix 1972, 399–400; Stanley 1976, 115–35).
114. See e.g. Diod. Sic. 15.46.1–2 for an example of the dangers for *poleis* of receiving forces within their walls: in 374/3, the Spartans sent a fleet against Corcyra in order to help some oligarchs take that city; the twenty-two triremes dispatched to the city pretended to be sailing to Sicily in order to be received as a friendly force by the Corcyraeans in the plan to help the oligarchs occupy the city.
115. See O'Connor 2021b, 528–9. See also Xen. *An.* 5.5.19: Xenophon arguing that the Cotyorites showed their lack of friendliness to the mercenaries by neither admitting them within their city walls nor sending a market outside; both practices were evidently considered normal. Stanley 1976, 119–20 was wrong to think that *agorai* provided by *poleis* to passing military forces were always outside city walls.
116. Gallant 1991, 95 was therefore wrong to describe the markets provided by *poleis* to armies and navies as 'periodic'.
117. For this point and the rest of this paragraph, see O'Connor 2021b, 528 for full discussion.
118. See Rhodes and Osborne 2003, no.18, ll. 17–20 with discussion *ad loc.*
119. Compare Reger 1994, 79–80 for the case of Delos in the Hellenistic period.
120. Xen. *Hell.* 7.1.3: πλεῖσται γὰρ πόλεις τῶν δεομένων τῆς θαλάττης περὶ τὴν ὑμετέραν πόλιν οἰκοῦσι, καὶ αὗται πᾶσαι ἀσθενέστεραι τῆς ὑμετέρας (trans. Warner).
121. See Bresson 2016, 369 for examples.
122. See Erdkamp 2005, 193–4 for these quotes, and see generally 190–4.
123. Erdkamp 2005, 191–3.
124. See de Angelis 2016, 121, 232 for figures.

125. See de Angelis 2016, 295–6, 312–13 for other evidence of export and trade in grain from and within Sicily in the Classical period.
126. See Fischer-Hansen, Nielsen and Ampolo 2004, e.g. 266 (Croton), 273 (Locri), 279 (Metapontum), 290 (Rhegium), 299 (Taras), 304 (Thurii).
127. See again Barat 2012, 239; Gallo 2015 for discussion.
128. See Xen. *An.* 5.1.13 with Gallo 2015, 49.
129. Gallo 2015, 49–50.
130. The mercenaries had to continue the march by land from Cerasus since there were no ships available in the city (Xen. *An.* 5.4.1).
131. Xen. *An.* 5.6.2: the mercenaries at Cotyora thinking that only the Sinopeans (not the Cotyorites) were able to provide sufficient ships to transport the army.
132. Lee 2007, Table 1.
133. See also Xen. *An.* 5.6.19 for the incidental presence of Sinopean and Heracleot maritime traders at Cotyora.
134. Xen. *An.* 6.6.3: ἤδη δὲ ἦν πολλὴ πάντων ἀφθονία· καὶ γὰρ ἀγοραὶ πάντοθεν ἀφικνοῦντο ἐκ τῶν Ἑλληνίδων πόλεων.
135. Xen. *An.* 6.2.3: 3,000 *medimnoi* of barley groats, 2,000 jars of wine, twenty cattle, and 100 sheep.
136. Xen. *An.* 6.1.15: 3,000 *medimnoi* of barley groats and 1,500 jars of wine.
137. See also Xen. *An.* 6.5.1: Already before this, a ship from Heraclea arriving at Calpe bringing barley groats, sacrificial victims, and wine.
138. Xenophon makes no mention of an *agora* being provided to the Cyreans by the Sinopeans: either the *xenia* provided by the Sinopeans were sufficient for the Cyreans' five-day stay outside the city (Xen. *An.* 6.1.17); or, more likely, the Sinopeans did provide an *agora* to the mercenaries but nothing sufficiently strange or controversial occurred in relation to this *agora* for Xenophon to include it in his narrative.
139. The Cyreans were staying at Trapezus in January and February of 400: Lee 2007, 35 and Table 1. Their halt at Perinthus took place in the deep midwinter of 400/399: see Xen. *An.* 7.6.24 with Lee 2007, 41 and Table 2.1.
140. The remarks above on the isolation of Cerasus and Cotyora apply to Trapezus, too. See also Xen. *An.* 5.1.4 for lack of trading ships during the Cyreans' stay at Trapezus. The mercenaries instead, in order to have enough ships to leave Trapezus, had to attempt to capture passing trading vessels as they coasted by the city (Xen. *An.* 5.1.10–11, 5.1.12, 5.3.1). For Perinthus, see Xen. *An.* 7.3.13 for Cyreans lamenting that winter meant the absence of ships which might transport them home. See Erdkamp 2005, 191–3 for the sailing of trading ships generally being restricted in winter.
141. Xenophon mentions that supplies were scanty in the *agora* provided by the Trapezuntians in an assembly held after the mercenaries had already spent thirty days encamped in some Colchian villages near Trapezus: see Lee 2007, 36 n.122.
142. Xen. *Hell.* 3.2.1: Derkylidas ἐβουλεύετο ὅπως ἂν μὴ ἐν τῇ φιλίᾳ χειμάζων βαρὺς εἴη τοῖς συμμάχοις . . . Derkylidas spent the winter plundering the villages of Bithynian Thrace in order to supply his army (Xen. *Hell.* 3.2.1–2).
143. See again Diod. Sic. 14.108.1–2, with Frontin. *Str.* 3.4.3 and esp. Polyaenus, *Strat.* 5.2.10 for Dionysius' very large (τηλικαύτην) force.
144. Both quotes come from Van der Spek, Van Leeuwen and Van Zanden 2015b, 3.

145. See Parker 2004, 80–6 and esp. 83–4 for what follows.

146. See Garnsey 1988, 74 and Bresson 2016, 429 for producers and sellers in Classical Greece being generally free from state control in marketing their grain.

147. See Erdkamp 2005, 295–6; Bresson 2016, 254–5; Bresson 2022, 231.

148. On the inverse relationship between fixed prices and quantities of food supplies made available for sale in markets, see Erdkamp 2005, 293; Bresson 2016, 433.

149. Bresson 2022, 221–2. See also Bresson 2016, 102–10, esp. 109 for this idea although, first, it needs to be emphasized here that there was no direct taxation-in-kind in the Classical Greek world (Littman 1988 is still a serviceable introduction on this point); and, second, the contrast drawn in Bresson between Greek and contemporary Mesopotamian state control of surpluses is overdrawn (Van der Spek 2017, 603).

150. Finley 1987, 117 with Saller 2005, 224–5; Launaro 2016, 237–8. Finley (1999, e.g. 60, 124, 125, 133) also accepted it as uncontroversial that cities could not be perfectly self-sufficient and needed to import and export goods in order to meet their (materially and culturally determined) subsistence wants and needs. See also Launaro 2016, 237–8 on this point.

151. See Finley 1970a, 13–14.

152. See e.g. Finley 1999, 105, 107, 138. Saller (2005, 225) tries to acquit Finley of a primitivist position on markets in the Graeco-Roman world by quoting Finley's statement that peasants were part of a 'wider economic system' and by stating that Finley 'noted that peasants specialized in cash crops for markets if they lived close enough to urban areas or sites of religious festivals'. This misrepresents Finley's position. First, Finley's focus throughout his discussion of peasants was on their self-sufficiency (and its wider economic effects); he wrote explicitly that peasant 'subsistence farming is by definition not market farming, not the production of cash crops' (1999, 107). Second, Finley mentions the possibility of peasants near 'larger towns, international shrines (. . .) or (. . .) more or less permanent army camps' specializing in cash crops to meet the demand of these sites. But he quickly dismisses this possibility: 'I suspect, however, that good land so located would have attracted the wealthier landlords (. . .) with their speciality products, and that it was in those strata, rather than among the peasants, that the suppliers of city-army-shrine needs were normally to be found' (1999, 107).

153. Finley's pessimistic views in *The Ancient Economy* on their potential performance discouraged work on markets in the Greek world until recently, as Harris and Lewis note in their valuable discussion of recent and past scholarly work on the subject (2016, 3–9).

CHAPTER 3
ECONOMICS OF CONFLICT IN THE ANCIENT GREEK MEDITERRANEAN

Manu Dal Borgo[1]

Based on Thomas Piketty's book *Capital in the Twenty-First Century*, Walter Scheidel argues in *The Great Leveler* that democracy tends to follow violent upheavals.[2] Organized violence, such as war, requires mass mobilization. War imbues the wage-earning masses with bargaining power which puts pressure on elites and reduces inequality. A powerful leveller was the mobilization of an ancient Greek navy for the maintenance of sea power, on account of the relatively large number of men required to man and row the vessels.[3] This chapter will address war as it affects property rights broadly rather than specific civic rights.[4] Property rights underpin the transparency of ownership and accountability for transactions and, therefore are the notions which will act as the foundations for strategic choices amongst historical actors. The two case studies we investigate are, first, the primitive economic institutions that emerged in Homeric Greece, and second, Athens' financial policy during the Peloponnesian War.

Sections 1 and 2 summarize the domain of warfare in the ancient Greek economy. Sections 3 and 4 present a game theoretic case study of the Homeric war economy and its similarities to a game of social contract. Section 5 argues that the emergence of the complex financial institutions of the Classical period set constraints on Athens' military funding mechanisms during the Peloponnesian War. Section 6 provides a detailed introduction to the different ways of costing the war and the current debate on how to recreate Athens' financial war strategy from that evidence. Finally, Section 7 presents a highly stylized simulation of the Peloponnesian War as a strategic network model of city-state actors (*poleis*), their economic strategies and payoffs. Section 8 concludes with some suggestions for future research into the economics of conflict in the ancient world generally. For the orthodox classicist, this study may appear reductionist; this is a result of the mathematization of historically nuanced arguments.[5] Political and cultural events should be analysed in conjunction with economic phenomena, not as one and the same.

1. War and the ancient Greek economy

Economics of conflict is the study of the trade-off between appropriation and production. In standard economic theory, the usual assumption is that property rights are perfect and costless. That is, when people agree terms, those terms are assumed to be clearly understood by all and that all parties fulfil their obligations without fail. To reflect the realities of war, in the emerging specialist field called the economics of conflict, property rights are neither perfectly nor costlessly enforced.[6] These economists employ game theory, which allows for market imperfections, to understand how a city-state allocates resources in times of war. Each city-state's labour market allocation today from peacetime work to military service, for example, may determine tomorrow's distribution of power from losers to victors among warring city-states. Power in the form of assets, both commercial and political, is the output of war.

War was profitable,[7] not always but mostly, and the right to booty was an 'eternal law' (*nomos aidios*, Xen. *Cyr.* 7.5.73). Violence for profit, or booty (*leia*),[8] was more often localized in the seizure and raiding of coastal territory.[9] Many Homeric heroes talk about raiding for livestock and slaves (e.g. *Od.* 9.39–42; *Il.* 1.165–8).[10] A 'booty-chaser' (*leister*: Homeric, later *leistes*) could act autonomously or under the instruction of a powerful leader who sought to outsource raiding at a more localized level. Homeric rulers incentivized 'border wars between neighbours', keeping enemies and allies weak and by implication their costs of war low (Thuc. 1.5.1–3). After the Greco-Persian wars, raiding was diverted largely to the open sea and coastal cities according to Thucydides (1.15.1–2). In all–out war or small-scale raids, plunder was seized by combatants and the division of the booty was done by leaders based on merit, a practice dating back to Homer, and by prearranged agreement, more common later in the Classical period.[11]

There were often disagreements about the division (Justin 5.10.12; Xen. *Hell.* 3.5.5; Plut. *Lys.* 27.2). At times, leaders would divide profits from the sale of slaves, for example, and leave combatants to plunder for themselves the loser's camp, city or land. Booty consisted of metal objects, especially weapons and armour, cloth, other movable property, livestock, enslaved captives, especially women and children, profits from the sale of land and money in the form of silver and gold bullion, which later included coinage (first introduced in Lydia around 600 BC).[12] Armies are by nature mobile and by necessity sold booty on the spot. As such, they were often accompanied by merchants (*kapeloi*) who supplied the army or were visited by maritime exporters (*emporoi*) who redistributed the loot to more favourable markets.[13] Merchants were expected to accompany armies and Greek armies retained officers charged with the sale of booty, *laphuropolai* (Xen. *Ages.* 1.18). Booty served to pay for a combatant and oarsman's needs during the campaign (Plut. *Cim.* 9). In the Classical period, booty as a substitute for wages is less common, since armies expected generals and city-states to pay wages up front and not in arrears. Yet, plunder was always to be part of military funding.

The orthodox view on the violent seizure of assets is that small-scale raiding, often referred to as piracy, is constant throughout history. Currently the modern state holds a monopoly on sanctioned forms of violence, small and large scale, both interstate raiding and war among coalitions. Vincent Gabrielsen calls the distinction between the 'raid' and 'war' a 'conceptual segregation' of how the violence producer behaves. The raid is supposedly more demographically and economically destructive and it challenges the central authorities who are entrusted with 'protecting those under its control'. It is a 'fundamentally ideological opposition'.[14] The Thucydidean premise that protection from piracy is achieved through a collective agreement to invest in fortifications permeates this type of discourse (Thuc. 1.6.1). I argue that this distinction is not solely ideological. Both forms of violence were (and are) economic choices with clear benefits and costs to the decision makers who operated within their specific institutional constraints.

Economic decision-making in these highly imperfect markets of the ancient world are a burgeoning field of study. For the Classical period, Allain Bresson argues that city-states made strategic decisions weighing the economic and political consequences of choosing between domestic commerce and the external commerce of grain.[15] Josiah Ober went further and designed the *King, City and Elite* game with Barry Weingast, a Stanford political scientist, that described the Hellenistic-era relations among kings, *demos* and elite who each, in turn, have to choose whether to fortify the city-state, vote for military investment and lend support to the democracy, or not.[16] Adding to this literature, the game theoretic analysis of warfare and its economic implications are used in this chapter to describe the imperfect markets for loot and for peacefully traded goods during war, and how these markets transformed with the evolution of city-state institutions in ancient Greece.

2. Homer and Hesiod

The economic 'realities' of the Iron and Archaic periods are elusive, veiled by the poetic fictions of Homer and Hesiod, such that the 'daily life' that the poems disguise are difficult to retrieve.[17] Further, little survives that lends itself to any form of economic quantification. Archaeological data is at best used as proxy data. Meanwhile, textual analysis results in circular arguments that are, for example, from Homer for Homeric Greece. This type of data however is advantageous for a diachronic view of ancient economic behaviour. We shall test the economic implications of the reported behaviours and interactions and see whether these make sense within a larger picture of economic development in section 7.

Hesiod's primary focus was on agriculture and trade as means of livelihood, contrasting with the martial exploits and acts of piracy present in Homeric epics. Nonetheless, Hesiod set war and trade on an equal footing. To Hesiod, the goddess of Strife has two facets which can explain the desire of mankind to accumulate or seize wealth. Strife is competition. Strife is both destructive and productive. She inspires both the toil of war (*Theog.* 224–30) and competition among tradesmen in the production of goods (*WD* 11–35). On a household scale, Hesiod in the *Works and Days* expects a landowner every summer after the harvest to set sail by sea either to trade or to raid, to either increase his current income or to escape debt and hunger, respectively (*WD* 655–6, 663–5). Another good time for sailing is in spring and again Hesiod expects men to be trading or raiding (*harpaktos*, *WD* 678–86). He does not endorse this mischief (*kakon*), namely, sailing, given the risk of losing your cargo to storms and other raiders.

Hesiod diffidently does not refer to large-scale war as a mechanism to acquire wealth despite acknowledging the regular practice of raiding for plunder. He instead treats wealth, acquired by whatever means, as a product of an intergenerational economic ethic of labour, agreements and offspring (*WD* 370–82):

> Let the wage promised to a friend be fixed; even with your brother, smile –and get a witness; for trust and mistrust alike ruin men. Do not let a flaunting woman coax and cozen and deceive you: she is after your barn. The man who trusts womankind trusts deceivers. There should be an only son to feed his father's house, for so wealth will increase in the home; but if you leave a second son you should die old. Yet Zeus can easily give great wealth to a greater number. More hands, means more work and more increase. If your heart within you desires wealth, do these things and work, with work upon work.

Homer between 750–700, however, is very alive to the productive aspects of warfare in these three categories – labour, agreements and offspring. All the heroes are taking part in the Trojan War expecting to profit from plunder in no small measure. It is the 'unfair' partition of spoils which sets the stage for the *Iliad* and the breakdown of the informal contract between Achilles and Agamemnon to fight side by side. In the epic, an economy both of tangible profit and intangible pain are intertwined. In book 11, we read that Agamemnon's labour of war is compared to the labour pains of a woman giving birth (*Il.* 11.267–72):

> But when the wound dried up, after the blood stopped flowing, Agamemnon, the son of Atreus, was pierced by pain. As a piercing, cruel arrow strikes a woman in the agony of labor, shot by the goddess of labor pangs, the Eileithuias, who are Hera's daughters, in charge of cruel birth-pangs – even so sharp pains pierced Agamemnon.[18]

The simile seamlessly provides the reader with an example of the tangible profits of war. Working for plunder is compared to bearing children, since 'more hands means more work and more increase' (Hes. *WD* 380). This is a unique description of the division of labour between men and women that sheds light on the value of labour in the Homeric economy. Like a mother producing and giving birth to a baby at great physical cost with the expectation of profit from 'more hands', the man trades his own blood on the battlefield for honour (*time*) and wealth. On a macroeconomic scale, blood and dead bodies pays for both intangible *time* and tangible wealth from plunder. Plunder in exchange for dead bodies is a common *topos* in Homeric economic thinking.[19]

In the context of development economics, it does not follow that the absence of a market economy implies that gains from trade go unexploited and that resources were misallocated.[20] On the state level, the war economy of *time* is where power and honour are the gains from trade from the suffering of the masses.[21] On an individual level, each warrior risks his life in the hope of profiting from battle. All men collectively cooperate, as they agree to fight together, in order to produce the output of war, be it victory or defeat. For each household, the outcome of war comes at the expense of losing a male and risks future aggregate family income, as Hesiod made evident. A state's power is the ability it has to achieve an end in the face of conflict and it depends on several households simultaneously cooperating and competing with each other.

This is why a foundational concept in the economics of conflict is that the contenders' relative commitments to conflictual labour determine how the aggregate income will be distributed among them.[22] This plays out more clearly in the textual evidence of the Classical period, but already in Homeric economic thinking, relative commitment is very much tied to the balance between peaceful and conflictual activity. In agreement with Hesiod, A. W. Gomme has argued that by the Classical period, *polis* armies mobilized during certain times of the year that were well known to be the campaigning seasons 'at the beginning of spring' and 'when the grain was ripe'.[23] The choice between trade and violent seizure was a regular consideration for agents of the ancient Greek economy. Each man had a choice to either kill or plough. Communities were either producing for sale or seizing for sale.

The choice between engaging in agriculture or participating in military campaigns in the Archaic and Classical *polis* was predominantly a civic decision. Unlike the individualistic pursuits often glorified in modern interpretations, ancient Greek citizens were subject to the needs and decisions of their city-state. Military service was compulsory, with citizens typically drafted into the army or navy. This conscription ensured that the *polis* could effectively mobilize its resources for both agricultural production and military endeavors, reflecting a collective approach to the challenges faced by the community (e.g. Aristot. *Const. Ath.* 24).

3. Homeric conflict economy: a case study

From what we read, the Homeric economic system required local leaders to finance military expeditions supplying soldiers and oarsmen with provisions (*Od.*15.506–7) with the promise of a share of the spoils – which in effect are the expected wages from military service. In general, the financing of state activity was an interplay of leverage among rulers, elites and the *demos*. Local rulers would source provisions for expeditions on the spot with a public levy on the *demos* (*Od.* 19.196–8) or on the wealthier members of their community (*Od.* 8.389–99; 417–41; 13.10–12). Rulers would later reimburse contributions from the elite through an informal *ad hoc* taxation of the *demos* (*Od.* 13.13–15). Members of the community with privately owned ships were either coerced (*Od.* 14.235–9; 248–51) or volunteered (*Od.* 7.189; 8.34–9) to deploy their ships for state use. Although local rulers were empowered to take executive decisions on the allocation of resources, private or public, it was done with some sort of communal approval which took the shape of an assembled number of elite men (*Od.* 7.189). Extraordinary expenses were footed by the elite, while regular expenditure was financed by the wider population (*Il.* 17.225–6 (*laos*); 17.248–51 (*demos*)).[24] Loot paid for the army in the ongoing campaign and was brought back and divided to pay off the initial investment (*Il.* 11.686–8, 698).

Failure to comply with a demand for military service could also result in one's assets being taken. This type of confiscation seemed to operate in the Greek and Trojan rules of conduct alike (*Il.* 13.669 (Greek); 18.300–2 (Trojan) cf. *Od.* 16.424–30, ML 20.41–2). Punishment could sometimes go beyond a mere fine and end in death (*Il.* 3.56–7) or exile (*Od.* 16.376–87).[25]

War could be a very lucrative business. The spoils of war in-hand are the realized wages from military service. These were collected into one deposit and were divided by executive order. The partition of the spoils was fair (*isos*), which does not mean equal (*Il.* 1.124–6). Shares were discriminated according to merit and status. Leaders or rulers received a lion's share accrued from their status, where prizes went to leaders and exceptional fighters (*ll.* 9.334). Further shares of food were meted out to the leaders as well.[26] Each ruler decided how much an individual or group received, including himself. There is no surprise that the unfair partition of plunder in favour of a leader was common (*Il.* 1.163–8; 2.225–33; *Od.* 10.40–2). Hesiod referred to local rulers as 'gift-eaters' (*dorophagoi*, Hes. *WD.* 39, 221, 264).

Leaders were further beneficiaries of informal trade tariffs or indirect taxes. Traders gifted goods to the leader supposedly to gain access to the local market (*Il.* 23.741–5; 7.467–75). Our evidence is from the market set up by the Greek camp during the Trojan war (*Il.* 7.467–75):

> And ships full, many were at hand from Lemnos, bearing wine, . . .And for themselves alone unto the sons of Atreus, Agamemnon and Menelaus, had Euneus given wine to be brought them, even a thousand measures. From these ships the long-haired Achaeans bought them wine, some in exchange for bronze, some for gleaming iron, some for hides, some for whole cattle, and some for slaves.

After the spoils were divided, soldiers needed somewhere to trade them, specifically here, for wine. Many Greek merchant ships carried Thracian wine to the Greeks in the Trojan war (*Il.* 9.70–3). These particular tradesmen wished to gain access to the goods seized and slaves taken by the soldiers on campaign. These temporary markets attracted traders of all kinds. The Phoenicians played no small role in provisioning and trading with the Greek army (*Il.* 23.740–5):

> Then the son of Peleus straightway set forth other prizes for fleetness of foot: a mixing bowl of silver, richly wrought; . . .seeing that Sidonians, well skilled in deft handiwork, had wrought it cunningly, and men of the Phoenicians brought it over the murky deep, and landed it in harbour, and gave it as a gift to Thoas.

The centralization of wealth in the hands of a few was tempered by the community's acquiescence to the allocation of those resources. Rulers were in charge of distribution, but were also facilitators of the logistical practicalities for soldiers to have access to a market. Whereas the Homeric economy favoured the wholesale seizure and retail sale of assets, this specific form of appropriation was not the same for all peoples. Appropriation is a rapacious seizure of goods, but equally it can mean to seize and control the market itself.

One of the earliest recorded peoples to control maritime trade were the Phoenicians. Assyrian texts refer to the Phoenician kings of Arados, Tyre, Sidon, Byblos and other cities as 'kings of the seacoast.'[27] The Hebrew Bible presents the Phoenician kings of Tyre (Ezek. 28.2, 26–8; 1 Kings 9.27) and Sidon (Isa. 23) as enthroned on the sea. In a *scholium* or marginal comment on the above *Iliad* passage, a commentator writes that 'to a supreme degree the Phoenicians were the first to plow the seas' (*Schol. Il.* 23.744, for the Phoenicians/Sidonians at sea: *Od.* 13.271–86; 4.285–307; 15.403–84). Homer acknowledges that the Phoenicians were 'famous for their ships' (*nausiklutoi*, *Od.*15.415) and goes as far as to imply that the Sidonians do not live in Phoenicia (*Od.* 4.83–4; 14.285–307). Phoenician traders profited from the exchange of goods and slaves with other Phoenician cities, with other coastal cities and especially from temporary markets for troops at war. Almost all traders in the Homeric poems are Phoenicians which indicates how the Greeks perceived their control over maritime trade and how specialized they had become in foreign trade at this time. By the Archaic period, the Phoenicians were sailor-merchants par excellence, with a taste for piracy in the form of slave trade.[28] War and trade are inextricably linked as a 'unifying force'.[29]

Metaphorically, the contest is often between an elephant and a whale: land powers regularly seek to put an end to or control sea powers. Goods circulate more quickly by sea, thus revenues are realized more quickly. Navies are an economic threat to land-based powers. According to Thucydides (1.4), the legendary king Minos 'likely' brought an end to piracy to bring in more revenue (*prosodos*) with the effective control of the Aegean under one rule.[30] Piracy is merely a form of small scale predation as opposed to the organized grand scale of war. Herodotus supports another early candidate besides Minos among the first sea–power suppressors 'in human history'. He writes that Polycrates in the 530s also desired 'the rule of the sea' (3.122.2). What we can say for certain is that the Persians took to ruling the sea-faring Phoenicians toward the end of the Archaic period. Around 530–525 BC, after Egypt's failed expansionary naval ambitions (Hdt. 2.161.1, 2.182.2), the Persians put in motion plans to control the Phoenician naval force (Hdt. 3.34.4). The Persians themselves were compelled to do so. Herodotus writes that they were 'not seafaring' (Hdt. 1.143.1; 151). It is only after 530, that Cambyses takes control of the sea with Phoenician assistance – sailors and captains – as their prevalence in the Greco-Persian war demonstrates.[31]

4. Social contract in the Homeric Age

A game theoretic interpretation of the Homeric economic system has rulers make a strategic choice between piracy and war. Rulers played a social contract game with each other which is very similar to the stag hunt game – so named after Jean-Jacques Rousseau's allegorical description: 'If it was a matter of hunting a stag, everyone well realised that he must remain faithful to his post; but if a hare happened to pass within reach of one of them, we cannot doubt that he would have gone off in pursuit of it without scruple.'[32] To hunt a hare is to have a sure reward: the value 1 in the matrix (see Matrix 3.1). However, to successfully capture a stag, all participants need to forge and commit to a social contract or tacit agreement to hunt the stag together: the value 2 in the matrix. Otherwise, one hunter risks not capturing either, should the other decide not to hunt the stag after all: the value 0 in the matrix.[33]

Likewise, the Homeric economic system was a struggle between the gains from piracy compared to the gains from war. If a household chose to pillage for its livelihood, it could live off of piracy, so argued Thucydides (1.5.1):

> For in ancient times both the Greeks, and those barbarians, whose homes were on the coast of the mainland or on islands, when they began to find their way to one another by sea took to piracy. They were commanded by powerful chiefs, who took this means of increasing their wealth and providing for their poorer followers. They would fall upon the unwalled and straggling towns, or rather villages, which they plundered, and maintained themselves chiefly (*ton pleiston tou biou*) by the plunder of them; for, as yet, such an occupation was held to be honourable and not disgraceful.

However, for more profitable investments such as sacking a larger fortified city, it required the joint effort of many people. The sure payoff from piracy, or at least the less risky

		Hunter 2: Stag	Hunter 2: Hare
Hunter 1	Stag	2,2	0,1
	Hare	1,0	1,1

Matrix 3.1 Stag hunt.

		Ruler 2: War	Ruler 2: Piracy
Ruler 1	War	**Share spoils of war**	Both agree to go to war but Ruler 2 defects
	Piracy	Both agree to go to war but Ruler 1 defects	Each raids separately

Matrix 3.2 Homeric coordination.

payoff, was an attractive alternative to the higher, yet riskier, returns from war. War was profitable only if the sack was successful. In addition, the spoils from war were then divided, as we hear from Homer, very often unfairly. With higher risks and the very real threat of returning home empty handed, war was attractive for its potential higher returns, but still riskier than piracy. This type of Homeric strategic thinking is a variant of the stag hunt and thus a similar coordination dilemma.

The Homeric 'no pain, no gain' assessment of economic incentives and decision-making conflated peaceful trade with violent appropriation. Piracy and war were undeniably important contributors to trade (Thuc. 1.13).[34] These trends persist into the Archaic period. Polycrates' maritime aspirations allowed him to enrich Samos by importing goods from many other Aegean cities,[35] literally filling (*eneplese*) Hellas with all types of foods.[36] The most prominent ship of the Archaic age was the penteconter; its primary use was for trade and only secondarily for war. Privately owned ships were mobilized for war at public expense.[37] This system, however, was less than perfect since it relied heavily on social contracts, under which property rights were imperfectly enforced.

The feud between Agamemnon and Achilles is an *exemplum* of the very high transaction costs that arose from unenforceable property rights. Agamemnon, the sceptre-holder (*Il.* 2.108) and commander of the suitors of Helen, triggered the defection of one of his rulers as a result of asymmetric information about how much that ruler was worth to the investment of Troy (*Il.* 1.171). This resulted in a disagreement regarding the costs of death as it pertains to the rentability of long-term cooperation versus short-term profits. In the pursuit of household income, death as a cost of conflict can cripple economic development and the very existence of a household. The effects of the sharply increasing death toll of war or plague on the ancient economy are well known. Although there are exceptions, a phenomenon regularly observed is that a reduced labour supply increases the bargaining power of wage earners.

The *Iliad*, set in the tenth and final year of the war, is a story of how Achilles bargains for rewards that should reflect his current valuation. Achilles' 'wage' or stake in the returns for military cooperation likely changed since he first set foot on the Trojan beach. With almost a decade of losses to the Greek camp and a recent plague, Achilles's value as a fighter could have only increased. If a ruler like Achilles in the command of a substantial number of troops retreated from the agreed coordinated attack of a hardened target city, such as well-fortified Troy, it could cripple, risk and potentially cause the whole military expedition to fail. Achilles time and time again values himself in terms of dead Achaeans (*Il.* 1.454, 16.237, 18.76–7). This would result in all the other participant states incurring their sunk costs in having provisioned the army, up to that point, and then unable to realize their profit. During the late iron age, efforts toward institutional change were made to centralize rule to increase logistical efficiency and the extraction of public revenue, but most importantly to help to better the valuation of the costs of conflict, so that large scale ventures would not easily fail. These changes fuelled international maritime trade and colonization, which intensified economic growth from Sicily to the Black Sea[38] and the emergence of transit trade hotspots for slaves and war booty, such as Crete.[39]

5. Evolution from the Archaic to the Hellenistic economy

Under the rule of law, Archaic communities attempted to regulate these imperfectly enforced mechanisms of exchange. The Persians were the first to establish annual tribute collection (Hdt. 3.89.1) and to enforce dispute resolution regulation among its allies in order to put an end to border raiding (Hdt. 6.42.1). This prevented losses to imperial revenue, which was assessed by the size and productivity of the territories.[40] Local authorities called satraps were appointed positions that held civil and military authority. Subjects paid tribute and provided troops for the satraps' and Great King's wars. Sparta in the early sixth century was the *hegemon* of the Peloponnesian league that also obliged members through treaties of alliance to supply troops. However, the league was not financially regulated, despite the Spartans' reputation for civic meddling, helping to impose oligarchic constitutions among member *poleis*.[41] Athenian imperialism largely borrowed the Persian instruments of imperial finance after the Greco-Persian war and was the wealthier for it in the Classical period.[42]

Throughout the Archaic Mediterranean, there is evidence of a burgeoning legal system to secure the property rights of sellers and buyers through a public record of land sales and litigation over assets. Although the evidence is predominantly from Athens, similar types of property records are found at Tenos, Miletus, Samos, Camarina and several Northern Greek cities.[43] Commodity or wants-traders from the Archaic period appear to have reduced the risks of exchange between buyers and sellers with letters on amphorae in the transport of both small- and large-scale ship cargoes. These letters on jars and further documentary evidence of customs fees being met at port left a paperwork trail which led to higher and higher degrees of information exchange – that is, there was less information asymmetry between buyers and wholesalers at the port or retailers in the *agora*. Athens, unlike other cities, after about 480, had no local Attic transport amphora production. The lack of production was surely due to a sufficient supply of imported jars. Increased literacy, standardized weights, measures and coinage allowed for even more transparency and standardization in the valuation of goods and services.[44]

By the Hellenistic period, ship-wreck archaeology shows even more evidence of larger cargoes, which is indicative of a higher frequency in direct trade.[45] In step with the growth in trade from the Archaic to the Classical eras, the Hellenistic age saw the regular movement of even larger armies as a result of the arms race between Alexander's successors.[46] The Homeric economic system of war and trade evolved dramatically. Institutional development of the Archaic allowed for a reduction of asymmetric information and promoted the transition of the ancient Greek economy from a Homeric conflict economy to a Classical centralized financial system.[47] Centralization increased state funding for conflict, notably in sea and siege warfare toward the end of the sixth century and in infantry warfare in the fifth century.[48]

6. The Peloponnesian War: a case study

Under Solon, Homeric social contracts spill over into the design of Athenian Archaic financial institutions. The *kolakretai* or 'ham-collectors' allocated resources from central funds on behalf of the community (*FGrH* 324 F36) while the *poletai* or Sellers imposed levies and made spending decisions, much like a king (*Ath. Pol.* 47.2–4). In the Archaic period *poletai* worked with the captaincies or *naukrariai* (*Ath. Pol.* 8.3), who were entrusted with a financial duty to collect taxes, specifically *eisphora*, but also cavalry and ships (Pollux *Lexicon* 8.108).[49] A defining quality of *eisphorai* is that they were *ad hoc*.[50] In Classical Athens, *eisphorai* were direct taxes, levied on a person's wealth, and used to finance war.[51] In 478/7, a financial office dedicated to reducing the risks in joint military ventures was established. These officials were called the 'Treasurers of the Greeks', the *Hellenotamiai*, and they managed the funds collected from the Delian League. The League was an Athenian-led confederacy of allies born to protect its members from 'barbarian' invasion and thus prevent any disruption to the Greek sphere of trade and livelihood (Thuc. 1.96). Athens from that point onward went to war with lower and lower relative costs, adding an annual income of tribute and imperial revenues of around 600t to her budget (Thuc. 2.13.3). Booty and permanent imperial revenue, from mine concessions (Thuc. 1.101.3, Amphipolis), cleruchies (Diod. 11.88.3; Thuc. 3.50.2; *IG* i^3 237) and taxes on trade[52] created unprecedented volumes of surplus revenues. *Eisphora* that had been vital to public finance was no longer needed and re-emerges only in the Peloponnesian War.

Thucydides notes that Athens' loss of the colony of Amphipolis in 424 was a severe hit to Athenian revenue. Without access to timber, mines and possibly revenue-bearing sacred land,[53] the fear of a cascade effect on other allies to surrender or defect was very

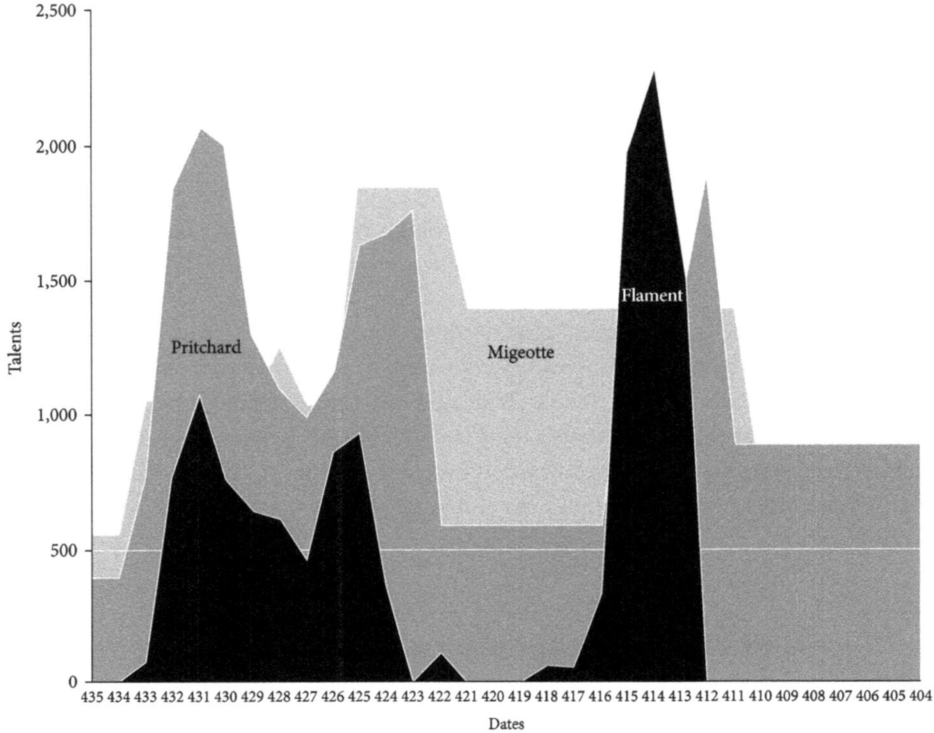

Figure 3.1 Athens' military revenue/expenditure streams from 435–404.[56]

real.[54] The alliance would dissolve if funds dried up. With fewer members, the heavier the financial burden would be on those remaining. Evidence of disaffection and revolt among the allies is strongest for the 450s and especially after the failure of the Sicilian Expedition in 413.[55]

Athenian military revenue and expenditure during the war is a problem which many scholars have investigated, but only a handful have costed.

The various streams of revenue – tribute, loans, taxes, trierarchies and other reserves – have led two scholars to attempt a full costing of the war. Léopold Migeotte's and David Pritchard's estimates for military revenues, looking at the line graph in the light and medium greys, respectively, propose similar trends for Athenian financial expenditure.[57] There are, however, two apparent discrepancies. In one case, they appear to disagree with regard to spending in the years immediately preceding the war as well as during the Archidamian war (433–423 BC). This is due to Pritchard opting for the more precise year-by-year estimate of expenditure, whereas Migeotte calculates on the basis of a ten-year average spending trend. If we were to convert Pritchard's discrete figures into a ten-year average, we would arrive at a close 1,485 t.[58] compared to Migeotte's 1,333 t. (upper limit estimate).[59] Still, there is real divergence between them, in that, unlike Pritchard, Migeotte does not see a sharp drop in military spending starting with the Peace of Nicias

(421 BC) and ending with the launch of the Sicilian Expedition (415 BC). Pritchard believes that this period is characterized by a 70 per cent drop in military expenditure compared to the 420s.[60] Furthermore, Migeotte maintains that numbers were stable until the 410s, which included trierarchic contributions, sacred loans, plunder, the sale of prisoners and the collection or extortion of money and taxes. After 410, Migeotte adds two possible levies of *eisphora* (in 410 and 407/6), but these do not disagree with Pritchard's estimates after the Sicilian expedition (after 413 BC). The values for all of the extra-ordinary streams of revenue are completely unknown, such is the variability of the profits from war and other expedients (cf. Thuc. 8.23.3),[61] but Migeotte believes that the *eisphorai* and loans would each have amounted to several hundred talents and that plunder could also have reached several thousand talents from 410 to the end of the war in 404.

Cristophe Flament, dark grey in the graph, reports significantly lower estimates.[62] Flament arrives at his estimates via a different route to the previous two scholars.[63] Instead of estimating expenditure from the evidence on revenue streams of fiscal accounts and loans, as attempted by Pritchard and Migeotte, Flament extrapolates military expenditures from Thucydides', Xenophon's and Diodorus Siculus' campaign accounts. In the main, he estimates the cost of each reported campaign by multiplying the *number of combatants*, *duration of campaign* and a daily *wage rate*.[64] The daily wage of a hoplite soldier, he assumes, is one drachma a day for the most part (except for Potidaea and the Sicily expedition in 422 for which he uses two drachma a day), and assumes the standard cost of 200 drachma a day for a trireme. He does not include the trierarchy nor cavalry contributions, which depress his numbers considerably. These he disregards, since these were part of the annual expense of the city and not an extra-ordinary military expense as were the specific campaigns.[65] He cuts off his estimations at the start of the Decelean war. Flament assumes that, with the replacement of tribute with the *eikoste* or 5 per cent import/export maritime tax in 413 BC (Thuc. 7.28.4), *polis'* participation in troop maintenance declined drastically and was effectively nothing after 411 BC (cf. Thuc. 8.76.6). During this period, the Athenians expected a Persian subsidy to kick in (Thuc. 8.47.1–48; Arist. *Pol.* 5.4.13),[66] albeit in vain (Thuc. 8.56), which contributed to the fleet, with over 100 triremes, becoming ever more financially autonomous through raiding and extortion.

With respect to the data itself, the first two fail to include the *ad hoc* contributions made by the Sicilian allies in 427/6 BC (*IG* i³ 291), which records a contribution as meagre as 11 t. (l.28) to another that is over 160 t. (l.18).[67] Also they do not consider that distinct makes of ships vary in troop or cavalry cargo capacities (e.g. *triereis tacheiai*, 'fast triremes', versus *triereis statiotides*, 'troop-carrying triremes' Thuc. 6.43) and that ships may have carried fewer than the maximum load.[68] These addenda would not have altered the order of magnitude of the figures, in any event.

The conclusions we draw from these estimates are that Migeotte believes that, over the twenty-seven-year period of the war, expenditure was hump-shaped and weighted slightly toward the beginning. Pritchard's and Flament's estimates are more U-shaped, because both agree that the 420s saw little military expenditure. Pritchard's and Flament's estimates track closely during the Archidamian war whereas Flament's figures feature a slight lag, understandably, as a result of their different accounting methods. Pritchard, however, sees heavier expenditures after the Sicilian expedition and Flament at the beginning. Pritchard accounts for the 1000 t. reserve utilized in 412 BC (Thuc. 2.24.1; 8.15.1),[69] whereas Flament accounts for the costs of simultaneous extra-Sicilian campaigns around the Aegean. As we can see, different estimation methods and sources can lead to very different pictures in financial terms, even though the orders of magnitude are the same, which may be an indication that we are not far off the true figures. Combining different measurement techniques and comparing them is a vital part of any sensitivity analysis.

Pritchard and Migeotte, however, present a more consistent strategic spending stream, whereas Flament adopts a more radical view of the final phase of the war, in which state military finance disappears completely in the 410s.[70] These different spending streams represent almost polar opposite stories of the type of financial decision-making of the Athenians, especially in the later years of the war.

In agreement with Flament's interpretation, Lisa Kallet – in both her monographs on Athenian finance – shows how Thucydides describes this extortion policy as Athenian folly and that indeed 'state piracy' became normal practice.[71] Piracy is prominent in Thucydides' narrative of the war itself, even though it is most explicitly used to explain the economic growth of Greek *poleis* in the Archaic period.[72] Flament argues from inscriptional evidence that from 410 to 408 the army, but especially the navy in the Hellespont, operated with almost complete financial autonomy supposedly securing subsistence through raiding.[73] This is telling given the fleet was previously in charge of collecting tribute.[74] If tribute alone was indeed running at about 900 t. a year,[75] in order for the maritime merchant tax of 5 per cent to be more profitable than tribute, the value of the goods in circulation throughout the empire must have been close to 18,000 t.[76] But how could merchants be safe or even trade with unaffected settlements with all this raiding? Trade must have suffered, at least, some form of network disruption.[77] It begs the question of whether the fleet targeted allied regions as well.[78] It is no surprise that there is an explosion of revolts between 413 and 410 after the introduction of the 5 per cent tax.[79]

It may be posited that the allied and non-allied merchants were being plundered by a growing number of privateers and very possibly by those who were meant to protect them – the Athenian fleet.[80] At the same time, merchants that relied on sea-borne trade had to pay an unprecedented high merchant tax on their goods; previously, since 420, they had been taxed at 1 per cent.[81] Athens likely antagonized the wealthy merchants and farmers among their allies.

At the same time that Athens is replacing tribute, which likely taxed the aristocracies more heavily, she is on campaign to instate oligarchies in allied states. According to Thucydides, this was done to 'overthrow the *demos*' (Thuc. 8.64.2, 64.4, 65.1, 68.1, 4, 86.2, 9) or 'destroy the *demokratia*' (Thuc. 8.47.2, 63.3).[82] Bargaining power, political and economic, is transferred entirely into the hands of the elites alone, cemented by the Oligarchic coup in 411 (Thuc. 8.48).

This type of predatory financial planning against the *demos* is clearest in Thucydides' own treatment of the subject. In 428/7, a continuous stream of revenue through the extortion of money (Thuc. 8.3.1) was preferred to *ad hoc* levies on the wealthy denizens of the empire (Thuc. 3.19):[83]

> The Athenians, needing additional money (*chrematon*) for the siege [of Mytilene], although they had for the first time levied a tax (*esphoran*) on themselves (*kai autoi*) of two hundred talents, sent out twelve ships to collect money (*argurologous naus*) from their allies, with Lysikles and four others in command.

Raiding as a form of funding had persisted throughout the Sicily expedition and increased dramatically after Athens' defeat in 413 (Thuc. 6.62.3–4). As a consequence, the *demos* push back and begin defecting.

A decree seeking to standardize the weights and measures throughout the Athenian empire was rolled out within two years of her defeat in Sicily.[84] It required mass restriking of allied coins into Athenian owls. However, the sequence of allied revolts rendered the effort moot.[85] The tribute paid by the estimated 200–400 allies of the Delian League was replaced by the 5 per cent harbour tax in 413 BC (Thuc. 7.28.4). From this point onward we see a spike in revolts: Chios, Rhodes, Miletus, Teos, Lebedos, Aerae, Clazomenae, Methymna, Mytilene and Oropus in 412/11 BC; Abydos, Lampsacus and Thasos in 411 BC.

Whilst revolts are multiplying, Samos, a tribute payer (Thuc. 7.57.4), undergoes an internal revolution where the popular party (*demos*) overthrows 'the landholders' (*geomoroi*) (Thuc. 8.21.1).[86] Whereas tribute was likely locally funded by wealthy individuals, harbour tax was paid directly by the poorer merchants and consumers. For places like Samos, Lampsacus, Thasos or Euboea, the elimination of the tribute was a tax burden that was shifted away from the owners of capital (i.e. trade contractors, bulk commodity producers and landowners) onto merchants and consumers (i.e. renters, traders and wage-earners), either unchanged in its entirety or partially. This meant that the effective purchasing power of wage-earners likely declined. A tax cut of 5 per cent on gross profit for a farm or industry owner did not necessarily mean that employed merchant wages went up by 5 per cent, but instead, more likely wages increased only partially, if at all, given there was no inter-*polis* enforcement mechanism of which we know. As a consequence the army lost a 'risk-free' source of provision, and the market naturally was flooded with loot instead, such that the Thebans could purchase slaves and other plunder relatively cheaply from the troops garrisoning at Deceleia (*Hell. Oxy.* 17.4). Allies and non-allies became targets. In 409, we are told of the Athenians' ravenous pursuit of plunder in Lydia. They first raided for their common store, seizing money, slaves and other booty (*leia*). Later they set off on a separate raiding missions to obtain private plunder (*idia leia*, Xen. *Hell.* 1.2.4–5).

The Athenian empire, like Agamemnon did Achilles, under-valued its allies, or at least under-valued the large revenue-generating part of the *poleis*, the *demos*, who required lower risk for their business activities. Only then would cooperation with the empire continue to be attractive to them. This resulted in disaffection and revolts among the allied *demos*, since the problem was exacerbated by Athens' military maritime policy to raid settlements to provision the fleet from 413 until around 410.[87] However, there is evidence that the policy continued down to the end of the war.[88]

Who was responsible for this move toward predatory financial planning? Thucydides first points to the Periclean policy against wealth taxes as a policy of financial prudence (1.141.5):

> It is reserves (*hai periousiai*) that maintain wars rather than forced contributions (*hai biaioi esphorai*).

Pericles' argument is also made by Archidamus, who admits that the Spartans lacked the market economy from whence to source public wealth and neither would they tax themselves. (Thuc.1.80.4) According to Lisa Kallet, Thucydides believed that 'the *eisphora* of 428 reflected poor financial management and foresight and that Pericles himself, had he still been alive, would not have resorted to such measures'.[89] The increasing reliance on raiding and the additional move to impose an indirect tax on allies to fund the military had its inception in Pericles' anti-*eisphora* campaign. Although Thucydides' admiration of Pericles steers his audience to believe that a wealth tax policy was a bad or sub-optimal move, it appears it would have been a good or an optimum strategic move after all.[90] Thucydides' elite bias is laid bare. He chastises the Athenian *demos*, without revealing that it was an oligarchic policy all along to place the tax burden on the allied *demos*, which led to the mass defection of allies in the years following the Sicilian expedition.[91]

7. Network model and a simulation of the Peloponnesian War

All previous sections have helped to design the actor distribution, their strategies and payoffs, in order to construct a stylized economic model of the Greek world at an unspecific time before 431 BC.[92]

This network of nodes represents the economic power of each city-state (a *polis* from this point on is referred to as a 'state'). On the left-hand side of the network are the states located geographically in the Peloponnese. The states represented are a mixture of the traditional Elis, Arcadia, the Argolid, Laconia and Achaea inspired by the regions of the states in Homer's *Catalogue of Ships*.[93] At the center, Megara connects the geography of the Peloponnese with mainland Greece, due to the controversial trade blockade imposed on her by Athens' Megarian Decree in *c.* 432 (Thuc. 1.139.1, Ar. *Ach.* 115–203, 501–625, 719–66). On the right-hand side, I constrain the map to Aetolia to the west, Thessaly to the north and Euboea to the east. A single node in the bottom-right corner denotes the Ionian city-states and coastal frontier Persian satrapies connected via the sea primarily to Athens and Sparta.[94] This unique geography is meant to display the immediate sphere of influence of both warring states – Sparta and Athens.

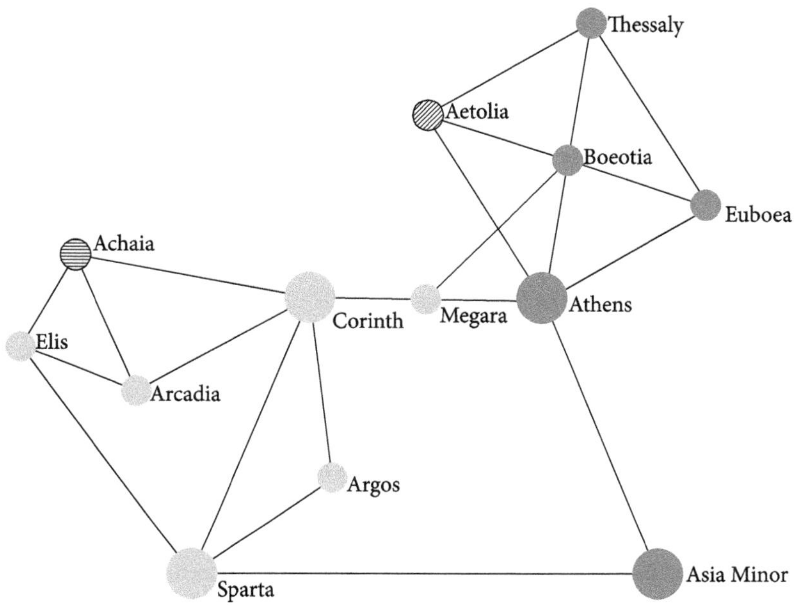

Figure 3.2 *Polis* network game.

What do the colours mean? The light grey states are Sparta's allies, the darker grey are Athens' allies and the remaining nodes with lines are independent states with no coalition. Before explaining the particular mechanics of how nodes interact, if all the states began as independent states, the map above is the state of the world that was the most likely to appear as an intermediary state between the initial state where all nodes were independent and the final state where one node became a hegemon. Boeotia nicely sits in the Spartan alliance; it was incorporated sometime during the Thirty Years' Truce preceding the war (Thuc. 1.111–15).[95]

The mathematics of the model and the code itself can be found on github for those who wish to dissect it, reuse it and transform it.[96] The code was developed by myself and Dr Cong Chen, and our findings were formally presented to the Network group at the Faculty of Economics, University of Cambridge, in 2020.

The map of the world is a network of nodes or states that have access to neighbouring states. The model parameters are such that each state has a sum of resources that is allocated to military or public investments, in economic terms, into fighting or productive efforts.[97] This is the 'guns and butter' problem interpreted as a public goods problem. Property rights are assumed to become stronger when the state invests in public security improving inter-*polis* trade and taxation, whereas investment into campaigning is motivated by private incentives that lead to the seizure of enemy territory and are to the detriment of trade. Equally, we can interpret this allocation policy of peace or war, as continued tax revenues and loans (on *demos* and elites) versus plunder, which as recent scholarship agrees dominated the latter half of the Peloponnesian War.

Each node's resources increase by a fraction with peace and also trade.[98] Likewise, every fight comes at a cost. At the start of a simulation, each state has the same amount of resources as everyone else, except for Athens, Sparta, Corinth and Asia Minor which are given larger but equal resources to represent their market power. Resource size is visible in the size of the node. Throughout the simulation, each state has an allocation policy of 50/50 except for Sparta which is given 80/20 in favour of fighting, as it is a state notorious for prioritising military investments. Sparta's allocation is arbitrary and meant to represent a particular preference, wherein its magnitude is non-significant.

The initial state of the world starts with all nodes as independent states.[99] The simulation randomly selects one node for each round to start the game, then that node decides whether it will fight any of its neighbouring nodes. The node chooses to fight based on a weighted expectation of its probability of winning multiplied by the benefits it would gain from an opponent's resources and a state's probability of losing multiplied by the cost of losing its resources. If the expected benefit minus cost payoff is positive, that state fights; otherwise, the simulation randomly selects another node. This random node selection and payoff comparison goes on until a hegemon node succeeds in taking over all other nodes. In every round, all nodes choose whether to defect from their alliance depending on the size of the coalition. The larger the alliance, the more likely someone is to defect.

Table 3.1 shows the results from 500 simulation runs lasting 300 pair-wise contests between states for each simulation. Each run began with all states being independent and would stop when one node would be first to take over all the other nodes and become a hegemon. Sparta is the hegemon 135 times out of 500 simulation runs, thus the most likely to win the war with 27 per cent. Athens is second place with 20 per cent and Achaia is a surprising 5 per cent. The Achaeans in the north Peloponnese retained significant independence and were probably not part of the Spartan alliance until after 417 BC.[100] The category 'Leavers' are the coalitions that were growing into potential hegemons, suffered defections and then were unable to reach a hegemonic state of the world by the end of the 300 turns.

Findings were that more military investment makes for a likely hegemon, as is the case for Sparta. More highly connected nodes experience much higher growth, as they

Table 3.1 Simulation output

Number of times as first hegemon in a 300-turn simulation, out of 500 runs		
'Athens'	20%	~100 runs
'Achaia'	5%	~22 runs
'Sparta'	27%	~135 runs
Leavers	43%	>200 runs
No-one	5%	~24 runs

have more opportunities for trade profit and can eventually eclipse smaller nodes, as for Athens and Achaia. What is enlightening is that this simple set up tracked some significant historical results using very coarse strategic behaviour. Our simple model leads to understandable output.

This *polis* network public goods game and Ober's recent work on the history of rationality and the game theoretic analyses of the Peloponnesian War have kindred ways of thinking; notably, the coalitions, hegemon versus subject incentives, uncertainty and expected payoffs will be familiar.[101] The principal difference is that our model is a generalizable dilemma played by all players sequentially – where every state aspires to hegemony, deals with the incentives to invest in peace or war and chooses to revolt or not. The other difference is that we simulate stochastic repeated interactions among players to provide output analysis for finite-horizon measures (i.e. simulation with fixed number of runs, here 500). For the generalizable solution, it is not within the scope of this chapter to provide a theoretical equilibrium solution for this network game. Two obvious extensions to the model would be to investigate steady-state systems, where each simulation runs infinitely until it reaches an unchanging state of the world, and to vary the connections amongst nodes.

8. Future research

The economics of conflict can provide us with simple tools to make generalizations about diachronic economic behaviour, which puts our scant and arbitrary pieces of evidence into a manageable format. The current perspective in this chapter is macroeconomic. On a microeconomic level, further investigation of different military suppliers would improve our view of these macroeconomic transformations, such as the birth of the weapons manufacturing industry. Microeconomic factors such as economies of scale, innovation and capital accumulation are the *proximate* causes of economic growth, unlike institutional change which seeks out long-term growth.[102]

The economics of conflict theory, to my knowledge, does not address the fact that ancient Greek warfare relied on individual soldiers to supply and arm themselves with their wages, as opposed to being financed by the state, as with modern states. In these types of models, the calculation of an outcome of war is described by the well-known *contest success function*. It is a weighted probability of success that assumes that the greater number of well-equipped soldiers one state has, relative to the enemy, the more likely that state is to win. The allocation of public funds to military training and equipment in the modern military does not depend on private wealth, wages and the market demand for arms as it did for the ancients. Military success is a macroeconomic decision for modern armies and not a household problem as it was for the ancient Greeks. I intend to discuss these themes and the adversarial competition for arms and armour in a subsequent publication.

Table 3.2 Migeotte

Migeotte*

Year	*Tribute*	*Trierarchy/ Property Tax*	*Loans*	*Public Funds*	*eikoste*	*Eisphora*	*Reserves*	*Current fund of Athena*	*Silver/Gold Objects*	*Plunder*	*Annual Totals*
435	383.33[1]	65[2]	33.33	74						0	555.66
434	383.33	65	33.33	74						0	555.66
433	382.5	135.83	466.66	65.83						0	1050.82[2]
432	382.5	135.83	466.66	65.83						0	1050.82
431	382.5	135.83	466.66	65.83						0	1050.82
430	382.5	135.83	466.66	65.83						0	1050.82
429	382.5	135.83	466.66	65.83						0	1050.82
428	382.5	135.83	466.66	65.83		200				0	1250.82
427	382.5	135.83	466.66	65.83						0	1050.82
426	382.5	135.83	466.66	65.83						0	1050.82
425	1180	135.83	466.66	65.83						0	1848.32
424	1180	135.83	466.66	65.83						0	1848.32
423	1180	135.83	466.66	65.83						0	1848.32
422	1180	135.83	466.66	65.83						0	1848.32
421	1180	120		?						90[3]	1390.00
420	1180	120		?						90	1390.00
419	1180	120		?						90	1390.00
418	885	120	58[5]	?						327	1390.00
417	885	120		?						385	1390.00
416	885	120		?						385	1390.00
415	885	120	350	?						35	1390.00
414	885	120		?						385	1390.00
413	Replaced w/ *eikoste*	120		?	1000					270	1390.00
412	Replaced w/*eikoste*	120		?	1000		1000			-730	1390.00

411	Replaced w/*eikoste*	120	?	1000				270	1390.00
410	172.5	120	?		200[6]	50[4]	75[4]	82.5	700.00
409	172.5	120	?			50	75	282.5	700.00
408	172.5	120	?			50	75	282.5	700.00
407	172.5	120	?		200	50	75	82.5	700.00
406	172.5	120	?			50	75	282.5	700.00
405	172.5	120	?			50	75	282.5	700.00
404	172.5	120	?			50	75	282.5	700.00

*Migeotte 2014, 565–8, all page references are in parentheses. Where M. provides upper and lower limit estimates, I take the average of the limits to calculate the annual total. **[1]** Net tribute figures. From the *aparchai* tax contributions, gross tribute is extrapolated and compared to literary sources (439–43). Both net tribute and its tax contributed to military expenses *only* and not to the construction of the Acropolis (571–5) M. estimates tribute ran at 382.5 t. for the first eight years and 1,180 for the following four years for an average of 648.33 from 433/2 to 422/1 (twelve years) and thereafter an average between 611–666.66 from 421/0 to 404/3. **[2]** Trierarchic contributions are the average of M.'s upper and lower limit range from 70 to 60. As to annual total expenditure, M.'s average from 433/2 to 422/1 is 1333.33 (567). To arrive at this figure, M. sums his upper limits and divides the total by 12. The total expenditure above is slightly different. Here, I take the average of his limits for each source of revenue to arrive at an average total expenditure. M. maintains the proportion of tribute and triarchies stable throughout the war, 44–48 per cent and over 8 per cent, respectively. (568) **[3]** Profits from plunder: M. estimates 'thousands of talents' between 421/0 and 404/3. I take M.'s annual average of expenses 1390 t. between 421/0 and 411/0 and subtract the estimates for tribute, trierarchy/property tax, *eisphora*, reserves, current fund of Athena and silver and gold objects for each year. There would be a surplus of revenue in 412, which is why plunder is negative in this year. Surplus paid back loans. Total plunder is about 4000 t. **[4]** M. has 'hundreds of talents' from 410 to the end of the war. I arbitrarily assign 50 t. a year on average for the current fund of Athena (and the other gods). Part of the funds ranged from 80 to 39 t. in *aparchai* tax every four years from 431/0 to 414/3 (442–3). M argues the fund had around 180 t. on account in 410/9 (*IG* I³ 375) which was a combination of *aprachai* reserves, individual offerings as well as fines and tax on the sale of confiscated goods (484–90). As to silver and gold objects, there was no less than 500 t. according to Thuc. 13.4–5. I estimate an average of 75 per year. **[5]** Loans from 421/0–404/3 (487, 567) of at least 408 t. There is evidence of another five loans of over 10,000 drachma (*IG* I³ 370–80, 86–7). M. argues some made before 412 and others before 408. **[6]** Both *eisphora* attained 'many hundreds of talents' (567). I give a conservative estimate of 200 for each year to match the 428 contribution which is disputed to be the standard or above the standard amount.

Table 3.3 Pritchard

Pritchard*

Year	*Tribute*	*Loans*	*Internal Surplus*	*Eisphora*	*Imperial Income*	*Annual Totals*
435	400[1]					400
434	400					400
433	388	76	100		212	776
432	388	1145	100		212	1845
431	388	1370	100		212	2070
430	388	1300	100		212	2000
429	388	600	100		212	1300
428	388	200	100		212	1100
427	388	100	100	200	212	1000
426	388	261	100	200	212	1161
425	1200[2]	130	100	200	212	1642
424	1200	163	100		212	1675
423	1200	253	100		212	1765
	Fixed Operating Costs[6]		**Variable Operating Costs**		**Reserves**	
422		402				594[3]
421		402	*Melos siege*			594
420		402				594
419		402				594
418		402	*Peloponnese & Thrace Campaigns*			594
417		402				594
416	402		*Scione siege*			594
415		402	*Macedon campaign/Sicily Expedition*			1366[4]
414		402	*Sicily Expedition*			1366

413	402	*Sicily Expedition*		1366
412	354		1000	1891 [5]
411	354	*Samos siege*		891
410	354			891
409	354			891
408	354			891
407	354	*Arginusai*		891
406	354			891
405	354			891
404	354	*Aegospotami*		891

*Pritchard 2012, 2015, 2019 **[1]** Supplemented with Ober 2015c, 245 values for 435–434 BC. **[2]** Tribute reassessment in 425 was calculated according to Athens' 'anticipated military spending' which in turn was based on military spending in the recent past and on short-term requirements. (2018, 165); *IG* i³ 71.61–181 evidence for 1460 t.; Plut. *Arist.* 24.3 for 1300 t. after 429/8; Andoc. 3.8–9 for 1,200 t. after 422/1; Ar. *Vesp.* 656–60 for 2000 t. after 423/2; Pritchard settles on 1200 t. from 425/4 onward. **[3]** P. argues that from 422/1 + five years (Peace of Nicias) saw military spending at 'around 30%' of the ten-year average from 433–423 (i.e. 445 t.), which includes cavalry wages, sailor wages, the maintenance of the fleet and other military assets (2015, 98; 2012, 44). P. elsewhere writes that spending 'could have easily been around 40%' (i.e. 594 t.: 2018, 167). **[4]** P. argues costs of over 4,000 t. for the Sicily expedition. (2015, 98) He follows Blamire (2001, 114) who adds 3,000, 300, 120 and notes the existence of a lost figure. From P., I extrapolate 3,000 (416/5, Blamire), 600 (I assume) and around 500 (414/13, Blamire) = average over three years is in excess of 1,000, which agrees with his assumption that values returned to the same level to those before the Peace. **[5]** P. argues for about 60% of the average level of spending from 433/2 to 423/22 (2012, 45 ft.171; repeated in 2015, 99; 2018, 167), with intense spending on ship building at the start of the Ionian war and a rise in costs on manning fifty extra ships at Arginusai and eighty extra ships at Aegospotami. I do not add the regular expenses in 'wages for other land-based troops defending Athens and its countryside, [and] the cost of shipbuilding' since they are not costed. I suspect these costs would have amounted to 300 or less, in line with P.'s 320s estimates. P. believes the archer corps shrunk after Sicily therefore I halve their wages (i.e. 96 talents/2) in the fixed operating costs which brings down the total to 354. (2018, 167–8) **[6]** Fixed operating costs are 402 t. (2018, 166) which are the cavalry corps (146 t.), twenty guard ships (135 t.), two messenger ships (25 t.) and the archer corps (96 t.).

Table 3.4 Flament

Flament (example tables)

433/2	**Campaign**	Corevra	(Thuc. 1.45.1–2, 50.5)*							**Annual Total**
		No.	**Daily wage**	**Days**	**Total in talents**					
	Triremes	30	200	<75	<75					
	Campaign totals:				**75**					**75**
432/1	**Campaign**	Peloponnese	(Thuc.2.17.4. 23.2)			Potidaia	(Thuc.2.70.2, 3.17.3)**			**Annual Total**
		No.	**Daily wage**	**Days**	**Total in talents**	**No.**	**Daily wage**	**Days**	**Total in talents**	
	Triremes	100	200	120	400	23	200	150	230	
	Hoplites	1000	1	120	20	4600	2	150	115	
	Archers	400	1	120	8					
	Campaign totals:				**428**				**345**	**773**
431/0	**Campaign**	Megarid	(Thuc.2.31.2)			Euboia	(Thuc.2.26. 32)			
		No.	**Daily wage**	**Days**	**Total in talents**	**No.**	**Daily wage**	**Days**	**Total in talents**	
	Triremes					30	200	90	90	
	Hoplites	10000	1	40	66 3/4					
	Light Troops	?	1	40	?					
	Metics	300	1	40	20					
	Campaign totals:				**> 86 3/4**				**90**	
		Peloponnese	(Thuc.2.56, 57)			Potidaia	(Thuc.2.58.2)			**Annual Total**
		No.	**Daily wage**	**Days**	**Total in talents**	**No.**	**Daily wage**	**Days**	**Total in talents**	
	Triremes	100	200	40	133 1/3	23	200	360	276	
	Hoplites	4000	1	40	26 2/3	3000	2	360	360	
	H reinforced					1600	2	180	96	
	Cavalry	300		40						
	Campaign totals:				**160**				**732±**	**> 1068 3/4**

430/29	**Campaign**	Potidaia	(Thuc.2.56.2, 58.3)			Akarnania	(Thuc.2.6B.7)			
		No.	**Daily wage**	**Days**	**Total in talents**	**No.**	**Daily wage**	**Days**	**Total in talents**	
	Triremes	100	200	40	133 1/3	30	200	30	30	
	Hoplites	4000	1		40	26 2/3				
	Campaign totals:				**160**				**30**	
		Naupactos	(Thuc.2.65, 80.4)			Lykia and Karia		(Thuc.2.69)		
		No.	**Daily wage**	**Days**	**Total in talents**	**No.**	**Daily wage**	**Days**	**Total in talents**	
	Triremes	20	200	210	140	6	200	30	6	
	Campaign totals:				**140**				**6**	
		Chalkidiki	(Thuc.2.79.1–7)			Potidaia	(Thuc.2.70)			
		No.	**Daily wage**	**Days**	**Total in talents**	**No.**	**Daily wage**	**Days**	**Total in talents**	
	Triremes					23	200	180	138	
	Hoplites	2000-430	1	30	7 and 5100 dr.	3000	2	180	180	
	Cavalry	200	1	30						
	Campaign totals:				**7.85**				**318**	
		Megarid	(Thuc.4.56)							**Annual Total**
		No.	**Daily wage**	**Days**	**Total in talents**					
	Hoplites	10000	1	60	100					
	Campaign totals:				**100**					**761.85**

Flament, 2007 [1] * Flament, p.123–4 on the duration of the campaign with Hornblower 1991 ad 1.50.5 on dispatch of reinforcement fleet 'not long after.' [2] ** Hornblower 1991 ad 3.17.2; troop numbers here are problematic. Contrary to the text, troops staying throughout is unlikely given the 'normal besieging practice of withdrawing perhaps half of an investing force once the siege was established.' [3] ± Note that this value should be less, given 1,050 men died of the plague in the midst of the siege. (Thuc. 2.58.3).

Notes

1. I would like to thank the British Academy for funding this research project at the University of Cambridge and to the participants of the International Conference on Ancient Warfare and Economics 2016 at UCL organized by Chris Carey, Hans van Wees, Roel Konijnendijk and myself, for their excellent feedback on the draft. I also would like to thank the attendees of the Wolfson Ancient Warfare Wednesdays webinar series, organized by Cezary Kucewicz and myself, for feedback on a second draft of the paper. For the helpful comments and discussions on drafts, I am grateful to Cong Chen, Antonio Cabrales, Roel Konijnendijk, Mark Pyzyk, Cezary Kucewicz, Lisa Kallet, Josiah Ober and Stephen Hodkinson. A profound thank you goes to Chris Carey, whose entirety is a *ktema es aiei* and whose mentorship so much more than an *agonisma*. He has inspired us and will continue to inspire us all through his person and works.
2. Scheidel 2017, 199n.35, where he does admit that 'just as in the modern period, there is no compelling evidence that democracy by itself curtails inequality'. This chapter offers one possible avenue for further investigation.
3. Piketty 2014; Scheidel 2017, 164–7, 188–99. Conclusions drawn from results in Ober 2015a, Hodkinson 2000, Van Wees 2004, Scheidel 2005.
4. In agreement with the development economics literature, e.g. North and Thomas 1973, North 1990, North et al. 2009 and Acemoglu et al. 2005. For a concise definition of property rights in socio-economic development, see Szirmai 2015, 530–1.
5. See Manning and Oliver 2017 on Ober 2015a, for the types of criticism to this approach.
6. Economics of conflict, see Garfinkel and Skaperdas 2007; property rights in ancient Greece generally, see Economou, Kyriazis 2017.
7. Garlan 1977; Finley 1985, 76–7; Pritchett 1991, 338–504.
8. Pritchett 1991, 77–86.
9. Van Wees 2010, 224.
10. Walcot 1979.
11. Pritchett 1991, 363–73.
12. Pritchett 1991, 375–425.
13. Pritchett 1991, 325–438, esp. 425.
14. Gabrielsen 2007, 252.
15. Bresson 2016, especially 433–5.
16. Ober 2015a, 310–4, 321–8.
17. Raaflaub 1998. Morris' use of epic poetry as evidence for the Early Iron Age down to the eighth century (2007, 232) is opposed by Osborne (2007b, 295, 298) for whom Homer and Hesiod represent exaggerated and over-simplified worlds, respectively, with very limited historical value. I assume both authors are close contemporaries and that they reflect Archaic practice, as well as Iron Age practice when supported by the archaeology.
18. Trans. Wilson 2023.
19. Troy as plunder in exchange for bodies: Solon 4.9–20, *harpage* plunder in exchange for dead youths; Aesch. *Ag*. 438–44, Ares is a trader, *chrusamoibos*, the 'gold-changer' of corpses for well-made urns; cf. Aesch. *Ag*. 534, Paris pays for his crime with *harpage*, plunder. Cf. Troy as an opportunity for plunder generally: *Ilioupersis, Sack of Troy*.

20. Acemoglu et al. 2005.
21. Holmes 2007, 49–53.
22. Hirshleifer 1991.
23. Gomme 1945, 5.
24. See Morris 2007, 231–41, esp. 237 for the general state of property rights in the Early Iron Age.
25. Van Wees 2013a, 17–23.
26. *Il.* 4.259–63; 343–6; *Od.* 13.8–9, cf. Xen. *Const. Lac.*15.2–4 with Hdt. 6.56–7, 7.103.1.
27. Kestemont 1983, 62–3.
28. *Od.* 3.68–74; 9.252; Hdt. 1.1–4 on the Phoenician abduction of women; 2.54–6; 4.196; Quinn 2018, 48–52; Garlan 1989, 189–94.
29. Quinn 2018, 82.
30. Kallet-Marx 1993, 24–27.
31. Phoenicians in the Persian fleet: Hdt. 1.143; 3.19; 5.108–9; 6.6–17, 25, 28, 33–4, 41; 7.23, 25, 96–8; 8.85, 90, 100; cf. 7.165; Byblos not until 425 BC: Hdt. 7.89; Phoenician naval equipment in the Persian fleet: Hdt. 7.98, with Thuc. 1.16, 'Darius used his Phoenician fleet to conquer the islands.'
32. Jean-Jacques Rousseau, 'Discourse on Inequality' (1754), translation from Skyrms 2001.
33. For a detailed introduction to game theory and how to interpret matrices, see Dal Borgo 2015. In brief, there are two Nash equilibria in this game, the cell (Stag, Stag) and (Hare, Hare). For each player, the first equilibrium is higher risk yet with a potential higher reward of 2, whilst the latter is less risky since it has an assured reward of 1. The payoffs in each cell of the matrix represent ordered preferences and are not comparable among players (i.e. not cardinal preferences). These theoretical and visual generalizations are powerful tools to represent strategic thinking given a set of constraints and player incentives.
34. Gabrielsen 2001, who discusses piracy in the Hellenistic age where the evidence is clearest.
35. *FGrH* 539 F2; Alexis: *apud* Ath. 12.540d.
36. Clearchos: *apud* Ath. 12.540e; cf. Ar. *Eq.* 813–15.
37. Van Wees 2013a, 31.
38. Morris 2004; Scheidel 2004; Morris 2013.
39. Chaniotis 2005b, esp. 107.
40. How and Wells 1912, Appendix VI.8.
41. De Ste. Croix 1972, 298–9.
42. Raaflaub 2009, on Athenian and Persian instruments of imperial finance.
43. Harris 2016 with Faraguna 2000; see Bresson 2016, 339–80 on the evolution of Greek international trade networks that operated in line with the principles of comparative advantage for bulk commodities and provided free-riding opportunities for more expensive products.
44. Van Wees 2013a, 107–33.
45. Lawall 2016, 268–71.
46. Archibald 2011, 46–51; at 48, she notes that 'movement was not necessarily the result of rational and willed planning'. This should be kept in mind for all economic activity not only piratical and rapacious practices in the ancient Greek economy.

47. Van Wees 2013a; Migeotte 2000.

48. Van Wees 2004.

49. Van Wees 2013a, 42–3; on *poletai*, Rhodes 1981, 552–7.

50. Dem. 3.5; cf. Thuc. 3.19 for first literary mention of funding, here for the siege of Mytilene; Fawcett 2016, 156, for Athenian settlers in allied *poleis* as liable for *eisphora* in 446/5; Hestiaia, *IG* i[3] 41, ll. 38–9.

51. Van Wees 2013a, 44–8, argues that *naukraiai* are replaced by demarchs in the reforms of Cleisthenes and in the fourth century they transformed again into war tax-symmories (*FGrH* 323 F8).

52. Fawcett 2016.

53. See Thuc. 3.50.2 for liability to such dues on Lesbos.

54. Thuc. 4.108.3; cf. [Xen.] *Const. Ath.* 2.7, for the strategic importance of ensuring the continuous supply of timber for the construction of triremes; Kallet-Marx 1993, 172–6.

55. Osborne 2000, 75–9, 95–7.

56. Migeotte, Pritchard and Flament employ the usual chronological division of events following Gomme (1974, 716–21). Athenian archon succession table: e.g. 432/1 for the first year of the Peloponnesian War in the archonship of Pythodorus which began in July/August of 432. In the above graph and the appended tables below, I display the leading year 432 and not the half year format 432/1. This is for the benefit of visualization only, and the usual chronological schema should be kept in mind. The graph and explanation, excluding the tables, are reproduced from Dal Borgo 2022 with permission of Palgrave Springer Nature.

57. Pritchard 2012, 39–45; 2015b, 91–9; Migeotte 2014, 565–9, provides comparable estimates. See Appendix for details.

58. Pritchard 2012, 43.

59. Migeotte 2014, 567, see Appendix: L. Migeotte, note 2.

60. Pritchard 2015, 98.

61. Kallet 2001, 252 notes that at 8.28.3–4 the Spartans 'appear to have been duped' in the prices paid for the sale of their captives.

62. Flament 2007, 169–77.

63. Flament 2007, 143–89, not cited by Pritchard until 2019.

64. Flament 2007, 137–43.

65. Flament 2007, 179.

66. Flament 2007, 179–82; cf. Pritchett 1991, 390–1; The Persian subsidy was received by the Spartans instead and amounted to 5000t. (Isoc. 8.97). Lysander in 405 BC brings back to Sparta an unspent sum of 470t. (Xen. *Hell.* 2.3.8). Athens had already considered Persian subsidies a possibility in 431 and 424 (Thuc. 2.7.1, 4.50.3). Thucydides' Pericles explicitly makes the point at the outset of the war that Athens does not require Persian subsidy because her naval resources are far superior to any others (2.62.2). Ironically, Pericles also notes that the downfall of the Peloponnesian league will be through want and delay of money (*ta chremata*, 1.142.1 cf. 1.121.3).

67. Gabrielsen 2007, 267; for the date of the inscription, see Ampolo 1987.

68. Hornblower 2008, Appendix 2, for a full breakdown of numbers and their attendant uncertainties. Other instances, *stratiotides/hoplitagogoi*: Thuc. 6.31.3, 8.62.2; cf. *IG* i[3] 60 ll.12–13. *Hippagogoi*: Thuc. 2.56.2, 6.25.2, 31.3, 43; Ar. *Eq.* 595–610; *IG* ii[2] 1627.241.

69. Kallet 2001, 246–50.

70. Kallet 2001, 250 for a similar view.

71. Kallet-Marx 1993, 246–50 with Kallet 2001, 200–2; cf. Arist. *Pol.* 1256a.37, piracy as a natural form of acquisition. Also note the problem with tribute collection in 420s: e.g. *IG* i^3 71, Kallet-Marx 1993, 191.

72. Thuc. 2.69, to protect merchant ships from pirates, and 6.104, Spartans operate like pirates in the Peloponnesian War.

73. Flament 2007, 182–9.

74. 430/29, Thuc. 2.69; 428/7, Thuc. 3.19.1–2; 425, Thuc. 4.50; 424, Thuc. 4.74.1 – in the Hellespont.

75. Samons 2000, 250–4.

76. Osborne 2000, 75; For evidence that tribute may have been reinstated around 410, Xen. *Hell.* 1.3.9–10 (evidence in 408 BC); Ar. *Ran.* 362–3 (evidence in 405 BC), references to payment of tribute; Samons 2000, 250–4.

77. Gabrielsen 2001, reiterates that the merchant, pirate and *prostates* intricate relationship by the Hellenistic period was a long-standing economic structure. My emphasis is on disruption that was more than usual.

78. Illyria and Aetolia; *IG* i^2 42, is a tax exemption from *eisphora* for the seizure of pirates, date around/after 420s; *IG* i^3 1032 (OR190) introduction of joint trierarchies and its monumental celebration with a list of sailors of Athenian triremes, date 412–405.

79. Euboea 413/12, Thuc. 8.5.1–2, 4–5, 411/10, Thuc. 8.95.5–7; Chios, 412, Thuc. 8.7, 8.9–10.1; Methymna, Mytilene 412, Thuc. 8.22, 24.2–5 (many allies shared Chios' risk); Rhodes 412/11, Thuc. 8.44.1–2; Samos 412, Thuc 8.21, *IG* i^3 96 (resisted revolt); Thasos 411/10, Thuc. 8.64.2–5, recovered in 407/8 Xen. *Hell.* 1.4.9, Diod. 13.72.1; Lampsacus, Abydos 411/10, attempted revolt Thuc. 8.61–2; cf. Thuc. 8.96.5.

80. Pritchett 1991, 381, 385 for a list of raids by hegemonial powers from the period after the Sicilian expedition. In 428, already the Athenians fund the siege of Mytilene with plunder (Thuc. 3.19.1) and the during the Sicily expedition as well (Thuc. 6.62.3–4). Gabrielsen 2001, 221 writes 'these occurrences, however, count for little in comparison with those from the period after 411, during which plunder and extortion became two of the financial props of naval campaigns.' At 224, he refers to the evidence of the hegemonial powers 'turning raider', mainly, Athens, Sparta, Carthage and Syracuse.

81. 420–406: 1% harbour tax, [Xen.] *Const. Ath.* 1.17; Ar. *Vesp.* 658; *IG* i^3 182, cf. generally *IG* i^3 62 with Osborne 2000, translation; 413: (*eikoste*) 5% import/export tax, Thuc. 7.28; 410: (*dekate*) 10% transit tax (on goods passing through the Bosporus) Xen. *Hell.* 1.1.22; Polyb. 4.44.3; 402/1: (*pentekoste*) 2% import/export tax, Andoc. *On the Mysteries* 133–4; Fawcett 2016, Table 1.

82. Mynott 2013, 540 n2.

83. Kallet-Marx 1993, 200.

84. OR 155.

85. Kallet and Kroll 2020, 121–2.

86. See Hornblower 2008, 808–9, for literature.

87. Cf. Xen. *Hell.* 1.3.8 for evidence of Chalcedon paying tribute in 408.

88. Ar. *Ran.* 363 for an *eikoste* collector at Aegina's harbour as late as 405.

89. Kallet-Marx 1993, 136.

90. As noted by Arcenas 2020, modern historians often conflate historical fact with Thucydidean interpretation.
91. Kallet-Marx 1993, 204.
92. Dal Borgo 2022, 47–102, discusses how the Peloponnesian War can be modelled as public goods problem, as a dynamic inter- and intra-state game of competing public and private incentives.
93. Pretzler 2007, for the ethnic connections among Peloponnesian states.
94. On Persia: Kuhrt 2007, 310–46, esp. 335–46, for the textual and epigraphic evidence during the war.
95. De Ste. Croix 1972, 123, 124, 335–7.
96. For the full code, gifs of the simulations, and the Network group presentation with detailed finite-horizon output analysis, <<https://github.com/ManuDalBorgo/Network-model-of-the-Peloponnesian-War>>
97. Finley 1965.
98. Harris's chapter 9, this volume, also corroborates the ancient Greek growth mentality towards war and markets.
99. Our model was inspired by Dziubinski et al. 2021.
100. Freitag 2009.
101. Ober 2022, 306–46.
102. North and Thomas 1973, 2.

CHAPTER 4
THE BALANCE SHEET OF ACHAEMENID WARFARE: GATHERING THE EVIDENCE

Christopher J. Tuplin

1. Introduction

For over two centuries, the dominant power in Western Asia and the Eastern Mediterranean seaboard was an imperial state whose heartland was in south-western Iran.[1] This state is conventionally described as the Achaemenid Empire because from Darius' seizure of power in 522/521 until 330 it was ruled by a dynasty of kings who claimed descent from one Achaemenes. Since Darius' predecessors – Cyrus, Cambyses and Smerdis (Bardiya) – were the descendants of Teispes (king of Anšan) and since Darius' imputation that this family and his own one somehow overlapped is highly suspect, the proper label to cover the empire's entire history is arguably Teispid-Achaemenid. For the purpose of the present chapter, however, this is a nicety of little significance. The empire was created and expanded to its largest extent by wars of aggression (generally framed as wars of defence or retaliation) and its maintenance until the arrival of Alexander was predicated on the capacity to deploy military force: in this respect there is practical continuity across the Teispid / Achaemenid dynastic divide, and in attempting to recover something of the economics of warfare it is legitimate to treat the entire period from Cyrus' defeat of the Medes to Alexander's defeat of Darius III as a single historical and discursive entity.

The evidence available to us about the empire does, of course, lie unevenly across time and space.

Greek literary texts (historiographical or otherwise) characteristically provide the elements of a long-term diachronic narrative from 550 to 330 in a way that non-Greek sources emphatically do not, although they do so more richly for the first seventy years (Herodotus) and last ten (the Alexander historians) than for the periods in between. In all cases there is inevitably a Hellenic perspective both in subject matter (the empire is of interest inasmuch as it impinges on Greeks) and intellectual, moral and ideological frame of reference.

Non-Greek written sources occasionally have a narrative character: the Nabonidus Chronicle, the Cyrus Cylinder and Darius' Behistun inscription are notable examples, and one might add Udjahorresnet's autobiography (a narrative of sorts of his relations with Cambyses and Darius) or the Egyptian-language version of Darius' Suez inscription (a very sketchily preserved narrative about the sending of ships between Egypt and Iran). But the narrative elements cover limited periods of time and the texts characteristically use narrative to celebrate the qualities of their author or to spin a story in a particular direction. That is also true of the non-narrative royal inscriptions that come after the Behistun inscription (mostly from the reigns of Darius and Xerxes), which articulate in symbolic and timeless fashion a royal ideology of cosmic order characterized by the king's unique relationship with the god Ahuramazda.[2]

In texts of this sort we *are* dealing directly with a type of high-level political discourse. But the great bulk of non-Greek written sources are the contemporary documentary records of more or less local and banal economic, legal or broadly administrative processes, into which politics obtrudes at best very indirectly and mostly not at all. Texts of this sort exist from Babylonia across the empire's entire history (both before and after Darius' accession), but the number drops dramatically after 484 BC and falls even further in the fourth century. In the south-western Iranian heartland, the Persepolis Fortification archive is a rich source for the two decades of Darius' reign that span 500 BC. The period is extended into the 460s by the overlapping but comparatively tiny Treasury archive, but then Iran falls documentarily silent. Egyptian documentation is much more sparse and perhaps most notable for the Aramaic texts from the Judaean garrison community of Elephantine (stretching for a little over a century until *c.* 400 BC) and a small set of Aramaic letters associated with the satrap Aršāma towards the end of the fifth century. Elsewhere there are Aramaic letters from late Achaemenid Bactria (some linked directly with another satrap Akhvamazda) and nearly 2,000 Aramaic ostraca from fourth-century Idumaea – a cache whose grand size is matched only by the grand difficulty of deciding exactly what economic or fiscal processes is being documented.[3]

The great bulk of all of this (and of other more scattered items from various places and in various languages) postdates Darius' establishment of the Achaemenid dynasty: only Greek narratives about Cyrus and Cambyses, some Egyptian material about Cambyses, and Babylonian documents pre-dating 522/521 buck this trend. Even so, Greek sources largely buy Darius' claim that his seizure of power maintained dynastic continuity by eliminating a usurper, while the Babylonian material shows remarkable continuity in character across Cyrus' conquest of Babylonia and Darius' emergence as king, with only a gradually increasing sense across Darius' reign that the impact (but perhaps not the fundamental nature) of Iranian rule may be changing. These facts about the sources and the simple circumstance that the Teispid phase was comparatively short (even if historically important) explain why what one thinks of as the headline features of Persian imperialism during the Greek Archaic and Classical periods are essentially those of the Achaemenid dispensation – features such as: rule by a Great King under the aegis of Ahuramazda, maintenance of a complex court that moved regularly between royal establishments great and small, provincial governance characterized by satraps, tribute and a bewildering variety of taxes, a military system that supplemented the Iranian core with subject levies and mercenaries, and distribution of the benefits of empire in real estate and other rewards to an *ethno-classe dominante* and others.

The purpose of what follows is to contribute to the present volume's investigation of the economic perspective of ancient warfare by rehearsing some basic data about the economics of warfare in the Achaemenid imperial system. This is an empirical undertaking, unburdened by theoretical models and keen to stress the unsystematic and unquantified nature of the evidence at our disposal.[4]

2. Income

For Aristotle, war was a natural mode of wealth acquisition.[5] For Xenophon, the general must be an *oikonomos* (*Memorabilia* 3.4.7–12). Persian grandees lived amidst bureaucratized supply mechanisms and managed personal portfolios of horticultural, arable and livestock wealth, so they should have been no worse off than elite Athenians in this respect.

In a royal inscription, the king figures threats to happiness as an (enemy) army, famine and the Lie (DPd). From these Darius asks his god Ahuramazda to protect his land/people. As Ahuramazda's tools include military action, one wonders if the army protects against famine by securing and protecting good land. But the text hardly positively suggests this. More specifically military items in royal inscriptions speak of the *kāra* (army/people: the word is ambiguous) making others fear the king (DPe) or celebrate the extent of Persian conquest (DNa);[6] and success in protecting or increasing imperial resources is not explicitly among the characteristics of the good king (DNb). In the real world military personnel are used against natural enemies: a letter from Bactria (ADAB A4) envisages redeployment of soldiers to gather a harvest ahead of locust attack. But this is not the stuff of royal rhetoric.[7]

By contrast, Xenophon postulates a strong reciprocal relationship between protective soldiery and tribute-generation, and evokes the distinction between local economic goods and exported tribute.[8] Less explicitly, one may compare *Cyropaedia*'s representation of Gadatas and Gobryas (with their militarily and materially productive landscapes) and its Armeno-Chaldaean paradigm for defence of an imperial area against external banditry.[9] Or there is a story in Aelian (*VH* 2.17) about *magi* predicting that the reign of Artaxerxes III would see much death and much agricultural prosperity: the two may be as much connected as contrasted. Or there is the alleged Persian view of Darius as a *kapēlos* (merchant).[10] A *kapēlos* gets income by selling something, Darius' fixed tribute is income, and what he sells is perhaps the militarily underpinned good order that generates that income. *Kapēleia* may not be a concept of economic analysis, but we are dealing with the commerce of warfare. At the same time, there is an ideological tension between *commerçant* and warrior: the *kapēlos* is a socially challenged cheat with no place in a military aristocracy or among truth-telling Persians, and we recall how the Lydians became *kapēloi* and musicians to lose their military ethos (Herodotus 1.155). Economic activity with moral overtones makes the economics of warfare tricky.

Greeks saw Persian aggression as motivated by material gain. Naxos is *kalē te kai agathē* ('fine and productive') and contains *khrēmata polla kai andrapoda* ('a lot of property and slaves'), and the next stop is Euboea, *megalē kai eudaimōn* ('large and prosperous') (Hdt. 5.31). Atossa fancies having Greek servant-girls (Hdt. 3.134), Dinon's Xerxes is impressed by Athenian prickly pears: anything good should be consumable by the king not as *xenikon* ('gift from a foreigner') but as his own property (690 F12). Mardonius says something similar in Herodotus (7.5) and Xerxes agrees that acquiring better land is a traditional motive, though the passage privileges inherited duty of conquest as a primary cause, and the earlier Herodotean narrative does not really stress material greed as the reason for the empire's creation and growth. After the 470s, the wars that we can see were fought to retain or recover sources of income rather than to acquire entirely new ones.

The profits of war are variform. Acquisition of territory permits imposition of taxes but also distribution of real estate to Persian beneficiaries. Xenophon affirms this as a rule at satrapal level (the *paradeisoi* of Cyrus, Pharnabazus, Tissaphernes or Belesys are tokens thereof) and lower down Asidates' Caicus estate is a nice example. Artayctes' appropriation of the Protesilaum is symbolic: Protesilaus unsuccessfully attacked the King's domain. His property was therefore forfeit to the King, and the King can assign it to a favoured subject.[11]

More directly there is booty. Persian armies can be merely destructive; but before turning its *temenos* into a profit-producing enterprise, Artayctes plundered the Protesilaum, a type of action attributed to various Persian armies and generalized by Diodorus' assertion that the Persians looted every Greek temple in Asia except that of Hemithea.[12] Secular looting also appears: Herodotus' account of the capture of Sardis provides a historical origin for centralized collection of booty (also a feature of *Cyropaedia*), and the noble Spithridates was famously cheesed off when deprived of booty by Spartans who *also* liked to control booty-collection. Meanwhile Dercylidas feared Tissaphernes and Pharnabazus would plunder Ionia; and volunteers flocked from Syria and Cilicia to an army in Cyprus for booty opportunities: that army was Persian-employed rather than Persian, but the distinction is of doubtful importance and forcible redistribution of some of the affluence resulting from over three decades of Cypriot peace is in any event an economic consequence of imperial military policy.[13] There is recognition that Persians liked prisoners both in punitive contexts (with talk of deportation to distant places) and elsewhere. At Iasus, Tissaphernes forewent material booty in favour of human at a knock-down price, perhaps for re-sale, perhaps for labour. Hecataeus at least partly anachronistically alleged Cambyses took Egyptian craftsmen to build Persepolis, Susa and Ecbatana. Herodotus' story of the Paeonians' deportation from the Strymon to Phrygia is paradigmatic – and concerns a region that produced the largest attested set of foreign workers in the Persepolis Fortification archive.[14]

What the economic historian (or, actually, any historian) misses here is numbers. Greek sources occasionally quantify Greek booty, including that taken *from* Persians: Agesilaus seized 70 talents (t.) at Sardis and 1,000 t. over his whole campaign.[15] But no Persian booty is quantified; and the only valuation of territorial assignment is Themistocles' 50 t. from Magnesia.[16] We are reduced to considering very global figures. Herodotus (3.95) alleged an annual tribute income of 14,560 t. That is only eighteen times Thucydides' figure for the income of Odrysian kings (2.97) and thirty times pre-war Athenian tribute – and allegedly less than Hellenistic kings got from a similar area (Monson 2015, 11). Tribute *proprie dictum* represents a surplus over-and-above local tax-and-spend, so the figure does not capture imperial turnover. Still, if that surplus *was* proportionately similar to the Athenians', it might not count as extravagant. But, of course, the status of the Herodotean figure is contested. Another set of figures is at any rate less contested, viz. what Alexander found in heartland royal treasuries.[17] At a generous estimate this was 250,000 t., a figure sometimes felt to betoken excessive thesaurization.[18] In Herodotean terms it is only 8.5 per cent of tributary income over 200 years (the 9,700 t. Athens once had on the acropolis was a higher percentage of *her* takings to date[19]), but, again, any such calculation depends on a contested number. So, even when we *have* figures, their utility is circumscribed. And a real imperial end-of-trading figure would have to embrace *all* resources in all storehouses and worker-accommodation at the relevant moment.

So far Greek sources. What do non-Greek sources offer? More insight into the fiscal complexities underlying production of tribute or (more generally) an operating surplus for the imperial government and/or its local agents – though with no better way of quantifying either the overall profits or, more than anecdotally, the individual income streams. More insight also into the assignment of estates to elite individuals: at least, we see estates in Egypt, Babylonia, Persepolis and Bactria, but not their assignment – though that *can* turn up lower down the ethno-social chain. The satrap Aršāma's letter instructing a subordinate to exploit local unrest to increase his estate's branded labour-force discloses something of the appetitive psychology of top Iranians,[20] but, even foreswearing value judgements, we can better appreciate this category of profit from military superiority and its interaction with the wider economic environment – though we cannot put a global value on any such estate and evidence of this sort is no more likely than that about fiscal and business activities in general to indicate that it is the profits of war that we are inspecting: the types of documentation in question have no reason to engage explicitly with a larger picture that is simply taken for granted. Cyrus' acquisition of material booty is mentioned three times in the Nabonidus Chronicle (ABC no. 7: ii 3, 17, iii 14 [Kuhrt 2007: 50–1]), an astronomical diary tells us that the king's son plundered an unidentified enemy in November 363 BC (AD -362 rev.5, in Hunger and Van der Spek 2006), and the looting of gold and silver from a temple is attested in special circumstances at Elephantine in July 410 BC (TADAE A4.5, A4.7, 4.8.). The presence of foreign workers in Persepolis may sometimes be the direct product of war, that of foreign population groups in Babylonia sometimes the product of Persian rather than Neo-Babylonian war – and in both cases we are dealing with substantial elements of the economic demography.[21] A Babylonian chronicle records the arrival of female POWs in Sidon in the 340s (ABC no. 9 [Kuhrt 2007: 412]); and a business document the sale of an 'Egyptian woman, plunder of my bow' on 31 December 524 BC (Camb.334 [Stolper 1998: 143]).

But the most striking relevant information is what the Aramaic and Akkadian versions of the Behistun narrative say about the numbers of dead and captured of 522–521 BC: see Table 4.1.[22] As John Hyland has shown (2014), there are legitimate grounds for suspicion about the historicity of the specific figures alleged, but this does not detract from the significance of the inclusion of this type of information in what is, of course, a propagandistic text. The phenomenon is very imperfectly paralleled in

Neo-Assyrian texts as a whole, effectively unparalleled in the last century of Neo-Assyrian history,[23] and quite unparalleled in the Neo-Babylonian era. So the way things are presented in the Behistun text is not a matter of immediate literary models: however much the details are manipulated, the material reflects what Persians did, not someone's notion of what such narratives ought to contain. And one of the things they did was count captives very carefully. In the Behistun narrative, a battle often produces more dead than captives, something not generally true in the few pertinent Assyrian cases. Whether this is an actual peculiarity of the fraught first year of Darius' reign or a literary adjustment enjoined by the propaganda context is impossible to know. But, although one might expect it to be otherwise, the general run of Greek narrative evidence does not figure Persians as vigorous practitioners of battlefield slaughter, and we should not assume they regularly preferred satisfaction of blood-lust or demonstrative carnage to the acquisition of useful human resources. But, in any event, there is a neat connection between the war of Behistun and the economics of the Persepolis Fortification archive.

3. Costs

Military activity presupposes costs, to which I now turn. Comparatively few texts say anything that directly illuminates those costs and how they were met. Moreover, military costs are hard to disentangle from the general economy. The provincial military environment was mostly local: economically speaking, it is part of the local economy, a specialized aspect of human resource management. The King's Dinner was a permanent charge but, if the king is on campaign, it is a special aspect of military logistics. And actually, as the king never travelled unprotected, his sustenance was always part of the military economy – hence Herodotus' view that the empire fed king and *stratiē* (army) all the time and Isocrates' talk of the king and his *peripolousa stratia* ('the army that went around with him').[24] Cities were assessed for the King's Dinner as they were for tribute (so Theopompus said) and that assessment is *inter alia* a military one.[25]

One might seek to avoid military costs. A successful demand for earth and water would earn less material capital, but at less cost – and there would still be ideological capital. Bribery would cost more but could still diminish overall costs. And when war *was* undertaken, the king and/or his agents might seem parsimonious: the Oxyrhynchus historian noted this general phenomenon, Isocrates crowed over some examples, Tissaphernes was serially evasive with money and ships, Conon journeyed to Babylon to beg for improved cash flow, and Artaxerxes III allegedly ordered satraps to disband mercenary armies because they were costing too much.[26] On other occasions a willingness to spend money made a real difference: one might instance the creation of a new Spartan fleet to replace the one lost at Cyzicus in 410 and the support provided to the Spartans by the younger Cyrus in 407–405. Meanwhile, at least when the king went to war, the associated conspicuous consumption (not just the extravagance of the royal retinue but perhaps even the deployment of non-combatant military contingents[27]) arguably meant that *more* was being spent than was objectively necessary: whether that is true depends on how much the visible representation of power was genuinely thought to contribute to the morale of one's own troops and the discomfiture of the enemy – what one might call a matter of ideological expenditure.

The Lydian Pythius allegedly offered Xerxes over a year's tribute for his expedition (Hdt. 7.28). This is an unusual association of *money* with preparation for royal warfare. Relevant mobilization passages do not characteristically talk of money, but (if of anything) of non-monetary logistics. Another exception is the Naxian expedition: to get it mounted Aristagoras offered Artaphernes a bribe and payment of all the costs (5.30). In return Artaphernes released 200 ships, men and fourth months' money for logistical maintenance. Moving away from purely textual sources, of course, few will doubt that (for example) the abundant fourth-century coinage of Cilician mints is a reflection of actual or planned wars in the Eastern Mediterranean;[28] and some may even feel that rather a high proportion of all coin-production across the western lands of the empire during the fifth and fourth centuries was driven more or less directly by the needs of the Persian military establishment.[29]

The Naxian expedition figures in another relevant problem. Diodorus claims that, in the case of the *Greek* ships in Xerxes' invasion of mainland Greece, the king supplied hulls, while the (Asiatic) Greeks supplied crews (11.3.7). Controversy rumbles about whether this was true in 480 – or indeed ever.[30] Herodotus' Naxian expedition narrative does create an impression that the 200 ships were separate from the Greeks manning them, but no other evidence matches or contradicts the Diodoran model unambiguously.[31] I do not aspire to quell the controversy. I merely observe that arrangements on the Aegean seaboard *were* perhaps distinct, actual ship-building on the Eastern Mediterranean edge of the empire had to be done by maritime subjects, and so economically speaking the issue is whether the state supplied money or deemed the cost taxation-in-kind. At a cost of a talent per trireme, the outlay for a fleet of new ships would be modest in relation to the empire's global wealth but perhaps not in relation to the wealth of individual subject communities. Of course, *building* ships for a specific operation is rarely explicitly postulated by Greek sources,[32] and a regular programme of building might have mitigated the problem. But we do not know there was such a programme; and the relative slowness and incompleteness with which fleets set sail tempts doubts.[33] Pharnabazus certainly provided money and materials in 410: this is our only actual information about the process of ship-building, and may not be typical.[34]

Providing ships is an extreme case of providing the weapons of war. The economic costs of weaponizing soldiers is largely beyond the interest of Greek sources: Diodorus' reference to large *paraskeuai* ('assemblages') of arms and missiles is unusual (16.40.6).[35] Herodotus itemizes the weaponry of subjects in the Army List (7.61–99), but it is in the field because the people holding it are in the field; and the economic implications of *their* deployment are largely elided. Except with mercenaries, Greek sources mostly either do not care or behave as if soldiers are levied from an ethnically defined group that owes military service. Only Xenophon clearly envisages land-for-service arrangements; the interplay of tribute and military organization which appears in the Mnesimachus inscription from Sardis and which some historians retroject to Achaemenid times is not the stuff of literary sources; and when literary sources mention unusual things – e.g. Cardaces – they do so unreflectingly.[36] It is rare for sources to individuate processes of mobilization. When Diodorus reports a year spent training an army for an invasion of Egypt (11.75), it is an unusual detail with balance-sheet implications, as an army is mobilized long before it can do anything to earn financial or political/ideological profits. I already noted Diodorus' unusual allusion to weaponry and the same passage also refers to *sitos* ('food provision') (16.40.6). Greek authors *are* occasionally conscious of such things – sometimes when things go wrong or become difficult,[37] but sometimes not: Artabazus enjoys the *episitismos* ('ability to collect food') of Phrygia, Lydia and Paphlagonia (Dem. 23.155) and gave money to Chares specifically to buy provisions (Diod. 16.22); another Artabazus recommends Thebes over Plataea because of the better supply chain (Hdt. 9.41); the troops of Aryandes demand and receive *ephodia* ('travel provisions') from Cyrene (4.203);[38] Anatolian satraps provided food for mercenaries sent to Perinthus (Diod. 17.75); attacks on Egypt in 373 and 343 involve ships carrying *agora* and other *matériel* (15.41, 16.40) and Cambyses arranged for water supplies in Northern Sinai in 526 (Hdt. 3.9);[39] the younger Cyrus was accompanied by a Lydian *agora* ('market') (which travelled with the barbarian part of his army: so it is not simply a function of Greek mercenaries being present), and his elder namesake in *Cyropaedia* offered rewards to those who might provide that sort of logistic support;[40] Datames also apparently employed merchants (*kapēloi*), while Tiribazus sent a soldier across the snowy landscape of Armenia in search of a source of provisions;[41] and Herodotus acknowledges food-supply issues in Xerxes' expedition, noting sitagogic ships (7.184, 186, 191), the separate supply-train of the Immortals (7.83), the King's Dinner (7.118–19), the creation of food stores in the Hellespont and North Aegean (7.25), and the existence of a *pratērion* ('selling-place') for those building the Athos Canal (7.23).[42] Planning was certainly needed (as Darius' ghost says in Aeschylus' *Persians*, Greece starves an 'over-numerous population'[43]), but little of what Herodotus reports is quantified, and we are left to imagine the economic distortions produced by stockpiling food in unusual places or diverting workers to canal-building.[44] (But the King's Dinner allegedly cost Thasos 400 t., and an Abderite reckoned his city had been half-ruined.[45])

So, what other quantifications are there? Pythius' supposed offer is problematically extravagant, but there are some more serious figures for global costs or contributions.[46] These are not grossly incommensurate with the figures encountered in Athenian military contexts.[47] David Lewis declared 5,000 t. for the Peloponnesian War an exaggeration without saying why or by how much. Since we can quantify neither Cyrus' personal resources, nor the tribute he assigned Lysander, nor the cost of bringing Phoenicians to Caunus (on the balance sheet, even if unproductive), nor the cost of rebuilding the Cyzicus fleet and providing *interim* subsistence for the crews-turned-seaboard-garrison, I am not sure that he was right. Fifteen thousand talents for the Evagoras War may be another matter: perhaps Isocrates generated that figure as ten times a notional annual cost on the pretence that it was a continuous ten-year war. Given a single injection of 2,000 t. at one point, a yearly average of 1,500 t. for years of actual operations might be acceptable.

Greek sources occasionally quantify systematic military arrangements. An annual 140 t. and 360 horses went to the Cilician cavalry garrison, and 120,000 unspecified units of cereal to the Persians of the Memphis White Fort and their mercenaries (*epikouroi*).[48] Not knowing the size of these establishments, we cannot evaluate the provision or fully assess such reports. With certain assumptions about rates of pay, we can reckon that the Egyptian resource maximally funded 10,000 or 15,000 persons (depending on unit of measurement) and wonder whether this included *epikouroi* throughout Egypt, not just in Memphis;[49] and we can conjecture that the Cilician resource provided 1,200 men, 2,400 mounts and replacement horses every six to seven years – though that is so utterly theoretical that it may not even be heuristically valuable. Something similar might be said of Christelle Fischer-Bovet's version of the Egyptian *makhimoi* (2013, 217–19). Herodotus pictured a vast hereditary class with allotments of twelve tax-free *arourai* (and special perks for royal bodyguards), implicitly occupying two-thirds of Egypt's arable land. Fischer-Bovet reduces this to 800 high-rank officers with 200 *arourai*, 8,000 middle-rank officers with 100, and 70,000 ordinary soldiers with 5 *arourai*, occupying under 20 per cent of the arable land.

We thus approach a basic question, the unit-cost of individual soldiers. Greek sources rarely elaborate on this except in mercenary or naval contexts, and even there rarely provide figures: without a few passages in *Anabasis* I, Thucydides VIII and *Hellenica* I, we would be poorly off.[50] In the Xenophontic model, we have *misthophoroi* ('mercenaries') in citadels and people in the *khōra* who receive *misthos* ('pay'), both maintained by the satrap; it is unclear whether the latter are true mercenaries (people with no stake save pay) and, concomitantly, what sort of *misthos* is involved.[51] The model does not identify the income stream supplying the *misthos*, although this *is* addressed in a statement about Babylon (*Cyr.* 7.5.69–70): *phrouroi* ('garrison troops') receive *misthos* to guard Babylon which is funded by Babylonians (to make them poor and submissive). The punitive element is appropriate in *Cyropaedia* because Babylon was the great erstwhile enemy. But one would expect the income to be locally derived, so what Xenophon says may be what he imagined generally true. *Mutatis mutandis,* it matches Herodotus on Cilicia and Egypt. Without prejudice to the *misthos-sitēresion* question that worries students of Greek mercenary-service,[52] at least one Greek historian knew Persian military personnel were not necessarily paid in silver: Heraclides observes that, whereas Greek mercenaries are paid in silver, royal spearmen and peltasts supported by the King's Table receive food from the king *eis hupologon* – a very rare phrase perhaps meant to stress that the payments are not casual but subject to the sort of accounting procedures we see in the Fortification archive.[53] What sort of income the mysterious Cardaces received in the mind of the one source who describes them as 'barbarians serving for pay' is hard to say.[54] I should add that expenditure on armies is not limited to pay and/or subsistence-in-kind: Greeks knew of the Great King as a giver-of-gifts, and this could extend to special rewards for good service, though the examples are not copious, mostly arise in mercenary contexts, and are generally not quantified.[55] Nor is expenditure on war limited to that on armies (even taking that in the widest sense): if Darius III actually spent 10,000 t. or 30,000 t. on ransoming the royal women captured after Issus, that could have been categorized as expenditure necessitated by the (unsuccessful) conduct of war.[56]

I have been speaking largely of Greek sources. I summarize what non-Greek documents bring under two broad headings.

First, military and general economic environments overlap. Jewish and Egyptian soldiers operate as private property owners.[57] Fortresses in the Persepolitan region and elsewhere are part of the normal worker-commodity nexus and interact with elite estates.[58] People labelled as workers (*kurtaš*, *gardu*) may occasionally be soldiers in Persepolis and Babylon.[59] Lance-bearers (the largest militarily-designated Persepolitan group) turn up inspecting or counting things of interest to the general administration, not necessarily in military or security contexts. A so-called ship-commander is responsible for the rations of workers. Soldiers in Bactria move travel-provision stores and clear sand from a caravanserai; one group are soldiers 'who go to markets' (whatever precisely that means). Others are diverted from wall- and ditch-building to harvest land ahead of locust attack.[60] The fact that Akkadian *ṣab* (man) and Elamite *taššup* (personnel) apply indifferently to officials, workers and soldiers is emblematic: being sure one is looking at real soldiers is hard in Persepolitan and Babylonian documentation – a problem exacerbated in the latter case by the prevalence of substitutionary cash-payment.

Second, what does the provisioning and remuneration of military personnel look like? The land-for-service model appears, with varying inclarities. The Bactrians just mentioned perhaps protected their own land against locusts. The 'bow-and-arrow-case of the Harku people' in a Persepolitan text (PFNN 1277) *might* be a military fiscal category, and it is possible that there was a tax on estates in the Persian heartland that provided support for the military.[61] Egyptian Demotic records produce two Hermotybians with 'revenue-land' and three others getting a taxable allocation of 30 *arourai* – an inexact match with Herodotus, perhaps because he misunderstood Hermotybians.[62] There are faint hints of 'military land' in Egyptian Aramaic documents, more credible at Memphis-Saqqara than Elephantine.[63] Above all there is Babylonia.[64] When temples supplied troops for state ventures, this was a tax-charge upon the temple. But there were also tax-groups called bows and pieces of land called bow-, horse- or chariot-fiefs. These were part of the fiscal-economic structure of Achaemenid Babylonia. But it is a matter of debate how *directly* either is linked to the actual military establishment – how far they illustrate military economics rather than a general economy which (eventually) might *inter alia* support military activity. Actual mobilization of fief-holders is exceptional. What a fief usually produced was tax, not a soldier. The same is true of bow-tax. So does the military designation mean the tax was hypothecated for military expenditure? Did the state regularly use it to hire professional soldiers? We do not know. Bow-tax texts almost always lack military context. The tax due from bow-fiefs consisted in 'King's Man, flour, *barra*, and the other dues of the royal house'. But, even if these are separate income streams, there is no guarantee they are expenditure streams or that King's Men did military rather than labour service. Our problem is that, lacking state archives, we see almost nothing of how the state spent its money. This also means, incidentally, that we cannot tell whether observed upward trends in general tax-take say something about military activity.

More direct types of payment also appear. Ostraca from Tel Arad in southern Palestine may record food-disbursements to military personnel (Naveh 1981).[65] Individual Babylonian soldiers, when visible, get silver as well as provisions. Egyptian Aramaic documents show two payment-types, *prs* and *ptp'*, the former silver, the latter food.[66] The latter term recurs in Bactria, though in a document not dealing with soldiers. Another document, naming Hystaspes the *karanos* (on the face of it a military leader), opaquely records a transfer of forty sheep. A third document shows the travel-provisions of Bessus at Maithanka in 337/6 as so huge that one guesses satrapal court-guards were among the beneficiaries.[67] The same guess is made about the Persepolitan Table of kings, queens and satraps,[68] while more specific indications of the provisioning of large numbers of military personnel on the move have been claimed to be present in some other Persepolitan texts.[69]

And what about quantification? Nothing can be said about Bactria. At Arad there are eighteen recoverable quantities of barley, but the period of time the allotments are for is never stated and nothing consistent can be inferred.[70] In Egypt, we have few pertinent texts. Four groups (Arabs, Medes, Men-of-the-Fortress, Men-of-Syene) get 36, 90 or 100 deben which *could* be a month's pay at 1 *deben* = 20 drachmae per month (equivalent to the initial basic pay of a Cyrean mercenary) – but the text might be Ptolemaic, the men might not be soldiers and the *debens* might not be silver. More reliably twenty-two members of the Syene garrison get 1 artaba a month, 2 get 1.5 and 30 get 2.5 per month; and there are individual records of at least 2 and 2.6666 ardabs. Many of these people are getting well above the 1 artaba per month basic Persepolitan ration.[71] In Babylonia, Jursa suggests (on a generous view of pertinent documents) that silver payments in military contexts ranged from 2–10 shekels per month; in a more tightly defined dataset I find nothing outside that range. That is higher than the full ration for non-military Persepolis Treasury tablet workers as expressed in silver, which varied from 1–3 shekels per month. But only the highest figure (definitely not standard) is of the same order of magnitude as basic Cyrean mercenary pay (at 1 daric per month). Babylonian silver payments often go alongside food-provisions, so the comparison may not be valid. Texts definitely referring to actual soldiers that admit of monthly calculations are very rare, and sometimes puzzling: six people guarding land against wild animals (only marginally soldiers) each get some twenty-five litres of foodstuff per day, which is a substantial amount. Egypto-Carians at Borsippa whom some identify as soldiers get a food ration (meat, beer, flour and seasoning) that is unquantified save that the meat element alone can be 2.25 shekels per month: they are living well.[72] Where the Persepolis documentation allows one to see or conjecture military pay, the phenomena sometimes exceed basic worker-subsistence in cereals by virtue of commodity offered (meat, wine) and/or rate of pay. And even putative soldiers on the basic 1 QA p.d. of grain might have been receiving something else that was accounted separately.[73] It is tantalising that an unpublished Persepolis Fortification seal (PFATS 0011) is reported as associated with 'significant rations … apportioned to military units in year 23' without details of the relevant tablets being given (Azzoni and Dusinberre 2014, 21). But the overall message for Persepolis, as for other *loci*, is that quantification is scant and hardly statistically cogent – quite apart (to reiterate) from uncertainties about the status of the persons whose income we are inspecting.

The sort of resource-management seen in the Fortification archive could clearly be used to underpin a military structure, and it provides a general background against which to understand e.g. Heraclides on the royal bodyguard (p. 87), various parts of Herodotus' picture of Xerxes' expedition (p. 86) or other non-Greek evidence about the maintenance of soldiers. But, replete though the documents are with numbers, they do not get us much closer to the economics of Persian warfare. The region to which they relate lies in the true imperial heartland. This is where the core *Persian* army came from – what one might think of as the defining military resource of the entire imperial enterprise. But the peculiar quality of that resource remains elusive, as does its role in explaining how the Persians were able so rapidly to overturn the established political geography of the world that lay to their west.

4. Conclusion

The blunt truth is that the balance sheet of Achaemenid warfare is destined to remain evocatively descriptive rather than mathematically robust. I end with another descriptive issue.

Lisa Kallet has drawn attention to the importance for Athenians of the principle that 'our strength is in our money'. How does this play in an Achaemenid context? Not at all in the verbal utterances of the Great King, whose strength is in Ahuramazda or in the men and horses of Persia.[74] But also not really in what Greeks imagine Achaemenids thinking. Pseudo-Aristotle's *resumé* of the royal and satrapal economies is predominantly interested in income (entirely so in the case of the satrapal one) and has no military dimension, whether in regard to income or expenditure.[75] Herodotus does not figure Darius' tribute reform as intended to improve the funding of further military conquest – and this despite the fact that the Athenians copied the system precisely as a way of maintaining (naval) military capacity.[76] Mardonius disdains fear of Greek money, but he says nothing about Persian. Demaratus (a Spartan exile among Persians) finds Greek strength in the qualities gained from resisting poverty, but he says nothing of Persian wealth. Xerxes takes comfort in the *fodder* his army has with it.[77] Alexander historians contrast the visible opulence of a Persian army with the sobriety of a Macedonian one.[78] And this is the key. In much Greek discourse, Persian wealth is a cause and sign of weakness. It is not the business of a text such as Aeschylus' *Persians* to suggest that wealth guarantees power. The king is the richest of men but easily mastered because everyone in his realm practises slavery not martial vigour: so says Xenophon's Jason of Pherae. He can hire many mercenaries – but they are *Greek* mercenaries and that proves his weakness.[79] Wealth leads to *truphē* ('self-indulgence'). Perhaps not everyone thought this. Some held that wealth and luxury characterized noble and courageous nations, though the view was perhaps only articulated to controvert it. The historian Heraclides maintained that the King's Dinner was an economically sensible arrangement that *inter alia* maintained elite military forces. Perhaps that is what a fourth-century Persian grandee would have said too. But Greeks preferred to go with the Arcadian Antiochus: the golden plane tree is too small to shade a cricket and, amid 10,000 cooks and servants, there are no men capable of fighting Greeks.[80] As with Darius the *kapēlos*, morality interferes with economics.

Table 4.1 Captives and dead in the Behistun narrative (Akkadian and Aramaic versions)

Single dead and surviving figure		
§33	Sagartia	dead/surviving = 447 [akk.]
§45	Kapishakana [Arachosia]	dead/surviving [figure lost] [akk.]
§46	Gandutava (Arachosia)	dead/surviving = 4579 [akk.]
§47	Arshada (Arachosia)	dead/surviving = 42xx [akk.]
		dead/surviving = [. . .]5 [aram.]
§50	(Arakhu) [Babylonia]	dead/surviving = 2497 [akk.]
No captives		
§18	Tigris (Babylonia)	killed all, no prisoners [akk.]
§19	Zazannu (ditto)	killed all, no prisoners [akk.]
§29	Izala (Assyria)	2034 d., [no c. figure] [akk.]
		2034 d., [no c. figure] [aram.]
Separate dead and captive figures		
§25	Maru (Media)	3827 d., 4329 c. [akk.]
		5827 d., 4329 c. [aram.]
§26	Zuzahya (Armenia)	827 d, xx06 c [aram.]
§27	Tigra (Armenia)	546 d., 520 c. [akk.]
		5046 d., 520 c. [aram.]
§28	Uyana (Armenia)	472 d., 525 c. [akk.]
		472 d., xx02 c. [aram.]
§30	Autiyara (Armenia)	2045 d., 1558 c. [akk.]
		2046 d., 1578 c. [aram.]
§31	Kunduru (Media)	34,425 d., [*lost*] c. [akk.]
		34,425 d., 18,01[-] c. [aram.]
§35	Vishpazatu [Parthia]	6346 d., 4346 c. [akk.]
§36	Patigrabna [Parthia]	6570 d., 4192 c. [akk.]
§38	Margiana	55,2xx d., 6572 c. [akk.]
		55,243 d., 6972 c. [aram.]
§41	Rakha [Persia]	4404 d., [2xxx] c. [akk.]
		35,404 d., [*lost*] c. [aram.]
§42	Parga (Persia]	6246 d., 4464 c. [akk.]
§45	?Kapishakana [Arachosia]	4579 d., 3760 c. [aram.][82]
§46	?Gandutava (Arachosia)	4579 d., 3760 c. [aram.]

Perhaps royal military parsimony reflects a profit-loss mentality (invest the minimum required to secure the result) crossed with an abiding older worldview that 'our strength is in our men'. But Darius III resisted Alexander quite energetically, and the empire did not simply fall because of economic weakness.[81]

Notes

1. Briant 2002 is the standard large-scale history. For more recent compact accounts, see Waters 2014a; Brosius 2021; and Llewellyn-Jones 2021. Jacobs and Rollinger 2021 is on an encyclopaedic scale. Kuhrt 2007 presents a history of the empire through annotated translations of primary sources.
2. Nabonidus Chronicle, Cyrus Cylinder, Behistun inscription, Udjahorresnet: Kuhrt 2007, 50–3, 70–4, 141–57 and 117–22 respectively. Suez inscription: Lloyd 2007; Klotz 2015. Royal inscriptions: Kuhrt 2007, 244, 300–6, 316–19, 334–5, 364–5, 403–9, 476–8, 492–9, 502–5, 554–5.
3. Persepolis Fortification archive: for a recent overview, see Henkelman 2021. Elephantine: the texts are distributed through Porten and Yardeni 1987–99; Lozachmeur 2006; Moore 2022. The secondary literature is enormous. For recent collections of studies, see Kratz and Schipper 2022; Folmer 2022. Aršāma: Tuplin and Ma 2020. Bactria: Naveh and Shaked 2012. Idumaea: Porten and Yardeni 2014–23.
4. This essay can in due course be read alongside my discussion of the intersections between Persian-employed mercenaries and the market: Tuplin (in press). For ideological aspects see Tuplin 2017.
5. *Pol.* 1255b37, 1256b1, 1256b23–27.
6. A similar idea (warfare characteristically happens at distant borders) is encoded in seal-stone combat images: see Tuplin 2020a, 375–9, 387–8.
7. For translations of the royal inscriptions cited, here see Kuhrt 2007, 486–7, 502–5.
8. Xen. *Oec.* 4.4–15.
9. Gadatas: Xen. *Cyr.* 5.2.28, 5.3.12, 15, 26; 5.4.2–3, 9, 29, 5.4.4–6; Gobryas: 4.6.2, 9. Armenia: 3.1.1–3.2.31. Tuplin 2014, 676–7; 2023, 475–6.
10. Darius *kapēlos*: Hdt. 3.89; Tuplin 1997.
11. General rule: Xen. *Cyr.* 8.6.10. *Paradeisoi*: Xen. *Oec.* 4.21, *An.* 1.2.7,9 (Cyrus), *Hell.* 4.1.15 (Pharnabazus), *An.* 1.4.10 (Belesys), Diod. 14.80.2 (Tissaphernes). On *paradeisoi* see Tuplin 1996, 80–131; 2019; Wiesehöfer 2021a. Asidates: Xen. *An.* 7.8.8–23. Artayctes and the Protesilaum: Hdt. 9.116. (A very profitable estate, if Artayctes could offer 300t. to his captors to secure his and his sons' release: 9.121.)
12. Asian temples: Diod. 5.63. Temple despoliation: Diod. 1.46, 1.49, Hieron. *In Dan.* 11.7–9 (Cambyses in Egypt), Hdt. 6.18, 6.101, 8.53–6, Aesch. *Pers.* 809–15, Isoc. 4.155–6, Diod. 16.51.
13. Sardis: Hdt. 1.88–9. Spithridates: Xen. *Hell.* 4.1.26–7, Plut. *Ages.* 11; Dercylidas: Xen. *Hell.* 3.2.14. Cyprus: Diod. 16.42.6. (One might compare the '*episitismos* [provisioning] of the Peloponnese' occasioned by Sparta's war against Elis: Xen. *Hell.* 3.2.26.) Other examples of booty collection include Hdt.1.161, Ctes. 688 F 8d (45), Polyaen. 5.44.5, 7.28.1, Diod. 11.13, 16.49, 17.7, Nep. *Dat.* 10–11. It is a feature of the fictive Persian world of *Cyropaedia*.
14. Punitive deportations: 4.203, 6.9, 6.19, 6.32, 6.101, 6.119. (Viewed in economic terms, one could possibly regard these as a reparation payment.) Iasus: Thuc. 8.28. Egyptian craftsmen:

Diod. 1.46 (anachronistic inasmuch as the development of Susa and Persepolis were largely or wholly Darian enterprises). Paeonian deportation: Hdt. 5.12–17. Skudrians: Stolper and Henkelman 2009. Other prisoner texts: e.g. Hdt. 1.161, 3.25, 6.96, 7.181, Diod. 14.35, 15.43, Ctes. 688 F 13(20). State use of prisoners as a labour resource was not wholly alien to Greek custom: Hdt.3.39 (Polycrates). Accounts of imprisonment in the Syracusan quarries in 413 (Thuc. 7.86–7, Plut. *Nic.* 28–9) do not dwell on any work the prisoners might have done. On Achaemenid deportations, see recently Rollinger 2018; Matarese 2021; Wiesehöfer 2021b.

15. Xen. *Hell.* 3.4.24, 4.3.21.

16. Thuc. 1.138. Magnesia was assigned as his bread. Thucydides provides no valuation for Lampsacus (wine) or Myus (*opson* [food]).

17. Alexander: Damascus: Curt. 3.13.6. Arbela: 5.1.10; Diod. 17.64. Babylon: Arr. 3.16.3, Curt. 5.1.23. Susa: Arr. 3.16.7, Diod. 17.66, Just. 11.19.4, Plut. *Alex.*36, Strab. 15.3.9, Curt. 5.2.11. Pasargadae: Curt. 5.6.9. Persepolis: Curt. 5.6.9, Diod. 17.71, Plut. *Alex.* 37. Ecbatana: Strab. 15.3.9, Diod. 17.80, Just. 12.1.1. Pursuit of Darius: Diod. 17.74, Arr. 3.19, Curt. 6.2.10. For a recent discussion of this and other aspects of Alexander's enrichment by conquest, see Holt 2016.

18. On this issue, see Bresson 2020.

19. 9,700 t.: Thuc. 2.13.

20. TADAE A6.10 (Kuhrt 2007, 819–20), with Tuplin 2020b, 180–96 and Ma 2020. Aršāma's postulated concerned about the impact of the Peloponnesian War on Egypt's maritime trade and (therefore) tax revenue (Hyland 2020) may have been less self-centred.

21. Foreign workers in Persepolis: Stolper and Henkelman 2009. That workers in the Persepolis economy might arrive as prisoners is now attested explicitly of Lycians, another ethnic group (like Skudrians: see n. 14) very well represented in the Fortification archive (Hyland 2022).

22. There are many uncertainties in the readings, especially in the Aramaic version, which I have not attempted to indicate. (For details about the Akkadian text see Hyland 2014, 177–80.) However, the tabulated figures give a fair enough impression. For an annotated translation of the Behistun narrative (DB), see Kuhrt 2007, 141–57.

23. Inspection of material in De Odorico 1995 suggests that the non-rounded exactness we find in DB is comparatively rare in Neo-Assyrian texts (fewer than 10 per cent of salient cases) and quantification of human victims virtually disappears after Sargon II. Quantified statements are much more likely to be about captives than the dead – fewer than 30 per cent of salient items involve quantifications of dead enemies, though this statistic is helped by the fact that, although rather common in Assurnasirpal's texts, quantified killing is virtually absent from Tiglath-Pileser III onwards. In Darius' text, by contrast, both categories are normally reported; and the variant in which a single figure is provided for captives *plus* dead is not paralleled in Neo-Assyrian texts. For general reflections on reporting of numbers in Assyrian military contexts, see Nadali 2020.

24. Hdt. 1.192, Isoc. 4.145. *Peripolousa stratia*: Tuplin 2014, 679; 2018, 23–4 n.35.

25. Theopomp. 115 F 113. King's Dinner: Henkelman 2010.

26. Earth and water: see recently Waters 2014b; Rung 2015; Klinkott 2016. Bribery: Lewis 1989. Parsimony: *Hell. Oxy.* 22, Isoc. 4.142, 153. Needing mercenaries for an invasion of Egypt, Artaxerxes II did not simply offer higher wages but encouraged peace in Greece to release mercenaries onto the market (Diod.15.38). Tissaphernes: Thuc. 8.29, 8.45–6, 8.85. Conon: Diod. 14.81; Artaxerxes III: schol. Dem. 4.19.

27. For that explanation of the Herodotean army list and the reviews at Abydus and Doriscus, see Kienast 1996; Briant 2002, 195–8. The costs of alleged regular local inspections of military

resources are, of course, another element in the balance sheet: such inspections are inferred from Xen. *Oec.* 4.6; *Cyr.* 6.2.11 (along with *An.* 1.1.2, 1.9.7; *Hell.* 1.4.3; and perhaps Arr. *Anab.* 4.1.5) and possibly exemplified in UET 4.109 and the Uruk mobilization texts from January 421 (BE 10.61,62, PBS 2/1 54,162,194, IMT 83, Lutz 1928 [Kuhrt 2007, 722 (no. 38)]; Stolper 1985, no. 117). See e.g. Briant 2002, 749, 980.

28. By way of quantification, de Callataÿ (2000a, 97) speculates that, at a conservative estimate, the coins of Pharnabazus and Tarkumuwa alone would pay 20,000 soldiers for twenty-six months at (the relatively high figure of) twelve staters per month; and he is prepared to envisage the number of coins involved (and so their military purchasing power) being twice as high. In a more recent general treatment of the military purpose of Cilician (and Pamphylian) coinage, he puts it differently: the output would have paid 39,000 soldiers for a year or maintained a force of 1,625 soldiers for twenty-four years (de Callataÿ 2023, 48).
29. This issue surfaces several times in Meadows and Bodzek 2023, but see Meadows 2023 in particular.
30. For recent brief comment, see Van Wees 2013a, 147–8. A different interaction of Persian ships and economic structures is provided by the same author's observations of the fiscal effects in mainland Greece of the need to confront Persian trireme fleets. Trundle 2010a on the monetization of warfare in the Greek world can also be read in this sense.
31. The fact that Cypriot rebels in Hdt. 5.109 lack triremes is perhaps the closest. Otherwise the best-attested boat owned by the state but used by others is the apparently non-military Nile boat whose punctiliouly budgeted repair is the subject of TADAE A6.2 (Kuhrt 2007, 727–9).
32. Building ships: Diod. 11.2, 14.98, Hdt. 6.48. Texts normally use more ambiguous terms such as *kataskeuazein* ('equip') or *hetoimazein* ('make ready').
33. For example, the 300 ships imagined at Xen. *Hell.* 3.4.1 never fully materialized. 300 is also Diodorus' figure for the infamous Phoenician fleet of 412 BC (13.36), of which at most 147 materialized (Thuc. 8.87).
34. Xen. *Hell.* 1.1.25 (cf. Diod. 14.98 for satrapal involvement).
35. Note also the provision of missiles and 'other things needed for war' to mercenaries sent by Persian satraps to assist Perinthus: Diod. 17.75.
36. Land for service: Xen. *Cyr.* 8.6.10, 8.8.20; Sekunda 1985; 1988; 1991; Klinkott 2022, esp. 275–82. Mnesimachus: Sardis VII.1.1, Henkelman 2018a, 40–2. Cardaces: Tuplin 2014b, 686–8.
37. Logistics fail: mutiny over food-supplies (Diod. 15.3: enemy action prevents merchants from conveying food from the mainland to Cyprus), army reduced to eating horses (Plut. *Art.*24), cannibalism (Hdt. 3.25). Logistics difficult: Darius in Scythia (Hdt. 4.130, 140; Polyaen. 7.12), Cyrus off-piste in the Middle Euphrates (Xen. *An.* 1.5.5–7).
38. One might regard *ephodia* (which recurs in a Persian context in Xen. *Hell.* 1.1.24) as the Greek equivalent of **pasābara-*, a word used both in Persepolitan (at least nine texts: *baššabara*) and Bactrian (ADAB C3:44: *pšbr'*) documentary sources, or **dauša-xwar(a)-*, attested just in Bactria (A2.1, C1:2,51 *dwšḥwr'*).
39. The information in Theop.115 F 293 about the 343 expedition may pertain to the King's Table rather than general logistical provision – though in simple balance sheet terms the distinction is perhaps nugatory.
40. Cyrus the Younger: Xen. *An.* 1.2.18, 1.3.14, 1.5.6. (Tissaphernes followed suit in the post-Cunaxa phase: 2.4.9, 2.5.30, 3.2.21.) Cyrus the Elder: *Cyr.* 6.2.38–9. O'Connor 2015 sees such *agorai* as at best supplementary suppliers of food (their primary role being to buy booty).

41. Ps.-Ar. *Oec.* 2.2.14 (a slightly opaque story, admittedly, and perhaps a problematic situation); Xen. *An.* 4.4.16 (only problematic because the soldier fell into the hands of the Greeks).

42. Xerxes was modest by the standards of Darius III: those managing *his* campaign in 333 had to cater for the women of the court as well (Arr. 2.11.9–10; Diod. 17.31.2, 17.32.2, 17.35.2–36.4, 17.37.3–38.4; Curt. 3.3.22–5, 3.11.21–6, 3.12.2–26, 3.13.1–15; Plut. *Alex.* 21, 24; Dicaearch. fr.64 Wehrli = fr.77 Mirhady [Athen. 557D-E]) – though the sources dwell more on the opulence of Persian encampments and the pathos of the women's fate than on brute logistics. We do, however, learn that porters were called *gangabae* (Curt. 3.13.7), a word attested in Elamite (*kanzapa* = **ganzapa*) in PF 1358. Henkelman (2011, 137) detects a similar group in the Elamite *lin-huttip* of Fortification archive texts. For the wider context of long-distance transport of valuable commodities, see Tuplin 2020b, 236–41.

43. *Pers.* 794: κτείνουσα λιμῷ τοὺς ὑπερπόλλους ἄγαν.

44. The Athos Canal was an exceptional enterprise, as was Darius' completion of Necho's Nile–Red Sea canal, an enterprise not solely motivated by economic or strategic consideration (Tuplin 1991). But (quite apart from in-campaign operations) resources must have been expended on humbler general infrastructure projects concerning e.g. roads and forts. Some Cilician expenditure (above, n.28) may have been on naval installations.

45. Hdt. 7.118, 7.120.

46. *Peloponnesian War.* Global cost: Isoc. 8.97: over 5,000 t.; Andoc. 3.29: 5,000 t. (doubted by Lewis (1989) 232.) Pharnabazus sent 25 t. when trying to get ships sent from Sparta (Thuc. 8.8). Tissaphernes pay-rate 33 t. per month (8.29). Cyrus arrives with 500 t. and can use *idia* and throne (Xen. *Hell.* 1.5.3); the 500 t. and much more had been spent by 2.1.11 (405 BC). Lysander had 470 t. left from *phoroi* allocated him by Cyrus (2.3.8). *Cyrus' insurrection.* Greek mercenaries cost 565 t. *Post-400 war with Sparta.* We know of at least 1,420 t. allocated to this (Diod. 14.39, Hell.Oxy. 22.3, Nep. *Con.* 4). *Evagoras War.* Global cost over 15,000 t. (Isoc. 9.60). Tiribazus gets 2,000 t. for war after naval success over Evagoras (Diod. 15.4). *So-called Satraps' Revolt.* Orontes has a year's pay for 20,000 mercenaries (Diod. 15.91), perhaps 800 t.

47. Potidaea cost 2,000 t. (Diod. 12.46) or 2,400 t. (Isoc. 15.113). Samos cost 1,000 t. (Isoc. l.c.) or 1,400 t. (Kallet 1993, 104). Archidamian War: Pritchard 2015b, 145 reckons an annual cost of 1,500 t.

48. Hdt. 3.90 (Cilicia), 91 (Egypt).

49. Tuplin 2020c, 300 n.34.

50. Xen. *An.* 1.3.21; *Hell.* 1.5.4–7; Thuc. 8.29, 8.45.

51. Xen. *Cyr.* 8.6.1–3, 9, 10, 16; *Oec.* 4.5–11, with Tuplin 1987, 167–75; 2016b.

52. That is, the question whether soldiers were paid an allowance for subsistence (*sitēresion*) as well as basic pay (*misthos*). See e.g. Pritchett 1971, 1–6; Krasilnikoff 1992.

53. Heraclides 689 F 2 (Kuhrt 2007, 610–11): *ta sitia para tou basileōs eis hupologon lambanousi* ('they get their food from the king *eis hupologon*'). *Eis hupologon* occurs in no other literary source (TLG) nor is it unambiguously present elsewhere (BGU 1216B2.147 and P.Tebtunis 895.85 involve restorations). Perhaps a missing verb is to be understood governing *eis* or perhaps *eis hupologon* is to be taken as an adverbial phrase (in-*hupologos*-manner or for-the-purpose-of-*hupologos*). In any event, the meaning of *hupologos* is the important problem. On the face of things it evokes a process of accounting, so that translations such as 'en guise de paiement' (Lenfant 2009, 282) or 'in return for their services' (Olson 2006, 194) or 'as compensation for their service' (Kuhrt 2007, 610) seem unsatisfactory. In documentary papyri, *hupologos* characteristically involves deduction (*hupologou* can mean minus or substract), and that idea can very frequently be sensed when the word or the associated verbs are used (both

literally and metaphorically) in other literary and epigraphic texts – and notably in the only other case known to me where it is associated with military pay, Polybius 6.39.15. Sensing things thus is to some degree a matter of perspective, and is easier in some cases than others. But there is a definite case for saying that Heraclides means the soldiers receive food as a deduction against some sort of predetermined account. But even if he means no more than 'against an account', the proposition is distinctive, and it is very suitable to the environment we see in the Persepolis Fortification archive, where payment *memoranda* typically record quantities of commodities that are to be set against the account of a relevant official or office.

54. Aelius Dionysius (ap. Eustathius ad *Iliad* 2.289 = 368.38): *ouk idion ti genos, alla misthou strateuomenoi barbaroi* (' not a distinct race of some sort, but barbarians serving for pay').

55. Hdt. 7.19, 26; Xen. *An.* 1.4.13, 1.7.4–8, 18, 1.9.1–27, *Hell.* 3.1.13, Diod. 15.9, 16.51, 52, Theop. 115 F 124, Plut. *Artox.* 6. Quantification: Cyrus offers each man 5 *minai* (over a year's pay by any reckoning) and a gold crown (*An.* 1.4.13, 1.7.7). There is no telling how valuable the gold crowns would have been, but the prospective outlay probably exceeds 1,000 t. and might well approach 2,000 t. The *mantis* Silanus was given 3,000 darics (equivalent of ten talents) for an accurate prediction (1.7.18). In a diplomatic context, Artaxerxes II allegedly gave the Athenian ambassador Timagoras 10,000 darics as well as other goods (Plut. *Artox.* 22). On Persian gift-giving and Greek perceptions thereof, see recently Ellis 2021.

56. 10,000: Arr. 2.25. 30,000: Curt. 4.11.6,12, Just. 11.12.10, Diod. 17.54.2.

57. TADAE II xiii–xiv; P.Louvre E2929, P.Loeb 41 = P.Hou 7, P.Loeb 44+49, P.Loeb 51.

58. DB §47 (Aršada fortress *and* estate). Persepolis: places designated as fortresses are mentioned quite often as part of the basic economic structure. PF 1857 links estates and grain stored at a fortress. Persepolis itself was in part a fortress (Tuplin 2021, 405, 411–12). In fact the common translation of *didā* (OP) and *halmarriš* (Elamite) as 'fortress' is misleading in suggesting a predominantly military function (Henkelman 2018a, 46 n.32). Henkelman 2008, 313, postulates that Taoce and Gabae (places named by Strabo in the same breath as Persepolis, Susa and Pasargadae and clearly visible in the Fortification archive) 'must have been of pivotal importance in the economic and, most likely, military structure of Achaemenid Fars'.

59. PFNN 1202, PFNN 2356; CT 22.74. Some think this could also be the case with the *ḥayla* of 'Armapiya in A6.8 (Kuhrt 2007, 816), though there is no particularly strong reason to take this view: see Tuplin 2020b: 131–46.

60. Lance-bearers: Henkelman 2002; 2017, 72–7; 2023, 246, 286. Ship-commander: PT 8. The ship-commander (Bakabada) is plausibly the Megabates later famous for his role in the Naxian expedition (Hdt. 5.32–5): see Henkelman 2023, 248–55 (redating PT 08 to 507/6–506/5 or earlier) and 275–80 (on Bakabada / Megabates). The workers are perhaps oarsmen or shipwrights: Henkelman 2023, 277. Travel-provisions and sand-clearance: ADAB A4. Soldiers 'who go to markets': ADAB A2 (the phrase could be translated differently). Locusts: ADAB A2.

61. Henkelman 2018a, 42–6; Tuplin 2020b, 161. The tax can be envisaged as a duty of service incumbent on the estate-holders.

62. 'Revenue-land': P.Cairo 50098+50102 (Vleeming 1991, 78), actually just post-First Domination . Revenue land recurs in P.Loeb 45, P.Moscow 424. Taxable allocation of 30 *arourai*: P.Ashmolean 1984/87 (Fischer-Bovet 2013). A Calasirian may get rations from a temple in CG 50060, but the case is not clear. See Tuplin 2020c, 310–11; 2020d, 48 n.166.

63. Variously inferred from Segal 24 (Kuhrt 2007, 715), 31, 46, TADAE A5.2, A5.5, B8.10, C3.5: see Tuplin 2020b, 298. Porten 1968, 300, doubted there was enough viable arable land around Elephantine. Things might be different elsewhere.

64. Stolper 1985; Jursa 2009; 2011; Manning 2021, 159–202.

65. Archaeological evidence of grain silos from other South Levantine sites has been thought to reflect storage facilities for military consumers: Tuplin 2014b, 677; Henkelman 2017, 86–92.

66. *Prs*: TADAE A2.3, A3.3, B4.2, B.4.3 = 4.4, D7.9, CG 29, 148, 162, 170, 235, 255, X11. TADAE C3.26 probably does not refer to soldiers. *Ptp'*: TADAE B3.13, B5.5, C3.14. For more details, see Tuplin 2020c, 296–7.

67. *Ptp'*: B2:2, C4:10,42, C5:8. An associated official, *ptpkn* (**piθfakāna-*), occurs in C1:47, C4:10,25. Hystaspes: ADAB C2, with Hyland 2013; Luther 2021. Bessus' provisions: ADAB C1: over 200 animals or birds, 4,990 quarts of three grades of flour, 120 *mariš* of Arachosian wine, sundries (oil, vinegar, sour milk and unidentified), further flour entries of uncertain status (over 4,000 quarts), 3,000 quarts of fodder; *and* material for divine offerings.

68. Table of the King: Henkelman 2010.

69. Tuplin 2014, 674–5; 2020b, 126, 161; Henkelman 2010, 705, 707, 711; 2017, 49, 167, 198; 2018a, 42–6; 2018b, 228–9; 2020, 216–17. A common feature of cases involving large groups is use of the term *taššup* ('personnel') and/or of labels such as *hallinup* or *haldabe* that have been claimed to designate soldiers. The provisioning of any lance-bearers (above, p. 88) who *were* engaged in military activities would also exemplify the payment of soldiers, and that applies to any other individuals with potentially military function-designations: but unambiguous examples are rare. Even those optimistic about finding soldiers in the Persepolis archives acknowledge that their presence is patchy, perhaps because the military was largely covered by a distinct administrative structure (Henkelman 2018b, 229; 2021, 891).

70. One can have 4 *seah* for one donkey, 1 *seah* for one horse, 4 *seah* 3 *qab* for a horse and a donkey, 1 *seah* 3 *qab* for 12 colts etc.; 3 *seah* 1 *qab* for plural horsemen, 4 *seah* for a single horseman.

71. Arabs etc: Smith and Martin 2009, no. 18 (Saqqara S.71/2 DP-31). Syene garrison: TADAE C3.14 (May 400). Other items: TADAE B3.13 (2 or more ardabs), B4.4 (2.6666 ardabs). For more details see Tuplin 2020c, 296–7 n. 21.

72. Babylonia: Jursa 2009, 257. 4 shekels p.m.: NCBT 958 etc. (Jursa and Hackl 2010, 651), YOS 3.171. 7.7 shekels p.m.: Dar. 154. 25 litres p.d.: YOS 7.156. The famous Gadal-Iama text (Lutz 1928 [Kuhrt 2007, 722]) allocates 60 shekels for provisions. Other Uruk mobilization texts allocate 20, 6 or 80 kor of barley for various combinations of silver, clothing, travel provisions and equipment. Borsippa Egypto-Carians: Waerzeggers 2006.

73. Persepolitan figures (rates are *per diem*): (1) Bakadadda the *pamanuyakara* (protection-maker: PF 1017) gives flour to horsemen, 2 @ 4.5 quarts, 8 @ 3 quarts. (2) Military unit (PFAT 054) coming from Bactria: at least 1 quart. (3) 259 'ship-men' going from Persepolis to Media (PFNN 2261) get 0.1 of a sheep each. Fort. 0472-101:07–9, 24–6 (Henkelman 2023, 277 n.95) also mentions ship-men, but their rations cannot be calculated. (4) A bow-and-arrow-case-carrier (PF 1560): 2 quarts of wine. Lancemen regularly 1 quart of wine, 1.5 quarts of flour. (But so-called 'lancemen' are by no means always engaged on military business: see above, n. 60.) (5) Turmašbada and companions, fortress-guards (a dozen texts): normally 2 @ 1.333 quarts of wine, 7 @ 1 quart; once 1 @ 2 quarts, 2 @ 1.333 quarts, 5 @ 1 quart. (6) Hindukka's Bezimatiyans *alias* fortress guards (PF 1946:17, PF 1591): 1 quart. (7) Several texts involving Karkiš (Carmanian satrap) assign large daily rations of flour (14,000, 21,400 or 32,310 quarts), wine (2,000 quarts) or small cattle (291 head) to *taššup* accompanying him. Perhaps these are 1 quart or 0.1 animal rations for large groups of soldiers.

74. See above, p. 81. Nor is that quite the message of the armed royal figure on *sigloi* and darics, though its presence is appropriate on what is, among other things, an instrument of military expenditure.

75. The text is succinct and theoretical in character (Descat 2020), but elimination of the military still seems remarkable.

76. Raaflaub 2009, 98–9.

77. Strength in money: Kallet 1994, 243. Ahuramazda: *passim.* Men and horses (and once chariots): DPd, DSf, DSp, DSs. DZc. (For translations of some of these, see Kuhrt 2007, 485–6, 487, 492–5.) Ps-Aristotle: *Oec.* 1345b19–1346a5. Mardonius: Hdt. 7.9a. Demaratus: Hdt. 7.102. Xerxes: Hdt. 7.49. (Coined and uncoined money is mentioned later by Artabazus as resource for bribery: Hdt. 9.41.)

78. Opulent/sober armies: Plut. *Alex.* 20, 23, Just. 11.10.1f, 11.13.5, 11; Arr. *Anab.* 2.11.10, Curt. 3.2.12, 3.3.14, 26, 3.10.9, 3.11.20, 3.13.7, 4.13.1-2.

79. Jason: Xen. *Hell.* 6.1.12. Greek mercenaries: Dem. 14.31, Plat. *Leg.* 697E, Xen. *Cyr.* 8.8.26, with Tuplin 2022, 245–6.

80. Wealth and *truphē*: Isoc. 4.151. *Truphē* good: Heraclid.Pont. 55 Wehrli and Aristox. fr.50, both quoted by Athenaeus, on whose reliability see Lenfant 2007. Rational economy: Heraclides 689 F 2. Antiochus: Xen. *Hell.* 7.1.38.

81. Tuplin 2014b.

82. The Aramaic text is awry here. It gives the same figures for two successive battles, while entirely omitting any other details (notably location and date) about the second. This is clearly a copyist's error. In the Akkadian text, 4,579 is the combined figure for dead and surviving (see above) at the second of the battles (Gandutava). We can be sure that the original source text did not claim that two battles produced precisely the same numbers of dead and captured.

CHAPTER 5
THE CORINTHIAN WAR (395/4–387/6 BC): SHIPS, WALLS AND MONEY

Annabel Florence

1. Introduction

Historians of Greek antiquity have long accepted the view that Athens, after the Peloponnesian War, lacked the necessary financial skills and monetary resources to fund any co-ordinated military programme and achieve its imperialist ambitions. This traditional view has been the *communis opinio* of scholarship on Athenian public finance for 200 years: from when August Böckh wrote *Die Staatshaushaltung der Athener* in 1817, to French historian Patrice Brun who, in 1983, argued that Athens' failure to organize its finances properly was 'la raison directe de la mort de la cité en tant qu' Etat indépendant'.[1] More recently, ancient historians have begun to re-assess this view. It is now argued that post-war Athens recovered faster than has previously been thought, and that it continued to do so throughout the century.[2] However, research on the public financing of Athenian military campaigns of the early fourth century is yet to reflect this more positive assessment. Inevitably when scholars discuss the bleak state of fourth-century Athens, the financing of the Corinthian War is their starting point. In most versions, an ill-equipped, ill-prepared and under-funded Athens joined Corinth, Argos and Thebes against Sparta for the sole purpose of re-establishing its empire.[3] Ancient sources covering the war such as Lysias, Xenophon, Diodorus Siculus, the Oxyrhynchus Historian and Aristophanes are cited selectively by historians to present post-war Athens as a city in chaos; a city that was so desperate to revive its empire it was willing to sacrifice its stability and security for the slimmest of chances. Contributing to this are the anti-democratic sentiments expressed by Xenophon, Plato and Isocrates who are critical of the democracy and its leadership, characterizing both as unstable, unpredictable and easily manipulated by demagogues.

Unsurprisingly, then, scholarship regularly presents as fact that Athens, despite its bold imperial ambitions, struggled to fund its military campaigns during this period and that its concern for its military finances was 'haphazard and improvisatory' and at times 'temporarily disabled or dysfunctional'.[4] August Böckh first argued this in 1817, when he wrote that Athens frequently experienced financial difficulties because it lacked the foresight and economy to manage its revenues properly.[5] Traditionally, scholars cite events from the Corinthian War that reinforce these characterizations of Athenian financial decision-making: the constant levying of *eisphorai* ('wealth taxes'), a seemingly desperate call for voluntary contributions of cash, a heavy dependence on generals raising money in the field, a reliance on the financial support of Persia, and the arbitrary rejection of peace when it was offered.

More often than not, historians writing about the finances of fourth-century Athens rattle off this evidence of poor decision-making in a perfunctory mention of the Corinthian War in their overviews of the state of the Athenian economy and its recovery after the Peloponnesian War.[6] Some merely recount the events of these first two decades without providing any comment on the financial implications of mounting the war's military campaigns.[7] Others, such as Barry Strauss, offer a narrative about the Corinthian War only as the context for the political, economic and social atmosphere at the beginning of the fourth century.[8] Then, there are those who take an in-depth look at the individual personalities of the war, for example Conon and Thrasybulus.[9]

Significant research has been done on specific areas relating to the funding of Athenian military campaigns in the fourth century such as the *eisphora*, *epidoseis*, foreign aid and monies raised by generals in the field.[10] Again, though, this research analyses the fourth century as a whole, and consequently discussions in relation to the funding of military operations during the Corinthian War regularly end up as summaries recorded in a few paragraphs at most. Despite an attempt by Patrice Brun in 1983 to calculate specifically the amounts received by the state through one or other sources of revenue, for example, the *eisphorai*, the costs associated with the military expenditure of the Corinthian War are yet to be determined. Disappointingly, this renders the figures generated by Brun meaningless. Predictably, then, the traditional story continues to be used to explain Athenian financial expenditure on warfare during the 390s and early 380s.

The problem in using the traditional view is that there is very little in this scholarship that connects the *dēmos*' financial decision-making during the Corinthian War to the events and the major campaigns of the war itself. Consequently, the financial decisions taken by the *dēmos* are assumed to be reactionary. Athens did indeed relentlessly levy *eisphorai* on its elite citizens during the early years of the Corinthian War. Wealthy Athenians were also called upon to make an *epidosis* ('voluntary contribution') of cash to the *dēmos*.[11] Yet these taxes were all imposed during a period when Athens had a limited number of troops on the ground. The possibility that Athens might have been accumulating cash reserves for some future use has never been considered.

Almost all scholarship on the Corinthian War focuses on Athens' opportunistic dependence on Persian subsidies to finance is military expenditure.[12] Scholars place significant importance on this aid, arguing that it gave the *dēmos* an exaggerated view of the state's financial strengths and abilities. So much so that it rejected a peace plan put forward by Andocides in 392/1.[13] Yet, the evidence for a connection between this aid from Persia and its contribution to the funding of Athenian military campaigns is minimal.

In their discussions about the financing of the Corinthian War, scholars regularly bypass any reflection on what Athenians saw as the priority of military finance and what drove their decision-making in this area. Traditionally, they put it down to 'unbridled imperialism'.[14] But there is more to it than that. The Athenians had long-held beliefs about military security and how to achieve it; bringing *sōteria* ('safety') and *dunamis* ('military might') to the city through the acquisition of ships, walls and money was fundamental to this ideology and consequently, is essential to any discussion on Athenian military financing.

It is the purpose of this chapter to re-examine the financial decisions made by the *dēmos* in response to the events of the Corinthian War and show that in fact Athens, far from mismanaging its military finances, held tight control over them. The chapter will address Athens' ability to manage its military finances, the ideology behind its decision making and the wisdom of its funding choices in three sections. The first, section 2 below, outlines the financial position of Athens as at the restoration of the democracy in 404/3. It will demonstrate that Athens during this period and up until the beginning of the Corinthian War did in fact manage its revenues and expenses extremely well. Section 3 examines the first stage of the Corinthian War from the summer of 395/4 to the winter of 391/0. It calculates the military expenditure over these five years and compares it to the total revenue generated by the *eisphorai,* the *epidosis* and Persian subsidies. It will examine how the state's concept of military security influenced its decisions about military financing during this period. The final section will detail and analyse the remainder of the financing of the war from 390/89 to 387/6 by costing Athenian naval campaigns. It demonstrates that Athens had put in place, from the very outset of the war, a well-considered financial plan to fund the costs of these campaigns.

Calculating the costs of Athenian military expenditure for the Corinthian War is fraught with problems; descriptions of battles from 390s and the 380s often lack the same level of detail found in those of the 370s. Consequently, my estimations of the costs to Athens of its land and naval campaigns during the Corinthian War fall short of providing an exact figure. Therefore, these figures should be viewed as rough 'ballpark' estimates. However, the exercise is important one. Establishing the amount of revenue that would have been necessary to cover these costs provides us with greater insight into Athens' public finances and allows us to evaluate the wisdom of its decision-making.

Ultimately this chapter aims to show that the traditional story of Athens' management of military finances during the Corinthian War needs adjusting to reflect that, in fact, Athens was quite deliberate and careful about its military finances during this time. Fifteen years after the Peloponnesian War, Athens had re-established itself as a maritime power within the Greek world by rigorously pursuing its concept of military security.

2. Athenian public finance in the aftermath of the Peloponnesian War

Losing the Peloponnesian War had come as a bitter shock to Athens; a greater shock still was that the city-state had also lost its empire, its Long Walls and its fleet. Scholarship has long held the view that post-war Athens was in dire financial straits. Towards the end of the fifth century, Athens had gradually lost its largest sources of revenue: imperial tribute and the silver mines. To add to its woes in 404/3, the Athenian *dēmos* was in debt to the Boeotians for 2 talents (t.) and to the Spartans for 100 t. Indeed, on the surface, with significantly less income, outstanding debts and its yearly financial obligations to its religious, civic and military affairs, it is not difficult to imagine that post-war Athens was in crisis. However, it is the purpose of this section to examine the state of Athenian public finances in the years immediately following the end of the Peloponnesian War and prove that this is not the case. Consequently, the section will cost the city's annual recurring fixed-operating expenditure relating to festivals, democracy and the military, and demonstrate that Athens did indeed have ample internal revenues to meet these expenses. In doing so, it will show how the *boulē's* supervision of financial matters allowed the Athenian *dēmos* to maintain tight control over the state's public revenues and expenses, enabling it to implement cost-saving measures where appropriate and to impose an *eisphora* when needed.

The Athenian *boulē* applied strict scrutiny to the state's public finances in the fifth century and this continued into the next.[15] At the beginning of the fourth century, the council members could expect to know the exact amount of anticipated revenues for the year as well as the anticipated annual expenditure. Given that Athens had lost its two main sources of revenue, the *boulē* would have held real concerns about maintaining the state's other income streams. Additionally, as the city began to recover from the Peloponnesian War and the chaotic rule of the Thirty, the council would have kept a watchful eye on Athens' public expenditure. It was the *boulē's* intimate day-to-day knowledge of public finances that allowed the Athenian *dēmos* to exercise control over its limited revenues and ensure that all of its vital expenses were able to be met.[16] Accordingly, the role of the council to advise the assembly on financial matters was critical to the successful management of the state's finances in the early days of the restored democracy.

This is particularly evident in a decision by the assembly to reduce the pay of the cavalry in 403/2. In a fragment from a speech written by Lysias dated to the same year, it is clear that the pay rates for *hippeis* ('cavalrymen', Xen. *Eq. mag.* 1.19) and *hippotoxotai* ('mounted archers', Thuc. 2.13.8) had come under scrutiny in the assembly (fr. 6.3.79–81 Gernet-Bizos).[17] After much debate, the pay rate for *hippeis* was slashed from 6 obols (ob) per day to 4ob per day, and the *hippotoxotai* from 12ob per day to 8ob per day (73–9).[18] The lowering of the cavalry's daily wages resulted in a saving of around 28 t. per year to the state's budget. This saving could have been allocated elsewhere, used to fund some other fixed operating cost, but there is no evidence for this. In fact, it is more likely that the *dēmos*, acting on advice from the *boulē*, knew that it did not have the revenues necessary to cover the state's total fixed operating costs for the year and consequently had no other option but to cut spending.[19]

Many scholars believe that cutting the pay of these cavalrymen and mounted archers was a form of retribution for their heinous crimes as part of the Thirty.[20] I prefer to think that it is based more on logic than emotion; if savings had to be made to fixed operating costs, then the military budget was one of the few places to make them. However, it was probably a combination of both. The importance of the religious, cultural and political activities of the democracy ensured that the festival program remained a financial priority of the state (e.g. Dem. 24.26–8).[21] These festivals, so essential for securing the favour of the gods and protecting the *polis* after the nightmare of the Peloponnesian War, also helped to alleviate the city's bleak post-war mood illustrated so vividly in the plays of Aristophanes (*Eccl.; Plut.*).[22] Additionally, as the *dēmos* had fought hard to restore the democracy, cutting the expenditure required to run the state seems disadvantageous. Athens would have had no plans to wage war in the immediate future and given that cavalrymen were part of the state's wealthy elite, it made good economic sense for the *dēmos* to cut costs in this area.

Additionally, around the same time the cavalry's pay was cut, Athens forced the cavalrymen who had served under the Thirty in 405/4 to repay their *katastasis* (Lys. 16.6–7).[23] The *katastasis* was a loan made by the state to any horseman who formally enrolled in the *hippeis* corps. Its purpose was to help new recruits to purchase a war horse.[24] Upon his retirement the cavalryman was required to repay the loan, while the state would then use that money to extend a loan to the recruit taking his place.[25] The value of a war horse depended not only on the horse's age but also its colour, how well it was cared for and its agility.[26] John Kroll argues that the maximum amount the state would lend was 1,200 drachma (dr).[27] However, a mount purchased for this price would more than likely be a horse better suited to racing than charging into battle (Ar. *Nub.* 21–3; Xen. *An.*. 7.8.6; Lys. 8.10).[28] Kroll bases his argument on lead tablets found in the Athenian Agora and the Kerameikos which document the colour, branding symbol, valuation and owner of a large number of cavalry horses from the third and fourth centuries. From these figures the total average price of a war horse can be estimated at around 700dr.[29] However, when only those horses dated to the fourth century are examined, the average price seems more likely to have been around 408dr.[30] In the year that the Thirty ruled Athens, the size of the *hippeis* corps was around 1,000 men (Thuc. 2.13.8; Xen. *Eq. mag.* 1.2, 9–10, 19; 9.3 maintains the same for the 360s).[31] The enforced return of the *katastasis* by these men, long before their retirement, would have netted the state approximately 68 t. in surplus revenue. Again, the cavalry offered the state the opportunity to punish those who had opposed the democracy and to generate revenue. What the *dēmos* did with this surplus is unknown; given that it was an unforeseen one-off windfall gain by the state and was not expected to be repeated, it seems unlikely that it would have been used to fund any annually recurring costs. It is also possible that the *dēmos* simply held the sum aside in order to help cover the costs of future loans.

The outstanding debts to Boeotia and Sparta presented the *dēmos* with a significant financial hurdle the moment the democracy took back its control of Athens. A speech written by Lysias in 399/8, *Against Nicomachus*, has been used as evidence that the state was in extreme financial difficulty because it suggests that Athens could not pay these outstanding debts.[32] We know from the speech that at the restoration of the democracy the Athenian *dēmos* owed Boeotia 2 t. (Lys. 30.22). We know too that the Thirty borrowed the much heftier sum of 100 t. from Sparta to fund their civil war against Athenian democrats (Lys. 12.59, 30.22; Isoc. 7.68; [Arist.] *Ath. Pol.* 40).[33] The speech seems to suggest that the Athenians have continually missed the deadlines for payment (30.22). Part of the case brought against Nicomachus accuses him of trying to defraud the city over two years when clearly he knew that public funds were needed to repay, among other things, these outstanding debts. This suggests that Athens did not have the internal revenues or surplus revenues to cover the costs of any large extraordinary expense.

The Boeotians decided not to wait around for Athens to find the money and extracted its 2 t. by raiding the Attic countryside (Lys. 30.22). According to Demosthenes, there was much debate in the assembly on how best to repay the larger amount owed to the Spartans (20.12). Evidently Sparta was issuing threats over the non-payment of the debt (Lys. 30.22; Dem. 20.12) and it seems clear that Athens was keen to have the matter dealt with as quickly as possible. The decision was made to levy an *eisphora* (Dem. 20.12).[34] It is difficult to determine an exact date for the tax. The speech itself offers no definitive answer. However, ancient sources appear to agree that an *eisphora* was levied during the amnesty period just after 403/2 (Dem. 20.12; Isoc. 7.68; [Arist.] *Ath. Pol.* 40.3). This suggests that Athens paid the debt rather more promptly than Nicomachus' accuser would have us believe. The Athenian *dēmos*, then, knowing it did not have the surplus revenue required to pay the debt, appears to have acted quickly and decisively to impose a wealth tax on its elite citizens.

It was the responsibility of the Athenian *dēmos* to authorize the spending of Athens' public revenue in three main areas: festivals, democracy and war.[35] Within each of these areas, Athens incurred costs that were required to be met every year. Classical Athens financed an extensive festival programme which included, among other festivals, the Great Panathenaia, the Lesser Panathenaia, the City Dionysia, the Lenaea and the Eleusinian Mysteries.[36] The number of festivals that the state administered during the fifth century does not appear to have been affected by the Peloponnesian War or its outcome. Therefore, we can assume that a full programme of festivals was celebrated at the beginning of the fourth century.[37] Epigraphic evidence indicates that the Great Panathenaia, one of the most expensive festivals in the Athenian calendar, was certainly celebrated in 402/1, almost immediately after the restoration of democracy.[38] Not only did Athens have the money to fund the celebrations in that year but it also paid for the introduction of a gold crown to be dedicated to Athena, as well as the addition of gold crowns to the prize lists for each of the victors in the musical *agōnes*.[39] David Pritchard estimates that in the 370s, the cost to the public purse of the Great Panathenaia alone was at least 12.5 t. and that overall the annual festival program required an investment of at least 50 t. by the state.[40] Therefore it can be stated with a degree of confidence that because the festival programme was not altered and because it continued to be celebrated, Athens had sufficient revenues to fund its extensive number of annual festivals.

In his book *Public Spending and Democracy in Classical Athens*, Pritchard has also estimated the annual cost of running the Athenian democracy for the 420s, 370s and 330s.[41] His calculations include costings for jurors, councillors, assembly-goers, magistrates, undersecretaries and public slaves. During the 420s, the democracy cost an extraordinary 156 t. 5,507dr per year.[42] This dropped to 98 t. 2,232dr in the 370s. We know that at the restoration of democracy the courts were fully operational, and the number of councillors remained the same.[43] The number of magistracies and undersecretaries would have been significantly reduced due to the loss of empire, and the number of public slaves was probably half that of the 420s.[44] Pritchard's figure for the 370s includes pay for 6,000 citizens to attend the assembly introduced in the mid-390s (Andoc. 1.87; Dem. 24.45–6; [Dem] 59.89; *IG* ii^2 102).[45] Consequently, the cost to run the democracy at the beginning of the fourth century probably fell slightly under its costs for the 370s, perhaps around 78 t.

During the period immediately after the Peloponnesian War, expenditure on the state's military fixed operating costs would have been minimal. This expenditure would have been restricted to the yearly recurring costs associated with the necessary maintenance of any full-time military personnel. This included the sailors manning the guard ships required to protect merchant vessels carrying corn from the Hellespont to Athens and to patrol the exposed Piraeus.[46] During the fifth century, Athens had employed up to twenty guard ships to police the seas and perform these duties ([Arist.] *Ath. Pol.* 24.3; cf. Thuc. 8.74.2–3).[47] At the end of the Peloponnesian War, Sparta, concerned with depriving Athens of the ability to launch a naval attack anywhere in the Aegean, permitted the city just twelve triremes (Andoc. 3.12). Given that the Piraeus, the Attic coastline and supply ships travelling the grain route had no protection from pirates or other raiding parties during the early years of the fourth century, all twelve of these ships were probably used in this capacity. The unprotected areas of Attica were more than likely at risk of being raided during the spring and summer of each year.[48] If all ships were fully manned for six months of the year, the state would be required to pay 72 t. annually in wages.[49]

Athens' main line of defence for the first decade of the fourth century was its cavalry corps. The city was required to fund the fixed operating costs of this permanent full-time force, which sat ready to respond immediately to any military emergency. In 404/3, the size of this cavalry corps was 1,200 men (Thuc. 2.13.8), made up of 1,000 *hippeis* and 200 *hippotoxotai*.[50] Using the new pay rates determined in 403/2, the annual cost of the *hippeis* to the state was around 41 t., and the *hippotoxotai* around 16 t.[51] This equates to a fixed annual wages bill for the cavalry corps of approximately 57 t.

There is no evidence to suggest that the Athenian military was called on at any time during the immediate post-war period to fight on behalf of Athens itself. However, sometime between 402/1 and 400/399 the Spartans required Athens to send troops to aid it in its invasion of Elis (Xen. *Hell.* 3.2.21–31; Diod. Sic. 14.74.4–12). Additionally, in 400/399 Athens dispatched 300 *hippeis* to support the Spartan general Thibron in Asia Minor (Xen. *Hell.* 3.1.4; Diod. Sic. 14.17.7). These horsemen had served in the cavalry under the Thirty (Xen. *Hell.* 2.4.1–10) and Xenophon tells us that the *dēmos*, rather callously, chose them to go in the hope they would die there. Xenophon also helpfully tells us that the Spartans were to pick up the bill for their wages as well, a potential saving of 1,200ob per day (or 1t. per month) to the fixed military costs of the state (*Hell.* 3.1.4).[52] The fate of these cavalrymen remains unknown; therefore, it is impossible to determine how long Athens enjoyed this saving and, consequently, the impact that this would have had on its annual defence expenditure.[53] Therefore, we can cautiously estimate that the annual total of Athens' recurring military fixed operating costs was approximately 129 t. (guard ships 72 t. + cavalry 57 t.).

No longer able to depend on the large revenue surpluses and cash reserves of the fifth century to help defray the fixed operating costs of the city, Athens had to rely on other sources of income to generate the revenue required to meet these expenses. A regular and dependable stream of income came from the annual sale of the rights to collect various taxes. For example, collection of the import/export tax, the tax on the sale of confiscated property paid by the buyer, a tax on foreigners, and the tax on certain land sales, to name a few.[54] In fact, the right to collect the *pentekoste,* the 'import/export tax' of 2 per cent on all imported and exported goods, raised 30 t. for the state in 402/1 and 36 t. the following year (Andoc.1.133–4).[55] Other internal revenues came from court fines, the sale of confiscated property, and the rents from sacred and public land ([Arist.] *Ath. Pol.* 47.2–48.2).[56] It was from these sources of revenue that Athens had to meet the expenses of the city, most importantly the annually recurring fixed expenditure that was essential for the state to function.

My calculations above suggest that from the beginning of the century to the start of the Corinthian War, the state required internal revenues of at least 257 t. to meet its annually recurring fixed operating costs. The *merismos*, a process whereby the state's known annually recurring revenues were allocated, by law, to specific areas of expenditure, was in operation by 386/5 (*IG* ii^2 29=RO19).[57] Rhodes argues that, despite being slow to evolve, the *merismos* was more than likely introduced during the revisions to the Athenian law code in the late fifth century.[58] If these internal revenues fell short of the amounts annually required to fund the state's festival programme, the democracy, and its fixed military expenditure, public services would cease to operate (e.g. the law courts in 348: Dem 39.17). There is no evidence to suggest that Athens could not fund its annually recurring fixed operating costs for the entire period of the Corinthian War. Items of expenditure were keenly debated in the assembly by the *dēmos* and arguments centred on whether or not the state could afford the expense. Orators arguing for or against any expenditure proposed for approval were expected to provide accurate details to the assembly on how much the expense would cost, how it was to be funded and where, if necessary, additional funding would come from (e.g. Dem. 14.20–8).[59] Therefore, the *dēmos* was not at liberty to spend money it did not have.[60] Consequently, the annual internal revenues received by the state from 404/3 to the start of the Corinthian War cannot have totalled less than the required 257 t. Based on this, not only did the *dēmos* approve the state's fixed operating costs but it also knew it had the money to do so.

With all its fixed operating costs accounted for by internal revenues and an *eisphora* levied to pay off the extraordinary debt to Sparta, the evidence presented here demonstrates that in the years leading up to the Corinthian War, Athens had tight control over its finances. This directly contradicts the idea that, during the beginning of the fourth century at least, the Athenian *dēmos* was 'haphazard' or 'dysfunctional' in controlling its finances. From 403/2 to 395/4, the *dēmos* knew with some certainty where its money was coming from and it knew exactly where it was to be spent. The institutional design of the Athenian democracy ensured that with the supervision of the *boulē* the *dēmos* approved, and had the money to pay, all of the recurring fixed operating costs of the festival program, the democracy and the military. This also gave it the ability to foresee financial trouble spots and to attempt to control them, either by cutting expenditure, re-calling loans or imposing *eisphorai*. Demonstrably, the state had its financial house in order during this lead up to the Corinthian War; the next section will show that this control continued into the financing of the war itself.

3. The Corinthian War, stage 1: land warfare

As so conveniently demonstrated by Xenophon in *Hellenika*, the Corinthian War can be divided into two stages, with each stage identified by the type of war-making that dominated it. During Stage 1, 395/4–winter 391/0, all publicly funded Athenian warfare took place on land; during Stage 2, spring 391/90–387/6, naval warfare dominated. This section will concentrate on the military financing of the land wars during stage 1. Athens engaged in three significant battles during this period, at Haliartus, at Nemea and at Coronea. Minor engagements by mercenary forces make up the remainder of the land warfare over these years. Scholars usually argue that Athens financed its warfare during this period by levying multiple *eisphorai*, levying a cash *epidosis* and placing significant reliance on Persian subsidies. Arguments generally stress that Athens' heavy dependence on Persian financial aid and its obsessive imperialistic ambitions gave the state an inflated sense of its ability to withstand further warfare, and that this directly led to the *dēmos*' rejection of the peace plan put to the assembly by Andocides in 392/1. This section seeks to establish not only the variable operating costs of Athenian land warfare during this period, but also the capital costs involved in preparing for future warfare. It will show that the revenue generated was considerably more than Athens needed to finance its military commitments. It will suggest that the state created the *stratiōtika* ('military fund') to hold surplus cash reserved for future military expenditure and it will argue that it was because of this reserve, not Persian funding, that Athens rejected Andocides' proposal for peace. Importantly it will illustrate clearly that Athens was systematically acquiring money, and re-building its walls and ships in order to re-establish its *sōteria* and *dunamis*.

The build-up to the Corinthian War was marked by an intense political atmosphere at Athens. Strauss notes tensions between the rich and poor, rural and urban dwellers and oligarchs and democrats.[61] Tangled up in this mix was Athens' strong desire to restore its empire (e.g. Xen. *Hell.* 3.5.10; *Hell. Oxy.* 9.3, 10.2; Isoc. 5.63, 6.154, 9.52, 9.54f; Diod. Sic. 14.39.3; Nep. *Con.* 2.1, 5.1f; Justin 6.3.4f). There were two distinct sides to the argument: those who preyed on the lingering anti-Spartan sentiment and actively campaigned to restore the empire immediately (*Hell. Oxy.* 9–10; Xen. *Hell.* 3.5.1), and those against this who urged caution and patience, fearing that should Athens not follow the terms of the peace, it would suffer a form of retribution similar to the rule of the Thirty and the loss of its democratic government (*Hell. Oxy.* 9.1). Thus, both public opinion and the decisions of the *dēmos* were regularly conflicted. However, between 403/2 and 395/4, several events occurred that fuelled Athens' confidence to take on Sparta again: the decision by Sparta to send one of its kings, Agesilaus, to campaign in Asia Minor far away from his homeland; the defection of Rhodes from Sparta; the formation of a defensive alliance between Athens and Thebes; and the temptation of Persian gold. A key indicator that the mood at

Athens had changed, and that all uncertainty about whether or not to challenge Sparta had been resolved, was the unanimous decision by the *dēmos* to send Athenian troops to aid Thebes against Sparta at Haliartus in 395/4 (Xen. *Hell.* 3.5.16; cf. Ar. *Eccl.* 195f). This was a crucial moment for Athens; there was no turning back, sending troops to Haliartus meant war with Sparta.

4. Variable-operating costs: land warfare

The *dēmos* voted to send a contingent of hoplites and cavalry under the command of Thrasybulus to Haliartus (Xen. *Hell.* 3.5.17–24; Plut. *Lys.* 28–9; Diod. Sic. 14.81.1–4; Paus. 3.5.3, 9.32.5; Dem. 18.96; cavalry: Lys. 16.13). Just how large this contingent was is unknown. Our main ancient sources for this battle, Xenophon and Plutarch, provide different, and at times confusing, accounts of the action. Both agree though that Sparta sent two forces to Boeotia, one under the command of Lysander and the other under Pausanias (Xen. *Hell.* 3.5.17, Plut. *Lys.* 29). We only have troop numbers for Pausanias: 6,000 (Diod. Sic. 14.81.1). Both authors agree too that Lysander arrived first and, not waiting for Pausanias, attacked Haliartus and was killed. Pausanias arrived the day after the battle (*Hell.* 3.5.21; Plut. *Lys.* 29).

Xenophon's account of the battle has the Athenians deployed in the field alongside the Thebans but not actually fighting (*Hell.* 3.5.22). Plutarch has them securing the city whilst the Thebans fought the Spartans alone (*Lys.* 28.3) and following on later to assist with the continuing battle (29.1). Lysias, giving weight to Plutarch, seems to imply that the Athenians did indeed actively participate in the fighting (16.15–16). If we accept Plutarch's version, the Athenian force had to be large enough on its own to defend the city from a possible attack by Pausanias' 6,000 troops en route to meet with Lysander. The Spartans, outnumbered by the combined forces of Athenian and Theban hoplites and cavalry, instead of launching a fresh attack requested a truce to collect the dead (*Hell.* 3.5.23).[62] Therefore, we can speculate that total Athenian troop numbers at Haliartus were probably between 5,000 and 6,000; perhaps even as many as 6,000 hoplites and 600 cavalry.[63]

After the Theban victory at Haliartus, Athens and Thebes strengthened their alliance against Sparta by joining forces with Corinth and Argos (Diod. Sic. 14.82.1). By the spring of 395/4, this anti-Spartan alliance had established a general council at Corinth (Diod. Sic. 14.82.2) and then, by the summer of 395/4 had ultimately gathered for battle on the banks of the Nemea River (Xen. *Hell.* 4.2.14–23; Diod Sic. 14.83.1–2). Athens sent 6,000 hoplites and 600 cavalrymen to fight at Nemea (Xen. *Hell.* 4.2.17). Sparta was the victor in this clash and the two sides met again just a few weeks later, in August 394/3, at Coronea (4.3.10–21). Similar sized forces went into battle and again Sparta set up a victory trophy.

The cavalrymen deployed at Haliartus, Nemea and Coronea were all part of Athens' permanent cavalry corps. Consequently, their wages were already covered by internal revenues (see above). The hoplite army, however, was an additional cost for the state to cover. These costs obviously depended on the length of time the army was away from Athens actively fighting and hence were highly variable in nature. Ancient sources suggest that the pay rate for an Athenian hoplite varied throughout the fourth century. However, William Loomis has convincingly argued that an Athenian hoplite's daily gross wage in the first half of the fourth century was 1dr (6ob), consisting of a payment for service (μισθός) 4ob and a payment for rations (σιτηρέσιον) 2ob.[64] Therefore, the daily cost to Athens of its hoplite contingent at Haliartus was the relatively small figure of around 6,000dr, or 30 t. per month. Just how long Athenian troops were at Haliartus is difficult to determine. However, given that the Athenians were first assigned the duty of protecting the city of Thebes, and were then called to fight at Haliartus and to help defend that city during the retreat of the Spartans, it is possible that the Athenian troops were on campaign for, at the most, two months. The sources provide no indication that light-armed troops participated in this battle. Therefore, it is reasonable to suggest that this campaign would have cost the *dēmos* 60 t.

Again, due to the nature of the sources it is difficult to pinpoint when the Athenian forces left Athens for Nemea later that year and when they finally returned. For argument's sake, because they departed in the spring of 395/4 and the battle at Coronea took place at the end of August 394/3, I will assume they were absent from Athens for five months.[65] Therefore the state would have been required to pay the hoplite army's variable operating costs of 90 t. in 395/4 and 60 t. in 394/3.

In 393/2 an allied mercenary force of peltasts was established at Corinth by Conon, the Athenian general who commanded the Persian navy (Androt. 324 F48=Philoch. 328 F150).[66] These skilled warriors became famous throughout Greece, most notably for defeating Sparta at Lechaeum in 390/89 (Xen. *Hell.* 4.5.11–18; Diod. Sic. 14.91.2).[67] We have no precise numbers for this group at its inception, however we do know that in 389/8 Iphicrates took a force of 1,200 mercenaries to the Chersonese (Xen. *Hell.* 4.8.34).

In its first year, the mercenary force was paid for by Conon from his own pool of Persian funds. However, upon Conon's death in 392/1, it seems that the Athenians became financially responsible for the wages of these men (cf. Dem. 4.24). A mercenary peltast was paid wages of 1dr per day (Thuc. 7.27.1–2), thus the additional cost to Athens' military expenses would have been a total of 6 t. per month (36,000dr).[68] However, evidence suggests that the state contributed little, if anything, to the maintenance of this specialist force and that Iphicrates paid his men by plundering the countryside (Xen. *Hell.* 4.4.15–16, 4.8.35–6).

There were no more large-scale hoplite battles after Coronea and for the remainder of the Corinthian War land warfare consisted of skirmishes between the Spartans and this mercenary force at specifically targeted garrisons in and around Corinth.[69] Despite this, we do get fleeting references from Xenophon that Athenian hoplites were still active in Corinth after Coronea. These men, it seems, served as garrisons to keep watch over the walls of Corinth and Sicyon and therefore would have continued to receive a daily wage (*Hell.* 4.4.14). Again though, soldier numbers are lacking and, consequently, a figure for this expenditure cannot be included in my calculations. Nonetheless, the very existence of this group indicates that the variable operating cost associated with land warfare over the five years between 395/4 and 391/0 totalled considerably more than the 354 t. which can be calculated.[70]

5. Capital expenditure: land warfare

By making the unanimous decision to support the Boeotians at Haliartus, the *dēmos* had immediately placed Athens in a vulnerable position; the walls and fortifications of the Piraeus, demolished at the end of the Peloponnesian War (Xen. *Hell.* 2.2.20), had not, as yet, been rebuilt. Consequently, the city remained open to attack. It would have been essential for Athens to begin rebuilding the walls as soon as its troops began preparing for warfare.[71] Building accounts dated to Skirophorion (June/July) 395/4 confirm that work on these fortifications had already begun before the army had been dispatched to Nemea (*IG* ii^2 1656.1–2). The *dēmos* continued to pay for the reconstruction of the walls and were aided by Conon who funded the reconstruction of a large section of wall in 393/2 (*IG* ii^2 1657; Xen. *Hell.* 4.8.10; Diod. Sic. 14.85.3). Unfortunately, the inscriptional evidence is fragmentary and therefore no estimate of the cost of this capital expenditure can be made.

6. Sources of revenue for land warfare, 395/4–391/0

Now that Athens had committed itself to the Corinthian War, funding it would have been a major priority of the *dēmos*. The traditional view is that Athens, without access to large cash reserves and its imperial revenue, had little alternative other than to levy its extraordinary property tax, the *eisphora*, on its wealthy citizens to pay for its war-making.[72] Consequently the long-held belief is that, as it had done towards the end of the fifth century (Lysias 21.3), Athens funded its military expenditure between 395/4 and 391/0 by levying multiple *eisphorai*, beginning the instant hostilities resumed at Nemea.[73]

6.1 Eisphora

The *eisphora* was an ad hoc, emergency wealth tax levied, usually, in times of war (Thuc. 3.19; Lys. 21.3).[74] Ancient sources provide evidence that the *dēmos* repeatedly levied the tax during the first years of the Corinthian War (e.g. Isoc. 17.41) and that it took its toll on the wealthy. Writing in 390/89 or 389/8, Isaeus states that *eisphorai tosautai* ('so many *eisphorai*') have been levied to fund the Corinthian War (5.37). In 388/7, the speaker of Lysias 28 sympathizes with jury members by reassuring them that he too has suffered from the oppressive taxes that have recently been levied by the *dēmos* (3). In another speech written by Lysias sometime just after 390, the speaker claims that a certain Aristophanes and his father had contributed to many *eisphorai* over the past four or five years (19.29).

Modern scholarship argues that between 394/3 and 390/89 Athens levied four *eisphorai*.[75] It is possible to pinpoint the dates that at least three of these *eisphorai* would have been levied: 394/3, 393/2 and 392/1. It is also possible to suggest a legitimate date range for the fourth and final *eisphora* believed to have been levied in this period. A legal speech written by Isocrates written in 393 suggests that two *eisphorai* were levied in the war's first years (Isoc. 17.41):

> In addition to this, when a special tax was imposed upon us and other men than I were appointed registrars, I contributed more than any other foreigner and when I was myself chosen registrar, I subscribed the largest contribution ...

Relying wholly on Isocrates as evidence for these two *eisphorai* presents difficulties. His works are generally considered unreliable: full of bias, errors and exaggerations.[76] In this particular speech, the banker Pasion is accused of appropriating money which Isocrates' client, a young metic, had entrusted to him. In order to fend off any potential claim by Pasion that the money was the repayment of a loan, the young man intends to present evidence that he was quite affluent at the time and thus would not have needed to borrow money (17.40). He uses his contributions to the two *eisphorai* as additional evidence to support his claim. The point is important to his argument: how could he make such large contributions to the war tax if he lacked the necessary funds to do so? The members of the jury, and wealthy citizens reading a copy of the speech after the trial, would have been well aware of the number of *eisphorai* levied by the time the trial came to pass, but not the amounts paid by individual metics. Therefore, it is more likely that Isocrates exaggerated the value of his client's contributions to the war tax, not the number of *eisphorai* that had been levied. Consequently, Isocrates' claim that two *eisphorai* were levied in the first years of the war seems acceptable.

Fighting at Nemea began in the spring of 395/4 and continued at Coronea through to the summer of 394/3 (Xen. *Hell.* 4.2.14–3.10).[77] Therefore there is a tendency to assume that, in order to fund these two campaigns, Athens first levied the tax sometime before this campaign season began.[78] However, the speaker of Lysias 19 suggests that *eisphorai* began being levied sometime after Conon's victorious naval battle against the Spartans at Cnidus during the mid-summer of 394/3 (29). This places the date of the first *eisphora* at around the late summer of 394/3; that is, after the hostilities at Coronea had concluded.

The second *eisphora* was likely to have been levied the following summer, in 393/2.[79] It had to be in either the summer or the autumn of 393/2 in order to fit with the claims of Isocrates' client. Additionally, in the winter/spring of 393/2, after Agesilaus had captured Lechaeum, the assembly had voted to call an *epidosis* from its citizens (Isaeus. 5.37).[80] This suggests that an *eisphora* had already been levied earlier in the year and that the *dēmos* was reluctant to impose the tax again so quickly; consequently, instead of levying another *eisphora* it called an *epidosis*.[81]

Aristophanes' fourth-century play *Ecclesiazusae* indicates that a third *eisphora* was levied probably in the summer of 392/1, more than likely just after the arrest of Conon at Sardis (825–9).[82] Whilst Aristophanes does not expressly call the tax an *eisphora*, it was clearly an ad hoc tax that had recently been levied for a specific reason. Given that it was imposed at a time when Athens had begun to build a new fleet of warships, the tax fits the general description of an *eisphora*.

The fourth *eisphora* levied during this period has no conclusive date. However, Lysias 19 states that many *eisphorai* were paid by a certain Aristophanes, not the playwright, during the four or five years after Conon's success at Cnidus in the summer 394/3. Aristophanes and his father Nicophemus were executed at some point after the ships they were sailing to Cyprus were captured by the Spartan general Teleutias in the spring of 391/0 (Lys. 19.7; Xen. *Hell.* 4.8.24). Consequently, for Aristophanes to have contributed to his last *eisphora,* it must have been levied sometime before he was captured, so sometime during early 391/0. Therefore, it is safe to say that the *dēmos* levied an *eisphora* in 394/3, 393/2, 392/1 and 391/90.

If we accept these dates and if we accept, as the majority of scholars do, that the tax was levied at the minimum rate of 1 per cent on the total taxable wealth of Athens (6,000 t.: Dem. 14.49), then the *eisphorai* levied during the first stage of the Corinthian War raised a total of 60 t. per year or 240 t. in total.[83] On the other hand, Matthew Christ makes the very sensible argument that up until 378/7 there is no evidence that Athens kept a record of the capital wealth of its citizens for the purposes of calculating *eisphora* payments in such a way, as it did for its metic population. Accepting Christ's argument permits the possibility that Athens levied these *eisphorai* at a set amount as it had done in the fifth century.[84] Given that the *dēmos* had no trouble immediately after the restoration of the democracy with raising the 100 t. to clear its debt to Sparta (see above), it is very tempting to suggest that each *eisphora* raised 100 t., or a total of 400 t. over the four years.

It is clear from this evidence that Athens did not use the *eisphora* to fund its land warfare, as has traditionally been thought. The first levy of the tax occurred after the final land battle at Coronea and it continued to be levied during a lengthy period of limited military activity. It is possible that the revenue generated from these *eisphorai* was used to defray the costs associated with keeping the hoplites and mercenary peltasts active in Corinth. However, given the nature of the *eisphora* as an emergency funding strategy, and the amount of revenue each one was expected to generate, it is unlikely that these small costs were the reason behind the levying of the tax. Therefore, the consecutive levying of *eisphorai* suggests that Athens was systematically building up its cash reserves in order to finance a larger military objective.

6.2 Sōteria and dunamis

The clue as to what drove Athens to consistently and relentlessly impose these *eisphorai* on its wealthy citizens in order to create a large surplus of cash, becomes clear upon the examination of the legal and political speeches of the early fourth century. This corpus of public discourse highlights the importance Athens placed on restoring military security to the state. In fact, decisions regarding the democracy's military finances are inexorably tied to the Athenians' concept of salvation and power, its *sōteria* and *dunamis*. For the Athenians, the building-blocks of this ideology were ships, walls and money.[85]

In the law court speeches written by Lysias in the early fourth century, the orator uses the importance of *sōteria* and *dunamis* to the city in order to re-enforce his arguments. In doing so he consistently makes reference to ships, walls and money. His speeches remind jurors that the loss of the state's triremes, and the destruction of its ship sheds and its Long Walls after the Peloponnesian War exhausted the city's *dunamis* (13.46–7); that treasonous acts against the state are like handing over the city's walls and ships to its enemies (28.11); and that those who embezzle money from the city carelessly disregard the importance of repairing the ship sheds and the city's walls (30.22). In the speeches, appeals are made to the jurors to make their decisions based on his client's, or the accused's, treatment of the fleet: condemn them if they contributed to its destruction (12.38–40, 95, 99; 13.34, 46–7, 30.22); save them if they protected it (13.15–16; 18.5–6). In other speeches he makes the point that the *sōteria* of Athens too was dependent on the protection offered by its navy (18.5–6, 26.3–4) and its walls (18.5–6). In fact, in the speech *On the Property of Nicias' Brother*, he poignantly states that Eucrates '. . .preferred to die while working for your *sōteria* rather than see the walls being destroyed, the ships handed over to the enemy and your democracy enslaved. . .' (5); and in *Against Epicrates* he stresses the importance of money to military security by lamenting 'what hope of *sōteria* is there when the survival and non-survival of the city is dependent on money' (27.3).

This same ideology is central to Andocides' speech to the assembly in 392/1, urging it to accept peace with Sparta and put an end to the Corinthian War. His argument to the *dēmos* was a simple one: that military security can only be achieved through peace, not the continuation of war. In his speech, he focuses on the fact that in the past only *agatha* 'good things' have come to Athens through peace (3.4). He details these *agatha* as the fortification of the Piraeus and the building of the Long Walls (5, 7), the building of new ships (5, 7, 8), the increases in the number of cavalry and archers (5, 7), and the imperial income and large cash reserves kept on the acropolis (7–9). All of these things, achieved in peacetime, he says, allowed Athens to acquire great *dunamis* (4, 9) and *sōteria* (12). In contrast, he argues, when Athens sought to continue the Peloponnesian War and lost, Sparta stripped the city of its walls and ships so that it might never acquire *dunamis* again (30, 31, 39). He stresses that in Athens' current situation it has no money and no fleet (15) and therefore no *sōteria* and no *dunamis*, but peace now with Sparta will restore them (14, 23, 12).

The idea that ships, walls and money were critical to military security was not a new one. In his *History of the Peloponnesian War*, Thucydides makes it abundantly clear that in the fifth century *sōteria* and *dunamis* depend unquestionably on ships, walls and money.[86] For example, he writes that in his speech to the assembly on the eve of the Peloponnesian War, Pericles assured the people that they would be safe because they had the protection of the Long Walls, a strong fleet and plenty of money (2.13.2–4). Aristophanes' plays of the fifth century provide more evidence: in *Banqueters*, written in 428/7, money must be spent on ships and walls (fr. 230); in *Birds* (415/4) the state's children, slaves and wealth are protected by high walls and long ships (378–80); and in *Lysistrata* (411/10) the women are convinced that war will end if only they can cut off the supply of money from the acropolis (175–9, 488, 496).

Lisa Kallet argues that for fifth-century Athenians *dunamis*, and consequently *sōteria*, was seen as something tangible; something achieved through the generation of revenue, the accumulation of cash reserves and then, ultimately, expenditure on war-making.[87] Despite the loss of imperial revenues, Athenians of the fourth century felt no differently. Therefore, a desire by the *dēmos* to generate cash reserves would have stemmed from Athens' own priorities when it came to military security and the safety of the people. Ostensibly then, Athens levied *eisphorai* every year for four years in a deliberate attempt to systematically build up its own cash reserves in order to rebuild its fleet and restore *sōteria* and *dunamis* to the city.

6.3 Epidosis

An *epidosis* was the calling for voluntary contributions/donations from Athenian citizens and metics by the *dēmos*. The *dēmos* would determine the type of donation required, the size of the donation and what it would be used for.[88] For example, during the Persian Wars and the Peloponnesian War, there were times when the state called for elite citizens to voluntarily supply triremes at their own expense (Hdt. 8.17; Xen. *Hell.* 2.3.40).[89] We know from Isaeus that an *epidosis* requesting donations of cash was called in the winter or spring of 393/2 (5.37). By the summer of 393/2, the Athenian treasury was holding cash reserves of potentially 120–200 t., so the fact that the *dēmos* felt it needed to call an *epidosis* later that year to raise even more funds is baffling. What is not known is how much revenue was raised from the voluntary contributions, nor, in fact, the reason why it was called at all.[90] This frustrating lack of information means that this particular *epidosis* receives very little attention from scholarship on the Corinthian War, and we are left with the impression that it was nothing more than an improvisatory cash-grab by the state.

An *eisphora* had already been levied earlier in the year; consequently, the additional levy of an *epidosis* would have put further financial strain on the city's elite. The evidence for *epidoseis* levied at Athens in the early fourth century is limited. Those we know of levied in other *poleis* were used to fund construction projects like cult buildings, fortifications and harbours.[91] Later in the fourth century and in the third, Athens used *epidoseis* to fund expenditure on, for example, securing grain (*IG* II^3 1, 430 – circa. 337) and protecting the countryside during the harvest season (e.g. *IG* II^3 1,1011 – 248/7). Isaeus makes it clear that the *epidosis* of 393/2 was called after the Spartans had captured the Corinthian port of Lechaeum (5.37). After taking control, the Spartan general, Praxitas, destroyed large sections of the Long Walls connecting Corinth with its harbour (Xen. *Hell.* 4.4.13), and this offered the Spartan army a clear and unobstructed path directly to Athens. In fact, Xenophon states quite clearly that the Athenians feared a direct attack (*Hell.* 4.4.18):

> Now the Athenians in their turn were also intimidated by the strength of the Spartan force. They were quite concerned that the Spartans, having torn apart the Long Walls of the Corinthians, would then directly attack themselves . . .

The Athenians would have perceived their own walls to be at risk. The very thing that represented salvation and security to the city and which, for that matter, had only just been restored was under threat. It could be that Athens, spooked by the Spartan threat, thought that the accumulated cash reserves would not have been enough to fund an adequate defence of the *polis* and called the *epidosis* in order to increase the war chest. Therefore, it suggests that Athens levied the *eisphorai* and an *epidosis*, not to fund its current military operations, but to build cash reserves in anticipation of a greater battle.

6.4 Surplus revenues

Building up the state's cash reserves was not limited just to levying *eisphorai* or *epidoseis*. The accrual of annual revenue surpluses played an extremely important role in Athens' ability to fund its warfare during the 390s. Traditionally, scholars have argued that early fourth-century Athens was not able to generate annual surplus revenues after its defeat in the Peloponnesian War.[92] However, Athens had been able to defray the variable operating costs of its land warfare, in addition to the capital expenditure on the rebuilding of its Long Walls, before the *dēmos* had begun to levy any *eisphorai*. In order to do this, it must have had access to other avenues of funding. Presumably, raiding the territories of the men they were marching with and fighting with was not an option. Yet nothing can be found in the ancient sources to indicate that the *dēmos* attempted to raise any additional revenue to cover these costs.

What is known is that as the decade progressed, the annual internal revenues of the state increased. For example, immediately after the restoration of the democracy, harbour tax revenue rose from 30 t. (402/1) to 36 t. (401/0), a jump of 20 per cent (Andoc. 1.133–4). This revenue would have continued to grow through the 390s as the importance of the Piraeus continued to grow as a centre for trade in the Greek world (Isoc. 4.42; Xen. *Hell.* 5.19–24).[93] Additionally, at some point during the first decade of the fourth century, total annual revenues had increased sufficiently to fund the introduction of assembly pay at 1ob per day. By 392/1, the *dēmos* had been able to increase that amount to 3ob per day, an annual cost to the state of 20 t. (Ar. *Eccl.* 184–6; *Plut.* 171; [Arist.] *Ath. Pol.* 41.3).[94] Therefore, Athens was clearly generating more revenue each year than was required to cover its annual fixed operating costs. That the state was able to defray the costs of its land warfare in 395/4 and 394/3 without raising extraordinary revenue indicates that, at some point between the restoration of the democracy and the outbreak of hostilities at Haliartus, the *dēmos* had begun to accrue its annual surplus revenue. This means that the state must have accumulated between, at least, 210 t. and 354 t. (150–222 t. for 395/4 and 60–132 t. for 394/3) in revenue surpluses from the beginning of the fourth century, an average of 35–59 t. per year.

6.5 Stratiōtika

By 391/0, after levying *eisphorai* and an *epidosis* in addition to accruing its annual revenue surpluses, Athens potentially had access to significant cash reserves to pay for its military expenditure. With a surplus of such a size sitting in reserve a strong argument can be made for the creation of the *stratiōtika*, if not immediately after the restoration of the democracy, most definitely in the early years of the post-war era. The *stratiōtika*, administered by its own treasurer ([Arist.] Ath. Pol 43.1), held the state's annual surplus revenues ([Dem.] 59.4), the collected *eisphorai* ([Dem.] 50.8, 10), probably the cash *epidosis*, and any booty acquired on military campaigns.[95]

In the late fifth century, Athenian imperial revenues set aside for warfare expenditure were held in a fund administered by a group called the *hellenotamiai* ('treasurers of Greece'). These treasurers disappear from the historic record after 403/2.[96] Generally, so too does the belief that Athens had a specific fund set aside to pay for its military expenditure. In a discussion on the *stratiōtika*, George Cawkwell argued that because warfare continued throughout the fourth century, a fund similar to the one administered by the *hellenotamiai* must have existed.[97] The mention of the *stratiōtika* on an inscription dated to 374/3 provides the evidence that, by the 370s at least, the Athenians did indeed use such a fund to pay its military expenses.[98]

An exact creation date for the fund has proved elusive. However, writing before the discovery of the inscription, Cawkwell – using Demosthenes and other sources – correctly argued that the *stratiōtika* was being used in the 370s. In a note to his discussion, he suggests that because Athens was at war in the first decade of the fourth century, the Athenians must have set aside money raised specifically for military purposes into a fund similar to that which the *hellenotamiai* had administered. He then argued that whatever fund was used to hold these revenues in the 370s was more than likely created in the 390s for this purpose.[99] Cawkwell's theory must be right. Once Athens had begun accruing any annual surplus revenues and then levying *eisphorai* during periods of no military action, it would have been essential for record-keeping purposes that the *dēmos* create a fund in which to place this money to ensure it was used for war. Tantalisingly, Angelos Matthaiou has argued more recently that the treasurer of the fund is first mentioned in an inscription which can be dated, by the hand of its stone cutter, to between 400 and 390.[100] Unfortunately, that critical word, 'στρατιωτικῶν', does not appear on the stone and is supplied entirely by Matthaiou over two lacunose lines.

From the restoration of the democracy until the decision to send troops to Haliartus, Athens, for fear of punishment, had gone out of its way to follow the terms of the peace and to do exactly what the Spartans had ordered them to do. To have re-established the fund under the administration of imperial treasurers would have been a dangerous move and would have openly signalled to Sparta any plans the Athenian people may have held to restore the empire. With cash reserves fulfilling an important role in contributing to the *sōteria* and *dunamis* of the state, the introduction of a separate fund in which to record this money would have been crucial. Consequently, Athens created the more commonly named and less grand *ta stratiōtika* and funnelled the *eisphorai*, the *epidosis*, annual surplus revenues and perhaps even the returned *katastasis* into it. I believe that it was this money, accruing in the *stratiōtika*, that gave Athens the confidence to reject Andocides' peace plan in 392/1 (see below).

6.6 Persian gold

In spite of this, modern scholarship unanimously believes that one of the most important sources of funding for Athens during the Corinthian War was the subsidies, both direct and indirect, that it received from Persia.[101] The arguments suggest that Athens would not have joined the Corinthian War, nor been able to defray the costs of the war, nor rebuild its fortifications or its fleet without Persian money. But importantly too, modern scholarship argues that it was the knowledge that Athens had the financial support of Persia that lead the *dēmos* to reject the peace terms put to the assembly by Andocides in 392/1. I disagree. I believe that modern scholarship has consistently overstated the importance of Persian financial aid to Athens during the early years of the fourth century.

Ancient sources suggest that Persia gladly offered financial support to any city state that it felt it could benefit from, with funding given in the form of gold or silver. Athens is often thought to have benefitted from a share of the 50 t. of Persian silver offered by Timocrates the Rhodian in 396/5 to entice the Greek mainland states to agitate for war against Sparta. At this time, political tensions at Athens about whether or not it was time to challenge Sparta and attempt to restore the empire remained high. Xenophon claims that politicians from Thebes, Corinth and Argos accepted the money but that the Athenians, though keen to wage war against Sparta, did not (*Hell.* 3.5.1–2). The Oxyrhynchus Historian, however, tells a different story (10.2), saying that certain people with a deep hatred of Sparta and a desire to involve the city in war *did* take the gold. The point to be made here is that the money was offered to politicians so that they would stir up anti-Spartan sentiment in their respective assemblies. Therefore, the money would never have reached the state's treasury, staying firmly in the pockets of the individuals intent on reigniting hostilities with Sparta. Consequently, there is no evidence to suggest that Athens directly received a cash payment from Persia in order to meet any of the military costs of the Corinthian War.

Athens' greatest benefit from Persian aid came in the summer of 393/2 when Conon, fresh from his naval victory over Sparta at Cnidus, sailed into the Athenian harbor with a fleet of 80 triremes and a ship laden with plunder and Persian gold (Xen. *Hell.* 4.8.1–12). Conon's purpose in coming to Athens was to assist in rebuilding the Long Walls and the fortifications of the Piraeus that had once provided safety and protection for the Athenian people and the Athenian fleet. Persian money supplied by Pharnabazus and from Conon's own purse funded the labour and material costs to rebuild these walls so important to Athens' defences (Xen. *Hell.* 4.8.10; Diod. Sic. 14.85.2–3).[102] As noted above, Conon also set up and paid the maintenance costs of the mercenary force at Corinth commanded by Iphicrates (Dem. 4.24; Ar. *Plut.* 173; Androt. 324F48=Philoch. 328F150).[103] The benefit of this force in Corinth meant that, if needed, it was possible to deploy Athens' large citizen army elsewhere (Xen. *Hell.* 4.4.14).[104]

Christoph Flament argues that lines from the play *Plutus* by Aristophanes indicate that Persian money also funded the new pay rates for assembly attendance (171).[105] Flament gives the impression that he believes the King's money is directly responsible for the increase in state-funded assembly pay. I do not believe his interpretation is quite right. The 'him' in the line 'Doesn't the assembly get held because of him?' in Flament's interpretation suggests that the character Carion is talking about the Persian King. However, when the line is read in context, the 'him' obviously refers to the god Wealth. Flament's idea, though, is not far wrong. The influx of silver from Conon through the employment of labourers for the Long Walls and the increase in trade for the materials and tools needed would have provided a much needed injection into the economy of Athens.[106] In fact, there was such an abundance of silver in the *agora* that the state voted to abolish the emergency copper currency it had struck towards the end of the Peloponnesian War and return to silver coinage (Ar. *Eccl.* 815–23).[107] Some of this silver may have made its way into the treasury, via the harbour tax presumably, boosting state revenues and thereby allowing a politician like Agyrrhius to propose an increase in assembly pay (Ar. *Eccl.* 183–8, 289–310, 380; *Plut.* 329f; [Arist.] *Ath. Pol.* 43.1).[108]

A popular theory amongst scholars is that Persian money rebuilt the Athenian fleet and that Conon was using his fleet to re-establish Athens as a power in the Aegean.[109] Persia had a history of offering city-states financial aid to build-up their fleets (For example, Isoc. 8.97; Xen. *Hell.* 4.8.10–11; 4.8.16). This claim appears to be supported by Xenophon (*Hell.* 4.8.12):[110]

> When the Spartans heard that Conon was using the King's money to rebuild the Athenians' walls, to maintain his fleet, and to win over to the Athenian side both the islands and the cities on the mainland they decided to inform Tiribazus . . .

However, there are some obvious problems with this theory. First, of course Conon is using Persian money to maintain his fleet; it is a Persian fleet, it belongs to the Great King. There is no evidence to suggest that Conon and Persian money were funding the building of Athenian triremes at this point. A speech delivered by Demosthenes in the 350s lists all the great and honourable things Conon had done for Athens whilst commander of the Persian fleet; among them is the rebuilding of the Long Walls, but nowhere does he mention the rebuilding of the fleet (20.68–71). As a strong navy forms an essential part of the Athenian ideology about *sōteria* and *dunamis*, it is difficult to see why, if Conon had been responsible for rebuilding the Athenian fleet, Demosthenes would have left this information out. The real benefit Athens received from Conon's triremes was that while they policed the Aegean, the limited Athenian fleet did not need to; the grain route and trade were protected.[111]

Ancient sources are in agreement that Conon's loyalties, although he was working for Persia, were with Athens and that his aim whilst commanding the fleet was ultimately to bring about the restoration of the empire to Athens (Isoc. 4.154, 5.63, 9.54f; Diod. Sic. 14.39.3; Nep. *Con.* 2.1, 5.1f; Justin 6.3.4f; Dem. 20.69).[112] By 393/2 Sparta had lost its power over a significant number of its possessions in the Aegean; its fear then that, at that particular moment, Athens was growing in wealth and power because of Conon would seem justified. However, these islands and cities had been won over to Persia by Conon *and* Pharnabazus, and it was to Pharnabazus that these states gave gifts and money (Xen. *Hell.* 4.8.2).[113] There is no evidence to suggest that Conon and his fleet were involved in any conflict, either on behalf of Athens or Persia, from the moment he arrived in Athens in 393/2 until his death the following summer.[114] That said, Luca Asmonti quite legitimately suggests that Conon had something to do with bringing the islands of Lemnos, Imbros and Skyros back under Athenian control before the peace talks at Sardis in 392/1.[115] These islands were crucial to the safe passage of Athenian grain ships from the Bosporus to Athens, and the state had lost them at the end of the Peloponnesian War (Andoc. 3.12). Xenophon implies that by 392/1 they once again belonged to Athens (*Hell.* 4.8.15) but does not provide any information on how they came to be so.

Given that the King acknowledged the importance of these islands to Athens by specifically referring to them as belonging to the city-state in his terms for peace (Xen. *Hell.* 5.1.31), it is difficult to see that he would have strongly objected to Conon helping the Athenians recover them. Additionally, if Conon had been using the King's resources openly to benefit Athens in any other way, there is little chance he would have turned up in Sardis to oversee peace negotiations for fear of his life.[116] Conon's loyalty to Artaxerxes is clearly still strong in 392/1 when he obeys a summons by Tiribazus to return to Sardis on the pretext of being sent to the King (Nep. *Con.* 5.3).[117] Therefore it is hard to accept unequivocally that Persian money was responsible for rebuilding the Athenian fleet, or that Athens was using Conon's fleet to restore its power in the Aegean.

7. Andocides' peace plan

In the late summer or early autumn of 392/1, Athens sent three ambassadors with plenipotentiary powers to peace talks in Sparta. The land warfare in Corinth was at a stalemate; neither side was securing any ground. Athens' options were limited; it was peace or naval warfare and at this stage Athens was still without a fleet of its own. At the conclusion of the talks the ambassadors returned to Athens and Andocides submitted the peace plan, with a recommendation that it be accepted, to the assembly for debate (Andoc. 3).[118] It was rejected. Scholarship suggests there were several reasons for this rejection but that underpinning them all was the knowledge that Athens had the financial backing of Persia should it need it.[119] However, I believe that the financial support of Persia had little to do with the Assembly's rejection of the peace.

As we have seen, Persia supplied no direct financial assistance to Athens during the first years of the Corinthian War. In addition to this, Conon died in the summer of 392/1 (Lys. 19.39, 41; Isoc. 4.154; Nep. *Con.* 5.4) and with his death Athens lost its strongest link to the Persian King and his money.[120] Strauss is right to argue that any Persian aid to Athens stopped with the death of Conon.[121] The subsidies to the mercenary force at Corinth funded by the general certainly appear to have ceased; Xenophon reports that Iphicrates began plundering raids in and around Phleious and Arcadia in 392/1 (*Hell.* 4.4.15–16).[122] Conon had been in the unique position of enjoying a close relationship with Athens and, via Pharnabazus, the Persian King.[123] The ancient sources give away no names that suggest that anyone took on Conon's role in the relationship and yet Conon's fleet was said to be made up of many Athenians (*Hell. Oxy.* 1.25, 5.1, 16.30; Isoc. 4.142).[124]

It can be assumed that Conon's Persian fleet remained a Persian fleet after his death and was not somehow appropriated by Athens.[125]

Flament argues that Persian subsidies continued to Athens through the satrap Strouthas, an Athenian sympathizer the King placed in charge of the Ionian states in Asia (Xen. *Hell.* 4.8.17–19).[126] However, there is no evidence either that Strouthas developed a special relationship, such as Conon had with Pharnabazus, with any Athenian general. In contrast to Pharnabazus, who regularly met and sailed with Conan, Strouthas remained in Asia Minor fighting land battles against Spartan forces, so it is difficult to see how he could have given any financial assistance to Athens from such a distance. Experience too had taught Athens that not all of Persia's satraps felt as favourably towards it as the King did (e.g. Tiribazus funding Sparta on the quiet – 4.8.16). Consequently, Athens knew when it rejected the peace that it had no trusted middle-man for any negotiations with Persia. Therefore, the *dēmos* would be in no doubt that depending on Persian money to fund any military expenses generated from a continued war constituted a serious risk. I believe the Athenians rejected Andocides' peace plan in part because the state had accrued a surplus of cash in the *stratiōtika* large enough to build a fleet and launch an ambitious naval campaign.

Athens had continued its tight control of its military financing during the first stage of the Corinthian War. Its revenues exceeded its expenditure and consequently the state began to accrue surplus funds from quite early in the 390s. The evidence presented here indicates that Athens was deliberately and systematically accruing cash reserves by levying *eisphorai* and an *epidosis*. By the end of 392/1, Athens had almost done enough to restore its *sōteria* and *dunamis*; it had its walls and it had its money, now it needed its ships. Sometime prior to winter 392/1, the Athenian *dēmos* had debated the possibility of launching a fleet in the assembly (Ar. *Eccl.* 197–8). We know too that at some point, possibly even during this debate, Thrasybulus had made a promise to the *dēmos* that in return for leading this new fleet he would 'make the city powerful and free' (Lys. 28.4). The following year in the late winter of 391/0, the beginning of the second phase of the Corinthian War, that is precisely what Athens gave him permission to do. Athens had anticipated the eventuality of being involved in naval warfare and had had the foresight to prepare its military finances in order to meet that commitment.

8. The Corinthian War, stage 2: naval warfare

From late 391/0 to the signing of the King's Peace in 387/6, Athens was constantly engaged in naval warfare. Conon had done his job well for the Great King: the Spartan navy had been chased from the Aegean. The time was right for Athens to take the initiative and begin its attempt at rebuilding its empire. Athenian naval campaigns began in winter 391/0 when Thrasybulus sailed out of the Piraeus with forty brand new triremes (Lys. 28.4–5). Athens had not involved itself in naval combat for fifteen years, but the launch of Thrasybulus' campaign marked the beginning of four years of intense seaborne warfare. The cost to the state of building and maintaining a fleet and its crews was enormous.[127] Thrasybulus' forty triremes were only part of a large number of ships launched in the first years of the Athenian naval assault: during the war over 116 triremes and twelve transport ships had departed the Piraeus on military operations. By its end, Athens had a fleet of at least sixty-eight triremes on active duty spread as far south as Cyprus and as far north as the Proconnesus.[128] Not included in these figures are the instances where Xenophon simply states that 'a large number of ships' departed. Athens was left with just twelve triremes at the end of the Peloponnesian War (Andoc. 3.12). Therefore, it would have been necessary for the state to build most, if not all, of these ships.

To illustrate the immense cost of naval warfare to the state this section will calculate the costs associated with the Athenian naval campaigns of the Corinthian War. This will include an investigation of the capital costs of building, fitting-out and storing the triremes, as well as the variable operating costs of wages for military personnel involved on campaign. Importantly, this section will examine just how the Athenian *dēmos* paid for this military expenditure by identifying three key revenue-raising strategies employed by the state: the accumulation of cash reserves, the expectation that generals would find funds in the field, and the re-establishment of regular external streams of income.

The calculation of the total cost to Athens of its naval program during this period presents difficulties. My calculations in this section depend almost entirely on Xenophon, who provides some figures for ship numbers but then includes those vague references to 'large numbers of triremes'. Clearly there were many more ships than we know about. Lengths of campaigns, numbers of men and methods used to transport large numbers of soldiers are missing. However, my figures are still valuable. By using the data I am able to extract from Xenophon, I can establish a minimum estimate of the cost to Athens of these campaigns. The size of this figure will give us an idea of why the Athenians made the financial choices they did and allow us to assess whether their decisions were indeed haphazard and improvisatory or part of a methodical financial strategy.

9. Capital costs of the fleet

An important component of Athenian military expenditure was the capital cost of building and fitting-out triremes. Up until the end of 391/0, the Athenian fleet appears to be practically non-existent. Of the twelve triremes that remained after the Peloponnesian War, Demaenetus, we are told, borrowed one to abscond to Conon in 396/5 (*Hell. Oxy.* 9.1). Xenophon does not mention the event, and if it did happen it is not certain that the ship did in fact belong to the state, for the council denied any knowledge of his actions (*Hell. Oxy.* 9.2). Additionally, it is likely that the *dēmos* donated ten of these ships to Evagoras of Cyprus in 391/0.[129] None of the ancient sources indicates that Athens was involved in ship-building during the land-war years of the Corinthian War, and with Conon patrolling the seas between 395/4 and his death, there was no pressing need for Athens to consider constructing a fleet. Therefore, if the ancient sources are followed, by 391/0 Athens had in its war fleet one, possibly two, ageing triremes.

However, in the spring of 391/0, for the first time since the end of the Peloponnesian War, a fleet of forty warships, led by Thrasybulus, sailed out of the Piraeus on active duty (Xen. *Hell.* 4.8.25). Therefore, at some point prior to this date, the *dēmos* had voted in the assembly to build and to fit out these triremes (Lys. 28.4–5; Diod. Sic. 14.94.2). The construction of this fleet more than likely began in the summer of 392/1 after the imprisonment of Conon at Sardis and his subsequent death (Xen. *Hell.* 4.8.16); without Conon and his fleet patrolling the Aegean and protecting Athenian interests, Athens simply had no alternative but to begin building its own ships.[130] Victor Hanson argues that the construction of one trireme could possibly have taken up to 6,000 man-days to complete.[131] Thus, according to the availability and the level of craftsmanship of shipwrights and their staff, the construction of one trireme could take between two and eight months.[132] We have no evidence to suggest precisely when this ship-building programme began. However, if we assume that construction started immediately after the rejection of Andocides' peace proposal in late summer/early autumn 392/1, and that Thrasybulus sailed out sometime in the spring of 391/0, Athens would have had around eighteen months to build all forty ships. This suggests that Athenian shipwrights managed to build, on average, two to three ships per month. This, in turn, suggests that twenty ships were constructed during 392/1 and another twenty during 391/90. Pritchard has estimated that the cost to build and fit out a trireme was around 1 t. 1,234dr.[133] These forty triremes then would have required a total capital outlay by the state of 48 t. 1,360dr, or 24 t. 680dr in both 392/1 and 391/90.

Eighteen months after Thrasybulus had sailed out of the Piraeus with his newly built and freshly equipped warships, the *dēmos* dispatched Iphicrates, in command of eight triremes and 1,200 peltasts, to the Chersonese to check the activity of the Spartan general Anaxibios. The construction of the eight triremes would have cost the state 9 t. 3,872dr. Problems arise with calculating Iphicrates' capital costs when transport for his 1,200 peltasts is considered.

'Fast' battle-ready triremes had just enough space on deck to transport an extra thirty troops if necessary.[134] However, those troops were required to sit closely packed together and remain still for long periods as the extra weight and any movement adversely affected the mobility and stability of the trireme.[135] The *stratiōtis* or *hoplitagōgos* was a trireme used specifically to transport hoplites and other military personnel into battle *en masse*.[136] These transport ships, or troop carriers, were generally older triremes that were no longer fast enough or light enough to manoeuvre during battle. These triremes were often modified by broadening the hulls, increasing the span of the decks (Plut. *Cim.* 12.2) and by the addition of bulwarks (Plut. *Them.* 14.2).[137] The only aging triremes to which Athens had access for Iphicrates were the remnants of Thrasybulus' fleet, and these were still relatively new. However, under the command of Agyrrhius, these triremes had been ordered to assist in the crisis at Rhodes (Xen. *Hell.* 4.8.31; Diod. Sic. 14.99.4). To accommodate the volume of additional troops required for the Sicilian expedition in 415, Athens used forty *hoplitagogoi*, each of which carried a reduced crew plus an additional 100 soldiers (Thuc. 6.31, 43).[138] Eager to ensure that Anaxibios was kept away from Athenian interests in the Dardanelles, Athens would have been keen to transport the men to their destination as quickly as possible using these vessels. The transport of 1,200 men would have required the construction of twelve new *hoplitagōgoi*. On the assumption that these ships cost around the same as a 'fast trireme', this would have added approximately 14 t. 2,808dr to the state's capital expenditure.

At the same time as Iphicrates was making his way to the Chersonese, Athens also fitted out ten triremes to deal with Spartan assaults on the Piraeus from Aegina (Xen. *Hell.* 5.1.2). The mission on which these new ships were used did not go well, and subsequently it was necessary for Athens to fit out 'a large number of ships' to aid those already at Aegina and bring them home (Xen. *Hell.* 5.1.5). Xenophon's use of the verb *πληρόω* ('fill') suggests that the hulls of these triremes were already constructed and that the *dēmos* has voted merely to furnish the ships with the appropriate fittings and equipment. This is probably true but given that Athens had virtually no fleet from 404/3 onwards, these ships would still have to have been recently constructed.

Another thirteen ships under the command of Eunomos were fitted out and sent to the island when the attacks began again some months later (Xen. *Hell.* 5.1.5). In this passage, Xenophon uses the verb *ἀντιπληρόω* ('fill up with men') in place of *πληρόω*, meaning this time that the *dēmos* had voted to fully man the ships. This indicates that the ships in Eunomos' fleet were probably the original ten sent to Aegina and three of the 'large number of ships' built for the previous mission. At a minimum, these thirteen ships would have cost the state 15 t. 4,042dr in addition to the unknown cost of the remainder of the 'large number of ships'.

In late 389/8 under the leadership of the Athenian generals Diotimos, Demaenetus, Dionysios, Leontinos and Phanias, twenty-four triremes were dispatched north to Samothrace, Thasos and other territories close to Iphicrates in the Chersonese (Xen. *Hell.* 5.1.7, 5.1.26). Following them in 388/7, Chabrias led at least ten warships to Evagoras in Cyprus (Xen. *Hell.* 5.1.10) and Thrasybulus of Kollytos commanded another 8 (Xen. *Hell.* 5.1.26). It is likely that seventeen of those ships sent north had to be newly constructed.[139] Again, given Athens began the decade with virtually no fleet, at least thirty-five additional triremes would have been built and fitted out at a cost of 42 t. 1,190dr. Chabrias also had 800 peltasts under his command to transport as well as additional ships and hoplites (Xen. *Hell.* 5.1.10). Given that the peltasts were probably transported to Cyprus on board these additional ships or through the use of the transport ships already built, we can safely estimate that Athens spent at least 130 t. 1,272dr on the construction of ninety-six 'fast' triremes and twelve transport ships between 392/1 and 388/7.

In addition to building its fleet, the *dēmos* would have ordered the construction of *neosoikoi* ('shipsheds') to house these new ships; keeping them safe, secure and dry until required for active service. These large buildings accommodated the hulls during construction and later permitted craftsmen to perform maintenance and repairs to ships when needed.[140] The shipsheds built in the fifth century, at a cost of 1,000 t., were destroyed at the end of the Peloponnesian War along with the city's Long Walls (Isoc. 7.66; Lys. 30.22).

Zea was the main military harbour in the Piraeus and it was here that these shipsheds would have been constructed.[141] Jari Pakkanen summarizes the minimum costs for the construction of ten shipsheds in Zea harbour during the early fourth century. In this comprehensive study, Pakkanen measures in man-days the skilled and unskilled labour necessary to construct the shipsheds, the manufacturing costs of scaffolding, roof tiles, clamps and dowels, as well as the transport costs of the materials needed, such as stone and timber. This comes to a total of around 40,000 man-days or 4,000 man-days per shed. In order to place a monetary value on these hours, Pakkanen applies a standard wage of 1dr per man-day across the board.[142] Loomis warns against using a 'standard wage' to provide reliable financial data. He argues that there are too many variables and inconsistencies in what we know.[143] However, we know that the types of skilled and unskilled workers required for the construction of the shipsheds were similar to those working on the Erechtheion in 409/8, who were paid 1dr per day. It is possible that these wages may have increased after the fifth century.[144] Therefore, for the purposes of ascertaining an approximate figure for the cost to construct a shipshed we will accept Pakkanen's methodology. Initially, the state would have to accommodate the forty new triremes built for Thrasybulus. Therefore, the construction of forty shipsheds over two years would have cost around 13 t. in both 392/1 and 391/0. With Athens constantly dispatching its newly built warships on campaign from 390/89 onwards, the number of shipsheds required for use at any one time would have been less than the number of triremes in the fleet. Additionally, it was not unheard of for ships to remain berthed in the open air (*IG* ii^2 1611.6).[145] Athens had at least sixty-eight ships in its fleet at the end of the Corinthian War, therefore we could estimate that the *dēmos* ordered that at least another twenty shipsheds be constructed by 388/7; a cost of 13 t. Therefore, the Athenian *dēmos* spent, at the very least, a total of 169 t. 1,272dr on the capital expenses of its shipbuilding program between 392/1 and 388/7.

10. Variable-operating costs of Athenian fleet, 391/0–387/6

An Athenian trireme required a crew of 200 men, who were each paid 1dr per day. Therefore, the monthly wage of a trireme crew was 1 t.[146] The sheer volume of men required to take part in a naval campaign and the length of time the fleet was at sea ensured that these variable costs were regularly extraordinarily high and, at times, difficult to predict (Thuc. 6.31.5).[147]

Unfortunately, given the nature of the sources, it is difficult to pinpoint a departure date for Thrasybulus' fleet in late 391/0. However, based on what is known, it is thought that he campaigned constantly for at least eighteen months to two years before his untimely death at Aspendus in 389/88 (Xen. *Hell.* 4.8.30).[148] Diodorus maintains that at some point Thrasybulus lost twenty-three of his triremes in a wild storm (14.94.3), a fact omitted by Xenophon.[149] Thrasybulus was making his way to Rhodes where the Spartan Teleutias sat with thirty-seven triremes (Xen. *Hell.* 4.8.24) and consequently recruited additional triremes from Chios and Mytilene (Diod. Sic. 14.94.4; Xen. *Hell.* 4.8.28).[150] Using the more conservative estimate of an eighteen-month campaign, and with a fleet of forty ships for twelve months and seventeen for six months, the wages bill for his campaign would have been in the order of 582 t. ((40 ships x 1 t. x 12 months) + (17 ships x 1 t. x 6 months)).

Iphicrates' campaign began in 389/88 and finished at the signing of the peace in 387/6, lasting almost two and a half years. The crew of his eight ships would have earned wages of 224 t. (8 ships x 1 t. x 28 months). Additionally, his peltasts would require around 171 t. ((1200 x 1dr/day x approx. 855 days)/6000dr) to cover their wages bill. This would have cost the state a total of 395 t. A lack of evidence regarding crew numbers and length of time at sea prevents the calculation of the cost of wages for the troop carrier crews. The length of time Eunomos' thirteen and the other fitted-out vessels spent travelling to and from Aegina is also unknown and therefore makes the calculation of wages for these campaigns almost impossible. However, using a conservative estimate of one to two months and adjusting for ship losses, these fleets combined probably cost the state around 48 t.

Of the remaining forty-two warships, we know that twenty-four spent from late 389/8 to the end of the war on active duty.[151] A further eighteen ships departed the Piraeus in the summer of 388/7. However, eight of these, commanded by Thrasybulus of Kollytos, were captured by the Spartans reasonably early in the campaign (Xen. *Hell.* 5.1.26). Therefore, the remaining thirty-four crews would have cost the state a total of approximately 693 t. in wages, inclusive of Chabrias' 800 peltasts. This brings the total wages bill for Athenian naval campaigns during the Corinthian War to, at the very least, a staggering 2,289 t. Significantly, this figure indicates that Athens was spending a substantial amount each year on war-making during a period in which it was, traditionally, viewed as financially destitute.

11. Funding the capital costs and variable operating costs of naval warfare

It is very clear from Xenophon that in 391/0, Athens knew that naval warfare with Sparta was imminent (*Hell.* 4.8.25). In order to defeat Sparta and restore *sōteria* and *dunamis* to Athens, it was critical that the state had the funds to build its fleet and that, when naval warfare broke out, it had the funds to maintain that fleet for the duration of hostilities. The combined capital costs and variable operating costs of Athens' naval program are indeed overwhelming at a total of around 2,2458 t. This was a substantial financial commitment. It was also a level of commitment that required adept financial handling. With so much at stake, Athens could not simply 'wing it' and rely on improvisatory strategies to defray its military expenditure. The *boulē* would have been under immense pressure to ensure that all of Athens' military expenses could be met. It successfully achieved this through three different strategies: the accumulation of cash reserves, the expectation that generals would find alternative sources of income whilst on campaign, and the re-establishment of regular external streams of revenue.

11.1 Cash reserves

The construction of a new Athenian fleet in 392/1 would have required Athens to have immediate access to a large sum of money. The *dēmos* would have anticipated this need for cash reserves by accruing its annual surpluses and other extraordinary revenues in the *stratiōtika* (see above). Brun claims that an additional *eisphora* was levied in 389/8 specifically to fund the naval expedition to the besieged garrison at Aegina.[152] However, his evidence for this is weak. He argues that because the assembly voted to equip the large number of ships sent to Aegina, we must assume that an *eisphora* was levied to fund the exercise. This assumption is surely predicated on Brun's argument that Athens had no cash reserves or surplus revenue of its own, and therefore no other way to fund such a project. Using a law court speech written by Isaeus, Brun also argues that an *eisphora* was levied in 387/6.[153] The speaker claims that he could not bring his law suit earlier because at the end of the war he 'had unfortunate difficulties with the public treasury' (10.20). Debtors to the public treasury were denied their citizen rights and therefore could not engage in litigation.[154] Brun again makes an assumption. He argues that the speaker's debt was unpaid wealth taxes from an *eisphora* which therefore must have been levied in 387/6. However, the debt could just as easily have been an outstanding fine or rent owing on sacred land or any number of other issues.[155] Additionally, it does not necessarily follow that the money owed belonged to an *eisphora* that had just been levied. Reforms to the collection of the *eisphora* are introduced in the 370s to address the issue of accumulated wealth taxes that are outstanding from a number of *eisphorai* levied at different times.[156] Consequently, Brun's arguments for *eisphorai* in 389/8 and 387/6 are difficult to accept.

In any event, it is clear from the law-court speeches of Lysias around 389/88 that the heavy levying of *eisphora* had taken its toll on the state's elite citizens (28.3–4, 29.4, 9). Consequently, the *dēmos* may have been reluctant to continue imposing the tax with such regularity. With no evidence to support the additional levying of *eisphorai* after 391/0, or evidence that any other extraordinary revenues were received by Athens during this period, these accumulated cash reserves must have funded the construction and fit-out of approximately 108 war and transport ships (169 t. 1,272dr.).[157] Therefore, it can be confidently stated that Athens had the means to cover fully the capital costs of its fleet. However, building the fleet was one thing, the variable operating cost of maintaining that fleet for the length of the war was quite another.

11.2 Money raised by generals on campaign

During most of the fifth century, with access to imperial income and other secular and sacred funds, Athens would dispatch its generals with enough money to cover the wages of their soldiers and crews; even sending additional funds when campaigns continued for longer than anticipated. For example, Thucydides and inscriptional evidence shows that in 440 the treasurers of Athena paid over 1,276 t. to cover the wages of the crews of 60 ships over a 9-month campaign to Samos (*IG* i³. 363; Thuc. 1.117.2–3; see also *IG* i³.364; Thuc. 1.45, 1.50–1; *IG* i³. 370.134–5, 375.34–7; and Thuc. 6.93.4, 94.4).[158] In the fourth century, this was impossible. The *dēmos* could send only minimal funds with its departing generals, enough perhaps to cover wages for the first few weeks of the campaign or at most one month (Thuc. 6.31.5).[159] During the Corinthian War, if we assume the crews of all 116 ships and the 2,000 peltasts dispatched from the Piraeus received an amount to cover one month of their wages bill, the total cost per year to the state would be 40 t. for 391/0, 64 t. for 389/8 and 22 t. for 388/7. These small stipends could easily have been funded through the cash reserves accumulated in the *stratiōtika*.

However, the crews and peltasts were at sea for extensive periods and consequently the *dēmos* had to fund at least a further 2,173 t. to maintain its men for the duration of the war: 120 t. in 391/0, 411 t. in 390/89, 406 t. in 389/8, 820 t. in 388/7 and 415 t. in 387/6. These amounts were too large for the balance in the *stratiōtika* to cover. Without substantial and continuous funding from the state to help defray these costs, the Athenian generals were compelled to employ other methods to raise the revenue needed to pay their men and maintain their ships. Their most profitable option, used reasonably successfully during the Ionian War and also by Conon after Cnidus (Xen. *Hell.* 4.8.9), was to self-fund in the field.[160] Under these circumstances, generals were at liberty to seize booty, to plunder land and to impose levies on both allies and enemies alike (Dem. 8.24–6).[161]

For example, in 390/89 Thrasybulus plundered territories and exacted money from cities as far north as the Bosporus and the Hellespont, in and around Lesbos and Chios, and down the west coast of Asia Minor around to Aspendus in order to pay his men and maintain his fleet (Xen. *Hell.* 4.8.28–31). Iphicrates, likewise, relentlessly plundered the territories around him and set forth on voyages up the coast of the Chersonese to gather money to pay his men (Xen. *Hell.* 4.8.35–6). The *dēmos* sanctioned these methods of revenue collection (Dem. 8.9; 21.3; Diod. Sic. 16.57.2–3; Lys. 28.5–6); any money raised in excess of what was needed was deemed to belong to the state and was handed over to the treasury upon the generals' return to Athens (e.g. Dem. 20.17–80; 24.11–14).[162] Collecting revenue in this way was a deliberate strategy put in place by Athens to meet the extraordinary variable operating costs of paying its men.

Admittedly, this approach could be viewed as improvisatory and haphazard. Relying on these methods was certainly risky: Thrasybulus lost his life trying to fund his fleet's payroll (Xen. *Hell.* 4.8.30; Diod. Sic. 14.99.4). Indeed, despite the impression that Thrasybulus and his generals were successfully funding their campaign through these methods, Lysias' prosecution speech *Against Ergocles* claims that remnants of the general's fleet were in fact 'breaking up because of a lack of money' (28.4). Thrasybulus and two of his generals, Ergocles and Philocrates, had been summoned back to Athens in 389/8 to face accusations of misappropriating the funds they had collected (28; 29). The trials are generally thought to have been politically motivated, brought against Thrasybulus and his colleagues and associates by his enemies at home.[163] As such, it suits the purposes of the prosecution to claim that Thrasybulus and his generals have kept the funds they have raised for themselves instead of ensuring that their ships were in good, seaworthy condition ready for combat and the defence of Athens. No other evidence can be found to suggest that any other generals were unable to maintain the seaworthiness of their ships.

In fact, the Athenian generals used these methods with great success. One of the most serious threats to the strength of the Athenian fleet was the risk of desertion by its crews (for example, Thuc. 1.31.1, 143.1, 7.13.2, 8.57.1; Xen. *Hell.* 1.5.4; [Dem.] 50; 49.15). A lack of pay or pay rates below what was expected could see crews refusing to row, as happened in 388/7 to the Spartan harmost at Aegina (Xen. *Hell.* 5.1.13); or even threaten to defect to the enemy ([Arist.] *Oec.* 1350a).[164] There is no evidence of Athenian crews deserting, or threatening to desert, the fleet at any time during the Corinthian War. Therefore, men were being paid well and presumably on a timely basis. Consequently, relying on its generals to raise sufficient revenue in the field to fund their campaigns was a calculated risk by the *dēmos* and it formed a deliberate part of Athens' overall plan to restore military security, *sōteria* and *dunamis*, to the state.

11.3 External sources of revenue

The next part of Athens' plan was to re-establish, in line with Athenian foreign policy, external sources of revenue that were vital to keep funds flowing into the state's cash reserves.[165] Consequently, in 391/90 the *dēmos* ordered Thrasybulus to sail north to the Hellespont, which at the time was free of hostile ships (Xen. *Hell.* 4.8.26), and secure alliances with the cities there. Thrasybulus' mission in the north achieved great success. He formed alliances with the Thracian kings and many other Greek cities in Asia Minor, the North Aegean and Thrace and established a democracy in Byzantium. The hostility and resentment engendered by the imposition of the *phoros* ('tribute') on its allies during the fifth century, prevented Athens from imposing any such levy on its new allies. However, Thrasybulus was able to re-introduce the 10 per cent tax (*dekate*) on shipping from the Bosporus originally imposed by Alcibiades in 410, and he imposed a 5 per cent tax (*eikoste*) on Thasos and Clazomenae (4.8.26–7; 1.1.22).[166] Athens enjoyed the monetary gain from these achievements for at least the following eighteen months (4.8.31), and quite possibly up until the Persians placed their support behind Sparta in 387/6.[167] The importance of the general's achievements to Athenian public finances is confirmed by Iphicrates' immediate deployment to the Dardanelles after Thrasybulus' death to ensure that all his hard work was not undone (4.8.34).

Most scholars argue that Thrasybulus was in fact originally ordered by the *dēmos* to go to Rhodes, but that after sailing out of Athens he 'changed his mind' and, ignoring the instructions of the *dēmos,* headed to the Hellespont.[168] Consequently, the strategy to re-establish external revenues in the north is attributed to the general himself, not to the *dēmos*. The evidence for this argument lies in the description of the event by Xenophon. Robin Seager claims that Xenophon 'expressly states' that Thrasybulus' expedition was intended to go to Rhodes. Seager is surely wrong here. Xenophon actually says (*Hell.* 4.8.25):

> οἱ δ᾽ Ἀθηναῖοι νομίσαντες τοὺς Λακεδαιμονίους πάλιν δύναμιν κατασκευάζεσθαι ἐν τῇ θαλάττῃ,ἀντεκπέμπουσι Θρασύβουλον τὸν Στειριέα σὺν τετταράκοντα ναυσίν.
>
> The Athenians for their part now realized that the Spartans were again deploying a naval force, so they sent out Thrasybulus of Steiria with forty ships.

The use of the verb ἀντεκπέμπω suggests that Thrasybulus was sent out, not specifically to challenge the Spartans, but in response to the knowledge that Sparta was building up a fleet.[169] This is entirely plausible. Xenophon does not provide any detail on what the general's specific orders were. Athens would have known at this point that naval warfare with Sparta was imminent, therefore in order for it to provide military security to its people the *dēmos* had to ensure that the fleet and its future were protected; small annual surpluses would not be sufficient. This meant that establishing external income streams would have been its top priority. If that is the case, it does not follow that Athens would have ordered Thrasybulus immediately to Rhodes. In the next sentence, Xenophon merely says that Thrasybulus 'made no attempt to help Rhodes' and then provides an insight into the general's thinking for heading north. Diodorus Siculus, who gives a brief account of the expedition, mentions Rhodes only as Thrasybulus' final destination after his exploits in the north (14.94.1–4).

It is generally argued that it was Thrasybulus' own imperialistic ambitions for Athens that caused him to disregard his orders.[170] There are some problems with this argument. Athenian generals, despite being away from Athens for long periods, had limited authority when it came to military operations.[171] Issued with explicit orders from the *dēmos* prior to their departure on campaign, they were expected to maintain communication with Athens for the duration of their mission.[172] Literary sources from the fifth and fourth centuries provide evidence that generals sent intelligence reports back to the *dēmos*, which in turn dispatched advice on whether to continue as planned or change tactics.[173] A good example of this during the Corinthian War is Iphicrates' campaign in Corinth. After his defeat of the Spartans at Lechaeum, Iphicrates believed that he could capture Corinth for Athens and sent word to the *dēmos* for instructions. Diodorus says that at Athens the idea was 'met with public opposition' (14.92.2), and consequently the general was ordered not to proceed with his plan.

Athenian generals were faced with the very real prospect that they would be prosecuted for any conduct whilst on campaign that did not comply with the instructions or expectations of the *dēmos*.[174] Generals could be called back to Athens to face trial at any time: in the middle of a campaign (e.g. Ergocles and Philocrates around 389/8 – Lys. 28, 29), at the end of their commission or even years later (e.g. Adeimantus in 393/2 for Aegospotami, Dem. 19.191).[175] Often, the penalty a general faced, if found guilty, was death (Lys. 29.2).

Consequently, the *dēmos* would have issued Thrasybulus with explicit instructions about his mission before he left. It would have been well informed about his whereabouts and all his activities. Additionally, if any of his actions had not complied with its instructions or expectations, he would have been recalled to Athens to face prosecution and more than likely execution.[176] Indeed, the Athenian general Timotheus was tried in 373/2 on a charge of abandoning an ally in need for failing to reach Corcyra within an appropriate timeframe (Plut. *Mor.* 836D; [Dem.] 49.9). Therefore, it is difficult to accept that Thrasybulus would have sailed to the Hellespont, in direct contravention of orders telling him to go to Rhodes, simply because he 'changed his mind' and wanted to follow his own agenda. Thrasybulus' mission seems to have been, first and foremost, about the pursuit of Athenian foreign policy: establishing alliances, protecting the grain route, and re-establishing the state's external revenue streams. Even if, as Strauss suggests, Lysias implies that it was Thrasybulus himself who proposed the idea to the assembly (28.4), the decision to go north and establish these streams of income lies undoubtedly with the *dēmos*.[177]

If we go back to Athenian public discourse and the definition of the Athenian concept of military security, it is clear that a priority of this ideology was that cash reserves were critical in order not only to build a fleet but also to be able to maintain the strength of that fleet. Obviously, during the Corinthian War, to achieve the first part of its goal, the construction of the fleet, the *dēmos* aggressively taxed its wealthy citizens and accumulated cash reserves. By forcing its generals to fund their variable operating costs through raising revenue in the field Athens was able to maintain those ships and fulfil the second part of its objective. Importantly though, it was essential for Athens to re-establish regular streams of income that would replenish its cash reserves and assist in funding its military campaigns.[178] This was achieved the instant the fleet was back on the seas, its generals ordered to place maritime taxes on other Greek states in accordance with Athenian foreign policy. Clearly Athens' tight control of its public finances continued throughout the Corinthian War.

12. Conclusion

The Corinthian War ended in a similar fashion to the Peloponnesian War: a significant portion of Athens' fleet was trapped in the Propontis, and Sparta again threatened the Athenian grain supply (Xen. *Hell.* 5.1.29). The Persian king had again placed his support behind Sparta, providing it with additional ships and money. Athens simply did not have the funds to compete against the combined forces of its enemies, and so it capitulated. Regardless of this rather disappointing end to the war for Athens, it is important to look at just what the state had achieved over the first fifteen years of the century. It had raised enough cash to build a fleet of at least ninety-six triremes and twelve transport ships, it had rebuilt its Long Walls and had re-fortified the Piraeus, it had regained the islands of Lemnos, Imbros and Scyros, and it had taken the first steps towards re-establishing itself as a major regional power.[179] In 387/6 it had more than sixty-eight triremes on active campaign throughout the Aegean and the Mediterranean. The difference this time was that Athens retained all these strategic assets as part of the terms and conditions of the King's peace.

This chapter has challenged scholarship's traditional story about the Corinthian War. Through a thorough investigation of Athens' public finances, and the funding choices made by the *dēmos* in response to the events of the war, the chapter has made some significant changes to that story. It has shown that, despite losing its largest income streams, the Athenian *dēmos* proactively sought to restore *sōteria* and *dunamis* to the state by trying to minimize its military expenditure and maximize its revenues. Importantly, the chapter has demonstrated that, contrary to the traditional story, the *dēmos*' immediate post-war priority was to accumulate cash reserves in the military fund by generating annual revenue surpluses, levying multiple *eisphorai* and an *epidosis*. Thus, the *stratiōtika* must have been created in the early years of the 390s, or possibly even towards the end of the fifth century as tax revenues on trade began to increase, as a depository for these funds. This parallels how the Athenians accrued their cash reserves in the fifth century.

Establishing the likelihood of accumulated funds in the *stratiōtika* during the first decade of the fourth century forces us to rethink the way we view the wisdom of some of Athens' choices during the war, in particular its rejection of Andocides' peace plan in 392/1. It removes Persia as the only potential money source for funding the military campaigns that the rejection of the peace was certain to ignite. Admittedly, the *dēmos* was not generating large surpluses at this time and its cash reserves could make only a small contribution to defraying the large variable operating costs of its naval campaigns. However, having the ability to generate an annual surplus, no matter how insignificant, meant that Athens had quickly established stable and secure income streams on which it could depend. Therefore, it eliminated the need for the state to gamble the safety of its people on the unpredictability of Persian support.

Clearly, decisions regarding military finance during the Corinthian War were driven by the state's concept of military security. The restoration of *sōteria* and *dunamis* to the city was the chief priority of this ideology. The belief by Athenians that *sōteria* and *dunamis* could be achieved only through the acquisition of ships, walls and money manifests itself in Athens' financial strategies to fund the Corinthian War. These strategies demonstrate that the Athenian *dēmos* attempted to anticipate the costs of its future warfare, thought carefully about how it was going to fund that warfare, and prepared accordingly. The accusation that the *dēmos* lacked the foresight and financial skills to organize its military finances properly is demonstrably inaccurate. A ruling body without such skills is capable only of reactionary decision-making; it cannot plan for future military expenditure and adapt and reform where necessary, nor can it hope to pursue and to maintain a steady approach to its national security.

What emerges here is that Athenian financial decisions made during the war about the funding of its military operations were far from 'haphazard and improvisatory'. The *dēmos* based its decision-making on a clear perception of what was required to bring military security to the state and its people. Consequently, it developed and executed successful financial strategies designed to acquire its ships, walls and money. The traditional narrative of the Corinthian War must change to reflect this new, more positive appraisal of Athenian financial management. The state managed to fund a total of, at the very least, 3,829 t. in military expenditure over the eight and half years of the Corinthian War. The evidence presented in this chapter has addressed Athens' ability to manage its military finances, the ideology behind its decision making and the wisdom of its funding choices. It has shown that Athens set out to create military security through a very deliberate, systematic and adaptable financial strategy. It fell just short of its goal, but the lessons learned in the 390s and early 380s provided the keys to success in the next decade.

Notes

1. Böckh 1817; Brun 1983, quote 185. See also, Croiset 1973; Andreades 1933; Ehrenberg 1943; Kagan 1961, 323, 326, 329; 1995, 16; Mossé 1973; Finley 1975, 90–3; Austin and Vidal-Naquet 1977, 131, 144; Burke 1978, 143; de Ste. Croix 1981, 293.
2. Strauss 1986, 42–69; Cohen 1992, 219; Harding 1995, 108; 2015, 85; Akrigg 2007, 39; Migeotte 2014, 581; Cecchet 2015, 119–22, 138; Ober 2015b, 224; Roberts 2017, 297.
3. Kagan 1961, 326; Hamilton 1979, 258; Seager 1967, 105.
4. Austin 1994, 557; Cartledge 2001, 109.
5. Böckh 1828, 584.
6. E.g. French 1991, 36; Austin 1994, 557.
7. E.g. Buckler 2003, 75–183.
8. Strauss 1986, chapters 4, 5 and 6.
9. See Cawkwell 1976; Seager 1967; Asmonti 2015.
10. See Brun 1983; Flament 2007; Migeotte 2014; Gabrielsen 2007; 2013.
11. Pritchett 1991, 473; Fawcett 2016, 14.
12. For example, Böckh 1828, 584; Kagan 1961, 329; Austin 1994, 556; Flament 2007, 194.
13. Böckh 1828, 584; Austin 1994, 556; Pritchard 2015b, 49, 55; French 1991, 56; Strauss 1986, 137; Flament 2007, 194; Kagan 1961, 328, 321–41; Roberts 1980, 105.
14. Seager 1967, 105–6.
15. Pritchard 2015b, 19–20.
16. Kallet-Marx 1993, 229–30; Rhodes 1972a, 88–113; Pritchard 2015b, 19.
17. Grenfell and Hunt 1906, 49–55; Stroud 1971, 297; Pritchett 1971, 22–3; Bugh 1988, 131, 221; Van Wees 2004, 67.
18. Loomis 1995, 230–6; Pritchard 2015b, 99, 107–8.
19. Loomis 1998, 131.
20. Stroud 1971, 298–9; Krentz 1982, 116–17; Lintott, 1982, 176; Strauss 1986, 102; Bugh 1988, 129, 131–3, 222–3; Spence 1993, 217–18; contra Loomis 1998, 46.
21. Pritchard 2015b, 17; Rhodes 2013, 206.
22. Pritchard 2015b, 40.
23. Kroll 1977, 98 n.37 suggests that it was the same year as the pay cut, 403/2.
24. Kroll 1977, 97–8; Pritchard 2015b, 106–7.
25. Kroll 1977, 98.
26. Blaineau 2015, 169–98.
27. Kroll 1977, 89; Spence 1993, 274–7; Blaineau 2015, 235.
28. Kroll 1977, 89
29. Kroll 1977, 89; Blaineau 2015, 229.
30. Kroll 1977, 89; Spence 1993, 274–7; Pritchard 2015b, 106.
31. Hansen 1991, 316; Burgh 1998, 154–6; Pritchard 2015b, 107. Spence 1993, 100 argues that this figure is theoretical and that the actual number was never more than 650 men; Blaineau 2015, 229.

32. Böckh 1828, 584.
33. Lysias claims it was the oligarchic faction running Athens *after* the Thirty were exiled that borrowed the money; Demosthenes states that it was the Thirty tyrants.
34. Thomsen 1964, 178; Brun 1983, 26; Migeotte 2014, 520.
35. Pritchard 2015b, 1, 16.
36. Pritchard 2015b, 41 table 2.2.
37. Osborne 2007a, 14–15; Pritchard 2015b, 12.
38. Shear 2001, 553–9
39. Shear 2001, 553–9.
40. Pritchard 2015b, 39 table 2.1.
41. Pritchard 2015b, 52, 89.
42. Pritchard 2015b, 89.
43. Pritchard 2015b, 47–60.
44. Pritchard 2015b, 82–6.
45. Pritchard 2015b, 62.
46. Pritchard 2015b, 109.
47. Pritchard 2015b, 109.
48. Brun 1983, 151; Pritchard 2015b, 109.
49. Monthly wages for fully manned trireme: 1 t. Therefore, 6 months x 12 triremes x 1 t.=72 t.
50. Bugh 1988, 221; Van Wees 2004, 67.
51. With Loomis 1995, 230–6; Pritchard 2015b, 108.
52. 300 *hippeas* x 4 obols/day.
53. Bugh 1988, 130.
54. Fawcett 2016, 154, table 1 for a complete list of taxes.
55. Fawcett 2016, 159–60.
56. Austin 1994, 545.
57. Rhodes 2013, 217 calls the process 'devolved budgeting'.
58. Rhodes 2013, 217.
59. Pritchard 2015b, 16.
60. Rhodes 2010, 367.
61. Strauss 1986, 57–63.
62. Vaughn 1991, 48.
63. This number is probably about right given that later in the year Athens was to send 6,000 hoplites and 600 cavalry to Nemea to fight the Spartans (Xen. *Hell.* 4.2.17).
64. Pritchett 1971, 20; Loomis 1998, 47–9.
65. Cf. Seager 1994, 102.
66. Strauss 1986, 133; Seager 1994, 105; Flament 2007, 194; Asmonti 2015, 203.
67. Trundle 2010b, 155.
68. Loomis 1998, 44. (1,200 peltasts x 1dr/day x 30 days= 36,000dr)

69. Although Athens did send hoplites in full force to re-build the Corinthian Long Walls at Lechaeum in 392/1.
70. 395/4 Haliartus + Nemea 150 t.; 394/3 Coronea 60 t. + 2 years of mercenary peltasts 144 t.
71. Seager 1994, 101.
72. Thomsen 1964, 180; Flament 2007, 191; Austin 1994, 580.
73. Thomsen 1964, 180; Brun 1983, 26; Flament 2007, 92.
74. De Ste. Croix 1953, 31; Thomsen 1964, 11; Christ 2007, 53.
75. Thomsen 1964, 181; Brun 1983, 27.
76. Cawkwell 1982, 319; Hunt 2010, 242; Ober 2011b, 248; Pritchard 2013, 57.
77. Seager 1994, 102–3; Strassler 2009, 136 n. 4.3.10a.
78. Thomsen 1960, 181; Brun 1983, 26.
79. Brun 1983, 27.
80. Thomsen 1964, 180.
81. Thomsen 1964, 180.
82. Sommerstein 1998, 209–10; Strauss 1986, 140.
83. De Ste. Croix 1953, 47–53 argues that throughout the fourth century most, if not all, *eisphorai* were levied at 1 per cent. Brun 1983, 57; Strauss 1986, 54; Flament 2007, 93 agree. Aristophanes claims that the tax imposed during 392/1 was levied at 2.5 per cent and was expected to yield 500 t. This would mean the taxable wealth of Athens was 20,000 t. Clearly, the tax rate and the expected yield are exaggerations by the playwright.
84. Christ 2007, 59; Thomsen 1964, 181.
85. Pritchard 2018; Ober 1978, 125; Kallet-Marx 1993, 6, 96, 133 focusing on money and naval power.
86. Kallet-Marx 1993, 96.
87. Kallet-Marx 1993, 133.
88. Gabrielsen 1994, 200.
89. Rhodes 2013, 205; Gabrielsen 1994, 203.
90. Migeotte 1983, 134–9, discusses this *epidosis* but only in terms of the process. He does not comment on what it may have been for.
91. Pritchett 1991, 474.
92. Ober 2015a, 499.
93. Austin 1994, 543.
94. Loomis 1998, 22; Sommerstein 1998, 154; Pritchard 2015b, 60–1.
95. Rhodes 2013, 219; Gabrielsen 2007, 270; Cawkwell 1962, 380.
96. Rhodes 2013, 213–5.
97. Cawkwell 1962, 380–1.
98. Stroud 1998, 1–140; Although Migeotte 2014, 432 places it in the early 370s around the time of the second Athenian alliance. With Brun 1983, 74–182; Flament 2007, 206–7, 223–31.
99. Cawkwell 1962, 381 n.1.
100. Matthaiou 2009, 83–7; Tracy 2003, 351–63; Rhodes 2013, 219 n. 107.

101. Böckh 1828, 584; Kagan 1961, 328, 329, 344; Strauss 1986, 127; French 1991, 36; Flament 2007, 194; Gabrielsen 2007, 267; Austin 2008, 556; Pritchard 2015b, 1, 7.
102. Strauss 1986, 127; Asmonti 2015, 198.
103. Asmonti 2015, 203.
104. Buckler 2003, 112.
105. Flament 2007, 193.
106. Flament 2007, 194.
107. Flament 2007, 194; Sommerstein 1998, 209.
108. Seager 1967, 104.
109. Buckler 2003, 133; Asmonti 2015, 208.
110. See also Diod. Sic. 14.85; Nep. *Con.* 5.1–3.
111. Sommerstein 1998, 155.
112. Strauss 1986, 128–9; Seager 1967, 99–100; Asmonti 2015, 19.
113. Cf. Seager 1967, 101.
114. See Seager 1967, 102 n.66.
115. Asmonti 2015, 203.
116. Strauss 1986, 128–9.
117. Cawkwell 1976, 276.
118. See Strauss 1986, 147 n. 62 for date; Sommerstein 1998, 3 concurs. Seager 1994, 108 says the talks took place in winter, but this would have been after Aristophanes' play *Ecclesiazusae*, in which the rejection of the peace is mentioned (202), would have been performed at either the Lenaea (January or February) or City Dionysia (March) during the winter of 392/1. Scholarship tends to favour the Lenaea (see Dearden 1976, 8) and if this is the case there is simply not enough time for the peace talks, Andocides' speech to the assembly, forty days of debate and deliberation by the assembly and for Aristophanes to include the event in his play and then have its performance for Seager to be right.
119. Hamilton 1979, 253, 258; Strauss 1986, 142.
120. Asmonti 2015, 175.
121. Strauss 1986, 152, 167 n.5.
122. Trundle 2004, 81.
123. Asmonti 2015, 35, on Conon's diplomatic skills. Buckler 2003, 54.
124. Strauss 1986, 125.
125. Conon died in Cyprus, so it is more than likely that the fleet ended up with Evagoras.
126. Flament 2007, 194.
127. Gabrielsen 2007, 257.
128. Clark 1990, 58; Gabrielsen 1994, 127.
129. Cawkwell 1976, 274.
130. Seager 1967, 107 n. 110 presumes a date of 391/0.
131. Hanson 2006, 262.
132. 8 months = 25 men/ship, 4 months = 50 men/ship, 2 months = 100 men/ship
133. Pritchard 2015b, 105.

134. Morrison, Coates and Rankov 2000, 152–7.
135. Morrison, Coates and Rankov 2000, 263; van Wees 2004, 221.
136. Morrison and Williams 1968, 247–8; Casson 1971, 92–3; Gabrielsen 2007, 266.
137. Morrison, Coates and Rankov 2000, 153.
138. Morrison and Williams 1968, 247–8; Casson 1971, 92–3; Van Wees 2004, 222, 311 n. 20; Gabrielsen 2007, 206.
139. Xenophon's 'large number of ships' probably totalled only ten: based on ten triremes sent in the first contingent (*Hell.* 5.1.2); thirteen with Eunomos (5.1.5) and then ten again with Chabrias (5.1.10).
140. Blackman 2013, 25.
141. Rankov 2013, 437; Morrison, Coates and Rankov 2000, 4, 128.
142. Pakkanen 2013, 63–71.
143. Loomis 1998, 232–9.
144. Loomis 1998, 233.
145. Morrison and Williams 1968, 181.
146. Loomis 1998, 57–8; Pritchard 2015b, 110.
147. Gabrielsen 2007, 257–8.
148. Cawkwell 1976, 273–5.
149. Cawkwell 1976, 271; Seager 1994, 114 accept Diodorus; contra Buck 1998, 116.
150. Strauss 1986, 152.
151. Xenophon gives the impression that these ships remained on campaign in and around the Thracian Sea until they became trapped by the Spartans in the Propontis in 387/6 (*Hell.* 5.1.7–26).
152. Brun 1983, 27.
153. Brun 1983, 27.
154. Forster 1927, 356; Edwards 2007, 163.
155. Böckh 1828, 385.
156. See Christ 2007.
157. 96 triremes + 12 transport ships.
158. Gabrielsen 1994, 115.
159. Timotheus is allegedly given just 13t in the 370s (Xen. *Hell.* 6.2.11–12); Gabrielsen 1994, 117.
160. The last decade of the Peloponnesian War: (411/10) Xen. *Hell.* 1.1.20, 22; (410/9) 2.2, 4, 17; (409/8) 3.3–4, (408/7) 8–10; (407/6) 4.8–11; 5.20; (406/5) 2.1.16.
161. Gabrielsen 2007, 268–71.
162. Pritchard 2015b, 103; Pritchard 2014, 8.
163. Roberts 1980, 110–14; Todd 2000, 286.
164. Gabrielsen 1994, 121–3.
165. Seager 1967, 110–11; Strauss 1986, 152–3; Bresson 2016, 305.
166. Seager 1967, 110; Buckler 2003, 157–60.
167. Fawcett 2016, 162, citing Demosthenes 20.60, believes the 10 per cent tax was still in place in 355.

168. Seager 1967, 109; Buckler 2003, 157; Strauss 1986, 152; Cawkwell 1976, 271; Strassler 2009, 168.
169. Definition confirmed by LSJ.
170. Seager 1967, 110; Cawkwell 1976, 270, 275; Rhodes 2012, 115.
171. Hamel 1996, 176.
172. Hamel 1996, 176.
173. See Hamel 1996, 176–8 for extensive list of primary sources.
174. Hamel 1996, 180.
175. Hamel 1996, 181, 187.
176. Indeed, as has already been noted, Thrasybulus and his generals were recalled to Athens for discrepancies in the accounting of the revenues they had raised.
177. Roberts 1980, 109; Strauss 1986, 153.
178. Kallet-Marx 1993, 185.
179. Although it remained without gates until 378/7.

CHAPTER 6
WAR AND THE *TECHNĒ* OF PUBLIC FINANCE
Mark Pyzyk

1. Introduction

The link between state power, warfare, and fiscal activity is a common thread in Classical history, starting with Herodotus and Thucydides. The ancient Greek case – characterized by increasingly capable states, generating ever more revenue, waging bigger and bigger wars – aligns with modern theories that link states' fiscal capacity to military competition. It is a powerful theoretical lens to turn on ancient warfare and ancient state formation.[1] Thus, the pithy statement that 'war made states, and states made war' – referring to post-Medieval Europe – applies to ancient Greece, too.[2] But where Renaissance and Early Modern European states have left copious documentation to illustrate the micro-processes by which such extractive structures were developed and spread,[3] classicists remain largely in the dark. How did states learn to administer finances, extract revenue and generate wealth more effectively? Who did the learning? What manner of *technē* was practised and passed on? Lacking a large, cohesive body of ancient literature on this topic, work must be done to fill this gap.[4]

Philosophical and economic texts from the Classical period do provide tantalizing glimpses into Greek engagement with this topic, testament to the fact that – by the mid-fourth century – Greek thinkers were keen to grapple with the subject, especially in the context of military competition. Consider Xenophon's *Hieron*, which Leo Strauss called antiquity's most 'modern' political texts on account of its thematic and intellectual overlap with Machiavelli's *Prince*. Xenophon concretely illustrates the dilemma of the state through the person of the tyrant. In so doing, he sets up a moral no man's land that tyrants must navigate (*Hiero* 4.9, trans. Marchant):

> The despot with his abundance of wealth has less to meet his necessary expenses than the private citizen. For while private citizens can cut down the daily expenditure as they please, despots cannot, since the largest items in their expenses and the most essential are the sums they spend on the life-guards, and to curtail any of these means ruin.

This included a bodyguard, army, fleet, stone walls and so forth.[5] Xenophon's tyrant becomes a prisoner in his own city, constrained in ways that help explain his most objectionable behaviour. Hieron says, for instance (*Hiero* 4.11):

> Now, despots are not seldom forced into the crime of robbing temples and their fellow men through chronic want of cash to meet their necessary expenses. Living,

> as it were, in a perpetual state of war, they are forced to maintain an army, or they perish.

Among Classical texts, Xenophon's account is exceptionally sensitive to these dynamics. Other authors typically present such dilemmas as simple morality tales in which the tyrant's need for cash emerged from sexual or moral perversion. Agathocles of Syracuse, for instance, was said to have been a male prostitute, rising up from a humble origin as a potter.[6] Theopompus recounts the debauchery of Philip and his men, calling them 'athletes of injustice and wrong-doing' who spent much of their time drinking and playing dice.[7] The conflation of state spending and personal immorality was a common feature of anti-tyrannical writing.

Xenophon's tyrant is useful precisely because he is not presented in such moralized terms. The plight of Hieron is not unfamiliar to political scientists, sociologists, and comparative historians: it is simply the problem that states face under pressure of war. We have already mentioned the 'war makes states' school of historical sociology, most famously illustrated in Charles Tilly's *Coercion, Capital, and European States*.[8] The argument goes something like this. New military techniques and technologies, outperforming old ones, often require increased specialization, more men or particular machines of war. These put increased stress on state finances, which requires increased extraction from the state's subjects. States ordinarily resist these, either through prudence or laziness, but the pressure to intensify such activities can be existential. Tilly suggests, further that such schemes might develop along either 'coercion-intensive' or 'capital-intensive' paths – with capital intensive characterizing the more dynamic, increasingly effective states of northern Europe (in distinction, say, to the coercion-intensive systems of imperial Russia or the Ottoman empire). In this chapter, we focus on the mixed approach of Classical city-states and their Opportunist rivals (to borrow a phrase pioneered by Davies, describing the rising cohort of fourth-century autocrats like Philip of Macedon, Mausolus of Caria or Evagoras of Cyprus).[9]

The behaviour that Hieron admits to in the above quote is one example of how such pressures disrupt norms. States find novel and increasingly effective ways of squeezing money out of subjects, which often involves increased administration and strengthened state institutions. Such a process makes the next round of military innovation both possible and necessary, and so the cycle begins again, theoretically *ad infinitum*. Something like this underlay Cicero's point that the sinews of war were composed of money – if possible, infinite money.[10] One element that Xenophon identifies as desirable in the *Hieron*, if it can be achieved, is to find means of extracting wealth as 'painlessly' (*alupos*) as possible, because it minimizes the viciousness that a tyrant (or by extension, the state) needs to resort to in order to meet its needs.[11] However, with or without such ameliorative measures, war creates severe pressures that states either conform to or risk collapse.

That such a military revolution occurred, roughly between the mid-fifth and fourth centuries BC, is the scholarly consensus.[12] It is implicit in Thucydides, who speaks of the corrosive effects of total war, which drove states to increasingly desperate expedients to win battles and more ruthless forms of taxation to pay for it.[13] It is occasionally stated explicitly. Take, for instance, the Spartan king Archidamus, who – seeing a Sicilian catapult for the first time – cried out, 'By Herakles, Man's valour is no more!'.[14] War machines like the catapult were not the only such innovation. They were joined by more sophisticated navies, stronger fortifications, and increasingly specialized and professional soldiers (e.g., peltasts). Overall, this meant rapidly increasing military expenses, which states struggled to keep up with.

Scholarly accounts of the period remain fuzzy on the question of how states learned to cope with increased expenses. We assume that states did not continually reinvent the wheel – clearly there was a diffusion of fiscal technique. There have only been a few attempts to show how such dispersal might have worked.[15] This picture must be filled in further – in particular, because we know how expertise of this sort *cannot* have spread.

It could not merely have been a matter of attracting a number of technical specialists and paying them to produce a particular product (as one might in the case of a statue). This is easy enough when there exists a tangible good that yields obvious benefits. When we hear that Alcibiades kidnapped Agatharchus – a famous painter – and forced him to decorate his house, we are amused and horrified, but not impressed. Alcibiades coerced the painter to produce a concrete work of art, and the arrow between expert and product is uncomplicated.[16] But institutional technologies are trickier precisely because they are intangible. What, after all, does a financial administrator – tasked with generating more revenue for the state – produce? It is not, in fact, gold or silver coins (products of the mint, hammered out by specialist mint workers). It is instead a series of ordered routines and directives to various social actors (which might include mint workers), along with their implementation. At their most tangible, this may take the form of laws, statutes or decrees, preserved on stone, paper or some other medium. But we must assume that fiscal and monetary structures were seldom so formalized in the pre-modern world. This was fine because early financial systems were not really very complicated, and so could be administered relatively intuitively.[17] More often than not, in fact, such institutional structures were conflated with their visible manifestation – the hated tax collector. This matters because, for the transfer of effective financial institutions to occur, it is necessary that the state – either collectively, or in the person of the autocrat – articulate what exactly public finance is, in the first place.

We have seen that such recognition of *technē* might be uncomplicated (for instance, in the case of wall painting). One difference between wall painting and revenue generation lies in the character of their respective product. For this reason, those who had need of intellectual expertise faced challenges not simply in recognizing the components or structure of an expert field. The challenge, in the case of public finance, was somewhat more basic: the state actor had to realize that effective revenue generation was an expert field *per se*, with its own parts, instruments, and practices. We should not take this for granted. It is today hard to find an example of a state or society that has not, to some degree, internalized this insight (even ISIS – rhetorically and ideologically backward-looking – tried in the mid-2010s to attract experts in tax collection and administration, monetizing fields as conventional as banking fees and as unconventional as artifact looting).[18]

Such structures are not, however, natural. Lisa Kallet has argued that rhetors helped to develop and articulate such fiscal notions for Athenian audiences. This was, perhaps, the first time in world history that such policies were communicated to a mass audience that genuinely needed to understand – at some basic level – the issues at stake.[19] Outside of such financial cultures, however, the going was slow and uncertain. Likewise, the processes of generating and aggregating such revenues, which involved a series of economic assumptions, will not have been automatically obvious to all ancient state actors. If even such basic notions about money were not universal, then we may perhaps more easily imagine how assumptions about the relationship between political economy and taxation could have varied considerably between states. Thus, the process by which sophisticated financial activities came to be practiced, and the means by which they were articulated to ancient audiences, ought to interest us greatly.

This chapter focuses its approach through a particular conceptual lens: the *technē* of public finance and its evolution, beginning in the late fifth century – that is, of practising public finance as a *technē*, with its own components, responsibilities and practices, which were distinct from other parts of governance.[20] *Technē*, though mapping roughly onto our concept of expertise, is an old word given new conceptual meaning in the Classical period. As scholars like Roochnik and Cuomo have made clear, a robust and widespread debate broke out in the Classical period over the precise meaning of the word, one bounded by old definitions but expanding quickly and greedily (touching on an increasing range of epistemic phenomena, such as *empeiria* and *epistēmē*).[21] Such debates occurred across fields such as medicine, rhetoric, and the military arts, being mediated by philosophers and sophists. That they should have touched upon public finance is no surprise, but in modern scholarship on this topic, more often than not, the technē-centred frame is underdeveloped or outright ignored. Our focus on Book II of the *Oeconomica* is therefore an attempt to say as much as possible about this *technē* through the lens of the largest and most complete exemplar of its genre – the handbook for public finance.

The separation – or disembedding – of state finance from other spheres of politics (e.g., speaking in the assembly, formulating military strategy, etc.) is bound up in such technical formalization, such that – by the late Classical period – politicians could claim to specialize in state finance exclusively, to the virtual exclusion of other kinds of politics (something Pericles would not have dreamed of). In particular, I am interested in this period as a moment in which Greek administrative technologies – developed in the *polis* – jumped the rail (both politically and culturally) and migrated to the far edges of the Mediterranean world. The need for a text like the *Oeconomica* had been spelled out in the fourth century by Aristotle, who in the *Politics* (1259a4) recommended that a compendium of precisely such fiscal mechanisms be written, with the tacit assumption that such institutional technologies could be exported between *poleis* (it is unclear whether he thought they could move outside of the *polis*). With respect to this lost

Aristotelian text (most likely not the same work as the surviving *Oeconomica*), we really cannot say much. What is important that Aristotle carves out a typological space for this sort of work, identifying a clear demand on the part of fourth-century statesmen for such material.[22] It is obvious that others were thinking the same thing during this time, as evidenced by the *Poroi* of Xenophon, which fulfilled a narrower version of Aristotle's goal, proposing a specific set of policy recommendations for a particular city, Athens. Clearly, the genre was already being populated by work of considerable sophistication in the early fourth century.

This paper builds on the work of several scholars. Edouard Will and John Davies – the latter building on the former – have articulated the figure of the fiscal expert in the fourth century, as well as an account of Greek fiscal practices across that period. The two phenomena – expert and expertise – are linked, and their focus on particular experts like Chabrias helps to situate this emerging *technē* in a broader history of Classical Greece.[23] Trundle has developed elements in this story, too, in particular the relationship between autocrats and money.[24] Ober has integrated this framework into his broader picture of the rise and decline of the Classical *polis*, especially the notion that a transfer of expertise underpinned the success of autocratic states in the fourth century.[25] On the other hand, in the way that expression is as important as practice – and indeed, in the way expression helped to determine practice – Lisa Kallet's work on rhetoric and fiscality has been important, especially in so far as she outlines the economic thinking of the generation just prior to the fourth-century military-fiscal revolution.[26] All of these are foregrounded by a recent upsurge in scholarship on ancient Greek financial regimes.[27]

Taking cues especially from Davies, I focus on fourth-century autocratic regimes – the so-called Opportunists. Because they formed a distinct class of state in the fourth century, playing catch-up with *polis*-based states early in the century and eventually competing strongly with them toward its middle, they show the kinds of financial *technē* most in demand, its directionality (away from cities like Athens and towards the non-Greek periphery), and the means employed in building fiscal capacity in those states. In some ways, this ignores where the real action was – that is, in the Greek, *polis*-based world (particularly in Athens). However, this has been the subject of much literature in recent decades, and discussion of, for example, the Athenian liturgical system and its mechanisms (*antidosis*, symmories and so forth) would not much illuminate our topic.

I argue that, in the fourth century, Greek practitioners of public finance were becoming more technical in their thinking and operation. This included Athenians abroad (like Chabrias, Callistratus, Xenophon), Athenians at home (Lycrugus and Eubulus), as well as non-Athenians (Eubulus of Atarneus, Antimenes of Rhodes, Polydamas of Pharsalus). This technical trajectory is hard to trace, but can be interrogated through sources like the *Oeconomica* or the *Hieron*. The process was driven by Tilly-like military pressures and, in turn, helped to intensify those pressures by satisfying states' needs for revenue. This history, though barely visible in surviving evidence, is critical to understanding the shape of the late Classical and Hellenistic military revolutions.

2. Ps.-Aristotle, *Oeconomica* Book II

One of the challenges in dealing with this topic is that we actually know a great deal about at least one Greek city's history of fiscal and financial management, i.e., Athens. Unconsciously or simply through sheer necessity, scholars are tempted to treat Athens as a barometer for Greek financial development and as a model for the rest of the Greek world. It is tempting to think that financial mechanisms that developed in Athens, at least those sufficiently adaptable to other *poleis*, were inevitably diffused elsewhere. Some did.[28] But this should point back to the question of *technē*, not stop the line of inquiry. By what mechanism did they spread? Who spread them?

The technical handbook was a major literary genre that mediated Greeks' and Romans' relationship to professional expertise – such manuals both contain the elements of the craft itself and often sketch a history of the field, and especially the development of new techniques.[29] Almost none of these remain for state finance, however. This means that we should take care to examine the most prominent such text – Ps.-Aristotle's *Oeconomica*. I argue that its existence gestures to the existence of other such works, and to a market for expertise in this field, similar to that hinted at by handbooks of siege engineering or medicine, which have been preserved in greater number and which served to advertise the knowledge of experts to Hellenistic patrons and to show why expertise was important.[30] These are distilled portraits of a field's knowledge, not a replacement.

It is not controversial to say that the work entitled *Oeconomica* is strange. It appears in the Aristotelian corpus erratically and has a checkered transmission history. Thus, what has come down to us is uncertain in authorship and clearly combines several, originally separate, works. What is controversial, rather, is whether the text offers us anything of intellectual or historical value. Rostovtzeff, on one hand, called it 'one of the most interesting products of Greek speculative thought combined with practical sagacity', a sentiment some have shared.[31] Others see its insights as 'ranging, in the surviving manuscript, from the banal to the meaningless'.[32] I side with the former, albeit the *Oeconomica* reveals as much through hint and omission as through substantive insight.

The contents of the *Oeconomica* are diverse. Book I deals with household management, being in substance similar to Xenophon's *Oeconomicus*, though more in the style of a Peripatetic treatise. Book III, preserved only in Latin, treats family and marriage, and seems to be Neo-Pythagorean in character.[33] For our purposes, however, Book II is most interesting. It is missing from many Early Modern manuscripts, most crucially from the editions of Moerbeke, Oresme and Bruni (who preserved only Book I and III).[34] Departing from the other two books – which deal with domestic economy – Book II takes as its subject the finances and revenues of a state. It spends the bulk of its time, like Polyaenus in his *Strategemata*, recounting anecdotes that are meant to illustrate the principles of successful action.

Preceding these, however, is an analytical introduction on the meaning of *oikonomia* (1345b7–1346a30).[35] The author begins by describing the characteristics of the successful financial administrator: 'Whoever intends to practice economy properly should not be inexperienced, should be naturally talented, and in character industrious and equitable. For whoever lacks these elements shall err often in the matter they take in hand.'[36] This statement, though sensible, is far from original in Greek thought. Something like this had been recommended by Hippocrates for doctors, and by Isocrates for students of rhetoric.[37] Its appearance here indicates the author is working within a broader *technē*-oriented genre, the most prominent surviving examples of which are medical handbooks, whose contours had been set more than a century prior. It suggests too that – like many of those other technical treatises – a major goal was to guide potential patrons in seeking out such an individual (perhaps the author themselves) – teaching them just enough to know what they lacked.[38]

The author next claims there are four kinds of economies. The first is the royal economy (1345b19–27), the 'greatest and simplest'. Its primary role is fourfold: first, to regulate coinage, both in quantity and quality; second and third, to deal with 'outgoings' and 'incomings' (*exagogima* and *eisagogima*), deciding what tribute is desirable from dependents, and also what ought to be redistributed from the centre back to the periphery; fourth, and finally, to control expenditures (*analomata* – that is, the purchase of services and commodities that cannot be obtained internally).

The second type of economy is the satrapal (1345b28–1346a5). Here the list of revenues (*prosodoi*, which distinguishes them from the 'incomings' and 'outgoings' of the royal economy) is quite long. Most important is the tax on agricultural goods, collected in kind (*to ekphorion*). Then, in descending order, are revenues derived from the mining of metals, taxes on harbors (*emporioi*), farmland (presumably cash payments assessed on land, which is distinct from *to ekphorion*) and market centres (*agorai*). Next is a tithe paid on grazing animals, probably for pasturage. The final components are poll taxes and various taxes on craftspeople. The whole catalogue is described in extremely terse prose. A fuller, decompressed version of such *prosodoi* can be found in Xenophon's *Poroi*, which – although treating a *polis*, and not a satrapy – recommends all manner of (quite sophisticated, compared to Book II) legal and financial reforms to increase state revenues.[39]

The scope of the *polis*' economy – as described in Book II – is smaller (1346a5–7). The primary source of revenue here comes from the 'peculiar' products (*apo tōn idiōn*) of the land, which were presumably collected in kind. Such specialized products could be used by the city in various ways – either sold at market or deployed strategically. The Cyreneans, for instance, used their comparative advantage in grain growing, when there was danger of famine, to score political points and ingratiate themselves with other states.[40] A second source of revenue comes from markets and trade (*apo tōn emporiōn kai diagōgōn*), which would have been a tax collected in cash. A third – and depending on the state, by no means least important – are revenues derived from 'regular' (*apo tōn egkukliōn*) taxes.[41]

The household (1346a8–13) is least important, being smallest and least coherent in its aims. Its 'incomings' and 'expenditures' (*tas prosodous kai ta analōmata*) are comparatively tiny. Three primary components account for household revenues. The most important is land. The next are various kinds of regular income (the cryptic phrase *hē apo tōn allōn enkuklēmatōn* probably refers to profits from personal business, payment for personal services, etc.). The last are revenues from the investment of cash (*hē apo argúriou*). Ps.-Aristotle ends by introducing a final principle, common to all levels of economy: expenses should not exceed income.

It should be clear from Ps.-Aristotle's terminology that, while he thinks that the royal level is grandest, it is also entirely dependent on the satrapal and political. The royal economy is responsible only for *exagogima*, *eisagogima* – none of which are produced in the palace, but rather cycle through the imperial system – and *analomata*, flows of goods than are not redistributed back into it, but rather spent by the royal authority. The *prosodoi* – new wealth injected into the system – are produced at the midrange (in the satrapies and *poleis*), and not at the top. It is these outputs that the *Oeconomica* seeks to increase. Thus, the phrase 'greatest and simplest' becomes more understandable. The royal level is the simplest of the four because it merely distributes revenues produced elsewhere. The four-level framing, unique in our surviving economic literature, suggests that the author was writing for a patron in either a royal or satrapal position, hoping to impress upon them that he was familiar with all the levels of the economy, and, through knowledge of their interconnection, could provide insight into how these domains ought to be ordered (or re-ordered).

After laying out the four-level structure, the author turns briefly to a few principles by which the various economic levels should be mediated, without providing much detail.[42] First, the resources of the overall state must be gauged across levels to see what is available – among its cities and satrapies, what strengths can be marshalled? Second, what manner of revenue is lacking and what must be improved in order to extract the resources that the state needs? How can these be strengthened or increased? Finally, among current expenses, what can be cut with the least disruption to the state? Indeed, this fits well with the broader notion of the ancient technical treatise as a method of advertising expertise, rather than containing it wholesale.

Next comes the best known aspect of Book II – the anecdotes. As we've noted, the anecdotes in the *Oeconomica* are often described as, at best, uninformative or, at worst, non-sensical. Reading them together, however, can offer some insights into the dilemmas of late-Classical and Hellenistic states, if not concrete solutions. Through the flailing of these autocrats, we are especially reminded of the limitations of the early financial managers. The most prominent figure among this lot is Dionysius of Syracuse, who engages in remarkable, outrageous and, if true, likely ineffective strategies to generate state revenue.[43] Nothing in the text specifies whether this Dionysius was the Elder or the Younger. I assume it to be the Elder, who undertook the massive military effort to fight the Carthaginians, and who mobilized the whole population of Syracuse to produce weapons and to fight, as well to innovate in fields like siege technology (producing the early *gastraphetes* catapult) and naval warfare (the five-oared warship) – typical war-makes-states behaviour.[44]

Ten incidents portray Dionysius variously swindling and strong-arming his subjects. The most common motive was to pay for expensive military activity.[45] He employs a range of tricks, which includes confiscating women's jewellery, striking a tin fiat coinage and generally fooling his subjects into revealing their personal property. Here, one understands Hopper's perspective when he dismisses the whole of Book II as 'shifts and devices of a puerile and ineffectual sort'.[46] While true of various anecdotes, this sentiment ignores the analytical and insightful first section of Book II. And even allowing that the stories are of dubious historical value, one must recognize in them the motivation and dilemma of the tyrant or king (just like Xenophon's Hieron), who is so desperate for cash that he empties temples and robs his citizens. In Book II, Dionysius' Syracuse shows what painful fiscal devices look like – echoing the desire expressed in Xenophon's *Hieron* for more painless ones (which is to say, more technically sophisticated ones).

In the end, the promise of the *Oeconomica* to the historian remains just that, a tantalizing glimpse of a body of knowledge that was central to the function of the major Classical and Hellenistic states. By the third century, this expertise had been codified in such a way that its practitioners had not one, but several models to draw upon (as we noted, the four-fold schema that Book II offers does not appear elsewhere – I assume that it was one among several approaches that have not come down to us). Works like the *Oeconomica* would have been instrumental in advertising the expertise of the practitioner, while holding back the detailed knowledge needed to actually administer finances (something that could not be communicated through a handbook, in any case). It represents a mature, albeit irretrievably mostly lost, financial *technē*, represented in figures like Demetrius of Phaleron, who undertook precisely the sorts of financial strategies required for effective public finance – in the process raising revenues considerably.[47] These probably went hand in hand with his Attic census, the first up to that point, which would have helped render Attic residents as legible to, and hence taxable by, the state.[48]

3. The craft of public finance

The question of the authorship of Book II, or even its textual unity, cannot be resolved. We are left with, at best, a sort of billboard for the state of the financial *technē* at the time of its writing, probably at the end of the fourth or early third centuries BC. While post-dating the military revolution, Book II illustrates the explicitly technical direction that the field of state finance was moving in the mid-fourth century, coalescing on a *technē*-based model of expertise common to other fields (e.g., medicine, siege engineering, rhetoric, military tactics/logistics, etc.). Given the labour model on which engineers, doctors, and other craftsmen worked in the ancient world, it implies – parallel to any permanent bureaucracy within Hellenistic courts or within *poleis* – a free-floating cohort of independent experts, who moved from state to state offering their services to the highest bidder.

This sort of traffic in financial experts has been examined within a narrow band of existing scholarship, offering insight into the fourth-century diffusion of Athenian financial techniques, chiefly to Egypt and Macedon.[49] But if fourth-century statesmen lacked a handbook, how did such wisdom travel? Dionysius stands at one end of this period. Alexander and his generals stand at the other, deploying enormous resources through both imperial tribute and through the more complex revenue schemes that had emerged in the meantime (Demetrius of Phaleron's efforts in Athens provide a small window into this).

Most contemporary literature on this subject would not have helped these rulers very much, in practical terms, because discussion of state finance was usually embedded in a variety of non-technical genres. Thus, Athenian orators mention state finance endlessly, with some speeches taking fiscal institutions as their explicit subject (e.g., Demosthenes' *On the Symmories* or Isocrates' *Antidosis*). But these were meant to convert listeners to positions related to, but not wholly focused upon, public finance. Often the issue was civic and distributive justice rather than the precise structure of taxation. And to the extent that public finance comes up elsewhere – in histories, for example – it was simply to acknowledge its importance or to dwell on particularly curious stories (for example, Herodotus' story about the invention of geometry in Egypt, supposedly to help re-assess the tax liability of Egyptians who had lost land to the Nile's encroachment).[50] Through the fifth and fourth centuries (the *Oeconomica* was written, at earliest, in 306 BC), we have not a single technical treatment of the subject along the lines of contemporary Hippocratic texts. This was not because the handbook, as a format, was confined to medicine. Indeed, non-medical handbooks were pioneered in other field (for instance, Xenophon's manuals on hunting and horse-riding, or Aeneas Tacticus' survival manual for sieges).

The only surviving text dedicated to *dioikēsis* in this period is Xenophon's *Poroi*, whose purpose is explicitly to increase state revenues (*prosodoi*).[51] The *Poroi* was written as a rather narrow policy paper, mostly intended to capitalize on Athens' comparative advantage in silver mining, and not directly relevant to most Opportunist autocrats. If this literature produced technical handbooks along the lines of Hippocratic texts, we have no evidence for them. Nevertheless, it was probably indicative of a wider literature on state revenue and management – almost all of which has been lost. The *Poroi* is suggestive, indeed, for the kinds of financial mechanisms that might have been available to autocrats hiring financial experts – much of which could be quite sophisticated. Indeed, the *Poroi* puts into practice Xenophon's ambition, set out in the *Hieron*, to formulate and offer up comparatively painless fiscal mechanisms to states (in this case, Athens), the better to reduce strife within those cities while increasing their revenue.

Nevertheless, while the *Poroi* is suggestive of an emergent genre of literature on state finance, it is doubtful that it (or any number of other such texts) would have been sufficient in its own right to carry out real financial reforms. The expertise needed to do so, ultimately, would have been too great. Autocrats therefore must have relied upon non-textual sources for fiscal knowledge. Could their own experiences have filled this epistemic void? Some fourth-century autocrats were, indeed, themselves expert financiers. Polydamas of Pharsalus, for instance, was entrusted with the affairs of his city because he was reliable and, apparently, because he was good with money.[52] Hermias of Atarneus – or rather his predecessor Eubulus, who was rumoured to be a banker, before becoming tyrant – seems to have benefitted from a background in finance.[53] Such individual technocracy, however, was rare. Theopompus notes that Philip – as a soldier

– had almost no time to devote to the practice of public finance, and for this reason was 'the worst administrator of all men.'[54] Nevertheless, Philip ran a large, complex kingdom that produced and spent considerable revenues. Such a personal approach, however, would have been rather 'sticky'. If a ruler had to cultivate his knowledge of public finance in his own city and only then practice it expertly, there would be little scope for it moving to other places. So, if autocrats did not themselves always know much about public finance, and did not have a handbook from which to learn – how did they gain access to such expertise?

The most likely vector for such knowledge was the movement of individual Greeks, hired by autocrats to reform or manage their states' finances. Financial specialization does seem to have increased at this time, especially moving into the mid-fourth century. Modern historians and ancient writers often fixate upon the increasing specialization of fourth-century Athenian politicians (from jack-of-all-trades to military commander and orator, respectively).[55] This is true, of course, but it seems that further specialization was possible. Aristotle commented upon this in the *Politics*, noting that 'an acquaintance with [financial] devices is also serviceable for statesmen, for many states need financial aid and modes of revenue like those described, just as a household may, but in greater degree; hence some statesmen even devote their political activity exclusively to finance.'[56] He is likely referring to politicians like Eubulus and Lycurgus, whose appeal lay in their management of Athenian institutions like the Theoric and Stratiotic funds. We have no reason to think that either Eubulus or Lycurgus became advisors to foreign dynasts. Other Athenians, however, seem to have.

A figure like Callistratus is emblematic. A major politician in Athens from the early 370s to the late 360s, after being exiled on account of an *eisangelia* trial, he went to work in Macedon as an advisor to the king.[57] There, he reformed the harbour tax of a major port city (we don't know which – perhaps Methone).[58] Whereas before the city had required a one talent fee (paid in advance) for the right to collect the harbor tax (thus restricting the circle of bidders), Callistratus lowered this to ⅓ of a talent. This promoted competition, brought in new bidders, and in the end, doubled revenues from the harbor. Here we see an Athenian statesmen reform the fiscal practices of a foreign patron, improve institutional performance, and increasing revenue. Book II discusses this case among its financial anecdotes. Indeed, it is one of the few examples that has been received positively by modern historians, largely because it provides significant historical details (for example, naming a known, albeit minor, historical figure we know to have worked with the Macedonians) as well as outlining a plausible mechanism for financial reform.[59]

The northern Greek city-states (like Methone) would have presented a moderate, but certainly manageable, challenge for fiscal experts. The region was relatively monetized and had substantial economic and political contact with southern city-states. The real problems came, it seems, as one went further afield. The need to extract precious metal coinage under circumstances of low monetization helps to explain an otherwise odd story about Iphicrates, also in Book II, who counseled Cotys of Thrace on how to raise money for his mercenary army.[60] One possible reading is that Iphicrates had Cotys convert his mercenaries into farmers. Having done so, they were to sow three *medimnoi* of wheat each, handing over their crops for sale at market. This is possible but not believable.[61] When would such sowing have taken place? Would Iphicrates' soldiers really have waited patiently through the winter as the crops were watered (or even submitted to farming someone else's fields)? Could the sum earned possibly have covered not only the campaign season, but also the field labour involved? A more realistic reading is that the ones sowing were not mercenaries, but subjects of Cotys. The Greek does not make it altogether clear whom we should identify as labourer – the mercenaries or some local population.[62] But the latter reading is the only one that makes sense. Agricultural goods that would otherwise have circulated within a non-monetized economy were instead brought to market in order to generate state revenue. Whether the story is accurate or not, the lesson here is on how to monetize otherwise frozen value inherent in labour and commodities – of no direct use in war – in order to pay mercenaries, who expected silver. In Tilly's framework, this is a means of employing coercion-heavy state power to generate capital.

Other regions presented different sorts of problems, in so far as they might have been better organized, had longer statist traditions, and abounded in precious metal, but nevertheless been unable to extract revenue effectively.[63] Thus, the satrapies of North Africa and the Levant, though quite wealthy, had – until the late fifth century – primarily raised uncoined revenue to send to the imperial centre as tribute. Herodotus records that Egypt (which then included also Libya, Cyrene and Barca) sent 700 talents (t.) a year to the Persian King.[64] This was no small sum, but under conditions of fourth-century warfare, it was far from sufficient. Athens alone, a generation after the Egyptian rebellion, produced around 1,200 t.[65] The job of Chabrias was to improve upon this Achaemenid tribute total, and he seems to have done so by pursuing several convergent strategies. Edouard Will was the first to describe the reforms of Chabrias as a comprehensive programme, and Davies built upon this by embedding it within a broader history of Greek public finance.[66] Ober has continued this analysis in a more recent history of the fourth century.[67]

I wish to single out one particular element of this reform: the introduction of an *eisphora* by Chabrias.[68] Was this *really* an eisphora? While acknowledging the particular Greekness of the institution (as Will says, 'cet impôt est typiquement grec'), we may at least say that it was a direct tax, focusing both on individual households and on monetized revenues under circumstances of extraordinary military crisis. Questions remain, however. Did it, for example, include symmories? Did it encourage the kind of self-scrutiny (e.g., an Egyptian *timēma*) that might have allowed these groups to track wealth and to hold one another accountable? This is left out of the account. Nevertheless, the transfer of such a Greek fiscal institution to Egypt was a sign both of desperation, on the part of an autocratic government, and of the malleability of Greek fiscal tools.

In these examples, Book II of the *Oeconomica* – despite its defects – presents us with at least two plausible instances of fiscal reform undertaken by autocrats under the guidance of Greek experts. These were aimed, first, at generating emergency funds, but more to the point, were meant to extract precious metal from economies that, by and large, used coinage infrequently or not at all.[69] That these were facilitated by Athenian experts who were willing and able to export such fiscal tools to autocratic, non-Greek states, is not incidental to the question of technical formalization. Xenophon's *Poroi* provides supplemental evidence that these financial mechanisms could be quite sophisticated, especially when it came to states enjoying considerable natural resources (Macedon especially was able to draw on silver and gold mines).

This returns us to the initial question of this chapter: how does an increasingly formalized *technē* help to spread a series of capital- and coercion-intensive, extractive financial practices? And conversely, how might this demand have driven the development of a *technē* of public finance? Moreover, why were these fiscal experts seemingly all Athenian? On the last question, there are several possible answers. The first is historiographical: they 'seem' to come from Athens because the exploits of other experts, from other cities, were not recorded. A second reason for this prominence was that Athens, through its particular mix of overlapping civic institutions (the *boulē*, boards of *tamiai*, etc.) distributed fiscal knowledge relatively widely, making some basic fiscal literacy a necessity to participate in government.[70] This was magnified by a third consideration. By the fourth century, Athens had a long history of massive public spending. Thus, its existing institutional advantages were aided by long and intense exercise.[71] Rhodes might have filled a similar role in the late fourth and third centuries, and we see some prominent Rhodians, like Antimenes – who succeeded Harpalus as Alexander's financial administrator – work effectively outside of their home city.

It seems clear that, in the fourth century, fiscal expertise moved through individual experts and not handbooks. But the conceptual anchor of this paper has been the technical manual of Ps.-Aristotle, so we are left with something like double vision. In the first place, the increasingly technical practice of experts like Callistratus and Chabrias is important in its own right, telling us much about how fourth-century autocrats captured and deployed such expertise. But in the second, Book II is itself a monument to this increasing formalization, a mature representative of a financial literature that, in the fourth century, was barely in its infancy. An important dynamic within this technical sphere was to make explicit institutions and practices that Athenian (and other Greek) administrators had been developing across several centuries. One reason for this explicit formulation was to separate them conceptually from their political and cultural context, and then export them to environments entirely unaccustomed to Greek ways of life. The later anecdotes of Book II, many of which take place in the Hellenistic Near East, hint at this, paralleling the historical expansion of Hellenistic institutions into Mesopotamia and Central Asia.

4. Formalization and the mobilization of expertise

Several strands converge here: autocrats, experts and the *technē* of public finance. The overarching question was how states learned to increase their revenues and generally improve their finances. Ancient theories of public finance were central to this (however meager our surviving evidence), and growing technical formalization allowed states to learn more easily from one another. Expertise and experts were therefore critical to the fourth-century military-fiscal revolution.

Book II of Ps.-Aristotle's *Oeconomica* provides a backward-looking lens on this subject. It is a flawed text that nevertheless hints strongly at the trajectory of fourth-century fiscal practice – that is, toward formalization in state finance. The question, of course, was what happened in the century or more between Dionysius I and Ps.-Aristotle. It seems that the answer runs through the career of many individual experts. Some were, so to speak, part of a vertically integrated bureaucracy. This included financial officials like mint masters (for whom we have only scattered evidence) or large-scale financial officials such as the Ptolemaic *dioiketes*, Apollonios.[72] Others had mastered the fiscal machinery of complex states and were willing to share some of their insights with powerful patrons. Such experts came to the aid of states under enormous fiscal strain (Macedon and Egypt, certainly – but probably others, like the kingdoms of Mausolus of Caria and Evagoras of Cyprus). In so doing, they helped to perpetuate a virtuous – or vicious – cycle in which states made war, and in turn were remade by it.

It is unknown whether or not these early fiscal experts wrote their own treatises (certainly, we hear of none). Nevertheless, some degree of formalization had clearly already occurred by Chabrias' time, if only within the financial pressure-cooker of the Athenian state, poking through in non-technical fora such as oratory and comedy, or occasionally in text like the *Poroi*. Such technical knowledge had to be reworked in terms that might travel outside of this narrow political sphere, however. Formal *technē*, a conceptual model that by the fourth century had been applied across nearly all of the crafts, filled this need. What this accomplished was the universalization of political practices – removing them from the sphere of democracy or oligarchy, or even from the *polis* itself. The intellectual distance between Chabrias and Ps.-Aristotle is the intellectual space between the democratic *dioikēsis* of the Athenian statesmen and a more general *oikonomia* of the Hellenistic monarch.

There is, of course, uncertainty in this account, and no smoking gun ties these strands together definitively. But it allows us to explain elements of fourth-century history that are otherwise problematic (even if historians choose not to deal with them in most cases). It further establishes another commonality among the motley crew of fourth-century autocrats who are sometimes called 'Opportunists'.[73] How were autocratic states able to gain traction in this period, competing with or superseding Greek city-states that had been, up to that point, relatively unchallenged? The issue is clearly multi-causal, and unpacking these has created a fruitful locus for research over the last three decades or so. One approach has been to point to technology and expertise transfer in facilitating the creation of such competitors. To the extent that Opportunist states, Greek and non-Greek, gained sufficient state capacity to challenge (and then humble) the mainland *poleis*, they were able to do so by harnessing certain kinds of Greek technology and expertise.[74] Fiscal administrative tools were among these. Indeed, these mechanisms occupied a somewhat unique place, in so far as money facilitated all of the other transfers (of technology, of specialists, of material, ships, siege engines and even culture).[75] It is both the most critical import, and among the least visible, not merely in terms of historiographical visibility, as Davies says – though this is true – but also in terms of the product on offer.[76] The intellectual background against which this transfer occurred is important, because it cannot be imagined that it might have happened similarly in the fifth century – that is, before the shift toward an integrated, structured, and expansive concept of *technē* had been developed.[77]

How did fiscal experts convey their knowledge to such patrons? How did they themselves conceptualize it? Transplanting an institution like the *eisphora* – born in the Greek *polis* – into the remotest parts of the world required at least some sense of it as a distinct artifact, as opposed to an embedded cultural or political practice. It is for this reason that we must reckon with the tricky question of fiscal expertise as *technē*. That is because, by definition, *technē* makes the knowledge of the expert explicit, spelling out with some precision the parts, procedures, timing, and goals of a field of expertise. It is at odds with expertise as *empeiria* – that is, 'experience' – which, while effective in practice, remains unexamined and seemingly inherent to the practitioner. Plato often seized upon the inability of experts to articulate their field as evidence of their non-technical nature. Soothsaying and cooking fell into this category, because while they produced impressive results, they did so in a manner that remained inarticulable.[78] There are pragmatic consequences that flow from such technical formalization, or its lack, since it allowed specialists to present their product to patrons who might otherwise have only the faintest notion of what was on offer, along with some measure of what separated one specialist from another.

We would like to say much more about the precise history of this formalization – where, when, and through what individuals. We must admit, sadly, that this is impossible. We are left with a series of scattered data points from which to draw our conclusions. It is nevertheless clear that Athenian politicians of a certain kind *had* begun to specialize in state finance by at least the 360s and 350s BC. Aristotle, as we saw, spoke of such men in the *Politics*. That Chabrias and his compatriots – not quite so specialized, a full generation earlier – took such fiscal tools abroad indicates that this process of technical refinement was well on its way.

5. Conclusion

Let us return to the idea that 'states make war, and war makes states', which we can now see was one of the major processes driving this formalization: demand for fiscal knowledge. Specialists in state finance had a significant incentive to frame (or reframe) their expertise in a manner that made sense to potential patrons: technical literature was a major medium by which to do so. In this environment, a text like Book II of the *Oeconomica* becomes significantly more understandable – first, as a genuine attempt to summarize the expertise of the financial administrator (whether to other experts or to students), but second, as an attempt to communicate to kings and governors the kinds of technical knowledge they were in need of (whether they knew it or not). Those rulers, like Xenophon's Hieron or Pseudo-Aristotle's Dionysius (stand-ins for states, in general), were under tremendous pressure to raise revenue to fight wars, and were likely receptive to such promises.

One objection might be that such an explanation is too narrowly functional. It is true, of course, that technical fields develop along any number of lines, including purely creative ones. But we are talking about public finance, not painting or chariot-racing. To tell a story about the development of state finance in ancient Greece that does not take war as a primary driver seems to willfully ignore the problems faced by fourth-century states.

Consider Demosthenes' criticism that the Athenian state spent more on festivals than on defence. If true, it would indicate that the pressures of war could not have been so terrible, and that development in state finance might have had some other driver (a desire to please the gods or a taste for comedy).[79] However, if his contention had not already been obviously wrong, Pritchard has recently shown it to be so, demonstrating that warfare was undoubtedly the single largest line item in Classical budgets, growing year by year.[80]

Under such conditions, states explored multiple strategies to increase revenue. Some, as we have seen, imported experts, almost certainly at a high cost. Others, more fortunate, incentivized those already within their fold to work on the problem a little harder. Here, let us return to a passage we have already mentioned from Xenophon's *Hieron*. It falls, oddly, to the poet Simonides – Hieron's interlocutor throughout the text – to suggest one possible solution to his money problems: 'were it made clear that the discovery of some way of raising revenue (*prosodon*) without hurting anyone (*alupos*) will also be rewarded, this field of research too would not be unoccupied.'[81] He seems to be suggesting a prize for innovation in state finance, if not the establishment of a post for a professional official to manage the city's finances.

If we have, throughout, focused on the demand side of fiscal expertise – a focus that is shared by the 'war makes states' school – Xenophon here brings us face to face with a supply-driven perspective. States should aim at the invention of new fiscal tools and encourage experts to practice their craft more effectively by offering rewards to those with the necessary capability.

Here, remarkably, three intertwined phenomena all come together in a neat package. First was a demand for money, endlessly increasing on account of warfare. Second was the changing array of fiscal tools available to states. And – seated between these, facilitating the second, and sometimes improving on it – was an evolving field of expertise.

Notes

1. For detailed case studies of Athenian fiscal development, as related to military needs (and others), see Gabrielsen 1994; Van Wees 2013a.
2. Tilly 1990.
3. Brewer 1989.

4. Which is not to say such work has not been done, only that there is more still to be done. See Will 1960; Kallet 1993, 1994; Gabrielsen 1994; Davies 2004; Van Wees 2013a; Migeotte 2014.
5. Thus, Hieron notes (4.7) that, while the private man desires a house and a field, the tyrant seeks 'cities, plentiful lands, harbours, and strong forts' (ἢ πόλεων ἢ χώρας πολλῆς ἢ λιμένων ἢ ἀκροπόλεων ἰσχυρῶν).
6. Tim. *FGrH* 566 F 124b.
7. Theop. *FGrH* 115 F 225a–c.
8. The phrase is Tilly's. See Roberts 1956; Brewer 1989; Tilly 1990; Parker 1996; Morris 2014.
9. Davies 1983; Davies 1995.
10. Cic. *Phil.* 5.2.5: *primum nervos belli, pecuniam infinitam.* The Spartan king Archidamus voices a similar, possibly apocryphal sentiment: 'War does not feed on fixed rations' (Plut. *Sayings of Spartans=Mor.* 219a).
11. Xen. *Hiero* 9.9.
12. Trundle 2006, 66–8; Gabrielsen 2007, 256; Cuomo 2007, 41.
13. Thucydides focuses on the great *kinēsis* of war, which leads to stasis. See: Loraux 1986, though cf. Price 2004. Even when states collapse, as Athens did, innovations (in finance, tactics, and so forth) persist.
14. Plut. *Sayings of Kings and Commanders=Mor.* 191e; *Sayings of Spartans=Mor.* 219a. Translation is adapted from Babbitt.
15. Will 1960; Davies 2004; Ober 2015a.
16. Dem. 21.147; Plut. *Alc.* 16.4.
17. Thompson 1981, 159.
18. Clark et al. 2017, 29. That ISIS was actively advertising in western newspapers for administrative experts was reported in *Slate Magazine*. See Chodorow 2015.
19. Kallet 1994.
20. I rely here on a broadly Platonic definition of *technē*, adding to what has already been said that any such system ought to be teachable. For further detail, the reader may consult Roochnik 1996. Plato's views on *technē* were complex – too complex for our purpose here, which is to provide a working definition into which a manual like the *Oeconomica* might fit. The relevant components are: 1) explicitness (having a formal structure, set out as *epistēmē*); 2) effectiveness (that is, it ought to mitigate the forces of *tuchē* – or chance); 3) empirical grounding (passing from *empeiria* to *technē*); 4) teachbility. I am, of course, aware that public finance was not invented *ex nihilo* in this period, as work on Archaic public finance makes clear (Van Wees 2013a).
21. Roochnik 1996; Cuomo 2007.
22. Finley 1970b, 316–17.
23. Will 1960; Davies 2004.
24. Trundle 2006.
25. Ober 2015a.
26. Kallet 1994.
27. Van Wees 2013a; Migeotte 2014; Mackil 2015; Ober 2015b; Pritchard 2015b.
28. Davies 2004.

29. Kennedy 1959; Marsden 1971; Cuomo 2007, 7ff.
30. Cuomo 2007, 62.
31. Andreades 1933, 88ff.; Rostovtzeff 1941, 74; Baloglou 1998, 116; Zoepffel 2006, 54.
32. Finley 1970b, 316. See also Ampolo 1979, 119–30; Hopper 1979, 13.
33. Laurenti 1968, 137–57; Natali 1995, 102.
34. Menut (1957, 786) calls its transmission history 'strange and involved', and provides an excellent account of its medieval and early modern reception.
35. Much hinges on the meaning of the words 'economy' and *oikonomia,* in so far as the ancient and modern usage of the two terms differs. Both were used in a more traditional manner – being roughly synonymous – up to the nineteenth century. For a summary of the ancient meaning of οἰκονομία, see Reumann 1957; Natali 1995; Baloglou 1998. This is at odds with our contemporary meaning of 'economy', of course (i.e., the formal modelling of markets, prices, and wages that Finley insisted the Greeks had no conception of). I use the term 'public finance' or 'political economy' throughout to signal this difference (as opposed to the simple cognate – economy), though 'political economy' likewise veers into territory staked out by modern scholars (Andreades 1933, 81).
36. Ps-Ar. *Oec.* 1345b7–11. Translation of *Oeconomica* is mine throughout, unless noted.
37. Hipp. *On Technē* 8.36–41; *Aphor.* 1.1; Isoc. *Antid.* 189.
38. There is always the question of what audience was intended with technical literature. Specialists write for other specialists – be they doctors or catapultists – and for patrons, often at the same time. See Marsden 1969, 3–4; Cuomo 2007, 62–3.
39. Xen. *Por.* 1.2.
40. Bresson 2011, 74ff. The *Oeconomica* itself records several such instances: see Ps.-Arist. *Oec.* 1347b16 (Sparta); 1348b32 (the Selybrians); 1352a16 (Cleomenes of Alexandria); 1352a15 (Athens).
41. Aristotle uses this word to mean not merely taxes, elsewhere, but regular duties, such as those performed by the Spartan women, for the state's sake (Arist. *Pol.* 1269b35).
42. Ps.-Arist. *Oec* 1346a8.
43. On Chabrias's reforms, see Will 1960; Davies 2004. Bullock argued vigorously for the merits of Dionysius as a financier (calling him 'generalissimo', hinting at the contemporary comparandum he had in mind). His broad argument is unconvincing, however: see Bullock 1930.
44. Diod. Sic. 14.43.1.
45. Triremes: Ps.-Arist. *Oec.* 1349a25; 1349b32.
46. Hopper 1979, 13.
47. Duris of Samos (*BNJ* 76, Fr. 10).
48. Ctesicles (*BNJ* 245, Fr. 1). For standard theorization on legibility and financial extraction by the state, see Scott 1998.
49. Will 1960; Davies 2004; Ober 2015a.
50. Hdt. 2.109.2–3.
51. Xen. *Por.* 1.2. Zoepfell (2006, 55) summarizes modern debates over the ancient use of *dioikēsis*, whether it is synonymous with *oikonomia*, and the ways in which it is a particular field of activity in Athens, practised from a relatively early point.
52. Xen. *Hell.* 6.1.2.

53. Theopompus *FGrH* 115 F 291; Diog. Laert. 5.1.3. Both present particularly salacious descriptions. Other ancient traditions – more sympathetic – exist, including the paean of Aristotle for Hermias: see Wormell 1935, 74; Ford 2011, xvii, 18–19.

54. Theopompus *FGrH* 115 F 224: πάντων ἀνθρώπων κάκιστος ὢν οἰκονόμος.

55. So-called *hoi stratēgoi kai hoi rhētores* (Hyp. 5 F6).

56. Arist. *Pol.* 1259a34 (trans. Rackham).

57. Ps.-Arist. *Oec.* 1350a16–22.

58. This is the port from which Callistratus sets out in an intriguing story told by Demosthenes (50.46ff.). It may, but need not, indicate that this was where he was based.

59. Davies 2004, 508; Ober 2015a, 264–5.

60. Ps.-Arist. *Oec.* 1351a19–20.

61. This reading is supported by Zoepfell (2006, 621–2), who points to comparable occurrences under Iphicrates' command in Corcyra, wherein his trireme crews were supplied by working on Corcyrean farms. This example is not entirely parallel, in my opinion. Here, the sailors – otherwise unused while the army is active on land – are not paid from proceeds derived from the fruits of the land, but rather physically fed.

62. Ps.-Arist. *Oec.* 1351a19:'Εκέλευσε τῶν ἀνθρώπων ὧν ἦρχε προστάξαι κατασπεῖραι αὐτῷ γῆν τριῶν μεδίμνων.

63. Davies (2004, 493) notes that the coinlessness of the Egyptians – not absolute, but nevertheless pronounced – was a major problem for Chabrias.

64. Hdt. 3.91.2.

65. This is a minimum. The passage in Plutarch's life of Lycurgus claims between 14,000 t. and 18,650 t. passed through Lycurgus' hands in the twelve years he was in the fiscal ascendency. See: Plut. *Mor.* 841b.

66. Will 1960; Davies 2004.

67. Ober 2015a.

68. Van Groningen 1933, 164; Will 1960, 265; Davies 2004, 492.

69. But cf. Buttrey 1980; 1982.

70. We certainly do not want to overstate this point. Kallet (Kallet-Marx 1994) has noted the relative narrowness of Athenian fiscal expertise in the fifth century, with true expertise being restricted to the elite class. Even absent a larger study on this subject in the fourth century, however, it is safe to say that fiscal expertise was *more* widely dispersed here than elsewhere. For the notion that such institutions distributed knowledge, see Ober 2008.

71. Gabrielsen 2007, 256.

72. For mint officials and the *dioiketes* Apollonius, see Bresson 2015.

73. Davies 1983; 1995; Butler 2010; Ober 2015a.

74. Davies 1995, 35; Ober 2015a.

75. In the field of philosophy, to take one example, Xenocrates, Plato and Aristotle, were said to have received (respectively) 50, 80 and 800 t. for their services. For Xenocrates, see: Cic. *Tusc. Disp.* 5.91; Val. Max. 4.3.3; Plut. *Alex.* 8.5; Plut. *Mor.* 181e; 331e; 333b; Themistius 21 252a. For Plato, see: Diog. Laert. 4.9. For Aristotle, see: Ath. 9.58 (398e). These figures are almost certainly false, but probably establish the right order of magnitude (i.e., more than 10 t.).

76. Davies 2004, 493–4.

77. Roochnik 1996.
78. Plato *Meno* 99c; *Gorg.* 503e.
79. Böckh 1857, 370; Pritchard 2015a, 2.
80. Pritchard 2015a.
81. Xen. *Hier.* 9.9.

CHAPTER 7
WHO ROWED IN THE ATHENIAN FLEET FROM 479–405 BC?

Matthew Trundle

Did Athenian citizens row the ships of the imperial Athenian navy in the fifth century BC?[1] All manner of hypotheses have been proposed. Some have suggested that Athenian triremes were always made up entirely of citizen Athenian oarsmen and that it was exceptional for ships to be manned by slaves, foreigners or even metics.[2] Others have suggested slaves always made up a majority of oarsmen.[3] Some commentators argue for a mixture of crew-members that included citizens, metics and foreigners from both within and outside the Athenian naval *archē*; others include or exclude the use of slaves in addition. More recent cynical analysis of Greek warfare in general by scholars like Peter Hunt, Hans van Wees and Peter Krentz highlights an exploitative system across both land and naval warfare and thus one in which oarsmen were drawn from non-citizens and slaves as much as from citizens.[4] John Hale's 2009 book *Lords of the Sea* links the idea that Athenian citizens crewed Athenian ships and that as a result Athens was the birthplace of democracy. This connection between the naval service of the poor Athenian citizens and their military service in the fleet supposedly gave them political clout in the assembly. The book's subtitle – *The Epic Story of the Athenian Navy and the Birth of Democracy* – suggests as much.[5] The make-up of the Athenian fleet thus has major significance in political terms on both the military and social context of democratic Athenian society in the fifth century BC.

In the context of this array of possibilities for who crewed the Athenian fleet, what follows explores the possibility that Athenian trireme crew membership changed as the Athenian empire became more 'imperial' and as Athenian society became more monetized. Thus, I argue that Athenian citizens primarily rowed the Athenian fleets in the first half of the fifth century, but this changed at some time in the middle of the century. At some point, the navy began to incorporate increasing numbers of metics, non-Athenian citizens from within the *archē* as well as mercenary oarsmen from outside of the empire and finally increasing numbers of slaves as well. The likely transformation away from a predominantly citizen-rowed fleet occurred between the Battle of Eurymedon dated no later than the late 460s[6] and the revolt of Samos in 440–439 BC. As we will see the transformation had certainly occurred by the start of the Great Peloponnesian War in 431 BC. The introduction of more regular mechanisms of coinage payment after 460 BC helped to facilitate this transformation to a less national and more professional navy. Thus, the Athenian navy became a more mercenary and financially driven affair. The Athenian fleet increasingly enrolled non-Athenian oarsmen, including metics, foreigners from within their *archē* and slaves as the fifth century progressed. The underlying cause of this transformation of the Athenian navy from a citizen-rowed-fleet to an effectively mercenary one was the increased monetization of the Aegean, the Athenian empire and Athens itself. Coinage played an increasingly important role in the way in which the empire functioned and the way in which states and individuals interacted within it. In such a context, poorer Athenian citizens naturally sought out safer opportunities for making cash in this new economic environment than military service. Thus, interest in political service in Athens increased as explained by paid jury service within the law courts, and after the Peloponnesian War payment for assembly attendance. Citizens also had access to other forms of exploitative payments like renting out slaves to the mines or public work projects. Finally, slaves even found themselves rented out to the fleet itself. The irony inherent in this argument, however, is obvious for those who still believe in the connection between military service and political participation. As Athens became more democratic in the latter part of the fifth century the fleet was in fact becoming less Athenian, less political and politicized and more professional and mercenary.

The mythology of Athenian society's (and indeed of all Greek societies') connections between war and political life begins with Homer (*Il.* 12.290–328; 13.221–73; but see 2.212–44) and the poets (Hybrias, *Skolion* 909 Page). Idealized visions of the connection between political and social status and military service permeate Greek ideology.[7] Thus, Aristotle thought that early aristocracies occurred at a time when cavalry was significant. Later, as heavy infantry appeared, oligarchies replaced aristocracies and then navies created democracies (Arist. *Pol.* 1321a5–14). The Old Oligarch cemented the vision of a democracy based on the navy and an erosion of traditional aristocratic values (Old Oligarch 2.1). But both Aristotle and the Old Oligarch are aware that it does not necessarily follow that citizens have to do the rowing. The Old Oligarch even acknowledges the significant place of metics and foreigners in the fleet (Arist. *Pol.* 1327b11; Old Oligarch 11–12).[8]

Where did the Athenian naval crews come from? The first Athenian navies are likely to have been crewed by Athenian citizens and on occasion some metics. metic numbers probably grew considerably as the fifth century BC progressed and as Athens became an imperial city, thus metics likely made up fewer men liable for service in the early part of the century. Similarly, the Athenian fleet at the time of the formation of the Delian League must also have been primarily Athenian manned given the Athenian population base and, at least at that time, the likelihood of a lack of access to military markets in the Aegean. That stated, even in the early fifth century many states, especially smaller states like Aegina, crewed fleets with non-citizens. What is the evidence of the crews of early Athenian triremes? Thucydides (1.93.3) tells us that at the time of the Persian invasion in 480 BC, Themistocles considered that the Athenians had become a naval people (καὶ αὐτοὺς ναυτικοὺς γεγενημένους). A similar sentiment appears in Plutarch's *Life of Aristides* (23.5–24.3) whereby the Athenians of the immediate post Persian War period had become transformed away from farming Attica into a naval and money (*chrēmata*) focused people. It would be a leap to extrapolate from these statements that all Athenians were now in the navy, but it suggests the significant place of the fleet and the sea in the lives of the state and the people.

Early political developments potentially link Athenian citizens and the Athenian state to naval expansion even in the sixth century BC. The earliest evidence for naval organization suggests that the Demes of Attica and the Athenian citizen body established in the sixth century BC also had connections to the navy, even in Solon's constution. Hans van Wees has argued that Cleisthenes' late sixth century democratic revolution, in addition to reforming the state and the infantry, perhaps also restructured the already existent Athenian navy.[9] Indeed, it may well have re-organized the first version of something approaching a state navy. Thus, according to the *Athenaiōn Politeia* (21.5) Cleisthenes created new demarchs who replaced the *naukraroi*. At the same time, the demes or local 'villages' themselves replaced the *naukrariai*. In the fourth century BC, Cleidemus wrote that Cleisthenes had long before created fifty *naukrariai*, magistrates or ship-captaincies. He stated that these were similar to the symmories, or colleges of wealthy citizens who collectively funded the fourth century fleet (Cleidemus FGrH 323 F 8).[10] Van Wees therefore argues based on this that Cleisthenes created the original state-funded navy.[11] Thus *naukrariai* were simply part of the process that led to the fifth-century Athenian fleet.

There are dissenters against this narrative. Vincent Gabrielsen sees the *naukrariai* as simply overseers of the finances and administration of the early Athenian state, as their name potentially suggests.[12] This would then explain why according to Herodotus (5.71.2) the *naukrariai* assisted with the defeat of Cylon in 632 BC at a time when there was no Athenian navy at all (Hdt. 5.71.2). Similarly, other evidence shows that the *naukraria* was connected to administration prior to Solon (*Ath. Pol.* 8.3). Solon apparently had created twelve *naukraria*, three from each of his four tribes, for state financial administration (not necessarily naval). Van Wees goes far to explain these anomalies present in our later evidence and demonstrate how later writers like Herodotus, Thucydides and Aristotle confused the real roles of early officials called *naukrariai* and the *naukraroi* in the Athens of Solon.[13] He thus suggests in his *Ships and Silver, Taxes and Tribute* (see n.9) four challenges to later Greek sources to show they had important military oversight prior to Cleisthenes' revolution. Thus, first (pp. 44–6), the fragments of information preserved in out later sources, while offering no details of exactly what the *naukrariai* did, demonstrate they were important elements of Solonian Athenian political and economic life. Second (pp. 46–7), he argues that the nau- in *naukrarai* or *naukraroi* does in fact relate to those who have power over ships, and early state ships at that and not as earlier scholars have tried to show either something more generic or even temple finances from a connection to 'naos' related terms. Third (pp. 47–8), Van Wees highlights Pollux's second century CE *Lexica* (8.108), which gives more detail than Aristotle regarding their connection to the Athenian thirds as well as stating they were responsible for ships, cavalry and taxes and, therefore, were much more active in the military than Aritotle gave them credit. He also notes that Herodotus (6.89) states Athens had a fleet of fifty ships in 491 BC, which links neatly with Pollux's suggestion that fifty *naukrariai* oversaw the ships noted by Cleidemus in the fourth century (Cleidemus FGrH 323 F 8). Finally (pp. 48–53), Van Wees highlights their role in overcoming Cylon's conspiracy as far more logical if they had some military oversight and were more powerful than if they had been second tier local magistrates overseeing generic finance matters. He suggests later traditions (for example Thuc. 1.26 and Arist. *Ath. Pol.* 8.3) obscured the real nature of the Archaic *naukrariai* and played down the role of the navy and state finance in Solon's pre-Cleisthenic Athens from aristocratic prejudices and preconceived notions concerning the pre-Cleisthenic and democratic state.

Whether or not these early administrative units were connected to the navy, and it looks like they may well have been, then perhaps Cleisthenes absorbed the old *naukrariai* and *naukraroi* into his new deme-structure, which makes perfect sense. If he did, then Van Wees would also be right in seeing an original organization of fifty ships as the basis of the Athenian navy dating to Cleisthenes and not to Themistocles in 483/482 BC. Of course, any state navy would need a centralized system of governance, crewing and finance. The point for my purposes herein is that surely if the demes were themselves connected to financing and more importantly crewing the fleet then it is likely that citizens were also involved in naval service from the navy's pre-Themistoclean origins. In short then, the recruitment of naval crews had apparently been the concern of local administrative districts, and this was easily transferred to the new demes, which served similar roles also in other aspects of government.

The experience of the Athenians in the Persian Wars certainly suggests that citizens and other Athenian residents did, if needed, crew triremes and no doubt primarily as oarsmen given numerical requirements. Plutarch (*Themistocles* 7.1) explicitly states that Themistocles tried to get the Athenian citizens (*politai*) to embark on the triremes (τοὺς πολίτας ἐμβιβάζειν εἰς τὰς τριήρεις) in the initial panic concerning the Persian invasion. Herodotus (8.1.1) tells us that the Athenians provided 125 ships for the Artemisium campaign and that in addition to the Athenians serving in these ships the Plataeans served on them as well, despite their inexperience (Ἀθηναῖοι μὲν νέας παρεχόμενοι ἑκατὸν καὶ εἴκοσι καὶ ἑπτά· ὑπὸ δὲ ἀρετῆς τε καὶ προθυμίης Πλαταιέες ἄπειροι τῆς ναυτικῆς ἐόντες συνεπλήρουν τοῖσι Ἀθηναίοισι τὰς νέας). Does this suggest the Athenian citizens and metics by contrast to the Plataeans were themselves experienced crew? Perhaps.

The Themistocles Decree, questionable though it might be regarding its date, its reliability and its integrity, details clearly the crewing of triremes by citizens and metics of the city. The document may well be entirely apocryphal and relate only to its fourth-century context. In it, however, there is no mention of non-resident foreigners embarking on the 200 ships against the Persians, but simply citizen Athenians and metics (ll.12–13).[14] Later in the text, the inscription notes that only Athenians from the lexiarchic registers and the metics from the names lodged with the war archon will board the ships (ll. 27–31). This clearly illustrates that metics served, but nothing suggests their relative numbers to citizens or indeed the existence of foreign non-residents on board the Athenian vessels. Finally, the *Athenaiōn Politeia* (23.1; see also Plutarch, *Themistocles* 10.4) states that the Areopagus donated eight drachmas to each member of the Athenian fleet's crews who boarded the ships (ἐνεβίβασεν εἰς τὰς ναῦς) before Salamis. This does little to help explain the make-up of the fleet, but it is worth asking whether such an incentive payment was necessary in a time of national crisis. Perhaps the money was aimed at security for the families of those in service rather than a rather bald bribe for the men to enlist. The argument that the money aimed to care for the families has some support from the fact that the people of Troezen gave money to those who sought refuge with them (Plut. *Them.* 10.3). Plutarch explicitly attests that all Athenian men of military age boarded the ships for Salamis (τοὺς δ' ἐν ἡλικίᾳ πάντας ἐμβαίνειν εἰς τὰς τριήρεις, *Them.* 10.2). The Persian War evidence suggests Athenians and residents crewed the Athenian ships save for the Plataeans, who thus prove the rule.

The Great Persian War was exceptional given the extreme circumstances in which the Athenians found themselves. After the war Athens developed the basis of its later empire, the alliance known as the Delian League. The initial arrangements concerning the Delian League saw many small states assessed for tribute rather than ships and men – though several major states still sent ships and men to the alliance including Thasos, Naxos, Chios, Samos and the cities of Lesbos (see Thuc. 1.96.1–97.1; Plut. *Arist.* 5.18).[15] Blackman lists a host of smaller communities that either did or were likely to send triremes to assist the League's war effort. He argues that their military involvement with the League changed after the battle of the Eurymedon and that many smaller states switched to sending money to the league rather than military support. Thucydides is vague as to how this process occurred whereby Athenians did the fighting in Athenian owned ships. Blackman suggests following Thucydides (for example 1.99) and others (like Plut. *Arist.* 24) that the Athenians differed from their allies in their willingness, ability and physical readiness to serve on triremes.[16] For the allies, tribute payment may well have been less of a burden than providing ships and men.[17] In time all our sources agree that, either due to voluntary decision-making or enforced imposition, the allies paid tribute rather than fighting alongside the Athenians. Chios, Samos and the cities of Lesbos appear alone in continuing to serve as allies rather than as tributaries. Thucydides (1.99), Aristotle (*Ath. Pol.* 24) and Plutarch (*Arist.* 24) each demonstrate how the allies ceased sending ships and men and became ensnared in a tribute-driven system – ultimately in Athenian coinage – either voluntarily or as a result of revolts and the deliberate and enforced imposition of the *phoros* in coin onto states that failed to escape from an increasingly Athenian League.

Classical Greek navies in and of themselves did not need to be rowed by purely citizen or even native, that is local crews. Aristotle saw this point clearly enough in the *Politics* (1327b11). Several Greek naval powers must have utilized non-citizen oarsmen to man their ships. The island of Chios had a navy of 100 triremes at the time of the Ionian revolt. These ships fought at Lade. Herodotus (6.15) notes that forty elite citizens served as 'marines' on each of those triremes in the battle (ἄνδρας τεσσεράκοντα τῶν ἀστῶν λογάδας ἐπιβατεύοντας). It is unlikely that Chios has a citizen population large enough to crew all hundred vessels. Even in the Persian Wars states like Aegina utilized their non-citizen populations to complement fully their more than forty-five ships.[18] As with the navy of Chios, the 9,000 men required for such a fleet cannot have come from citizen oarsmen alone.[19] Thucydides (1.55.1) states that 800 of 1,050 rowers on Corcyraean ships captured at Sybota just prior to the Peloponnesian War were slaves (*douloi*). Corinth built ships and hired sailors from all over Greece ready for war with Corcyra (Thuc.

1.31). Sparta had a small navy prior to the last years of the Peloponnesian War, but the ships it did possess were likely rowed by helots.[20] Pericles went to great pains to allay Athenian fears that their enemies would lure skilled naval personnel from amongst their allies with money from Olympia and Delphi (Thuc. 1.143.1–2). The Athenians, therefore, appear no different to other states certainly in the latter half of the fifth century, but certainly by the time of the Peloponnesian War they had seen changes to the provenance of their trireme crews. Athens differed from other states in other ways too. As Pericles notes, their Athenian specialist crewmen gave them great advantages in naval warfare.[21]

Payment of wages in coin became the means of remuneration for naval crews in the empire.[22] This began with Athenians receiving payment, initially as much for naval training as for military service. Plutarch (*Per.* 11.4) tells us that Pericles regularly sent out sixty triremes with citizens (*politai*) under full pay for eight months a year.[23] As the fifth century progressed, coinage became increasingly important in the management of the empire and the payment of naval crews.[24] Decrees of the 420s BC illustrate well the increased amounts of tribute and its strict oversight as much as they also show the meticulous care and painstaking enforcement of the financial contributions of the allies within the empire.[25] In the context of imperial service, Pericles (Plut. *Per.* 12.3) famously justified skimming a sixtieth of the *phoros* because the allies provided neither ships nor men, but only money that belongs not to the givers but to the takers. There is though room in this passage to show that the receivers might pay others to do their bidding as the last sentence suggests, 'if they offer [that] for which they take' (ἂν παρέχωσιν ἀνθ᾽ οὗ λαμβάνουσι).

Thus, at least by 460 BC most states within the Athenian *archê* did not provide ships to the forces of the alliance, but only tribute in silver alone. When Athenians defeated a state, they took their ships. In turn, Naxos, Thasos and Samos lost the right to contribute ships to the Athenian cause and lost their navies in the process (Thuc. 1.98.4 for Naxos; 1.101.3 for Thasos; 1.117.3 for Samos).[26] The Aeginetans too lost their fleet once defeated by the league (Thuc. 1.105.2). Andocides (3.38) suggests that Athenian crews received pay from the Delian League tribute. Plutarch (*Cim.* 11.2; see also Thuc. 1.99.3) also suggests that Athenian crews were thus paid. A late source, Justin (3.6.4) adds that tribute was used for pay.[27] Blackman suggested that Athens may have supplied ships to states that did not possess them, at least initially.[28] He argued that as a result of confiscations and conquests Athens might well have owned something like 400 ships in 430 BC.[29] It is certain that by the 430s BC, after the failed revolt of Samos, only Chios and the cities of Lesbos provided triremes to the Athenian league.

The beginnings of Athenian naval dominance must, therefore, have been driven by Athenian citizen interest in military service in the early decades of the fifth century BC. Athens had fewer metics in the 480s BC than in the 430s BC. When the assembly voted to invest in a large fleet of triremes, we are told that personal profit lay at the centre of the decision. Athenians saw the potential to become rich through this large navy and crush Aegina at the same moment (Hdt. 7.144). Our sources refer to the Athenians on several occasions subsequently as both a naval people (Thuc. 1.99.2–3; Plut. *Them.* 4.3) benefitting as a community from the *archē* and well trained in military seamanship

(Arist. *Ath. Pol.* 24). Pericles' policy of sending out some 12,000 Athenians on sixty ships under pay for eight months a year (Plut. *Per.* 11.5) must have contributed to Athenian naval prowess and accustomed many Athenians to pay from naval service. It is also likely, therefore, that Athenians did row predominantly in the Athenian fleet in these early years. In 1927, Rachel Sargent championed the citizen oarsmen position. To her, 'military service meant freedom and she cites evidence for this in the fact that the Athenians freed slave-oarsmen whom they captured from enemy ships alongside the unique circumstances of Arginusae and the likelihood that newly enfranchised ex-slaves served in that engagement.[30]

Thucydides suggests that as a result of Athenians regularly serving on campaigns, the allies became no match for the Athenians who became better trained and more skilled at sea (Thuc. 1.99.2–3). Athenian crewmen are found on a ship captured by the Hestiaeans in 444 BC (Plut. *Per.* 23.2), though the Greek text actually states that when they captured an Attic ship they killed the men (ναῦν Ἀττικὴν αἰχμάλωτον λαβόντες ἀπέκτειναν τοὺς ἄνδρας); we thus assume them to be Athenians. Other evidence attests Athenians in naval service even in the 420s BC, as Aristophanes' *Knights* (542–4) alludes to a naval apprenticeship amongst Athenians[31] and Dicaeopolis describes Athenian oarsmen as saviours of the city (*Acharnians* 162). Significantly, Dicaeopolis' saviours of the city are actually the *thranitês*-people, or those who rowed the upper bench (ὁ θρανίτης λεὼς ὁ σωσίπολις), leaving the door open for others on the lower banks to come from elsewhere.[32] As already noted, however, even Pericles suggests in the last sentence that non-Athenians might receive pay for service (ἂν παρέχωσιν ἀνθ' οὗ λαμβάνουσι). The events of the Oligarchic coup of 411 BC, in which a democratic Athenian citizen fleet held out at Samos against the oligarchy at Athens, might demonstrate that the Athenian fleet was indeed 'Athenian', primarily thetic and democratic (Thuc. 8.73–7, 81–2). But even here, due to the sheer size of navies and their manpower needs, several thousand Athenians might still make up only a relatively small percentage of all the naval crews present. Nowhere does Thucydides state the numbers of Athenians present at Samos during this episode.[33]

We have already noted that from the middle of the fifth century BC, Athenians may only have made up a small percentage of crewmen on board Athenian ships (Ar. *Ach.* 162; Plut. *Per.* 23.2). There are plenty of references to non-Athenians present on board Athenian ships and even slaves. Thus, the Old Oligarch (1.11–12) speaks of the importance of non-Athenians to the fleet. Nicias' letter to the Athenians from Syracusan admits to large numbers of foreigners (ξένοι) in the Athenian fleet, even from the start of the expedition, who joined either by necessity (ἀναγκαστοὶ) or in hopes of great pay (μεγάλου μισθοῦ). Even slaves (ἀνδράποδα) had replaced oarsmen in the fleet as things deteriorated for the Athenians (Thuc. 7.13.2–7.14.1). Xenophon (*Hell.* 1.6.24) describes the fleet that went out to rescue Conon blockaded at Mytilene in 406 BC as manned by all men of military age whether slave (δούλους) or free (ἐλευθέρους). Finally, and of course well known to many, former slaves if not slaves themselves appear to have made up considerable numbers at the Battle of Arginusae in 406 BC (Xen. *Hell.* 1.6.26–38; Ar. *Ran.* 693–4 with schol. 694 = Hellanicus *FGrH* 323a F 25; see also Ar. *Ran.* 718–37,

1446–8). These instances are often dismissed by idealists as anomalies and the product of desperate circumstances, especially the Athenian disaster in Sicily and the action at Arginusae, but it is only from the assumption that Athenians always crewed Athenian ships and that democracy and naval power went hand in glove that these instances are seen as anomalies.[34]

Nicias' letter to the Athenian demos from Syracuse demonstrates the numbers of slaves and foreigners in his fleet, not to mention the role that money and mercenary activity played in their behaviour (Thuc. 7.13.1–7.14.2). In addition, his speeches at the end of the campaign try hard to rally a losing cause and are aimed as much at the allied crews as at the Athenians (Thuc. 7.61–4; 7.77–9).

Of some significance, the Spartans captured (and executed) only 3,000–4,000 Athenian citizens at Aegospotami from a fleet of around 171 ships (Plut. *Lys.* 11.2–13; Xen. *Hell.* 2.1.20, 27–32; Diod. 13.106.1–7). If fully manned, this equates to around 36,000 men. Admittedly some Athenian crewmen were killed in the capture of the vessels and Xenophon also refers to empty and undermanned ships, but on these figures alone the Athenians made up only 9 per cent of naval personnel or a staggeringly low number of seventeen men per ship.[35] If Athenians made up even a majority of the crews, then enormous numbers of them escaped or died in the process of the assault. Of course, we have no means of knowing how many specifically Athenian crewed ships were at the disaster, but Athenians more than likely made up only a relatively small minority of men actually in service.

One inscription (*IG*1^{3}1032) contains the lists of the names and status of four trireme crews. Citizens make up less than half the crews in each instance. In addition, slaves may proliferate. The least fragmentary list, that for Trireme Two, almost certainly contains the names of at least forty slaves and that for Trireme Three may contain as many as eighty-seven slave-oarsmen, or about half a full trireme compliment. The more fragmentary lists for Triremes One and Four suggest large numbers of slaves, but inconclusively. Unfortunately, the date for this important inscription cannot be determined, though it is certainly from the latter part of the fifth century BC and Graham dated it to 412 BC.[36] That slaves served alongside free men, both Athenian citizens and others, should really come as no surprise as building accounts for the Erechtheum construced between 421 and 406 BC illustrate clearly that free men, foreigners and slaves all worked together on the same building project (i.e. *IG* 1^3 474 and 476).[37] It was commonplace for slaves to earn incomes as agents of their masters. The fleet appears, therefore, to be no different at all to other working environments.

Can we conclude that Athenians served alongside non-Athenians in these latter years of empire and perhaps in fewer numbers than they had in the first half of the fifth century BC? It is tempting to see triremes manned by status, whereby Athenian citizens sat on the upper bench, as *thranitai*, and were paid more than those of the lower benches, the *zygioi* and *thalamioi,* who were perhaps comprised of metics, foreign subjects and even slaves (Ar. *Ach.* 161–2; *Ran.* 1074).[38] The very fact that the flagship of the Athenian fleet, the Paralus, had to be rowed only by Athenian citizens strongly suggests the rest of Athens' fleet did not and, therefore, it was not a citizen navy (Thuc. 8.73.5 and 8.74.1; Aeschin.

3.162, Poll. 8.116). Finally, the Spartans challenged Athenian naval hegemony with offers of higher pay to the islanders in the latter stages of the war. Lysander's four obols a day can have had an effect only if the Athenians relied heavily on mercenary oarsmen (Xen. *Hell.* 1.5.7; see 1.5.4, where Lysander makes the point explicitly asking for payment at a drachma a day).

Money in the form of coinage changed the nature of the Athenian fleet. Coinage provided the mechanism of remuneration from which, we can assume, Athenian citizens, metics, oarsmen from within and without the *archē* and even Athenian slave-owners gleaned wealth from the payment of slaves in crews, in much the same way as slave-miners enriched their owners at Laureion or slave-workers did in other industries. In this instance, money made citizens rich at the expense of the labour of others. We have already noted how other naval powers must have utilized non-citizen oarsmen to man their ships. Why would Athens be different? The rest of the allies in the Athenian *archê* provided money alone to support Athenian imperial campaigns. Their men must have served in some capacity on the Athenian ships. This is alluded to in several passages of Thucydides, as we have seen. As we have also seen, at the start of the war Athens' enemies hoped that they might draw non-Athenians away from the fleet with offers of money (Thuc. 1.121). Thus, Pericles allayed fears that the Spartans might appropriate the funds of the Delphic sanctuary also to attract the *xenoi* who served in the Athenian fleet into their service. Non-citizen-Athenian manpower played a significant role in the Athenian navy even in 432/1 BC.

Athenian imperial decrees and Thucydides illustrate clearly the central place of coinage in Athenian naval warfare. The mid-420s BC see increased tribute amounts and key decrees enforcing payment in Athenian coins. One of the means by which island communities secured such coinage could well have been in the military service for the Athenians. Island oarsmen received Athenian coins that returned to Athens as tribute in a neat economic cycle. After 412 BC, the Spartans through Persian funds manned their fleets eventually with offers of more pay than Athenian employers to the islanders of the Aegean.

The Athenian navy – and indeed naval warfare more generally – became increasingly mercenary in the latter third of the fifth century. The Athenian *archē* was also increasingly an economic empire concerned as much with coined money and its control and circulation as with political control of the Aegean. A case in point is the introduction of the *eikostē* of 413 BC, whereby goods were taxed at one-twentieth of their value as they entered the Athenian sphere (Thuc. 7.27.4).[39] This brought non-Athenian allies and non-tribute payers engaged in commerce within the *archē* into the Athenian economic world. Perhaps it became a mechanism to bring resources back into the empire that had flowed out of it and illustrates Athenian awareness of this phenomenon. The empire constantly pursued money, which played an ever-increasing role as an intermediary between the state and the fleet, and which is further reflected in the fleet's increasingly mercenary nature. Thus, the money of empire had produced a mercenary navy.

Aristophanic comedies of the 420s BC often highlight the role of money as a means to remunerate citizens for explicitly political rather than military service. It is possible to conclude that a main objective for Athenians during the Peloponnesian War was civic sinecure, rather than military risk. Three examples from Aristophanes illuminate this situation. The first comes from *Wasps* (1114–21). Cleon-Hater points to those Athenians whose goal was jury-service, feeding of the fruits of tribute, rather than doing their military service. The second from *Knights* (1350–4) shows that pay for jury service trumped military concerns for assembly goers; assembly-men would vote for their own pay ahead of building ships for war, as the Sausage-Seller says. And finally also from *Knights* (794–800) is a passage that perhaps requires a little more explanation to show that jury service was the goal of military expeditions and imperial control. The speaker in this passage states that Demos will one day sit in judgment in Arcadia at five obols a day. Until that time, Demos will receive three obols a day as his reward. Arcadians were ubiquitous mercenaries by the 420s BC.[40] This passage clearly shows the juxtaposition of the mercenary Arcadians who took wages for their military service versus the litigious jury-serving Athenians who seek political pay and avoid military service – and of course five obols a day for political or military service was an decent sum at that time.

In conclusion, Athenians served on Athenian ships in the early years of the empire, but in time the Athenian navy became increasingly mercenary, as metics, islanders and even slaves filled the benches of oarsmen within the Athenian fleet. Coinage fuelled this process creating the conditions not only for a professional navy, but also one that became increasingly less Athenian. For their part, Athenian citizens gleaned many of the benefits of coinage circulation in political service or even the exploitation of slaves in military service. An ironic spin-off of this conclusion, however, is that as Athens became more radically democratic its navy became less Athenian. The connection, therefore, between democracy and naval warfare looks tenuous at best.

Notes

1. I would like to thank the audience at the Australasian Society of Classical Studies in Adelaide 2015 where I presented this discussion for their questions, David Rosenbloom of the University of Maryland for many fruitful discussions on the topic of the Athenian navy and empire and Arthur Pomeroy of Victoria University of Wellington, for all his help and advice with this paper as well as Roel Konijnendijk for all his help and advice. All errors are, naturally, my own.
2. Thus, Sargent 1927. See also more recently Amit 1965, 33; Casson 1966, 35–44; Morrison, Coates and Rankov 2000, 117–18 who argue for the exceptional nature of the use of slaves as oarsmen.
3. See for example, Böckh 1817, 329; Bury 1951, 332. For metics in the navy especially see Clerc 1893, 71; Cloche 1934, 312. For various other positions on the integration of foreigners and slaves into the Athenian fleet, see Glotz 1931, 358; Kolbe 1899; Marsh 1943, 30; Romilly 1947, 69; de Ste. Croix 1954; Jordan 1972, 153–81.
4. For slaves at sea generally, see Hunt 1998, 83–101. For support of the non-Athenian presence amongst oarsmen, including slaves, see Graham 1992; 1998; Jordan 2000; Krentz 2007, 150; Van Wees 2004, 210–12; 2007, 295–8. For helots as oarsmen in the small Spartan fleet, see Bertosa 2005.

5. Hale 2009. In addition, excellent earlier but still recent textbooks do not equivocally address issues like this question in its specifics and so it has remained largely unscrutinized. For example, Rhodes 2006, 38, 153, 163, 384; Finley 2008, 33.
6. On the date of the Battle of Eurymedon, see Gomme 1950, 394–6; Meritt, Wade-Gery and McGregor 1939–53, 3.175–9; *CAH*^{2} 5.506–11; for an overview, see Rhodes 2006.
7. For good introductory discussions, see Van Wees 2007, 273–81 and (for navies) 295–8.
8. The date of the Old Oligarch remains disputed, but most likely the latter part of the fifth century BC. For a good brief introductory discussion, see Rhodes 2006, 116–17.
9. Van Wees 2010 and more recently 2013a. Important discussions have long suggested *chrēmata* here does not reflect 'wages', coinage or a transformation in practice, on which for example see Cairns 1984.
10. Gabrielsen 1994, especially 81–4, 186–91, 211–12.
11. Van Wees 2010, especially 224.
12. Gabrielsen 1994, 19–26; 1985; Haas 1985. See Androtion *FGrH* 324 F 4 for *theoroi* paid from naukleric silver. See also Rhodes 1993a, 151–3. Rhodes refers to Solon's overseas campaigns as requiring some financial duties, and he offers some support for Cleidemus.
13. Van Wees 2013a, 44–58.
14. See Meiggs and Lewis 1969, 2, 23. For discussion and the Greek text, see Jameson 1960.
15. For the league's organization, see Rhodes 2006, 14–21; for more detailed discussions, see Meritt, Wade-Gery and McGregor 1939–53; Meiggs 1972; Rhodes 1993b. For contrary discussions, see also Larsen 1940; Hammond 1967.
16. Blackman 1969.
17. See Rhodes 2006, 176.
18. Herodotus (8.1) states the Aeginetans had eighteen ships at Artemisium, and (8.46) thirty at Salamis as well as others at Aegina.
19. For full discussions, see Hansen 2006a; Kirsten 1964; Beloch 1886, 123, where the figure of 80,000 is arrived at through addition; Figueira 1981, 22–64. For further discussion of demography with examples, see Hansen 2006b.
20. Bertosa 2005.
21. On the connection of the specialists (*hyperesiai*) with Athenians, see especially Jordan 1972, 240–1; note Aristophanes, *Knights* 542–4 as evidence of an apprenticeship on board ships, but also note that Jordan 2000 argued that *hyperesia* were the lower-bank oarsmen and often slaves.
22. On payment generally, see Pritchett 1971, 3–30 for ancient references; Trundle 2004, 80–103, and especially 92–8; Loomis 1998, especially 33–9; Trundle 2010a.
23. On the veracity of this 'fact', see Meiggs 1972, 427.
24. For good discussions of the role of coinage in the Athenian empire, see Samons 2000; Blamire 2001; Kallet-Marx 1993; Kallet 2001; Mattingly 1968; Meiggs 1972; Meritt, Wade-Gery and McGregor 1939–1953; Samons 1993; Trundle 2010a.
25. Cleonymus (Meiggs and Lewis 1988, 68 = *IG* 1^3 34) in 426/5 BC, Kleinias (Meiggs and Lewis 45 = *IG* 1^3 34 = Fornara 98 in 425/4 BC) and a decree requiring the allies to use Athenian weights and measures and silver coins (Meiggs and Lewis 45 = *IG* 1^3 1453). See Blamire 2001, especially 111.
26. Thus, Blackman 1969, 185 states that Athenian control of ships enabled the provision of ships to allies who needed them. Blackman thinks changes to the *phoros* (from ship provision to

tribute) occurred after the Battle of Eurymedon. To him Cimon was significant in this process, though he also suggests an alternative later date of perhaps 454 BC if not the great battle's aftermath.

27. See Blackman 1969, 187–9.

28. Thus, Blackman 1969, 194, citing Andocides 3.38 who states 'that such states as possessed no ships should be supplied with them by us (i.e. the Athenians)'.

29. Blackman 1969, 196–9 for captured ships; 199–202 for surrendered ships; and 212 for the total of 400 ships in 430 BC.

30. Sargent 1927, 279 for 'freedom'; 277 for Arginusae. For references, see Ar. *Ran.* 718–37 and 1446–58; discussion Jordan 2000; 2003.

31. Amit 1965, 29–49.

32. Wallinga 1993, 181: Ar. *Ach.* 162, ὁ θρανίτης λεὼς (the people of the thranite oar). Thranitai were better paid because they were the best rowers and lead the stroke and as argued here because they were predominantly Athenians.

33. For good general overview of the episode, see Rhodes 2006, 160–5; see also Hignett 1952, ch. 10 and appendix 12; Taylor 2002; de Ste. Croix 1956b; Rhodes 1972b.

34. Thus, Jordan 1972, 220, argues that the demands of the Great Peloponnesian War made the Athenians use non-Athenian citizens.

35. Amit (n.2) 46 thinks the 3,000–4,000 men killed at Aegospotamoi represent the specialist crewmen (*hyperesiai*) and marines (*epibatai*) and therefore about 10–12 per cent of the men needed to crew each of the ships taken.

36. For discussion of *IG* 1[3] 1032, see Graham 1992; 1998. Masters and slaves rowed together as crewmen on the same ship and slaves definitely crewed too. Officers, citizens, foreigners and slaves are all listed on the inscription. A man named Euphronius, a metic, rowed alongside his slave Euphron on the same ship. Archedemus of Peparethus, thus a foreigner, also rowed with Timagenes his slave.

37. For the best discussions of the relevant material, see Lambert 2000, 157–60; Pakkanen 2006; Randall, Jr. 1953. Of 107 identified workers, only twenty-four are citizens, 39 per cent are metics and 19 per cent slaves.

38. For discussion of this problem, see Morrison, Coates and Rankov 2000, 33–6; Van Wees 2004, 206–31; Wallinga 1993.

39. For discussion, see Kallet 2001, 197–205. On the *eikostê*, see also Kallet 1999; Meritt, Wade-Gery and McGregor 1939–53, 158.

40. On Arcadia as a source of mercenary service, see Parke 1933; Griffith 1935, 237–8; Fields 2001; Roy 1999; Trundle 2004, especially 52–4.

CHAPTER 8

WOMEN ATTACHED TO ARMIES IN CLASSICAL GREECE: ECONOMIC COMMODITIES OR BURDEN?

Jennifer Martinez Morales[1]

How do ancient historians tackle the idea of gender in ancient military history? This is a question that a colleague asked me once, and I answered with the usual scholarly response that the main approach to women in ancient Greek warfare is to study them as active agents who engage in defensive behaviour, who go beyond their feminine roles established by society, and as the victims of war. But it is not so much a question of gender, but of recognizing that women are part of the social and economic realities of ancient Greek military history. If we accept that the ramifications of conflict make no gendered distinction, then we also must accept (although not in a straightforward manner) that the history of war makes no distinctions of gender. War happens to both men and women, and both men and women make war happen.

When it comes to economic value, we often think about fixed prices and specific amounts. But in a world where cash is not the main source of exchange, 'economic value' can take different forms in different contexts. In this case, I am interested in exploring how to measure women's economic value in the context of war. As we will see, the value of women is much more flexible than previously thought and depends on the military context (often shifting in the same war). Women could have entertainment value, for instance. But this does not exclude the possibility that at some point they could also have an economic value of a fixed price when sold. As Moses Finley once said: 'we have . . . to seek different concepts and different models, appropriate to the ancient economy, not to ours.'[2] Modern studies, like the comprehensive work of William Kendrick Pritchett, tend to prefer the explicit (but by no means simple) definition of economy in war. Until now, theoretical scholarship has focused on the traditional costs of warfare. For example, there is excellent research on the food supply of soldiers, the devastation of the rural economy, the distribution of arms and armour, military pay and looted property.[3] The reality is, however, that women do not fit easily into this picture.

In order to push debates forward, I will focus on two aspects of the economic realities of ancient Greek warfare: that is, the economic ramifications of having women in armies and military fortifications, and the economic ramifications of having women as war captives. This chapter investigates whether women attached to soldiers and armies in the Classical period were a hindrance to expeditions, valuable economic property, or a combination of both. It ultimately concludes that they were indeed both assets and burdens. This might seem almost too obvious to be worth concluding but it is nevertheless where the fragmentary evidence leads us. It aims to move us away from the idea that women in ancient warfare were static agents or persons whose lives revolved around some imaginary boundary beyond the confines of war. The definition used here is intrinsically related to economic assets – that of soldiers investing money, time and resources in women and obtaining benefits from this. Meanwhile the definition for economic burden is that which takes more from soldiers or hinders more an expedition than it gives back. In other words, an 'economic burden' is where there is an unequal exchange of resources (whatever these resources may be). In this chapter, I argue (i) that the economic implications of having women in armies and garrisons need to be analysed in each military context as this will invariably differ in each, (ii) that there is not one overarching economic model we can apply to women in the context of war, and (iii) that because of this we need to approach the evidence with a flexible economic framework. This is no easy task given that the evidence is fragmentary and it will hardly ever allow us to obtain answers to the types of questions we ask from it. But we can at least try.

Perhaps the best example that illustrates this complexity is the criticism of the Athenian general Chares. Theopompus (BNJ 115 F 213, trans. Morrison 2015) reports that:

> Χάρητός τε νωθροῦ τε ὄντος καὶ βραδέος, καίτοι γε καὶ πρὸς τρυφὴν ἤδη ζῶντος· ὅς γε περιήγετο στρατευόμενος αὐλητρίδας καὶ ψαλτρίας καὶ πεζὰς ἑταίρας, καὶ τῶν χρημάτων τῶν εἰσφερομένων εἰς τὸν πόλεμον τὰ μὲν εἰς ταύτην τὴν ὕβριν ἀνήλισκε, τὰ δ᾽ αὐτοῦ κατέλειπεν ᾽Αθήνησιν τοῖς τε λέγουσιν καὶ τὰ ψηφίσματα γράφουσιν καὶ τῶν ἰδιωτῶν τοῖς δικαζομένοις . . .
>
> Chares was both slothful and slow; moreover, he also lived for luxury. When he went on campaign, he brought around flute girls, harp girls, and common prostitutes. Also, from the monies brought for the conduct of war he spent some on this wantonness, the rest of it he left behind in Athens for those proposing and writing legislation and for those pleading cases for his private matters . . .

This example highlights how little evidence we have and how much we can glean from gems like this. This is a unique fragment in the whole Greek corpus. This passage is explicit about the presence of women in campaigns and it gives us an insight into the sort of soldier that could afford to bring women in their personal service (whether instead of or in addition to male personal attendants in another matter for future discussion). Additionally, no other source addresses women abroad from an economic perspective. This is part of the *topoi* of the fourth century BC, when generals were criticized for over-expenditure. But Theopompus' fragment makes it clear that women abroad in military expeditions were seen as a luxury. It is not every woman that is considered a luxury, however. Theopompus is much more specific than other sources on the types of women that are considered a luxury. Flute girls (αὐλητρίδας), harp girls (ψαλτρίας) and common companions (πεζὰς ἑταίρας) are all mentioned in this passage.[4] When our sources are not speaking of female captives, these are the types of women we should imagine accompanied armies abroad during the Classical period.[5] Women followed Greek armies in the service of soldiers and not only as captives of war. Theopompus is engaging in some very harsh criticism. The main problem is that money intended for war was being misused – and in a hubristic manner.

The narratives that mention women abroad with armies are those of Cyrus' mercenary army in Xenophon's *Anabasis* and Alexander's campaigns in Asia in the Alexander historians. Concerning the *Anabasis*, John Lee has argued that 'the Cyreans carried some things because they had to, and other things because they wanted to'.[6] Lee is referring to the equipment and essentials of the men, but women are part of this as well; the task is to discern whether they belong to the former or the latter of Lee's statement.[7] In a world where necessity and security are closely intertwined, sometimes it is very difficult to distinguish between the two. In what context would the ancient Greeks need women in expeditions? And at what point do women become a 'need' in a military context?

For the ancient Greeks, women are not needed in military expeditions in the sense that they are not required to be present (they are certainly not there to fight). The general consensus among scholars is that women are present on expeditions abroad for entertainment and sex.[8] If women are not required to be abroad, then we must explain their presence in these military contexts. Female captives of war, being acquired along the route of an army, are one of the most prominent groups of women who appear in our texts. Other women followed the expedition of the Cyreans not as captives, but as *hetairai* and entertainers (whether willingly is another matter).[9] Female companions (*hetairai*) are mentioned on several occasions in Xenophon's *Anabasis* – with Xenophon himself stating at one point that 'there were many *hetairai* in the army' (πολλαὶ γὰρ ἦσαν ἑταῖραι ἐν τῷ στρατεύματι) (Xen. *An.* 4.3.19). During the crossing of the Centrites River, for example, we hear how some soldiers ignored military orders to stay at their posts and went instead to look after their animals, baggage or women (Xen. *An.* 4.3.30):

> οἱ δὲ Καρδοῦχοι ὁρῶντες ὀλίγους ἤδη τοὺς λοιπούς (πολλοὶ γὰρ καὶ τῶν μένειν τεταγμένων ᾤχοντο ἐπιμελόμενοι οἱ μὲν ὑποζυγίων, οἱ δὲ σκευῶν, οἱ δ᾽ ἑταιρῶν), ἐνταῦθα δὴ ἐπέκειντο θρασέως καὶ ἤρχοντο σφενδονᾶν καὶ τοξεύειν.

> Now the Carduchians, seeing that those who were left were by this time few in number (for many even of those detailed to stay had gone off to look after pack animals or baggage or women, as the case might be), at that moment proceeded to press upon them boldly and began to sling stones and shoot arrows.

Lee argues that here we see initial signals of the start of a so-called 'new relationship' between the soldiers and the captive women.[10] 'The scrutiny in Carduchia, however', Lee claims, 'marked the start of a new relationship between the troops and their women; no longer simply captives, the women now became companions attached to individual soldiers'.[11] The use of the word '*hetairai*', however, suggests that these are not captive women but rather the female companions that the soldiers brought with them from the outset of the expedition. The terminology associated with this word is very complex.[12] But we should not see the actions of the soldiers in light of social and emotional values

– since this is something we can never know. These women are not captives turned *hetairai* in the abstract sense of the word. These women have always been *hetairai* and they are described by Xenophon as such.[13] It is safest to interpret the soldiers' refusal to obey orders in light of economic preoccupations.[14] From this point of view, it is far more likely that they broke rank to check on their property; the dangerous crossing makes this even more likely. The women have now indeed 'become valued members of the Cyrean community', as Lee argues.[15] But not because the soldiers cared for them emotionally, but because the nature of their value was very different. Both captive women and female companions (*hetairai*) were valued members of the Cyrean community not for their companionship but for their economic potential.

The women are mentioned after pack animals and baggage, both of which are considered property in any expedition. These *hetairai* are clear burdens during the crossing, or, at least, Xenophon portrays them as such. A protective manoeuvre even had to be implemented: Cheirisophus at the front, the baggage and camp followers in the middle, and Xenophon at the rear. The women also act as a distraction to the soldiers who are far more concerned with their property than with fighting. At other times, however, these women are part of the community at large, and cease to be a burden during the expedition. When the Greeks held games at Trapezus, we are told that the men were eager to show off because their spectators were watching them compete (Xen. *An.* 4.8.27):

> ἠγωνίζοντο δὲ παῖδες μὲν στάδιον τῶν αἰχμαλώτων οἱ πλεῖστοι, δόλιχον δὲ Κρῆτες πλείους ἢ ἑξήκοντα ἔθεον, πάλην δὲ καὶ πυγμὴν καὶ παγκράτιον ἕτεροι, καὶ καλὴ θέα ἐγένετο: πολλοὶ γὰρ κατέβησαν καὶ ἅτε θεωμένων τῶν ἑταίρων πολλὴ φιλονικία ἐγίγνετο.
>
> The events were, a stadium race for boys, most of them belonging to the captives (τῶν αἰχμαλώτων), a long race, in which more than sixty Cretans took part, wrestling, boxing, and the pancratium; and it made a fine spectacle; for there were a great many entries and, inasmuch as the companions of the contestants (τῶν ἑταίρων) were looking on, there was a great deal of rivalry.

The women are no longer burdensome because the men are at ease in a friendly city, or their burdensomeness is not what is at issue at this particular moment. The τῶν ἑταίρων spectating the competitions can refer to the men as well whose competitive spirit can be found throughout the *Anabasis* and Xenophon's work generally. This plural genitive can be either masculine or feminine, and the context ('many came down to watch') can also suggest that the competitors are inspired by the audience of their male comrades.

The most explicit example of women being burdens to an army is that of the ban on women reportedly introduced by Philip II of Macedon (Ath. 13.557b–e):

> Φίλιππος δ' ὁ Μακεδὼν οὐκ ἐπήγετο μὲν εἰς τοὺς πολέμους γυναῖκας, ὥσπερ Δαρεῖος ὁ ὑπ' Ἀλεξάνδρου καταλυθείς, ὃς περὶ τῶν ὅλων πολεμῶν τριακοσίας

> ἑξήκοντα περιήγετο παλλακάς, ὡς ἱστορεῖ Δικαίαρχος ἐν τρίτῳ Περὶ τοῦ τῆς Ἑλλάδος Βίου· . . .
>
> Philip of Macedon did not take women with him on campaign, as the Darius overthrown by Alexander did; even though he was fighting a war that involved control of his entire kingdom, Darius took 360 concubines along with him, according to Dicaearchus in Book III of *On the Greek Lifestyle*. . .

This is a much-debated passage in modern scholarship, mainly because it details Philip's practices regarding wartime marriage alliances for political advantage.[16] The passage is introduced merely because Satyrus, in his Life of Philip II, goes on to list the marriages of Philip to different women of diverse regions (e.g. Audata, Olympias and Meda, among others). According to Athenaeus, Philip 'did not lead women into war' (Φίλιππος δ' ὁ Μακεδὼν οὐκ ἐπήγετο μὲν εἰς τοὺς πολέμους γυναῖκας). We can only speculate on the reason behind this measure. But it may not be far-fetched to argue that by introducing this measure, Philip simply wanted his soldiers to carry the essential belongings on campaigns. Alternatively, he may have wanted to minimize the amount of unnecessary people accompanying the Macedonian army on campaign. Donald Engels argues that this was a measure introduced as part of the modifications that Philip made to the Macedonian army.[17] Whatever the reason for this, it seems that women are considered here by Philip as a burden and as a group which was not immediately necessary for expeditions abroad. The fact that this measure was even reported suggests that it was indeed common for armies to have women with them on expeditions abroad.

When women became too much of a burden abroad, measures were taken by commanders and generals to alleviate this liability in a way that would benefit the whole army. When Cyrus' army realized that Cheirisophus had not returned with the ships he promised he would bring back to the Euxine, they loaded women on board the small number of ships they had, which were not sufficient to transport the whole army back home (Xen. *An*. 5.3.1):

> ἐπεὶ δὲ οὔτε Χειρίσοφος ἧκεν οὔτε πλοῖα ἱκανὰ ἦν οὔτε τὰ ἐπιτήδεια ἦν λαμβάνειν ἔτι, ἐδόκει ἀπιτέον εἶναι. καὶ εἰς μὲν τὰ πλοῖα τούς τε ἀσθενοῦντας ἐνεβίβασαν καὶ τοὺς ὑπὲρ τετταράκοντα ἔτη καὶ παῖδας καὶ γυναῖκας καὶ τῶν σκευῶν ὅσα μὴ ἀνάγκη ἦν ἔχειν. καὶ Φιλήσιον καὶ Σοφαίνετον τοὺς πρεσβυτάτους τῶν στρατηγῶν εἰσβιβάσαντες τούτων ἐκέλευον ἐπιμελεῖσθαι: οἱ δὲ ἄλλοι ἐπορεύοντο: ἡ δὲ ὁδὸς ὡδοποιημένη ἦν.
>
> And now, seeing that Cheirisophus was not returned that they had not an adequate number of ships, and that it was no longer possible to get provisions, they resolved to depart by land. On board the ships they embarked the sick, those who were more than forty years of age, the women and children, and all the baggage which they did not need to keep with them. They put aboard also Philesius and Sophaenetus, the eldest of the generals, and bade them take charge of the enterprise.

Women are included here amongst the sick, those over forty years of age, children and 'all the baggage which they did not need to keep with them'. Xenophon's words acknowledge the fact that women were not necessary individuals in this type of expedition (much like the children and the aged). The word 'ἀνάγκη' literally means force, constraint or necessity. Earlier in the expedition the generals stationed themselves in a narrow pass (where every soldier needed to pass) in order to take away any items that they did not discard on previous orders. Some soldiers, however, still smuggled women past this checkpoint (Xen. *An.* 4.1.13–14):

> σχολαίαν γὰρ ἐποίουν τὴν πορείαν πολλὰ ὄντα τὰ ὑποζύγια καὶ τὰ αἰχμάλωτα, πολλοὶ δὲ οἱ ἐπὶ τούτοις ὄντες ἀπόμαχοι ἦσαν, διπλάσιά τε ἐπιτήδεια ἔδει πορίζεσθαι καὶ φέρεσθαι πολλῶν τῶν ἀνθρώπων ὄντων. δόξαν δὲ ταῦτα ἐκήρυξαν οὕτω ποιεῖν. ἐπεὶ δὲ ἀριστήσαντες ἐπορεύοντο, ὑποστήσαντες ἐν τῷ στενῷ οἱ στρατηγοί, εἴ τι εὑρίσκοιεν τῶν εἰρημένων μὴ ἀφειμένον, ἀφῃροῦντο, οἱ δ᾽ ἐπείθοντο, πλὴν εἴ τις ἔκλεψεν, οἷον ἢ παιδὸς ἐπιθυμήσας ἢ γυναικὸς τῶν εὐπρεπῶν.
>
> For the baggage animals and the captives, numerous as they were, made the march slow, and the large number of men who had charge of them were thus taken out of the fighting line; besides, with so many people to feed it was necessary to procure and to carry twice the amount of provisions. This decision once reached, they published the order to carry it into effect. When they had breakfasted and were setting out upon the march, the generals quietly stationed men in the defile and proceeded to take away from the troops such of the things specified as had not been given up if they found any; and the soldiers submitted, except in cases where a man had smuggled through a handsome boy or woman, for example, that he had set his heart upon.

Xenophon clearly states the reasons why the generals decided to take away unnecessary belongings at this point in the march. Two types of property are mentioned: baggage animals and captives. Again, just like the *hetairai* above, the captives here are mentioned alongside baggage animals – another type of property during the march. The women are among the captives mentioned. First, there was a preoccupation with numbers. There were too many animals and captives. Second, because of their large numbers, the march went too slowly and the men who were guarding them could not fight. Third, there was a preoccupation with supplies. The fact that the men had to find and carry double the food during the march proved too burdensome. These are the three main logistical reasons (as reported by Xenophon) why the generals decided to take away some of the property of the soldiers.

It is interesting to note that the property that some soldiers smuggled through this checkpoint was human property and not baggage animals. This tells us what these soldiers considered important or relevant at this moment in the expedition, which gives us an indication of the value the soldiers placed on both human and animal property and how they measured it against each other. In this case, Xenophon states that the soldiers 'desired' a handsome boy or woman. Consequently, the value of these individuals is superficial and physical, not economic.[18]

Why would the soldiers spend time, energy and food, and incur possible reprimands from their superiors, by smuggling these women and boys? On women that are clearly not essential in war? And in a territory that was unfamiliar and dangerous? One way of looking at this material is that women were considered a luxury in military expeditions abroad. If we remember the Theopompus fragment discussed above, we can see that the excessive expenditure was on women (Theopompus, BNJ 115 F 213).[19]

Besides the women's obvious sexual purpose, some of the women accompanying Cyrus' expedition are clearly the property of soldiers, and as such, they have an economic value. When the Cyreans entertained the Paphlagonian ambassadors, Xenophon tells us that an Arcadian was persuaded to bring a dancing girl (ὀρχηστρίς) he owned to join the festivities (Xen. *An.* 6.1.12–13):

> ἐπὶ τούτοις ὁρῶν ὁ Μυσὸς ἐκπεπληγμένους αὐτούς, πείσας τῶν Ἀρκάδων τινὰ πεπαμένον ὀρχηστρίδα εἰσάγει σκευάσας ὡς ἐδύνατο κάλλιστα καὶ ἀσπίδα δοὺς κούφην αὐτῇ. ἡ δὲ ὠρχήσατο πυρρίχην ἐλαφρῶς. ἐνταῦθα κρότος ἦν πολύς, καὶ οἱ Παφλαγόνες ἤροντο εἰ καὶ γυναῖκες συνεμάχοντο αὐτοῖς. οἱ δ' ἔλεγον ὅτι αὗται καὶ αἱ τρεψάμεναι εἶεν βασιλέα ἐκ τοῦ στρατοπέδου.

> Thereupon the Mysian, seeing how astounded they were, persuaded one of the Arcadians who had a dancing girl to let him bring her in, after dressing her up in the finest way he could and giving her a light shield. And she danced the Pyrrhic with grace. Then there was great applause, and the Paphlagonians asked whether women also fought by their side. And the Greeks replied that these women were precisely the ones who put the King to flight from his camp.

This is the first and only time we hear of a dancing girl with the army. This girl endured the same tribulations of the journey as the men, and her only purpose (as far as we know) is to entertain the soldiers. Her skills might give an indication of her high value and may provide an explanation as to why she was worth keeping during the march: (i) she knew the pyrrhic dance and was able to perform a grand spectacle, and (ii) the fact that a soldier had prior knowledge of another soldier's dancing girl suggests that she has performed in this way previously. Her entertainment value far outweighs the sharing of food portions and the burden she may cause during the march. Although in this scenario she is not earning money for her owner, this dancing girl is a vital investment for entertainment and ultimately, if sold later in a market, for profit. She is not only an economic investment but, indirectly, had a negotiating value as well. The Greeks were entertaining the Paphlagonians and seized the opportunity to win over the baffled ambassadors by using a woman performing under arms.

Thinking about the economic value of a woman brings one to another group of women who have a lot more, if not the most, economic value in ancient Greek warfare.

Female war captives are by far the most overlooked group of individuals in the history of ancient Greek conflict. They rear their heads only in discussions about tragic women, but it is often forgotten that real historical women were horribly affected in the most direct way possible by Greek warfare. Women who were taken during an expedition or after the fall of a city could be ransomed, sold into slavery or, on rare occasions, they could be let go without harm. I analyse here only those women acquired during an expedition abroad; this is because the fragmentary evidence allows for more discussion on this group of women. These women can be found in our sources under the general terms of *aichmalota*, which literally means captive 'taken by the spear', and *andrapoda*, which has been traditionally defined as 'four-footed human' and carries negative connotations.[20] This word, however, has been re-examined recently by Kathy L. Gaca who argues that the mercantile aspect of 'selling into slavery' should not be included in the traditional definition of this word.[21] It is the economic and, to some extent, the mercantile aspect that I am interested in.

Unfortunately, there is no explicit evidence for the exact monetary value of female war captives. We only find references in our written sources about the sale of war captives overall without distinction of gender. The people of Hyccara in Sicily, for example, were sold by Nicias and his Athenian generals in 415 BC for a total of 120 talents (Thuc. 6.62.1–4). There are, however, indirect indications in our written sources that the value of a woman captured in war depended on her previous associations with men, most often her family (including her husband or father).

Every captive taken in war, whether male or female, has a purpose. They could act as hostages, travel guides in foreign territory, or be used for negotiations and leverage, among others. Women, in theory, could be any of these (although interestingly enough we only hear of male guides). Like any other captive, women were captured for different reasons, but the second most frequent one was to offer them back to their friends and family for ransom.[22] The ransoming of female war captives was an economically advantageous activity for the victors. In 391 BC, the Lacedaemonian Diphridas captured and ransomed a Persian satrap's daughter and her husband (Strutha's daughter and her husband Tigranes) (Xen. *Hell.* 4.8.21):

> ὁ μὲν δὴ Διφρίδας ταῦτ᾽ ἐποίει, καὶ τά τ᾽ ἄλλα ἐπετύγχανε καὶ Τιγράνην τὸν τὴν Στρούθα ἔχοντα θυγατέρα πορευόμενον εἰς Σάρδεις λαμβάνει σὺν αὐτῇ τῇ γυναικί, καὶ χρημάτων πολλῶν ἀπέλυσεν: ὥστ᾽ εὐθὺς ἐντεῦθεν εἶχε μισθοδοτεῖν.

> Diphridas accordingly set about these things, and he was successful not only in his other undertakings, but particularly in capturing Tigranes, the husband of Struthas' daughter, and his wife also, as they were journeying to Sardis, and in obtaining a large ransom for their release, so that he was at once able to hire mercenaries with the money thus obtained.

Xenophon tells us that the amount Diphridas obtained for their release was large enough to hire mercenaries. We do not know the specific amount secured for their release, but we know that, as Matthew Trundle says, 'it was not cheap to pay mercenaries'.[23] The fact that Diphridas was in need of funds, and that he resorts to capturing this Persian noble lady, suggests that the capturing and ransoming of women was seen as an economically profitable military activity, especially when the women hailed from wealthy families. It was advantageous for two reasons: it was a large profit and an immediate profit. Another example that illustrates this can be found at the end of Xenophon's *Anabasis* when he captured the Persian Asidates, his wife, children and property (Xen. *An*. 7.8.22).

Once more we are ignorant of the amount Xenophon acquired during this plundering raid, but we can contextualize it by comparing his previous complaints that he was destitute, with his comments after the raid that now he was 'able even to do a kindness to another' (Xen. *An*. 7.8.22). This suggests that Xenophon made sufficient profit from the ransoming or selling of this Persian family and property.

Alexander, in his Asiatic expedition, captured numerous female captives. One of the most significant endeavours – for economic, military, and political reasons – is the capture of Darius' mother, wife and daughters after the battle of Issus in 333 BC (Arr. *Anab*. 2.11.9):

> τό τε στρατόπεδον τὸ Δαρείου εὐθὺς ἐξ ἐφόδου ἑάλω καὶ ἡ μήτηρ καὶ ἡ γυνή, αὐτὴ δὲ καὶ ἀδελφὴ Δαρείου, καὶ υἱὸς Δαρείου νήπιος· καὶ θυγατέρες δύο ἑάλωσαν καὶ ἄλλαι ἀμφ' αὐτὰς Περσῶν τῶν ὁμοτίμων γυναῖκες οὐ πολλαί.
>
> Darius' camp was stormed at once, and captured with his mother, wife, who was also his sister, and his infant son; two daughters were taken too, with a few noble Persian ladies in their suite . . .

Alexander managed to secure not only the Persian royal family, but also several women from other noble families. Elizabeth Carney sees the capture of these women as a 'potent set of symbols for that victory', while Maria Brosius sees them as 'part of the king's public persona during a campaign'.[24] These royal women are also the most economically valuable individuals attached to Alexander's army. In fact, Alexander kept these women for at least three years. Their presence cannot be merely explained in abstracts – Alexander must have realized that he had in his power the most important women of the world he was slowly acquiring. Therefore, they represented a great advantage in terms of leverage. By taking control of these women, he now had the upper hand against Darius.

Diodorus says that when Darius' camp was raided, the Macedonians, unaware of the identity of Darius' family, committed 'many improper acts through ignorance' (πολλὰ δὲ διὰ τὴν ἄγνοιαν ἀπρεπῆ πράττοντας) (Diod. Sic. 17.36.1–4).[25] We can see this as an example of the retrospective remarks so often found in Diodorus. But we can also look at it from the basic assumption that if the soldiers knew who these women were, they would not have behaved in the way that they did. These women were the most politically and economically valuable individuals in the enemy camp, and being part of the royal family, they would be of value either financially or for negotiating leverage at some point later. In fact, Darius was said to have offered 'in return for their three persons . . . thirty thousand talents of gold' (Curt. 4.11.7–8). Anxiety and concern for important female captives is almost always the result of a direct economic preoccupation. Parmenion illustrates this when he advises Alexander to release these women because they were slowing the progress of the march and accept the money that Darius was offering (Curt. 4.11.10–12). Here we see women as burdensome again, yet they are still kept in the army. We also see different points of view within the same army. Whilst Parmenion thought they slowed down the march and it was best to let them go, Alexander still decided to keep them. As far as economic commodities go, these women represented the ultimate ideal scenario for the acquisition of captives in war.

Captive women were often ransomed but they could be traded also for other items considered property in the ancient Greek world. Our earliest evidence for this trading practice appears in Homer's *Iliad* where captives are used as an economic currency to buy wine: '. . .the Achaeans bought their wine, some with bronze, some with iron, some with hides, some with whole heifers, and some again with captives' (ἄλλοι μὲν χαλκῷ, ἄλλοι δ᾽ αἴθωνι σιδήρῳ, ἄλλοι δὲ ῥινοῖς, ἄλλοι δ᾽ αὐτῇσι βόεσσιν, ἄλλοι δ᾽ ἀνδραπόδεσσι) (7.467). Human property taken in war is used in this legendary episode as something to barter and buy with. We also hear of women being given as prizes in competitions (Hom. *Il.* 23.177) and as gifts (Dem. 19.305–9). Although not set in a military context abroad, the story of the fate of the women of Olynthos after Philip's sack of the city in 348/7 BC sheds some light on the economic perspective of female war captives. Demosthenes, in his speech *On the False Embassy*, relates Aeschines' encounter with a man named Atrestidas (a former soldier from Mantinea serving under Philip) who had in his train thirty Olynthian women and child captives (αἰχμάλωτα) who were given to him as a gift from Philip (19.305–6).

We also hear the story concerning young unmarried girls from Pydna who were moved to Olynthos after their father's assassination in the hopes of a safer future. However, after Philip destroyed Olynthus, the girls became captives (αἰχμάλωτοι) 'digging in Philip's vineyard' and were being asked for by Satyrus as a gift from Philip (Dem. 19.193–5, Aeschin. 2.156, Diod. Sic. 16.55.3). Satyrus (a friend of the family) says that the girls will bring him 'no gain' (ἀφ᾽ ἧς ἐγὼ κερδανῶ μὲν οὐδέν) because he will have to provide them with dowries. 'I shall not', says Satyrus, 'permit them to suffer any treatment unworthy of myself or of their father' (καὶ οὐ περιόψομαι παθούσας οὐδὲν ἀνάξιον οὔθ᾽ ἡμῶν οὔτε τοῦ πατρός) (Dem. 19.195). When women were gifted after war, it was usually to make someone else profit. The story of Satyrus also puts in perspective Atrestidas' exceptionally large gift of thirty female captives – these women, we should assume, will be put to work (and not provided with dowries).

Therefore, having female captives in one's army was an economically viable endeavour intended only for profit. If the guarantee existed to sell or ransom these women back to their friends and family, then the soldiers would most likely prefer to hang on to them, even if this meant sharing their food portions, or protecting them through difficult and dangerous terrain. Having women during a military expedition guaranteed some form of profit, whether that is during the ransoming of captives, in the employment of a girl in negotiating parties, or trading her for other items. However, female captives may not be worth retaining in an army on the move when they are too much of a burden, if there is no market to sell them, or when their families have been killed in conflict (for instance, if the males died fighting and there is no one who will ransom them back).

On the logistics of female captives, women appear to be treated and allocated much like any other war captive. The most common pattern we find in our sources is that of the men being killed and the women (often grouped with children) being sold into slavery. They were both allocated to individual soldiers and kept under central control for eventual collective sale or ransoming. The latter was more common in Roman times but there are examples from the Macedonian royal families who could afford such large expenses (e.g. Plut. *Alex.* 7.2). The determining factor of the choice between these options seems to be the specific military context and perhaps the amount of economic reward to be gained from them. Xenophon, for example, explains that when the mercenary army was resting in place, the men were allowed to go out and plunder keeping whatever they obtained "but whenever the entire army set out, if an individual went off by himself and got anything, it was decreed to be public property" (*Anab.* 6.6.2). There is no reason to think that female captives were treated or dealt with any differently from male captives of war.[26] As property of the victors, both faced death, ransom, enslavement and could be treated with violence against their bodies. The evidence points to the harsh reality that the fact they were war captives (and therefore non-free peoples) made them both ideologically and economically the same – a *sōma* to be profited from.

Moving away from expeditions abroad, the economic prospects of women in military garrisons can be briefly addressed.[27] During the siege of Plataea (429–427 BC), Thucydides records 110 women in the military garrison as 'bread-makers' (σιτοποιοί, 2.78.4):

> ...αὐτοὶ δὲ ἐπολιορκοῦντο ἐγκαταλελειμμένοι τετρακόσιοι, Ἀθηναίων δὲ ὀγδοήκοντα, γυναῖκες δὲ δέκα καὶ ἑκατὸν σιτοποιοί. τοσοῦτοι ἦσαν οἱ ξύμπαντες ὅτε ἐς τὴν πολιορκίαν καθίσταντο, καὶ ἄλλος οὐδεὶς ἦν ἐν τῷ τείχει οὔτε δοῦλος οὔτ᾽ ἐλεύθερος. τοιαύτη μὲν ἡ Πλαταιῶν πολιορκία κατεσκευάσθη.
>
> And the men left behind to undergo the siege were only four hundred of their own number and eighty Athenians, besides one hundred and ten women to prepare the food. This was the number all told when the siege began, and there was no one else within the walls, slave or freeman. Such were the conditions under which the siege of the Plataeans was established.

The city had been previously evacuated, the women and children sent to Athens, yet they still chose to keep these female cooks as part of the military arrangements. The status of these women is still debated: some believe that they are slaves, while others argue that they are free and employed for their services as cooks.[28] Since *sitopoioi* could be employed (Thuc. 6.22) and were not by definition slaves but merely of low status, one is inclined to agree with the latter point of view. On the possible logistics for their organization, Jorit Wintjes argues that 'one woman … was assigned to prepare food … for every four men'.[29] One may propose that, from the perspective of an ancient Greek soldier, the women here represent a necessity. Given that they supported the men for two years, they can be seen as an economic investment in the long term. But, at the same time, it is easy to imagine these women being a hindrance due to their large numbers and the relatively small size of this garrison.[30] The presence of women in military fortifications, therefore, can be best understood as an unavoidable detail of ancient life under siege that must be accepted for the particular results of that siege. They are needed, but may perhaps be an economic burden, hence why Nicias is reported to have mentioned them in his speech against the Sicilian expedition: '… [we must take] bakers from the mills compelled to serve for pay in the proper proportion' (καὶ σιτοποιοὺς ἐκ τῶν μυλώνων πρὸς μέρος ἠναγκασμένους ἐμμίσθους: Thuc. 6.22).

We must return to the title of this chapter: are women economic commodities or a burden to military expeditions, armies and garrisons? The ways in which to move forward are to consider the possibility that depending on the military context, women were both economic assets *and* burdens. The economic framework proposed here is that women could shift between these two realities even in the same military expedition. The dancing girl who mesmerized the Paphlagonian ambassadors served both a diplomatic (immediate) and economic (long term) purpose. The flute girls, harp girls and prostitutes on whom Chares spent most of his war money had entertainment value. Female war captives of influential families wielded the most profit. But the women put on board the ships in Xenophon's *Anabasis* and those taken away from the soldiers were considered burdensome, cast off together with the baggage animals, children and the old men. Women are integral to the operation of armies and wartime economies; soldiers could profit from selling female war captives and this sometimes aided in the assembling of mercenary armies and it may have allowed soldiers to trade with others and to obtain supplies abroad. A call for flexibility in terms of how we approach women in military history is therefore put forward here.

Notes

1. I would like to express my sincere gratitude to the organizers of the conference from which this paper is derived and to the editors of this volume. Translations are from the Loeb Classical Library unless otherwise stated.
2. Finley 1973, 27.
3. See, for example, Hammond 1983; Thorne 2001; Pritchard 2012; for discussion see Konijnendijk and Osborne, this volume.
4. The phrase πεζὰς ἑταίρας deserves future examination, as it is mentioned only once in the whole Greek corpus. The phrase, I suggest, possibly refers to female followers of armies who (going by land or walking, literally 'on foot' (πεζός)) provided services to soldiers.
5. See also Plut. *Lys.* 15.4 and Xen. *Hell.* 2.2.23.

6. Lee 2007, 109.
7. Not that these are all of the options or that women are mere objects to be 'carried' by male mercenaries, but that because of the nature of their status, as 'non-freeborn' women, this gave these women no choice or voice as to whether they would be with the soldiers or not. Some argue that there could have been women that followed the army voluntarily (prostitutes in search of profit, for example), but if indeed these women existed, I gather that they would have been the minority and not the majority of women with the Cyrean army. On this romanticized view, see Kapparis 2017, 150 and n.9 below.
8. Cooking is one gender-specific activity in the ancient Greek household, but there is evidence to suggest that the men in military expeditions abroad could (and did) cook for themselves. See, for instance, Xen. *Cyr.* 6.2.31 where the men are expected to prepare their own food. When we do find women cooking for soldiers, it is always in the context of military garrisons in a city (e.g. Thuc. 2.78). The ordinary soldiers abroad would not have the luxury of having female cooks to bake and prepare their bread and daily rations. We do have evidence that, in the ancient Greek imagination, cooks in military contexts were not by definition all female (see Xen. *Cyr.* 2.2.2 for an example of a male cook). See Dalby 1992, 29 who argues in favour of soldiers cooking for themselves.
9. See Kapparis 2017, 150 for instance, who assumes that *hetairai* followed armies willingly: 'the slow moving campaigns of Cyrus against the Great King, or that of Alexander into the heartlands of Persia, might act like a magnet for *hetairai* willing to follow around their lovers, undoubtedly with a view to significant profit.' This romanticized and problematic view towards female followers of armies in the Classical period needs reassessing, but it is beyond the scope of the present chapter. On this matter, it is enough to say at present that not all women who followed armies did so willingly. Furthermore, those who would profit in this context would almost always be the soldiers themselves.
10. Lee 2004; 2007. The word *hetairai* is consistently used by Xenophon for female followers, while *andrapoda* and its related verb forms is frequently used for captives, including women.
11. Lee 2007, 270. This is because, according to Lee, 'The captives . . . realized that their captors had saved them from death at Carduchian hands' (2007, 270).
12. The word *hetaira* (female companion) needs dissecting as it covers a broad variety of sex workers. Henry 2012 defines it as 'an Attic euphemism for those women, slave, freed, or foreign, who were paid for sexual favours'. However simple and neutral this definition might seem, it has to be acknowledged that 'payment' for sexual favours was not always straightforward. *Hetairai* could receive payment in the form of gifts and gift exchanges. There is a long-standing debate in scholarship about the meaning and definition of the terminology associated to prostitution in ancient Greece. James Davidson (1997, 74–7) argues that the state of the discipline is without consensus because most scholars tend to group ancient women into what he calls the 'two-types model' of 'Wives and the Rest'. Davidson's call for diversity in the lives of different types of prostitutes and courtesans is very much welcome. There are different words for prostitutes in ancient Greece ranging from *hetaira* to *pornē*. The former has always been associated with a high-status prostitute whilst the latter has more 'street' and 'brothel' connotations. But McClure (2006, 7) rightly argues that a 'clear status distinction [between the words *hetaira* and *pornē*] . . . is not always evident'. Kapparis 2011 is the most comprehensive investigation into the vocabulary of prostitution in the ancient Greek world, while Futo Kennedy 2015 is now the most recent study on the social implications of the term *hetaira*.
13. See Kapparis 2017, 147, who understands these women as prostitutes following in the baggage train of this mercenary army.

14. Not that we should dismiss all other explanations; emotional attachments might be a possibility, however remote, especially when the value placed on attractive features is both physical and economic in the ancient world, but the realities of warfare indicate that when it comes to property, the economic aspect it is almost always at the forefront, especially in the case of mercenary armies. See Trundle 2004.
15. Lee 2007, 272.
16. Carney 2000, 52–76.
17. Engels 1978, 12–13.
18. Or at least that is how Xenophon portrays it – perhaps this was the only reasonable explanation Xenophon could think of regarding why the soldiers would ignore orders from their superiors.
19. None of our sources are more explicit on female followers of armies being a luxury than this. The word 'τρυφή' is used to describe Chares' economic extravagance. Robert J. Gorman and Vanessa B. Gorman (2014, 2) argue that the word has negative connotations: 'Its negative valorization is a matter of degree: taken to excess, it can degenerate in one of two contradictory directions. A person may emphasize τρυφή to such an extent that he forgoes military training, and thus becomes soft and unwarlike.' And this is exactly what we see in the case of Chares. He is described as slow and slothful, and as part of this he also 'lived for luxury'. It is perhaps worth noting that the women mentioned by Theopompus also appear in sympotic contexts so here we may have a metaphorical reference to corrupting luxury. See, for instance, Goldman 2015.
20. See, for instance, *Apophthegmata Laconica* where a Spartan captive corrected the booty seller who incorrectly said he was an *andrapodon* by saying that he was, in fact, an *aichmalotos*. Plut. *Mor*. 233C, 234C.
21. However problematic Gaca's arguments may be, this is still the most comprehensive study of this term: Gaca 2010, 123–7. More recent discussions appear also in Wrenhaven 2012.
22. The number one reason why women were captured in war was to sell them into slavery.
23. Trundle 2004, 81.
24. Carney 1996, 564 and Brosius 1996, 90.
25. See also Curt. 3.11.21.
26. They would embody the very definition of a common word for slaves – *sōmata*. 'In the Hellenistic Age, but sometimes as early as the fourth century B.C., the word "body" (soma) without any adjective was used to indicate the slave. This was meant to emphasize that a slave was exclusively or mainly a body, rather than a body of a particular kind' (Giuseppe Cambiano, cited in Pritchett 1991, 183–4).
27. Women's contributions to a city's defence continue beyond the Classical period and into the Hellenistic period. Great case studies are examined by Chaniotis (2005a, 109), who presents the example of Kourasio, a wealthy woman who funded the construction of a tower in the second century.
28. For the former, see Gomme 1956, 359; for the latter, see Wintjes 2010, 24.
29. Wintjes 2010, 23–4.
30. Fields 2006, 53.

CHAPTER 9
WARFARE AND MARKETS: SOME THOUGHTS

Edward M. Harris[1]

According to Herodotus (7.147), when Xerxes was at Abydos on the Hellespont, the Persian king saw ships sailing from the Black Sea with cargoes of grain on their way to Aegina and the Peloponnese. His advisors discovered that they were enemy vessels and asked Xerxes for permission to seize them. Xerxes then asked them where the ships were going. They replied that the ships were going to their enemies with a cargo of grain. Xerxes then answered that there was no reason for the Persians to seize the ships. After all, the ships were headed for the same destination as the Persians. Once the Persians arrived at their destination, they would need the grain; why not let these ships transport it there for the benefit of the Persians?

As with many stories in Herodotus, one cannot help but wonder if the tale was invented to portray Xerxes as an arrogant tyrant, who was so confident in his eventual victory that he could pass up an opportunity to harm his enemies by seizing their supplies of grain. The anecdote forms one of a pair about Xerxes' confidence in his victory. In the preceding section, Herodotus recounts how Xerxes ordered three Greek spies who had been caught at Sardis and condemned to death to be released and sent back to Greece so that they could tell their compatriots about the enormous size of the Persian army, which would induce them to surrender without a fight. But as the Italians say, *se non è vero, è ben trovato*. Whatever the historical veracity of the two stories, Xerxes' reply about the grain ships illustrates an important reality about the relationship between trade and ancient armies. Logistics play an important role for modern armies, which must organize supply lines to keep their troops maintained with food, equipment and fuel. During the Second World War, these supply lines might stretch over hundreds if not thousands of miles. The American forces in the Mediterranean and Europe were supplied by ships coming from ports on the east coast of the United States and those in the Pacific were supplied by ships coming from the west coast, especially cities like San Diego, San Francisco and Seattle, as well as by ships coming from Australia. By contrast, ancient armies depended heavily on local markets for their supplies and did not have the resources to transport food over long distances. This general point has been well made by Stephen O'Connor, who shows that the merchants who followed armies did so not to provide food but to acquire booty, which they could then resell at a profit.[2] For instance, when the Athenian expedition to Syracuse sailed from Corcyra to Sicily, they had to purchase supplies at markets in Rhegium and Messina (Thuc. 6.44.2–3, 50.1–2). When Cyrus marched his army from Ionia to the interior, he most often gained supplies at local markets (e.g. Xen. *Hell.* 1.5.6). Armies could not supply their needs with goods transported from home.[3]

I use this anecdote as an introduction to my chapter on warfare and markets. I have recently co-edited a collection of essays entitled *The Ancient Greek Economy: Markets, Households and City-States.* In the introduction to the volume, David Lewis and I show that the role of markets has generally been neglected in scholarship with a few exceptions up to about 2005, and the essays in the volume show first how the Greek city-states built the infrastructure necessary to promote the expansion of markets through legal institutions, by the use of coinage standards and by documentation for property ownership. The main themes of the volume build on an essay I published in 2002 on the specialization of labour and its role in promoting markets and market exchange.[4] I provided evidence for about 170 occupations – David Lewis has now refined this analysis and shown that there is evidence for roughly 276 names for occupations of which about 162 are genuine full-time occupations most of which are non-agricultural.[5] There is no reason to think that Athens was unique; as the late Claude Vial observed, most of the population of Delos was engaged in non-agricultural labour.[6] The rest of the essays show that participation in markets was not confined to the wealthy but extended to all social classes who produced for markets and purchased goods in the market for household consumption. The idea that the Greeks had an ideology of self-sufficiency is a myth based on a misreading by Finley, Austin and Vidal-Naquet of a key passage from Aristotle's *Politics*.[7] Our book is one of several recent books that finally recognize the importance of markets in the ancient economy. There are also the important collections of essays *Tout Vendre, Tout Acheter* edited by Chankowski and Karvonis (2012), *Agoranomes et édiles* edited by Capdetrey and Hasenohr (2012), *Pottery Markets in the Ancient World* edited by Tsigarida and Viviers (2013), *Die griechische Agora* edited by Hoepfner and Lehmann (2007), the book of Acton (2014) on manufacturing in Athens, the study of A. Eich (2006) of the Greek economy, and above all the impressive synthesis of Alain Bresson, now translated into English as *The Making of the Ancient Greek Economy* (2016). In 2016 there was a conference in Nottingham about professions in the ancient world, which among other topics challenged the assumptions of Finley, Millett and others about attitudes toward wage labor in Classical and Hellenistic Greece; a volume containing revised versions of the talks delivered at this conference has now been published.[8] We are in the middle of a sea change in approaches to the economy of Ancient Greece, which makes this volume about war and economy very timely indeed.[9]

This recent progress has moved the field beyond the assumptions (and assumptions is the right word) of what was called the New Orthodoxy in the 1980s and is still to be found repeated in the pages of *The Cambridge Economic History of the Greco-Roman World*, but challenges remain.[10] Some scholars have claimed that perpetual warfare among the Greek city-states inhibited the growth of markets and virtually eliminated the possibilities for economic growth in the Classical and Hellenistic worlds. For these scholars, the best way for states and individuals to gain profits was by booty from conquest and by slave labor. For instance, Paul Millett has asserted that 'exogenous shocks of famine, plague, and war took a heavy toll in the smaller economy of the Greek world'.[11] According to Paul Cartledge, as 'a vehicle for the distribution of goods, trade may have to take its place in the queue behind plunder and gift' and 'force, military force, remained the ideal economic specific, in the fourth (i.e. century BC) as it had been in the fifth'.[12]

The relationship between warfare and markets is a large topic; in this chapter, I would like to consider briefly four main topics and question the assumptions behind these statements of Millett and Cartledge.

The first is the destruction caused by war: how extensive and long-lasting was it?

The second is war and commerce: to what extent did warfare impede the functioning of markets and inhibit the growth of markets?

The third is war and profits for individuals: to what extent did wealthy individuals gain profits from warfare or through agriculture, craft-production and lending and to what extent did city-states and kingdoms gain revenues through booty as opposed to tribute and taxes?

The fourth is the demand for military equipment and supplies: to what extent did this demand promote the growth of markets and inter-regional trade?

1. The destruction caused by war

I start with the destruction caused by war in the ancient world, but preface my remarks with some modern history.[13] During the Second World War, the Allied forces conducted a massive strategic bombing campaign on the industrial areas, railroads, and ports of Germany and Japan. By the end of the war, the productive capacity of both countries had been severely reduced, and large parts of their cities had been completely destroyed. The following figures were produced for a report by Air Marshal Arthur Harris (fortunately no relation of mine) after the end of the war: Berlin 33%, Cologne 61%, Dortmund 54% Dresden 59% Düsseldorf 64%, Essen 50%, Frankfurt 52%, Hamburg 75%, Leipzig 20%, Munich 42%, Bochum 83%, Bremen 60%, Chemnitz 41%, Dessau 61%, Duisburg 48%, Hagen 67%, Hanover 60%, Kassel 69%, Kiel 50%, Mainz 80%, Magdeburg 41%, Mannheim 64%, Nuremberg 51%, Stettin 53%, Stuttgart 46%.[14]

According to Arthur Harris: 'the aim of the Combined Bomber Offensive . . . should be unambiguously stated [as] the destruction of German cities, the killing of German workers, and the disruption of civilized life throughout Germany. (. . .) the destruction of houses, public utilities, transport and lives, the creation of a refugee problem on an unprecedented scale, and the breakdown of morale both at home and at the battle fronts by fear of extended and intensified bombing, are accepted and intended aims of our bombing policy. They are not by-products of attempts to hit factories.' For Japan, I need only mention the names Hiroshima and Nagasaki, but many more cities suffered extensive damage. The bombing of Tokyo in Operation Meetinghouse on the night of 9–10 March 1945 resulted in over 100,000 civilian deaths and made over one million homeless.

Yet as early as the 1950s, the economies of both countries grew rapidly. In Germany, the rates of growth were between 9 per cent and 10 per cent per annum, and Japan enjoyed rates of 10 per cent growth per annum in the 1960s. By 1960, both countries were producing far more than they had before the war. Until it was displaced by China, Japan had the second-largest economy in the world by the 1970s. To take another example, the economy of Soviet Russia was devastated by the Civil War from 1918 to 1921, by the disastrous policies of War Communism, and by the starvation that resulted in large parts of the country. Yet by the late 1920s, grain production under the New Economic Plan (and before the ruinous collectivization drives starting in 1929, which led to the massive famine of 1932–3) almost equalled the levels achieved before the First World War. Now I would not claim that the economies of modern states were similar to those of the *poleis* in the ancient Greek world, but these examples should warn us that we should not assume that the impact of the damage caused by war is always long-term and that human communities cannot recover quickly from widespread devastation.

There can be no doubt that some Greek cities were extensively destroyed in the Classical and Hellenistic periods. One of the most notorious examples was the destruction of Olynthus by Philip II of Macedon in 348 BC (Diod. 16.53; Dem. 9.26; 19.196). Evidence for the siege was found in numerous sling-bullets, including one inscribed with the name of Philip's general Hipponicus.[15] Many of the houses on the site showed traces of intense burning, and the excavations led by Robinson turned up very few valuable objects, which were no doubt looted by the Macedonian soldiers.[16] In general, the site appears to have been abandoned after 348 BC even though some houses in the Northwest quarter were reoccupied after the siege, which reveals that the claim of Demosthenes (9.26) that Olynthus was 'so ruthlessly destroyed that a traveler would find it hard to say whether they (i.e. the cities of the Chalcidice) had even been inhabited' is somewhat exaggerated.[17] There is also good evidence from excavations about the Sullan destruction of parts of Athens in 88 BC, although the damage was mainly confined to the areas around the Kerameikos (see below).[18] In 354 BC Philip II forced the inhabitants of Methone to surrender and to abandon their settlement and move away. Recent excavations at Methone confirm that the site was abandoned in this period and not reoccupied.[19] After its destruction in 146 BC, Corinth appears to have been uninhabited or occupied by only a few settlers until it was refounded as a Roman colony in 44 BC.[20]

In other cases, however, the literary sources may give a misleading impression. For instance, Herodotus (6.19–20) informs us that in 494 the Persians laid siege to Miletus, took the city, killed most of the men, enslaved the women and children and plundered and burnt the shrine at Didyma. Those who were taken prisoner were transported to Susa and settled at Ampe where the River Tigris meets the sea. The land near the city was given to Persians, and the plain was given to Carians from Pedasa. From this account, one would conclude that Miletus ceased to function as a Greek *polis*. Yet a mere fifteen years later, Herodotus (9.104) tells us that there were Milesians ordered by the Persians to guard the passes around Mycale when the Greeks attacked there. They were numerous enough to pose a threat to the Persians, who did not allow them into their camp, and they joined forces with the Greeks after the battle and killed many Persians. As Norbert Ehrhardt has recently pointed out, the Milesians themselves did not see the year 494 and the years immediately following as a hiatus in the history of the city: in the late fourth century the Milesians published a complete list of *stephanephoroi*, their main magistrates, from the year 525/24 to the year 314/13, and there is no gap in the years after 494, indicating that they thought their community continued to function normally in this period.[21] If there had been any major disruption, we would expect to find some indication such as the years of *anarchia* in the Athenian archon list. There is a considerable amount of archaeological evidence for the destruction of Miletus, but rebuilding appears to have started very soon.[22] But the most significant evidence for the economic recovery of Miletus is the fact that the earliest entry for the payment of tribute by the city in 449 records a sum of 10 talents (t), one of the largest found in the Athenian tribute lists (*IG* i³ 263, (450/49), Column V, line 18 [*aparche* of 1,000 dr. = tribute of ten talents]). A similar recovery appears to have taken place at Eretria after the city was sacked by the Persians in 490 BC and its inhabitants enslaved and sent to Cissia on the Red Sea (Hdt. 5.99.1; 6.100.1). A decade later, the Eretrians were able to supply seven ships for the Greek fleet at Artemisium (Hdt. 8.1.2) and 600 soldiers (combined with those from Styra) for the Greek army at Plataea (Hdt. 9.28.5). On the other hand, the evidence for destruction at Athens in 479 is very extensive as demonstrated by Shear in an essay published in 1993, but that did not stop Athens from forming their league of allies in the following year and becoming the leading power in the Aegean for the next seventy years.[23] After its destruction by the Carthaginians in 409 BC, Selinus also recovered quickly under the inspired leadership of Hermocrates.[24]

Other passages in the literary sources describing extensive destruction must also arouse suspicion. Demosthenes (18.36, 41; 19.64, 141; cf Aeschin. 2.162) gives an alarming account of the treatment meted out to the Phocian cities as a result of their punishment by the Amphictyons in 346 BC, but Pausanias (10.33.8) states that they were refounded soon afterwards.[25] One of them, Elateia, appears to have been fortified again by 338 BC (Aeschin. 3.140; Dem. 6.15). Philip destroyed the city of Stageira, but either he or his son Alexander restored those who were in exile or enslaved to the city (Plut. *Alex.* 7.3; Diog. Laert. 5.4; Val. Max. 5.6. ext. 5). After Cleomenes destroyed Megalopolis in 223 BC, Antigonos Doson redistributed the land of the city and restored those who had been exiled a few years later in 217 BC (Plb. 5.93; Livy 32.22.10). The Thracians conquered, sacked and burned Lysimacheia in 198 BC, but two years later Antiochus III rebuilt the walls, ransomed some of the enslaved citizens, invited others in exile to return and attracted new colonists to the city (Livy 33.38.12–14). The claim made by Demosthenes (9.26) that Philip destroyed thirty-two cities in Thrace (which would include the Chalcidice) also invites skepticism.[26]

Isocrates (6.27), in his *Archidamus* of 366 BC, says that Thespiai was 'destroyed' (*anastatous*), and Demosthenes in his speech *On the Megalopolitans* delivered in 353/2 (16.4, 25, 28) gives the impression that Thespiai was not inhabited. Field surveys conducted in Boeotia over the past thirty years call these statements into question. On the basis of this evidence Snodgrass concludes that 'the population of fourth-century Thespiai, that is, of the *astu* proper, over the century as a whole was at least as high as, and in all likelihood higher than, at any time before or after'.[27] There also may have been building in the centre of the city in the 350s.[28] The Thespians were numerous enough to join in the destruction of Thebes in 335 BC (Diod. 17.13.5). As Snodgrass observes,

'Isocrates, Demosthenes and their like had political axes to grind' and it is doubtful that 'they or their rivals ever traveled to Thespiai to check their reporting'.[29]

Herodotus (6.46–7) reports that Darius ordered the people of Thasos to destroy their wall in 491, and Thucydides (1.101.3) states that after the Athenians besieged the city for two years, the people of Thasos agreed to tear down their walls again in 463 BC. As Grandjean however observes, 'ces démantèlements de rempart évoqués dans les textes ne sont pas aussi radicaux que la formulation utilisée pourrait le laisser croire'. It is likely that the people of Thasos were only required to open some breaches in the walls, to tear down some towers, and to level some parts of the curtain wall. In two places of the walls, the gate of Silenus and the gate of Hermes, where the stratigraphy can be established with some precision, there is no trace of any destruction in the fifth century BC levels.[30] According to Herodotus (8.127), Artabazus laid siege to Olynthus and captured the city, then cut the throats of the Bottiaeans living there before turning the place over to the Chalcidians. But Artabazus did not massacre all the Bottiaeans living there because there were so many Bottiaeans living in Olynthus later that they minted their own coinage separate from those of the Chalcidians.[31] At other sites such as Halai, which Sulla is reported by Plutarch (*Sulla* 26) to have destroyed, few traces of destruction have been found, and there is evidence that the site continued to be inhabited in the early Roman period.[32]

Even when there is good archaeological evidence to corroborate literary accounts of destruction, the finds from excavations sometimes reveal that the actual destruction was rather limited and that the city recovered quickly.[33] A good example is the Sullan siege of Athens in 87–86 BC. Three ancient sources describe Sulla's siege of Athens and its physical destruction. According to Plutarch (*Sulla* 12–14), Sulla's soldiers cut down the trees in the Academy and Lyceum to build siege-engines, then broke into the city between the Dipylon and Piraeus gates and slaughtered many in the Agora. He also burned the Piraeus and destroyed the arsenal of Philo. In another passage, Plutarch (*Mor.* 505a–b) states that Sulla almost destroyed (*mikrou ... kateskapse*) the city and filled it with slaughter and corpses. According to Appian (*Mithr.* 12.5–6), Sulla chopped down the trees in the Academy and destroyed the Long Walls to construct siege engines (cf. Strabo 9.1.15). Aristion, the commander in the city, burned down the Odeum of Pericles to prevent Sulla from obtaining wood to build siege engines for an assault on the Acropolis. Although Sulla did not allow the city to be burned, he permitted his soldiers to loot. Later he took some treasures from the Acropolis. Pausanias (1.20.4–7) offers fewer details but describes his treatment of the city as especially brutal. Some modern scholars have attributed much destruction to Sulla's siege, which caused long-term economic decline.[34] A recent study has, however, shown that despite the loss of life, there was little major destruction in the city, and recovery started soon after the departure of the Roman army.[35] The most damage appears to have been confined to the Kerameikos, where the Pompieion was destroyed.[36] There is little secure evidence for the destruction or damage to buildings in the Agora.[37] The Odeion was in fact burned down, but it was restored with the help of funds from King Ariobarzanes II of Cappadocia (Vitruvius 5.9.1; *IG* ii^2 3426).[38] There was also damage to the Asclepieion, which was quickly repaired.[39] On the other hand, the eastern part of the city appears not to have suffered any damage.[40] The archaeological evidence appears to confirm Plutarch's statement that Sulla destroyed Philo's arsenal, which was later used as a quarry.[41] By contrast, the harbor of Kantharos underwent restoration and development after Sulla's departure. An inscription dated to between 10/9 and 2/1 BC mentions that the *deigma*, the sample-market in the commercial harbor, was restored by a certain Magnus, who was probably the Roman general Pompey (*IG* ii^2 1035, line 47).[42] As Grigoropoulos observes, 'the volume and density of building activity of Imperial and Late Roman date that has been documented around the Kantharos demonstrates that, after the Sullan destruction, this area was redeveloped as the main harbour of the Piraeus. From the present evidence it would appear that the harbour experienced multiple phases of development to its infrastructure and remained operative from the first decades following the Sullan destruction right down to (at least) the sixth century AD.'[43]

A similar case is Delos in the first century BC. Several literary sources record an extensive destruction of Delos in 88 BC and another claims that the people of Delos were enslaved in 69 BC. According to Strabo (10.5.4), the general of Mithridates and the tyrant who encouraged Delos to revolt invaded the island and sacked everything. When the Romans regained control of the island, Delos was deserted (ἐρήμην) and remained indigent until Strabo's time. Appian (*Mithr.* 28) records that Archelaos, the general of Mithridates, captured Delos and killed 20,000 men, mostly Italians, gave the island to the Athenians and sent them their sacred treasures. According to Pausanias (3.23.3–4), Menophanes, another general of Mithridates, attacked the island and killed foreigners residing there and Delians. Phlegon of Tralles (*FGrHist* 257 F 12) reports that the pirate Athenodorus enslaved the Delians and destroyed the statues of the gods. Later C. Triarius repaired much of the damage and had a wall erected around the main settlement.

There can be no doubt that Triarius constructed a wall because several sections of the wall have been discovered from the House of Skardhana to the Stoa of Antigonus and to the south of the House of Hermes and south of the Agora of the Competaliasts.[44] Inscriptions confirm the role of Triarius in constructing the wall (*ID* 1855–8). Evidence for the destructions is harder to find. Some statues were mutilated for political reasons, but there are not many traces of other destruction. As Bruneau observes, particles of carbonized wood have been found in dirt floors, but this is true for all periods of habitation and are not numerous. They are more likely to form part of a pavement made from a mixture of cinder and small stones described by Vitruvius (7.4) and Pliny (*NH* 36.188).[45] In general, Bruneau notes 'l'exploration archéologique a également démontré que les dévastations ont été beaucoup moins importantes qu'on ne l'imaginerait d'abord sur la seule foi des dits historiens'.[46] Inscriptions dated to the imperial period are less numerous than in earlier periods but still reveal that political activity continued.[47] Roman coins from Augustus down to the fifth century CE have been found,[48] and lamps dated to the Imperial period have also been identified.[49] Aelius Aristides (50.32–77) reveals that the port remained in use during the second century CE. Once more, we see that the accounts of destruction found in the historians are greatly exaggerated.

As Hansen and Nielsen conclude in their survey of *poleis* destroyed in the Archaic and Classical periods: 'The overall conclusion is that annihilation of a *polis* seems to have been achieved in about a score of the 122 individually attested *poleis*. In the other cases the *andrapodismos* must have been partial and the destruction of the city superficial. (. . .) it can be shown that in most cases the destruction of the urban centre of a *polis* and the annihilation of its population must have been less effective and disastrous than appears from the accounts found in Herodotus, Thucydides, Xenophon, Demosthenes and Diodorus.'[50] A more thorough recent collection of evidence for the Archaic, Classical and Hellenistic periods confirms this general conclusion.[51] The claim of Ober that 'a Greek *polis* confronted a meaningful chance of being destroyed (. . .) as a result of the sack, of the central city and/or extermination, enslavement, or forced resettlement of the entire population' is untenable.[52]

In their accounts of campaigns, the Greek historians record relatively few examples of destruction and looting. For instance, the campaigns of Brasidas in Northern Greece in 424 and 423 BC did not do extensive harm to the local economy although they had serious consequences for Athenian tribute for a few years. Brasidas advanced through Thessaly with the help of local leaders without encountering resistance (Thuc. 4.78.1–6) and easily reached Dium (4.79.1). Instead of raiding Lyncus, he came to agreement with its king, Arrabaeus (4.83). Using a combination of promises and threats, he persuaded the people of Acanthus to come over to the Spartan side (4.84.1–88.1). Stagirus soon followed their example (4.88.2). With the help of some Andrians sympathetic to the Spartan cause, Brasidas took Amphipolis without a fight (4.102–3), and Galepsus and Oesyme also submitted peacefully (4.107.3). The cities on the Akte peninsula welcomed the Spartan general except for Sane and Dion, whose territories were ravaged (4.109.4–5). Brasidas next cooperated with conspirators inside the city to take Torone (4.110–14), and later Skione revolted after the general made an encouraging speech (4.120–1). The people of Mende followed suit soon afterwards (4.103). The only place he encountered significant opposition was Lecythus, which he took easily and razed to the ground (4.113–16). The joint campaign of Brasidas and Perdiccas against Arrabaeus achieved an initial victory before their troops were compelled to retreat before the combined forces of Lycestians and Illyrians, but inflicted no damage on the territory (4.124.1–128.5). The general Nicias was able to retake Mende without a siege (4.130.1–3), and Cleon regained control of Torone and Galepsos after brief assaults (5.2.2–3.6; 5.6.1), but none of these cities was sacked. The women and children captured in Torone were sold into slavery, but the men were freed on payment of ransom (5.3.6).

The Spartan campaigns in Asia Minor from 399 to 394 BC caused little damage and only had a temporary effect on trade and production. Thibron captured several cities without a fight and took a few small cities by storm (Xen. *Hell.* 3.1.6–7). When Thibron was recalled and sentenced to exile, it was for allowing his troops to plunder friendly territory, a practice to which later commanders put an end (Xen. *Hell.* 3.1.8; cf. 3.2.1). Dercylidas replaced Thibron and took Scepsis and Gergis, which submitted to him peacefully. He gained money to pay his troops by confiscating the property which

Meidias had taken from Mania after having her murdered (Xen. *Hell.* 3.1.20–3). The amount was so large that it provided wages to his troops for a year. To avoid Thibron's error, Dercylidas quartered his troops in places he later captured (Xen. *Hell.* 3.2.1). In his campaign against Pharnabazus, Dercylidas plundered Bithynia, but this tactic contained risks: the Bithynians attacked a raiding party of Greeks and their Odrysian allies, which resulted in many deaths (Xen. *Hell.* 3.2.3–5; cf 3.4.22; 4.3.22–3 for similar incidents). On the other hand, constant raids by an enemy might prevent a community from cultivating its land: ambassadors from the Chersonese reported to Dercylidas that Thracian attacks made it impossible for them to work in their fields (Xen. *Hell.* 3.2.8). But Dercylidas quickly put a stop to these raids by driving out the Thracians (Diod. 14.38.7) and erecting a wall across the entry to the Chersonese (Xen. *Hell.* 3.2.10).[53] Dercylidas also took Atarneus to prevent it from being used as a base for Chian exiles to raid the surrounding territory (Xen. *Hell.* 3.2.11).

Agesilaus succeeded Dercylidas and during 396 and 395 BC conducted a campaign against Tissaphernes, winning a battle against the Persians outside Sardis (Xen. *Hell.* 3.4.23–5). However, he left the area without plundering the land after receiving 30 t. from Tissaphernes to pay for his supplies (Xen. *Hell.* 3.4.26). Agesilaus then burned crops and ravaged the land in Pharnabazus' satrapy, but this lasted a very short time and could have affected only a small part of the area. Any damage done by the Spartan king would not have been extensive (Xen. *Hell.* 4.1.1). During the campaigns of all three Spartan leaders, no major cities were destroyed.

Unless a commander could capture the main cities in an area, any attempt to lay waste the land would inflict only temporary damage. When Agesilaus attacked Acarnania in 389 BC, he methodically devastated farm land, not advancing more than a mile or two every day (Xen. *Hell.* 4.6.4–5). The Acarnanians were able to withdraw into the mountains with their cattle, but even after Agesilaus was able to seize some of their cattle (Xen. *Hell.* 4.6.6), they still maintained control of their cities and resumed planting after the Spartans left (Xen. *Hell*, 4.6.13). The long-term economic effect from the destruction during this campaign was nil.

Alexander's campaigns included some devastating sieges, but most cities came over to his side without bloodshed. In his first campaign as king in 335 BC, Alexander razed the city of the Getai (Arr. *Anab.* 1.4.5), but left other cities in Thrace and Scythia unscathed. Later that year, the Greeks under his command dealt out harsh treatment to the rebellious Thebans: their city was razed to the ground except for the Cadmea and Pindar's house, and the entire population was sold into slavery (Arr. *Anab.* 1.9.9–10). Yet Thebes was the only city in Boeotia to suffer this treatment. Through brutal, the example of Thebes convinced other Greek cities to submit to the king without a fight. One should also recall that merely twenty years later Cassander gathered all the Thebans who survived and refounded the city (Diod. 19.53.2). The refoundation was supported by contributions from many parts of the Greek world including communities in Italy, Sicily, Arcadia, Athens, Cos and Cyprus (Diod. 19.54.2; Paus. 9.7.1–2).[54]

Alexander's march from the Hellespont caused little damage: he took Miletus without obliterating the city, and only destroyed houses near the walls at Halicarnassus (Arr.

Anab. 1.23.2–4). Other cities like Aspendus and Gordion surrendered without any violence (Arr. *Anab.* 1.27.1–4; 2.3.1–8). All the kings of Cyprus joined Alexander willingly (Arr. *Anab.* 2.20.6). The long siege of Tyre was clearly expensive for Alexander, but he replenished his coffers by selling the women and children into slavery after all the adult men were killed (Arr. *Anab.* 2.15.7–24.6). Some places near Tyre were sacked, but there was no extensive destruction (Arr. *Anab.* 2.20.5). The siege of Gaza did not take as long, and once again all the men were killed and the women and children enslaved, but the city remained intact and was repopulated with members of neighbouring tribes (Arr. *Anab.* 2.26.1–27.1). Life continued much as before, just with new residents. The conquest of Egypt was peaceful and involved no looting (Arr. *Anab.* 3.1.1–2). In fact, Alexander had an incentive to treat the natives well because he needed the revenue from their tribute (Arr. *Anab.* 3.5.4). There was a smooth transition from Persian to Macedonian control. From the time he crossed to Asia in 334 BC until 330 BC, the only place Alexander burned to the ground was the palace of the Persian kings at Pasargadai (Arr. *Anab.* 3.18.10–11). It is also interesting to note that the scorched-earth policies of Darius and Bessus failed to halt Alexander's advance (Arr. *Anab.* 3.19.2; 3.28.8).

One could of course point to the Spartan attacks on Attica during the Archidamian War, but these did not have as much impact as the occupation of Deceleia in 413, which made it impossible to work the fields and mines and resulted in the desertion of many slaves, whose number Thucydides (7.27.5) estimates to have been over 20,000. Yet despite this damage to the Athenian economy until the surrender of Athens in 404 BC, there were apparently no long-term effects.[55] As Victor Hanson has observed, the consequences of destroying crops were generally short term.[56] It is extremely difficult to destroy olive trees without completely uprooting them, and fields of burnt crops can be sown again quickly. All the available evidence indicates that the economy of Athens recovered quickly after the Peloponnesian War.[57] The public revenues of Athens fell sharply to 130 t. a year after the Social War (357–355 BC) but recovered quickly and reached 400 t. a year by the late 340s BC (Dem. 10.37–8).

The Greeks were certainly aware that warfare could interrupt economic activity and in some cases factored this possibility into their agricultural contracts. I give five examples.

1. *IG* ii² 2492 (345/4), lines 12–14. A contract from the deme of Aixone with Autocles and Auteas for forty years with rent of 152 drachmas a year. 'If the enemy prevents (work) or destroys something, the people of Aixone have a right to half the produce from the land.'
2. *SEG* 24: 151 (fourth century BC), lines 17–20: If the enemy destroy (anything) while Xanthippos is in possession of the land, he is to give half of what he takes from the land to the Teithrasians (. . .)
3. *IG* XII, 9, 191 (late fourth century), lines 13–17. Work contract from Eretria: 'If war will prevent Chaerephanes from draining the marsh and making it dry as has been written, let an equal amount of time be given to him when it is possible and peace returns, to the length of time the war prevented him (i.e. from working). If

war occurs and it is not possible to reap the land near the marsh, (. . .) let an equal amount of time be given him to the length of time he was prevented (. . .).

4. *IJG* 12, lines 152–4 (Heraclea – fourth century BC).
5. *SEG* 22:508 (Chios), lines A40–2, B42–3.

Yet even though these contracts indicate that destruction from war was a constant threat, they also give the impression that any damage caused would only last for a year or two and leave the renter free to cultivate the land after the enemy left. During an invasion, farmers might retreat to fortified areas and return after the enemy had left and resume cultivation.[58] The ancient historians fill their narratives with accounts of battles, raids and plundering, but one must bear in mind that Greek armies were not very large by modern standards and that their marches covered only small areas, leaving the territory of most city-states untouched. Fighting was confined to small areas, and long, drawn-out sieges were comparatively rare. The war between Athens and the Peloponnesian League may have lasted for twenty-seven years, but large parts of the Peloponnese, Aetolia and Boeotia never saw an Athenian army. In general, there is no reason to believe that the destruction caused by warfare had any long-term economic consequences.

One must also bear in mind the tendency of Greek and Roman historians to exaggerate suffering and destruction in their accounts. As Polybius (29.12) observes: 'For when dealing with a subject which is simple and uniform they wish to be thought historians not because of what they accomplish but because of the multitude of their books, and to make such an impression as I have described, they are compelled to magnify small matters, to touch up and elaborate brief statements of fact and to convert quite incidental occurrences into momentous events and actions, describing engagements and pitched battles in which the infantry losses were at times ten men or it may be a few more and the cavalry losses even fewer. As for sieges, descriptions of places and such matters, it would be hard to describe adequately how they work them up for lack of real matter' (trans. Paton).[59] In several cases, the evidence of archaeology confirms the warning of Polybius.[60]

2. Impact of war on trade

But what impact did warfare have on economic activity, trade and the expansion of markets? Did warfare inhibit the growth of regional and inter-regional trade to any large extent? Three cases studies will be examined.

The first is from Thasos in the fourth and third centuries BC. In an essay on the exports of wine from Thasos, the Bulgarian scholar Chavdar Tzochev has studied the Thasian stamped amphoras found at sites around the Aegean and the Black Sea such as Amphipolis, Maroneia, Abdera, Pella, Panticapaeum, Histria, Callatis and Athens.[61] These amphoras bear the name or device of a local official. Even though the dates of each official cannot be fixed with precision, they can generally be assigned to periods of ten to twenty years, which has enabled Tzochev to present several sales allocation graphs for the years from 392 BC to 198 BC. The stamped amphoras often also carry the names of fabricants – this term is used by amphora specialists to denote those responsible for production – and these indicate a gradual increase in production from 392 to the end of the fourth century, then a gradual decline with a sharp decline in exports to the Black Sea region around 250 with a complete halt in the next decade. Tzochev notes that raids and destruction may account for the decline in exports to the Cimmerian Bosporus and Callatis, but this does not account for other cities in the Black Sea such as Odessos, Mesambria and Tomis, which were flourishing in the Hellenistic period. The reasons for the decline in Thasian production are multiple, but they have far more to do with increases in production by Rhodes, Cnidos and Cos. What is striking, however, is the steady nature of these exports over a long period of time. These centuries were not a period when warfare was absent from Thrace, the Northern Aegean and the Black Sea regions – our sources inform us about fighting in the Hellespont during the Corinthian War culminating in the seizure of the straits by Antalcidas, civil war in Thrace in the 360s, Athenian battles with Cotys and Cersebleptes in the 360s and 350s, Philip's campaigns in the region in the late 350s and 340s, then the fighting among the successors of Alexander and the invasion of the Gauls in the 280s. Some of this fighting may have led to temporary disruptions, but did not alter the overall flow of exports from Thasos, which continued at a steady pace. As Tzochev shows, the producers of Thasos were not producing for the local market or disposing of an occasional surplus – they were producing for export on a regular basis and could find foreign markets in every period. This provides additional support for an important point made by Bresson in 1987 that the Greek *polis* was interested both in imports and exports, but generally ignored by British and American scholars (in particular by Horden and Purcell in their *Corrupting Sea*), despite its obvious relevance to their interests.[62]

The second case study is found in an essay of Tania Panagou, which is based on her University of Athens PhD thesis of 2010, and provides more support for Bresson's thesis.[63] Panagou shows that many Greek *poleis* exported large numbers of amphoras from many different communities to numerous destinations, some quite distant, over long periods of time. For example, according to Garlan, the number of known Rhodian stamps is 200,000, found at dozens of sites. What percentage of the total this represents we cannot tell, but the actual total must have been enormous. The numerous wars of the Hellenistic period appear to have no major impact on this trade. If there was conflict in one area, a community could easily find trading partners in other areas. And with a large number of ports to choose among, merchants could choose the one that offered the best prices.

The third example is from Corinth during the Peloponnesian War. According to Thucydides, whom we have no reason to doubt on this score, Corinth was hostile to Athens throughout the Peloponnesian War and also during the First Peloponnesian War in the middle of the century, roughly 462 to 445 BC. A study by Brian MacDonald shows that 136 Athenian pots have been reported in the North cemetery for the period 460 to 445, an incidence of near four Athenian pots per grave.[64] There is a decline in Attic imports from 445 to 395, but the decline starts during peace-time, not war-time. Despite the decline there is evidence for Athenian imports during the war. In two wells in the

Agora, there is additional evidence for Attic imports during the last third of the fifth century. From other excavated areas 'Catalogues by Boulter and McPhee (. . .) of published Attic imports (. . .) list fifteen kraters, four stemless cups, three squat lekythoi, one pelike, fragments of two closed vases, and an *epinetron* that span the period of the Peloponnesian War'. And imports continued from Corinth to Attica: 'Storage bins, jugs, askoi, lekanides, louteria, and mortars, all of Corinthian manufacture and dated throughout the second half of the fifth century.' We have no way of knowing who transported these goods, but in this case the war did not interrupt the flow of goods from one community to another. States were of course interested in the supply of goods for military use – Demosthenes (19.286) tells us about a ban on exports to Macedon passed by Timarchus – but there was no ban on the flow of non-military goods. And as Gomme pointed out over eighty years ago, ancient fleets could not stop commerce by maintaining blockades.[65] A trireme was designed for speed and had no space for sleeping quarters or for cooking food like a modern warship. A trireme had to land every day for its rowers to take meals and to rest. An ancient fleet could not have blocked a hostile coastline for weeks, let alone months, and cut off shipping for a long time. When Demetrius Poliorcetes wanted to cut off the supply of grain to the Athenians, he had to seize first Eleusis and Rhamnous (Plut. *Demetr.* 33.3), then Salamis and Aegina (Polyaenus *Strat.* 4.7.5) to block shipments (cf. Xen. *Hell.* 2.2.9). Antalcidas blocked shipments of grain to the Piraeus in 387 BC by seizing control of the Hellespont, not through a blockade (Xen. *Hell.* 5.1.28–9). Warfare had only a very limited impact on the flow of goods between regions and caused no long-term damage to economic growth.

3. The profits of war

But what about the gains from warfare? Surely military command offered one of the best ways of gaining profits in ancient Greece, some might argue. Let us look at the leading generals of Athens in the fifth and fourth century and the information about their property in John Davies' still valuable *Athenian Propertied Families*. Pericles had enough income for his own estates to fund a performance of a trilogy by Aeschylus, which included the *Persians*, in 473/72 BC, long before he commanded an army (*IG* ii^2 2318, lines 9–11). According to Plutarch (*Per.* 16.3–4), Pericles maintained his wealth through careful management of his estate, not from the profits of booty. Cimon's generosity to his poor demesmen of Lakiadai came from his landed property ([Arist.] *Ath. Pol.* 27.3; Plut. *Cim.* 10.1–2), which he inherited from his wealthy ancestors (Hdt. 6.35.1). It is possible that booty may have helped pay for the buildings attributed to him, but it is more likely that the state paid for these buildings from the proceeds of booty paid to the treasury. There is no reason to believe that Nicias gained any personal profit from his military campaigns; his wealth came from his mines worked by slaves (Plut. *Nic.* 4.2). Alcibiades was so wealthy that he was able to enter seven chariots at the Olympic games in 416, where he won first, second and fourth places (Thuc. 6.16.2; Athen. 1.3e),[66] but the money that paid for these expenses could not have come from booty because Alcibiades not yet been elected general. His money came partly from marriage to Hipparete, the daughter of Callias, not from warfare. Conon may have gained money from his military career, but his fortune probably came from his service abroad and not at the head of an Athenian army (Lys. 19.39–40). His fortune of 40 t. was impressive, but smaller than that of Pasion, who earned his money from banking, a shield workshop, and other investments.[67] Timotheus gained his fortune by an inheritance from his father Conon (Lys. 19.39–40), but his career in politics and the military caused him to fall into debt. He had to borrow money for his expedition in 374/373 ([Dem.] 49.3–8), to pay Boeotian trierarchs ([Dem.] 49.14–16) and to pay for entertaining Jason and Alcetas who came to Athens to support him at his trial ([Dem.] 49.22–4).[68] After several years as general, his financial situation became so desperate that he had to hire himself to the Great King ([Dem.] 49.3, 37, 60, 65). His military career ended after he was convicted at his trial and could not pay the enormous fine (Isocrates *Antidosis* 129). A military career at Athens was undertaken to win glory and political influence, not to gain profits. Any booty taken in war had to be turned over to the treasury (Dem. 20.77) and could not be kept to increase one's personal wealth. The same was true at Sparta where there were special officers who sold booty and turned over the money to the treasury (Xen. *Hell.* 4.1.26–7).[69] As Hodkinson has shown, the wealth of the Spartan elite derived mainly from the ownership of land and slaves, not from the acquisition of booty.[70] The plunder gained in this way might be substantial, but it was only a windfall profit and could not be counted on to provide a regular source of revenue. When Cimon captured Sestos and Byzantium, he sold the prisoners and their luxurious clothing, but the proceeds gave him enough money to cover pay and rations for four months; there was also much gold left over to contribute to the city's budget, but it could not have amounted to more than a few hundred talents (Plut. *Cim.* 9.4). Plutarch (*Cim.* 13.8) states that the booty acquired by Cimon in the late 450s helped to pay for southern wall of the Acropolis and the foundations of the Long Walls, but does not give a precise figure. Whatever the exact amounts, they could not have made a major contribution to the city's annual income, which Bdelycleon in Aristophanes' *Wasps* (658–60) performed in 422 BC places at 2,000 t. According to Bdelycleon, public revenues came from tribute, import and export duties, court fees, the mines, markets, harbours, the rental of public land and confiscations. One should also note that Bdelycleon does not include any booty in this figure, no doubt because its contribution to the annual figures when averaged over time was negligible. For instance, the slaves Nicias captured on Sicily brought in only 120 t. (Thuc. 6.62.2–3). The spoils gained by the Argives from their invasion of Thyrea in 414 BC amounted to only 25 t. (Thuc. 6.95).

In the fourth century, Demosthenes (20.77) reports that Chabrias captured a huge amount of booty after the battle of Naxos, including forty-nine triremes and 3,000 prisoners, and deposited 110 t. in the treasury. The figure for the ships captured at Naxos is probably an exaggeration,[71] and it is hard to tell if the figure of 110 t. includes the proceeds from the sale of the prisoners or not.[72] But even if the total figure were as high as 200 t., this would have been only half of the annual state revenue in the late 340s BC (Dem. 10.37–8) and only one-sixth of the annual state revenue under Lycurgus ([Plut.]

Vit. X Or. 842f). The booty gained by Chabrias might have defrayed military expenses for one year but not much longer: Cawkwell calculates that the Athenians spent 332 t. and 1,620 drachmas a year on their fleet, while Pritchard puts the figure at 401 t. in the 360s.[73] When campaigning in Thrace with Seuthes, the remaining Greeks of the Ten Thousand took 1,000 captives, 2,000 cattle, and 10,000 other animals and sold them at Perinthus. This provided pay for only twenty days (Xen. *Anab.* 7.3.48; 4.2, 5.2). Military victories just did not produce that much money either for individuals or for the state; booty could not be relied on to produce a constant income for the treasury.[74] The 60 t. gained by Iphicrates from ships carrying gold and ivory statues of Dionysius was used to the upkeep of soldiers and made no contribution to the public treasury (D. S. 16.57.2). More impressive is the plunder gained by Agesilaus from his campaigns in Asia Minor, which allowed him to send 100 t. as *dekate* to Delphi in 394 BC and implies a total amount of 1,000 t. (Xen. *Hell.* 4.3.21). This is the largest sum for the Classical period and was clearly exceptional.

But what about the Macedonians? After over twenty years of campaigns and collecting booty, Philip left the Macedonian treasury either with only 70 t. (Aristobulus) or 200 t. in debt (Onesicritus). Alexander may have gained much booty from sacking the treasures of the Persian king, but, as Frank Holt has argued, the majority of it would have been used to pay troops and defray military expenses; it could not have had a major stimulating effect on the economy of the Near East.[75] Polybius (2.62) provides several figures for booty but also criticizes Phylarchus for recording the inflated figure of 6,000 t. taken by Cleomenes from the spoils of Megalopolis and compares the more reasonable figure of 300 t. from the spoils taken from Mantinea.[76] The amount of booty taken after Pydna and valued at 6,000 t. was clearly exceptional (Plb. 18.35.4). On the other hand, the figure of 150,000 people enslaved by Aemilius Paullus in 167 BC appears to be greatly exaggerated.[77] By comparison, figures for the annual revenues from Ptolemaic Egypt range from 14,800 t. of silver and 1,500 artabas of wheat to 12,500 t. of silver.[78] Steady revenues from tribute and taxes made a greater contribution to public revenues than the occasional windfall from booty.

4. Demand created by military expenses

I end with my fourth point: we should not underestimate the amount of demand generated by the need for military equipment and its stimulating effect on the growth of markets. In one of the stranger statements in the *Cambridge Economic History*, von Reden claims that there was not enough demand in the Athenian economy to generate permanent markets.[79] As David Lewis has shown in our volume, this statement ignores masses of evidence and is quite untenable (of course, I mean that in the nicest possible way). The demand for military equipment such as helmets, spears, breastplates, greaves, and swords was constant and considerable. At the end of the fifth century, it kept many or most of 120 slaves busy all year round in the workshop of Lysias and his brother, who had seven hundred shields in stock in 404 BC (Lys. 12.19). Around 362 Apollodorus, when offered a choice between his father's bank and the shield workshop, he chose the latter because it produced a steady income of a talent a year without risk (Dem. 36.11). Here, the people's demand for shields kept Apollodorus' slaves hard at work. These shields were not purchased by the state, but were sold on the market. One might object that Athens in the Classical period was unusual, but as John Ma has shown, even small cities during the Hellenistic period maintained armies that needed armour.[80] Andrej Chankowski has recently traced the existence of the *ephebeia* in dozens of cities during the Hellenistic period.[81] These ephebes too needed armour, which would have been supplied by craftsmen selling on the market.

The Athenian fleet required vast amounts of wood, which could not be supplied by the forests of Attica.[82] In the fifth century the Athenians were able to secure a steady supply of wood after the foundation of Amphipolis in 437 BC, but the capture of the city in 424 BC by Brasidas cut off this source (Thuc. 4.108.1). To gain another supply of timber, the Athenians appear to have concluded a treaty with King Perdiccas of Macedon, who appears to have agreed to ship oars only to Athens (IG i^3 89, line 31) and later with his successor King Archelaus (*IG* i^3 117). Andocides (2.11) claims to have taken advantage of his hereditary ties with Archelaus to supply the Athenians on Samos with oars. The presence of Athenian owls in Southern Asia Minor with a significant concentration in Cilicia in the early fourth century BC indicates that the Athenians started to import timber from this area when the political situation in Macedonia was too unstable to allow for steady commerce from the region.[83] Later the Athenians resumed good relations with King Amyntas III (*IG* ii^2 102), and this led to a resumption of trade in timber from Macedonia (Xen. *Hell.* 6.1.11; [Dem.] 49.25–37). To make sails, the Athenians needed flax, which appears to have been imported from Egypt.[84] To combat shipworm and rot, a serious threat to wooden hulls, the Athenians needed to import *miltos*.[85] This commodity was so important that in the middle of the fourth century BC, the Athenians concluded a treaty with the island of Keos, which granted them a monopoly on the acquisition of *miltos*.[86]

Greek cities also needed to build walls, which required major investments and hired labor. There are few figures preserved for the costs of building and repairing walls, but the expenses could be considerable and would have pumped money into the local economy. Maier has collected the following sums for construction of fortifications: 1,686 drachmas for the construction of a tower at Eleusis (329/8 BC), 9,200 drachmas for the construction of a tower at Cyzicus (third or fourth century BC), 7,000 drachmas for the construction of a tower on Thasos (first century BC), 2,800 for the construction of a wall at Olbia (third or second century BC), and three sums of 890 drachmas, 5,010 drachmas, and 2,200 drachmas for the construction of a wall on Teos (around 200 BC).[87] Migeotte has collected inscriptions concerning subscriptions for the construction of fortifications, and the sums contributed are often substantial. A subscription from Erythrai dated to between 334 and 315 BC records around 170 contributions, about half of which provided a sum of 16,000 drachmas, and Migeotte believes that the total could have reached 28,000 drachmas.[88] A subscription from Colophon dated to between 311 and 306 BC for building fortifications raised between 165,000 and 300,000 drachmas.[89] A subscription at Chios dated to the third century BC produced 128 contributions and a sum of around 13,670 drachmas.[90] After the earthquake in 227 BC, the people of Rhodes had to rebuild their fortifications and asked for contributions from citizens. One subscription for a tower drew two contributions of 20,000 drachmas each, and Migeotte thinks that the entire sum may have around 250,000 drachmas.[91] Other subscriptions were smaller, such as one at Chios dated to the third century BC for around 13,670 drachmas and another at Naxos dated to the first century BC for a little more than 8,000 drachmas.[92] In each case, these sums may have been supplemented by payments from the public treasury. One might object that these were one-off expenses, but several of the contributions were for repairs and maintenance. One cannot claim that these examples are somehow exceptional: as Frederiksen has shown, there were a large number of cities building fortifications even in the Archaic period.[93] And cities that possessed fleets had to build shipsheds, whose construction would have involved large sums.[94] According to Isocrates (7.66), the ship sheds in the Piraeus cost the Athenians more than 1,000 t.

5. Conclusion

Each of these sections could be developed into a more lengthy study. An analysis of the information provided by the literary sources about the destruction of cities compared with the evidence gained from excavations is now the subject of a collection of essays with a detailed appendix edited by me and Sylvian Fachard. A more extensive study of the evidence provided by amphoras and other types of pottery could help to measure the impact of warfare (or the absence of any impact) on the flow of trade in different periods. More attention could be paid to the contribution of booty to state finances. The economics of building fortifications and equipping soldiers would also repay closer examination. Yet a general picture begins to emerge from these preliminary remarks: there is no reason to exaggerate the negative impact of warfare on economic production and trade. Warfare might be a good investment for some individuals and communities, but it was a highly risky one. Much safer in the long term was an income derived from agriculture, money-lending and craft production. For cities and kingdoms, more profitable over the long term was the revenue from taxes and tribute than the risky and intermittent gains from warfare. That is not to say that military expenditure did not make up a large part of the budgets of city-states and Hellenistic kingdoms. In fact, it might have had a stimulating effect on local economies and driven the expansion of trade. One must recall that even though the policies of Roosevelt's New Deal helped many Americans throughout the 1930s, it was only the boost in military spending during the years leading up to the Second World War that brought an end to the Great Depression.

Notes

1. I would like to thank Sylvian Fachard, David Lewis and Mirko Canevaro for reading an earlier version of this paper and for offering helpful suggestions. I would also like to thank the organizers of the conference, Manu Dal Borgo and Roel Konijnendijk, for their invitation to

participate. A shorter version of this chapter was delivered to the Department of Classics and Archaeology at Nottingham University in February 2019.

2. O'Connor 2015.
3. On the supplies for Alexander's army, see Engels 1980.
4. Harris 2002.
5. See Lewis 2021.
6. See Vial 1984, 355.
7. See Harris 2015 on *autarkeia* in Aristotle.
8. Stewart, Harris and Lewis 2020.
9. Ober 2015a claims that there was substantial economic growth in the city-states of the Archaic and Classical periods, but attributes the growth primarily to political factors and has relatively little to say about the expansion of markets and legal institutions. On this book, see the reviews of Vlassopoulos 2016 and Manning and Oliver 2017. Carugati 2019 makes a similar claim about 'credible commitments' in Classical Athens, but see the reviews of Harris 2022 and Nippel 2023 for an analysis of the errors in this work.
10. For the 'New Orthodoxy' of 1983 repeated without question in 2007, see Scheidel, Morris and Saller 2007, 10.
11. Millett 2001, 35.
12. Cartledge 2002, 27–8. Bresson (2016, 452) has claimed that the 'profit levels that could be drawn from war or simply from pure economic rents made it economically irrational to establish a free-market system. In the short run, these systems of predation which certainly created maximum insecurity, were much more advantageous than the supplementary profit that would have been made by opening up markets.' This statement exaggerates the income from booty (see section 3 of this essay) and seems to be at odds with the analysis in the rest of the book, which I find convincing against the views of Finley and his followers such as Millett and Cartledge.
13. This section draws extensively on Fachard and Harris 2021, 1–33.
14. Hastings 1979, 371–2.
15. Cahill 2002, 46.
16. Cahill 2002, 48–9.
17. Cahill 2002, 49–57.
18. See Parigi 2019 and Rogers in Fachard and Harris 2021, 288–318.
19. See Bessios, Athanassiadou and Noulas in Fachard and Harris 2021, 108–28. For more detailed analysis, see the contributions in Morris and Papadopoulos 2023.
20. See Williams, Bookidis and Slane with a contribution by Tracy in Fachard and Harris 2021, 258–87.
21. Ehrhardt 2003.
22. For the archaeological evidence, see Herda 2019 and Lohmann in Fachard and Harris 2021, 50–69 with references to earlier treatments.
23. Shear 1993 and Camp in Fachard and Harris 2021, 70–84.
24. On Selinus see Marconi in Fachard and Harris 2021, 84–128.
25. Cf. McInerney 1999, 281–3.
26. Griffith 1979, 371–6; Tsigarida 2011, 152–4.

27. Snodgrass 2016, 21.
28. See Snodgrass 2016, 14 and Schachter 1981–94, 1.217–18. See also Bintliff in Fachard and Harris 2021, 340–7.
29. Snodgrass 2016, 31.
30. Grandjean 2011, 370–1. Cf. Lawrence 1979, 115–16.
31. On the coinage of the Bottiaeans, see Psoma 2001, 101–8. See also Cahill 2002, 34, 307 n. 26.
32. See Coleman et al. 1992.
33. For a good summary, see Rogers in Fachard and Harris 2021, 288–318.
34. Hoff 1997.
35. Parigi 2019.
36. Parigi 2019, 57–75.
37. Parigi 2019, 76–93.
38. Parigi 2019, 102–3.
39. Parigi 2019, 104–7.
40. Parigi 2019, 123–30.
41. Grigoropoulos 2016, 252–3.
42. For the date, see Schmalz 2009, 10–11.
43. Grigoropoulos 2016, 249.
44. Bruneau 1968, 674
45. Bruneau 1968, 687–8.
46. Bruneau 1968, 684.
47. Bruneau 1968, 695.
48. Bruneau 1968, 696–7.
49. Bruneau 1968, 697–8.
50. Hansen and Nielsen 2005, 122.
51. See the online appendix to Fachard and Harris 2021.
52. Ober 2008, 81–2, who misrepresents the analysis of Hansen and Nielsen 2005, 122.
53. There was a wall across the Chersonese in the sixth century (Hdt. 6.39) and also in the fifth century (Plut. *Per.* 19) presumably for the same reason. For raids by Thracians on Sestos in the Chersonese during the late second century BC, see *OGIS* 339.
54. For the contributors, see also the fragments of an inscription about the contributions: *IG* VII^{2} 4 [= *SIG*^{3} 337] with a new fragment *SEG* 64:403 and the discussion in Kalliontzis and Papazarkadas 2019.
55. After the Athenians lost their fleet in the late fourth century, they adopted a different attitude toward the defense of the countryside in the third century BC. See Oliver 2007, 134–92.
56. Hanson 1998.
57. See Hanson 1998, 131–73. Chaniotis 2011, 128 asserts that the 'long-term impact of war on agriculture should also not be underestimated' but all the examples he provides relate to short-term damage.
58. For the function of fortified areas in the countryside as places of refuge for farmers, see Fachard 2012, 279–92.

59. On massacres as a literary motif in Roman historians of the Republic, see Barrandon 2018, 21–63.

60. See the essays in Fachard and Harris with the catalogue of destructions in the online appendix.

61. Tzochev 2015.

62. Bresson 1987. This essay has now been translated into English in Harris, Lewis and Woolmer 2016, 41–65.

63. Panagou 2016, based on Panagou 2010.

64. MacDonald 1982.

65. Gomme 1933.

66. For his liturgies and victories at games, see Davies 1971, 20–1.

67. For the fortune of Pasion, see Davies 1971, 431–5.

68. Davies 1971, 509–11 claims that the property of Timotheus was mortgaged, but the passages he cites ([Dem.] 49.22, 26, 34) mention nothing about real security.

69. See in general Pritchett 1991, 404–16.

70. Hodkinson 2000.

71. See Diod. 15.35.2 and Canevaro 2016, 317–18.

72. For discussion and earlier scholarship on the question, see Canevaro 2016, 318–19.

73. Cawkwell 1984; Pritchard 2015b, 112–13.

74. Pritchett 1991, 505–41 provides a useful list of references to booty in the Greek historians but never attempts to compare the proceeds gained from booty as a source of public income with the money gained from other sources of income. There is no analysis of the economic contribution of booty or any attempt to measures the costs vs. the profits of warfare.

75. See Holt 2016. Cf. Briant 2018.

76. See the figures collected in Pritchett 1991, 519–28.

77. See Forsén in Fachard and Harris 2021, 229–35.

78. See Manning in Scheidel, Morris, and Saller 2007, 454.

79. von Reden in Scheidel, Morris, and Saller 2007, 403.

80. Ma 2000.

81. Chankowski 2010.

82. On supplies of timber in the ancient world, see Meiggs 1982. On the costs of building and maintaining the Athenian fleet, see Gabrielsen 2017. On the demand for timber, see also Bissa 2009, 107–52.

83. See Psoma 2015. For Cilicia as an area producing timber in this period, see Theophr. *Hist. Pl.* 4.5.5.

84. Hermippus fr. 63 K–A.

85. For the problem of shipworm and rot, see Ar. *Eq.* 1308; Thuc. 7.12; Theophr. *Hist. Pl.* 5.4.4.

86. See Lytle 2013 on *IG* ii^{2}1128, who provides much evidence to refute the view of Rhodes and Osborne (2003, 280) that 'it is hard to see any functional necessity for Athenian import of ochre from Ceos'.

87. Maier 1961, 2.66. Tréziny 2001, 374 estimates the cost of constructing the fort at Epipolai, the largest fortification in the Greek world at the time (Diod. 15.13), not to have exceeded 2,900,000 drachmas.

88. Migeotte 1992, 211–13. Cf. the analysis of de Callataÿ 2000b on the military expenses in the budgets of Greek *poleis.* Chaniotis 2011 lists some expenses for military needs but appears to be unaware of de Callataÿ's more extensive analysis.

89. Migeotte 1992, 214–23.

90. Migeotte 1992, 178–82. On the rebuilding of Rhodes, see Bresson in Fachard and Harris 2023, 189–229.

91. Migeotte 1992, 105–8.

92. Migeotte 1992, 178–82, 165–7.

93. Frederiksen 2011.

94. On ship sheds, see Blackman and Rankov 2013.

CHAPTER 10

REPARATIONS CLAUSES IN TREATIES OF THE IRON AGE MEDITERRANEAN AND THEIR ECONOMIC IMPLICATIONS

John Davies

A substantial body of evidence from antiquity bears witness that victors in warfare might exact post-conflict compensation from their defeated opponents for the costs that they had incurred.[1] Though the terminology used in the relevant documentation was variable, the practice was often readily recognizable as the exaction of what would now be termed 'reparations' or 'indemnities' (for present purposes, the two terms are interchangeable). Unfortunately, their scholarly study presents an unsatisfactory picture. The reparations exacted from defeated opponents by the Roman Republic have attracted much attention,[2] those known from the Greco-Punic period far less,[3] and though the shadow of Versailles 1919 has understandably not been absent[4] there has been little inclination to broaden the discourse. One might, for example, have tried either to estimate the impacts of reparations on victors and vanquished by attempting to create a structural model, or alternatively to locate the data from antiquity within the frameworks that economists have created in order to interpret what they call with deceptive simplicity 'the transfer problem'. In consequence, though economists' discussions of reparations sometimes allude to the Roman-Carthaginian treaties of 241 or 201, or cite Keynes' description of the 1919 Treaty of Versailles as a 'Carthaginian Peace',[5] the comparison is not pursued. However amateurishly, this chapter is intended to initiate such a comparison, both as a suitable contribution to this volume and as a stimulus to a convergence of discourses.[6] Reasons of space firmly exclude any attempt to survey all known cases from antiquity of the exaction of reparations. Instead, it begins with a quartet of precursors, reviews a 'worked example' in detail, runs rapidly through various clusters of known examples from Classical antiquity and the patterns of action that they present,[7] reviews such categories of proxy data as might help us to assess how, and to what degree, winners and losers gained or lost from indemnity arrangements, and ends by glancing briefly at available economic theories.

1. First attestations

Since a systematic survey of documentation from the Eastern Mediterranean (see Appendix) yields no clear evidence for the exaction of reparations as defined above, the four cases of monetary payments after conflict which are known from Late Archaic

Greece seem to provide the first firm attestations of the practice. They are: (i) the exaction of 100 t. from the Siphnians by exiled Samians *c.* 525 (Hdt. 3.58.4), (ii) the stupendous fine (ζημίη) of 1,000 t. T which the Argives imposed upon the Sikyonians and the Aiginetans (500 t. each) for having given naval assistance to King Kleomenes in his invasion of the Argolid in 494 (Hdt. 6.92.1–2), (iii) the attempted exaction of 100 t. from the Parians by the Athenian Miltiades ca. 489 (Hdt. 6.133–5),[8] and (iv) the resolution of Carthage's earlier war with the 'Africans' over long-unpaid ground rent for the site of Carthage that was due under the initial agreement (Justin 18.5.14), a war which was ended by a monetary payment, not by force (19.1.3–5).

The problem is to decide how far these early examples were really 'reparations', i.e. compensation for losses of men and matériel incurred in war. Not all of them were – indeed one referee briskly but plausibly rates example (i), and possibly also (iii), as a 'racket'. Yet the Argives' claim in (ii) for 500 t. from each party was clearly an initial bargaining figure, for the Sikyonians got quittance by paying 100 t., and in (iv) one can be semi-confident that some arithmetical calculation of 'what was due' underlay the demand, even though the agreement was later dishonoured.[9] Nonetheless, their closeness in date to each other (and to the treaty discussed in section 2 below) is striking, and cannot be wholly due to the survival of Herodotos's text. Instead, behind this dossier one should dimly discern the impact of three new considerations. One was an awareness, which one can attribute to all parties concerned, of the recent increase in the availability of silver bullion from Laurion and southern Spain. A second was a similarly shared knowledge of the convenience of the new technology of stamped coin, and a third, perhaps reinforced by the battle of Sepeia, was an appreciation that for a community to agree to a specified loss of silver was both practicable and more bearable than the loss of adult manpower which a renewal of warfare would entail. Indeed, if Justin's information is reliable, the impact may have allowed the concept of reparations, on the basis of some estimate of 'what was due', to have taken shape independently in several regions of the Mediterranean in the late sixth century BC.

2. A 'worked example'

By good fortune, a salient episode in the history of Classical Greece provides a detailed 'worked example' and suggests that the three 'considerations' formulated above had taken root. In the same year, 480 BC, that mainland Greece was invaded by the army and navy assembled and led by the Persian King Xerxes, the tensions in Sicily between Greek colonialist occupation in the east and south and Carthaginian colonialist occupation in the west and north came to a head in the form of a major Carthaginian invasion. Met by Greek forces led by Gelon the tyrant of Syracuse, it encountered catastrophic defeat at the battle of Himera in summer 480.[10] The Carthaginians then sued for, and obtained from him, acceptable peace terms,[11] the two reliable provisions of which were that they were to pay an indemnity of 2,000 t. and to build two temples, in which copies of the treaty were to be deposited.[12] This seems to be the first fully documented example[13] in

Mesopotamian-Mediterranean history of a formal agreement in monetary terms[14] about reparations after armed conflict. That statement may seem over-bold, for Diodoros' lengthy narrative has suffered serious troop-number inflation, unhistorical decoration, and wildly pro-Sicilian partisanship, while its historiographical antecedents cannot be confidently unravelled.[15] However, what matters for present purposes is not its historical accuracy *per se* but its value as a model. It shows that the contending powers implicitly recognized as appropriate a complex conceptual structure of negotiation. No fewer than ten components of that structure are identifiable, of which two, the institutions of (1) 'treaty to end conflict' and (2) 'written document accessible to the public', each had a substantial back-history in Greece by 480 and need no further comment here. More closely pertinent is (3) the idea of recompense for the 'military costs incurred by the <aggrieved but victorious> party'[16] as an entity different from (4) 'booty acquired by victorious soldiers', from (5) 'booty acquired by the victorious polity',[17] from (6) 'equitable division of such booty',[18] and from (7) 'ransom of persons taken prisoner',[19] all five of these components being explicitly signalled in Diodoros' text.[20] One may go further, for the idea of recompense (component 3) was being understood not in symbolic but in quantitative terms (component 8) and also in terms of the silverization[21] of assessments of value (component 9). Whether one can actually identify, as a tenth component, 'calculation of recompense in terms of losses of men and *matériel*', is unclear, since Diodoros offers no figure for Greek losses: my guess (but it is a guess) is that (as with the instances cited above) the sum of 2,000 t. was fixed rather as a tidy round figure which reflected an estimate of ability to pay and the need to draw a line under the conflict.[22]

It is convenient to stay in Sicily and to follow this first regional cluster further in time. The Congress of Gela in 424 offers the next known case to embody some form of compensation.[23] That motif recurs eleven years later,[24] is absent from Dionysios's first two treaties with the Carthaginians,[25] but re-appears in his interim treaty of (?)389 with Rhegion. This used his victory at the Elleporos in order to exact 300 t., the surrender of her fleet and 100 hostages, and probably some obligations of supply.[26] The motif then reappears with the boot on the other foot in his third treaty with Carthage, this time in the form of a 1,000-talent indemnity payment by Syracuse, probably in instalments.[27] The pre-Roman sequence in Sicily ends with Agathokles as ruler of Syracuse taking with him a payment of 300 t. as the price of finally vacating Carthaginian soil in summer 306,[28] even though the balance of power was even and it was he who had sought to make terms.[29]

3. Other clusters (a): Greek

A second small cluster is detectable in the Aegean. The clear case is that of the revolt of Samos in 441–439, where we have no difficulty in linking Thucydides' report that the Samians were to repay the costs incurred by the Athenians in instalments[30] with the epigraphic (OR 138) and literary[31] picture of those costs, at least 1,200 t. and probably more. Moreover, that case may well not stand alone, for in the light of Thucydides' language about Thasos[32] and of the known history of the island's tribute payments,

Simon Hornblower has surmised that the same treatment had already been applied to Thasos in 463 in the form of an indemnity of 1,000 t., payable at 50 talents p.a. for 20 years, after which, precisely in 443, her tribute payments jumped from 3 t. to 30 t.[33] His hypothesis is undoubtedly on the right lines, and one might even speculate that the very similar treatment inflicted on Aigina *c.* 457 also contained an element of reparations for the costs of a very lengthy siege: Thucydides' silence is not decisive negative evidence.[34] If so, the procedures offer a contrast with the narratives of the creation of the Delian League, for the notion of compensation was there expressed not in terms of indemnity but in those of on-going conflict and tit-for-tat destruction (Thuc. 1.96.2).[35]

Thereafter, apart from a few marginal cases which I do not discuss,[36] the trail goes cold in Greece for 80 years, though Isokrates' report that Artaxerxes II spent 15,000 t. in his war of the 380s against Euagoras of Salamis on Cyprus is relevant insofar as it poses three sadly unanswerable questions, namely 'How did he know?', 'How was the figure reached?' and 'Was there a specific element of reparation in the tribute which the peace treaty of 380 re-imposed on Euagoras?'.[37] However, the theme of indemnity re-emerged with full, indeed vindictive, force in 346, with the Phokians sentenced by the Amphiktyones of Anthela-Delphi to pay no less a sum than 10,000 t. (perhaps originally 5,000 t., doubled as a penalty for non-payment) as compensation for their impiety in using the bullion of dedications made at Delphi for coinage to pay mercenaries in the Third Sacred War.[38] It is true that, as with other penalties inflicted by the Amphiktyones, the basic alleged tort was impiety against Apollo, not hostile military action, but that merely serves to remind us that, as with the collective Aegean reaction to the Persian destruction of temples in 490–479, the sense that reparations were due might have wider and deeper cultural roots than just those that were generated by what we might call 'secular' military aggression.

All the same, most of the later episodes of reparation-exaction from the Greek world[39] do seem to stem from such 'secular' action. One only requires notice, Athens' capitulation to the Makedonian viceroy Antipatros in September 322 at the end of the Lamian War. Here, the narrative in Plutarch's *Phokion* takes us back to the components identified above in Diodoros' post-Himera narrative. In Antipatros' words to the Athenian general Phokion, 'there will be peace and friendship with the Athenians ... (on other conditions, which I omit, and) ... by their paying off the moneys of the war and a penalty'.[40] Yet we have no idea how much was demanded or whether it was ever paid, and this may tell us something about Macedonian priorities, for, with one exception,[41] throughout the next three centuries there is a notable absence of explicit[42] reparation claims on the part of any of the Hellenistic royal regimes.[43] Even more strikingly, they also appear to be absent from Kretan treaties of the Hellenistic period[44] and from the very numerous known cases of arbitration.[45]

4. Other clusters (b): Roman Republic

If, in this cursory and selective review of evidence, I now turn to that for Roman behaviour, the picture is very different. The literary record shows a long series of treaties or truces requiring defeated opponents to provide reparations, typically of the expenses incurred by Rome in kind or coin during the campaign. It runs from the fifth century to the 80s BC and appears to offer a remarkable example of continuity of policy and practice, consistently applied by the Roman politico-military class for generations. The trouble is that the historiographic record is broken-backed. From 263 onwards, when the treaty with King Hieron II of Syracuse displays the policy in detail, down to the vengeful treatment of western Asia Minor in 83,[46] the literary tradition is consistent, detailed and credible.[47] On one occasion, moreover, the negotiations with the envoys of Antiochos III, that tradition explicitly reports Scipio's *consilium* before the battle of Magnesia as stating the hard-line legalistic view that 'in justice Antiochus should pay not half the expense but the whole, for the war was originally due to him and not to them', a view which Scipio himself reasserted after the battle.[48]

In contrast, the tradition in Livy and Dionysios reports earlier Roman military dealings with communities in Etruria and the Central Apennines as yielding a string of indemnity transactions. Many of Livy's reports use the stereotyped formula *frumento stipendioque impetrato* ('Grain and maintenance having been demanded'), which figures in his first report, of 475 BC,[49] while the terms *pecunia* ('money') and *aes grave* ('heavy bronze') enter the tradition from 394.[50] It continues[51] down to a notice of a one-year truce with Falerii in 293,[52] after which the loss of Livy's Books 11–20 prevents us from being able to follow the tradition for the next thirty years. That is unfortunate, since it was clearly historically reliable by the mid-3rd century and probably long before, but in the absence of reliable criteria commentators debate inconclusively about which earlier transactions can also be accepted as real. I cannot broach that argument in full here,[53] but note must be taken of Cornell's observation that the change of the formula in 394 can plausibly be connected with the reform of the army *c.* 406 that changed recruitment procedures and instituted pay for soldiers.[54] If correct, the implied role of money suggests at least a partial parallel with the start of the Greek sequence a century or so previously.

5. The raw data reviewed

All the same, the documentary record for the Greek and the Republican Roman worlds gives us a worthwhile corpus of raw data. They are economically important, for they could involve big money: not just the 1,200 t. or more that the Athenians recouped from Samos or even the 2,000 t. that Gelon got back from Carthage, but extending to the 15,000 t. that the Romans extracted from Antiochos III and the 20,000 t. that Sulla drained from the cities of western Asia.[55] Indeed, Philip Kay has reckoned that in just under fifty years (201–152) the Romans received some 27,280 t. in indemnities.[56] At the other extreme, even the 10 t. which Eretria and Histiaia promised each other shortly after 404 as indemnity for possible breach of treaty,[57] if demanded and paid over, would have made a significant hole in the public accounts of a Greek city. Yet there is surprisingly little direct evidence from antiquity of the effect of such international transfer payments on winners or losers.[58] We seem therefore – and disconcertingly – to be largely on our own in trying both to imagine a likely spectrum of effects and to identify such proxy data as might give us a handle on the problem.

Of course, any effort of imagination is coloured by knowledge of the effects which the provisions for German reparations that were imposed by the 1919 Treaty of Versailles helped to generate in subsequent history.[59] One has however to leave that knowledge aside and instead to locate indemnity provisions within a world of Iron Age economies with predominant agro-pastoral sectors, limited access (at least at first) to fiscal expedients, and very varied levels of monetization and liquidity of money supply. The obvious way into that context is to follow the trails generated respectively by demand and by supply, terms which are all too brutally appropriate for transactions conducted within the terms of a reparation-clause. Each trail needs separate consideration.

6. The fiscal trail generated by demand

The goods or monies that were transferred by demand on the part of the victorious power will obviously have entered its fiscal economy directly. There are hints in the earlier Roman tradition that reparations were exacted *en nature* – *vestimenta* and *frumentum* – and were calibrated in terms of the size of the Roman forces involved and of the length of the specific campaign: the agreement with the Hernici in 306 looks like one such, though it is unfortunately marred by a textual crux at the critical word.[60] However, in addition to *vestimenta* and *frumentum,* the terms demanded of various Etruscan cities in 294 and 293 included fines specified in pounds of *aes grave*: one may identify various possible reasons for the addition,[61] and one may perhaps assume that the difference in the sums demanded – 100,000 lb from Falerii, 300,000 lb from each of three others – reflects either the relative sizes of the communities or the relative degree of their malfeasance in Roman eyes. In any case, our problem is to estimate how much difference such reparations and the others I have cited made to the recipients.

Unquestionably, they conveyed very significant monetary and other advantage to the victorious state. In simple quantitative terms, the payments made by Samos – and perhaps by Thasos to Athens – were each more than twice Thucydides' figure for the annual tribute from the state concerned. The sums that went to and fro in Sicily from 480 to 306, however arbitrary the level at which they were pitched, will not just have recompensed rulers or regimes fiscally but will have created major opportunities for patronage and redistribution. The figures for fines imposed on the Etruscan cities in the 290s, if historical and accurate, were far from token, however hard it may be to assess their purchasing power or their routes of entry into the Roman fiscal and real economies. The later Roman sequence, certainly from the Treaty of Catulus in 241 onwards, will have had all the more impact for being paid in instalments and therefore coming closer to being a steady component of state revenue rather than windfall one-offs. And that is without taking into account the two most massive impacts, the settlement of Macedon in 167 that permitted the suspension of the payment of *tributum* within Italy, and the flood of money into Italy that followed the rape of the Asian cities after 83. Their effects can now be followed in detail in Kay 2014.

7. The non-fiscal trail generated by demand

There were wider, non-fiscal effects too, however. Three require mention. In a bipartite structural analysis, Tim Cornell has interpreted Roman policy and attitudes from the 330s to the 260s as driven by the network of alliances that Rome had created, not just because they allowed well-nigh continuous military activity as an instrument of policy with minimum risk to herself (and, we should add, at minimal cost), but also because, since those alliances were purely military, 'Romans had to engage in warfare if they were to avail themselves of the services of the allies and to keep the system in being'.[62] He then explains the complement to Roman action, the high level of allied loyalty, through a cost–benefit analysis of their status (though he does not call it that) which is the nucleus of a serious economic model.

Second, reparations, and especially the instalment system, may be viewed as an instrument of policy, for the obligation to pay so much annually had the effect of tying the debtor polity down and of restricting its independence of action. That can be sensed for Thasos and Samos, and was unquestionably true for Roman exactions from Catulus's treaty of 241[63] onwards. Indeed Erich Gruen has made the case that consistently '[p]olitics rather than economics took central place', with 'Rome cancelling Philip's reparation payments in 190 when he proved cooperative and valuable' but refusing the year before to accept indemnity payments from Carthage before they were due: while after 167 the indemnity from Macedon, payable annually *sine die*, turned indemnity into *tributum* itself.

Yet it was the third non-fiscal effect that was the longest-lasting, in the form of the inflation which has been diagnosed by Michael Crawford for the first two generations of the second century.[64] Unfortunately, it is impossible to distinguish the inflationary influence exerted by reparations from that exerted by the influx of booty and newly-mined bullion into Italy from all quarters of the compass after 200. There may be some reason to ascribe the greater impact to booty and new bullion, since their trails will have led through the hands of *privati* who will have wished to spend and display in a way that the state did not, but such a hypothesis is unprovable.

8. The trail generated by supply

I turn finally to the trail generated by supply, i.e. by the compulsory surrender of goods and metals by losers to victors. Though the transmitting entity will in all cases have been the loser state, it may be justified to suppose that the surrender of goods affected the welfare of its inhabitants differently from the surrender of metals, coined or otherwise. For example, insofar as they are historical, Rome's pre-coinage demands for grain or for *stipendia* in kind may be envisaged as having impacted immediately and directly on the granary holdings of households via some sort of organized levy, perhaps to have depleted seed-corn stocks, and perhaps to have caused serious short-term distress among those whose storage margins were thin. Demands for clothing likewise will have largely fallen on the labour of the female population, with no corresponding contribution to family assets. Whether a longer-term demand might have triggered a Hopkins effect of increased production on the part of that unfortunate population may be left to the imagination. In contrast, the initial impact of demands for metals, coined or uncoined, noble or base, will first have been on a royal or civic capital reserve if one existed, but then on some sort of *eisphora* system so that the community could recoup its outgoings, on a pattern already foreshadowed in the *Odyssey* (13.7–15). However, a severe level of demand would trigger a rise in 'taxation' and a need to raise short-term debt, with all the tensions and complexities that debt brings with it, especially in communities with only a limited money supply.

These are all, in economic terminology, negative wealth effects,[65] but they were real as well as perceived. The real tasks are to identify, to quantify, and to theorize: all are equally intractable. In order to 'identify', for example, the effects of specific reparation demands need to be distinguished from such other requirements and restrictions as the victor might choose to impose. The classic case is that of the provisions imposed on Athens by Antipatros after the Lamian War. As already noted, the size of the indemnity he imposed is not known: what is known, apart from the installation of a garrison, is his injunction that only those with property of a value of 2,000 drachmai or more (i.e. ⅓ of a talent) were to be full citizens, the remainder being encouraged to emigrate to Thrace.[66] Though subsequent events modified the terms, and though the extent of actual emigration is disputed,[67] there can be little doubt that the demographic basis of the fourth-century Athenian economic model was seriously and adversely affected: but that cannot be seen as a consequence deriving wholly from the indemnity that was imposed.

All the same, that example allows us to identify demography as one possible source of proxy data. A second, in theory, is coinage – sizes of issues, cessation, changes of style, weight standards, circulation patterns, or purity, and so on. The trouble is that it is often impossible to pin any such change directly onto the demands for reparations. There can even be negative evidence, for Samian and Thasian coinages continue after their revolts without much sign of impact,[68] and Georges Le Rider saw no unusual signs of strain in the coinage of Seleukos IV even though some payments of the indemnity inflicted on his father had been missed.[69] A third, also in theory, might comprise halts or slowdowns in public building projects or other major deployments of resources. The model might be the brake on projects in Athens that was imposed by one section of the second Kallias decree,[70] or the near-halt in work on restoring the Apollo temple at Delphi during the Third Sacred War which the temple accounts show us in detail. Unfortunately, only very rarely is the evidence fine-grained enough to allow us to detect such changes in momentum, let alone to create a clear link between them and a demand for reparations.

That leaves debt, especially that of the supra-regional kind which infested mainland Greece after the 190s and the Aegean after 83. Here too caution is necessary, because tensions over debts can be detected in regions which were not being directly mulcted by Roman decisions. That much said, there is a well-supported view[71] that the region where those tensions boiled over most damagingly into civil war, namely Aitolia after 189, was also that where the polity was experiencing the greatest difficulty in meeting Roman demands for reparations. However, in this context the problem with establishing a direct causal connection is that the issue of debt had already arisen in the earlier Aitolian crisis of *c.* 205, long before there was any question of defeat or reparation. One has to assume that here, as everywhere both then and now, debt was at the same time both an indispensable and ineradicable social mechanism *and* a potentially disruptive force.[72] Roman envoys eventually knocked heads together[73] in 173, but the fact that they had to do so by lowering interest rates in Thessaly and Boiotia as well as Aitolia suggests that reparations were a trigger as well as a cause, and that the macroregional money supply, a grotesquely unequal wealth distribution, and perhaps severe weaknesses in the administration of law were all also active ingredients.

The fifty-year desolation of the eastern Aegean states after 83 is a different matter. Even if the disruption of the earlier 80s is taken into account, it does little to mitigate the picture, known from direct evidence,[74] of the immediate and violently negative impact of the reparations that were imposed on their societies in 83. We know, too, that the ensuing need to raise loans with which to pay the consequential public and private debts caused substantial monies – very likely part of that same fund of abstracted bullion – to be recycled back into the region via the Roman money market at usurious rates of interest.[75] The whole episode could form an invaluable second worked example, both because further epigraphical evidence is now available[76] and because its scale ought to make it a viable basis for theorization.

9. Towards theorization

The difficulty is to identify a helpful model. Three offer themselves, of which one should be dismissed. One might hypothesize that capital depletion via reparations comprised the formal converse of the processes of capital-formation via external aid, remittances, foreign investment and loans to less developed countries that have been identified and discussed in development economics. However, the analogy encounters serious objections, for capital depletion by external *fiat* does not accurately mirror processes of endogenous capital formation,[77] most obviously because 'depletion' was top-down, peremptory and immediate, while 'formation' was a long-term, bottom-up process. In any case, of course, the principal effect may not have been a measurable gain or loss of GDP so much as an impact on mood and attitude among both victors and vanquished, as the last 100 years have shown us all too clearly.[78]

A very different model, formulated by Occhino et al.[79] in order to assess the losses suffered by occupied France after 1940, deserves closer consideration. It comprises two stages. The first uses the available historical evidence to construct an equation which includes all the variables necessary to represent the utility function of a household for the period concerned. The second stage uses all the available quantitative evidence in order to replace the variables by quantities, thereby allowing the haemorrhage of GNP during the Vichy regime to be measured, at least approximately. This model, too complex to reproduce here, poses a frustrating challenge. The equation itself could be adapted to ancient conditions well enough to complete the first stage, but would encounter insurmountable difficulty at the second stage. As with Kay's enterprising exploration of the economy of post-200 BC Italy,[80] the 'health warnings' would inevitably proliferate.

The third option is to invoke the theoretical structure which has been devised since the 1920s to accommodate 'the transfer problem'. Originally developed as a response to the 1919 Versailles Treaty,[81] it has proved to be widely applicable, e.g. to the post-1815[82] and post-1871[83] reparation payments made by France and to the obligations imposed on Iraq after the First Gulf War.[84] As sketched sixty years ago by Johnson, its core structure:

> can be separated into two problems for analysis. The first is whether the process by which the transfer is financed in the transferor country and disposed of in the transferee will affect each country's demand for imports (at unchanged prices) sufficiently to create the trade surplus and deficit necessary to effect the transfer. The financing and disposal of the transfer will tend to reduce the transferor's demands for goods and increase the transferee's demand for goods: both effects will tend to improve the balance of trade of the transferor and worsen that of the transferee, and the changes may fall short of, or exceed, the amount of the transfer. Unless the changes in trade balances are exactly equal to the amount of the transfer, there will remain a balance-of-payments disequilibrium which must be corrected by some adjustment mechanism.[85] (. . .) The second part of the transfer problem is whether the adjustment mechanism will be effective in restoring equilibrium. This problem really raises two subsidiary questions, one of direction and one of magnitude of influence.[86]

This poses a different challenge, since it is clear that modern economist/historians can use the model without difficulty. For example, Devereux and Smith (2007) begin by constructing a static model of two-region interaction for French post-1871 reparations, expand it by including other factors such as international debt, and then add such parameter variables as are required in order to model change through time. Their next step, just as with the internal model explored by Occhino et al. (2008), is to replace the variables in the various equations by data, but in order to reconcile the ensuing picture with known reality the authors finally also find it necessary to complicate the model still further by factoring in the impact of various internal or exogenous shocks.

Can historians of antiquity follow suit? In principle, yes: a comparable set of equations could be constructed on the same principles and be applied to reparation-stipulations from antiquity. The problem is that such a procedure is not simplified by the fact that we cannot assume, as all modern discussions[87] do, that there existed an international money market which could provide loans to the debtor state.[88] Nor can it be assumed that the existence of significant bilateral trade, both before and after the conflict that generated the reparations obligation, permitted the impact of reparations to be largely managed by adjustments in the terms of trade via the volume or price of traded goods. On the contrary, this 'worked example' of post-1871 reparations reveals that even for a polity wherein non-traded goods comprised two-thirds of GDP,[89] an accurate modelling of reality requires a high level of conceptual and mathematical complexity and an intimate knowledge of both data and environment. We cannot suppose that ancient realities were any less complex. Economic historians of antiquity who wish to disentangle the effects of post-conflict reparations are therefore faced with the unwelcome combination of complex equations and an extreme paucity of data with which to energize them.

This chapter simply reports a reconnaissance. It has been able to do little more than to identify one further aspect of the close interaction between war and economic life and to explore its extent and implications. Inevitably, too, it presents an ungainly mixture of academic dialects. That is the nature of the beast, because we are dealing with complex societies that were open to long-distance influences and pressures and cannot be analysed via one academic discipline on its own. At least, however, it has shown that, as an aspect of the economic and social effects of warfare, reparations deserve more attention than they have had.

Appendix I. The ANE material

Most, but not all, of the primary evidence which comes into range for the present chapter is assembled in the two published volumes of the series *Die Staatsverträge des Altertums*, its volume II (1962) containing treaties of the period from 700 to 338 BC and volume III (1969) containing those of the years from 338 to 200 BC. Volumes I and IV have never appeared,[90] though Bengtson's preface to vol. II reported that almost seventy texts from the Ancient Near East had been identified by Dr Einar v. Schuler for Volume I. (I do not know whether the papers for this assemblage have been preserved anywhere.) In its absence it would have been impracticable to review the pre-700 evidence for Kriegskostenerstattung or -schädigung, but the publication by K. A. Kitchen and P. J. N. Lawrence in 2012 of their monumental three-volume *Treaty, Law, and Covenant in the Ancient Near East* now permits an exploration of the 102 texts which they republish in full. (A range of other documents is listed in their vol. I 1082–1086, but for various reasons without texts or translations: I have not attempted to review them.)

Unfortunately their corpus appears to reveal nothing *ad rem*.[91] I have pursued all the entries under 'Compensation', 'Punishments (v)', and 'Ransom, redemption' which they assemble in their Index of topics (II 111–38), but none emerges from a clear post-conflict context or gives any explicit hint that some form of reparations is being specified. The nearest example is the provision in a treaty between Suppiluiuma I of Hatti and his vassal Aziru of Amurru that the latter was to pay an annual tribute of 300 gold shekels (Kitchen & Lawrence 2012, I No.58 A/B, §1 ii, 9–11), but though this reflects Suppiluiuma's determination to come down hard on Aziru's disloyalty[92] it is not represented as reparations. The same is true for a very well-documented example which would not have come within their purview, Sennacherib's first campaign against Babylon in 703. His own narrative records that

> (§60) 'I returned to Assyria with 208,000 men, a huge spoil, 7200 horses and mules, 11,073 asses, 5230 camels, 80,050 cattle, 800,100 ewes. (§61) This does not include the men, asses, camels, cattle and sheep which my troops had carried off and parcelled out among themselves'.[93]

Though the conceptual distinction between the booty acquired by individual soldiers and that acquired by the polity is clearly made, the emphasis is laid on the number of objects acquired, not on their value: still less is any attempt made to distinguish between compensation for the costs of the campaign on the one hand and net profit on the other.

Notes

1. The relevant definition in the OED s.v. 'Reparation', §5 d. is simply 'Compensation for war damage owed by the aggressor'.
2. Extended discussions by Meißner 2008; Kehne 2008; Müller 2008; Müller 2009; and Kay 2014, 21–42, especially 37–42. Szaivert and Wolters 2005, 150–5 provide a bare list (texts and German translations). Gruen 1984, 1.291–4; Crawford 1985, 23 with n. 31; Cornell 1995, 188–9; Chaniotis 2005a, 139–40; Oakley 2005, 539–41; and Serrati 2007, 488–9 provide briefer references. I find no explicit reference to the topic in Canfora *et al.* 1990, Eckstein 2006, or Campbell and Tritle 2013.
3. To my knowledge, only Fernández Nieto 1989. Pritchett discusses booty at length (1974, 53–100) but not reparations.
4. E.g. Meißner 2008, 246.
5. Thus the title of Mantoux's 1946 book. Add Sullo and Wyatt 2013, §5, and Oosterlinck 2008.
6. I am most grateful to the editors for encouragement, to Prof. Graziella Bertocchi (Modena), Dr Matthew Fitzjohn (Liverpool), and Prof. Kim Oosterlinck (ULB) for helpful references and bibliographic material, to my wife for helpful discussion, and to publishers' referees for helpful and pointed comments.
7. Since this chapter is intended to be accessible to economists, economic historians and historians of other epochs and regions, I add that the unit of large-scale monetary value used in the sources and therefore in this paper was the talent (abbreviated hereafter as 't.'), a weight equivalent to 26.196 kg. The consignments thus reported might consist of coin (usually of near-pure silver), but might equally comprise bullion, whether loose, as plate, or as bagged and countable units of hacksilber. All dates are BC unless otherwise stated.
8. Fernández Nieto 1989, 375–6.
9. However, the payment was later forcibly refunded (ib. XIX 2.4). For the episode, see Aubet Semmler 2001, 228–30.
10. Main ancient narratives in Hdt. 9.153–67 and Diod. 11.20–6, with Asheri 1988, 766–75. The recent excavation of mass warrior graves in the western cemetery of Himera (Vassallo 2011; 2016) has given sobering substance to the literary narrative.
11. *Staatsverträge* 2.131 (Diod. 11.26.2).
12. A third stipulation, that human sacrifice was to cease, is reported only by Theophrastos (F 586 Fortenbaugh ap. Σ P. *Pyth.* II 2) and is generally seen as not credible (thus, e.g., Jacoby's

Commentary on Timaios, *FGrH* 566 F 20), though an injunction to the same effect is said by Justin to have been issued to the Carthaginians by Xerxes' father Dareios (19.1.10–11).

13. For other quasi-relevant evidence, see Appendix I.

14. 'Monetary' in terms of weighed silver, not in terms of coin: Carthage herself did not coin until late in the fifth century, and the date of the first Sicilian-Phoenician civic coinages is debated (Manfredi 1995, 151–3; Visona 1998; Marcoe 2000, 105–7. In spite of its title, the discussion in Villaronga 1973 is concerned only with third-century issues.).

15. Devillers 1998, 150 n.6: but the strong case for Timaios was restated by Meister 1967, 41–3.

16. 'τὰς εἰς τὸν πόλεμον γεγενημένας δαπάνας' (Diod. 11.26.2).

17. About the disposal of which Gelon is reported to have made specific arrangements (Diod. 11.25.1).

18. Thus Diod. 11.25.1: 'by analogy with the number of those who took part in the fighting.'

19. Where Diodoros' references to 'a mass of prisoners' (11.22.6; 25.2; 25.5), however unbelievable the figures, are circumstantial and credible, but are incompatible with his report of Gelon's instruction to take no prisoners (11.22.4).

20. Roman practice and vocabulary for components (3) to (7) is reviewed by Kay 2014, 21–42. Whether the Roman state made quantitative calculations of due recompense is argued by Müller 2009: a rebuttal by Crawford is reported as forthcoming by Kay 2014, 22 n.5 but is not yet published.

21. Exposition and exemplification of the term in Van der Spek 2011.

22. I do not attempt to discuss the 'crown of 100 gold talents' which the Carthaginians gave to Damarete (Diod. 11.26.3) or to broach the problems of the Demarateion; see Green 2006, 81 n.106 for references.

23. Thuc. 4.65.1, a general decision of 'uti possidetis' carrying the exception that Morgantina was to belong to the Kamarinaioi on paying a specific sum of silver to the Syracusans. The stipulation remains irritatingly Delphic in the absence of explanation.

24. The Athenian commander Nikias offered the Syracusans full reimbursement of war-costs as recompense for the unhindered withdrawal of Athenian forces (Thuc. 7.83.2).

25. Respectively *Staatsverträge* 2.210, of 405 (Diod. 13.114.1), and 2.233, of 392 (Diod. 14.96.3).

26. *Staatsverträge* 2.240 (Diod. 14.106.2, 108.1).

27. *Staatsverträge* 2.261 (Diod. 15.17.5; Plato, *Ep.* 333a).

28. *Staatsverträge* 2.437 (Diod. 20.79.5; Justin 22.8.15).

29. Likewise, the payment of 300 t. by the Carthaginians to his mercenaries the previous autumn (*Staatsverträge* 2.436: Diod. 20.69.3; Justin 22.8.13) represented arrears of pay, not an indemnity.

30. Thuc. 1.117.3, with Shipley 1987, 113–22, reported in *SEG* 37:28.

31. Isoc. 15 *Antidosis* 111; Nepos, *Timotheus* 1: discussion in the commentary to ML 55.

32. χρήματά τε ὅσα ἔδει ἀποδοῦναι αὐτίκα ταξάμενοι καὶ τὸ λοιπὸν φέρειν (Thuc. 1.101.3).

33. Hornblower 1991, 158.

34. For the siege, Thuc. 1.105.2–3 and 108.4. Aigina's well-attested annual tribute payment was also 30 t. for at least fifteen years thereafter until it reappeared as a much lower level (9 or 14 t.) in 432/1.

35. Review of the bibliography in Raaflaub 1979.

36. *Staatsverträge* 2.217 (Sparta and Elis in 400) and 286 (Klearchos of Herakleia and a local dynast Mithridates in 364). The contributions which Timotheos exacted from Samos and other Aegean seaboard cities in the 360s (Isoc. 15 *Antidosis* 111–15) were no doubt forced, but were not reparations *sensu stricto.*

37. *Staatsverträge* 2.252 (Isoc. 9 *Euag.* 60 and 64; Theopompos, *FGrH* 115 F 103.10–11; Diod. 15.9.2). The questions in the text are regrettably not addressed by Meier 1994, 312–17; Briant 1996, 666–75; or Stylianou 1998, 184. Whatever the credentials of the figure of 15,000 t., it will surely have encompassed the expenses of the whole war against Cyprus and Egypt.

38. Sources and discussion in Davies 2007.

39. References in Fernández Nieto 1989, 379–83.

40. *Staatsverträge* 3.415: ἀπεκρίνατο φιλίαν ἔcεcθαι τοῖc Ἀθηναίοιc καὶ cυμμαχίαν ... χρήματα τοῦ πολέμου καὶ ζημίαν προcεκτίcαcιν (Plut. *Phok.* 27.5).

41. *Staatsverträge* 3.518 (Achaios at Selge-Pedlenissos in 218).

42. Demetrios did exact substantial sums (πολλὰ χρήματα) from the Boiotian cities after their revolt of 292 (Plut. *Demetr.* 39.4), but the unvengeful attitude which Plutarch reports of him discourages their identification as formal reparations.

43. Unless the enormous dowry which Berenike brought with her to Antiochos II as a component of the settlement at the end of the Second Syrian War was a covert indemnity payment to Antiochos on the part of Ptolemaios II (Otto 1928, 45; Will 1979, 239–40 and 241–2). See also Walbank 1979, 110, on Plb. 21.17.6 for the problem of accounting for the 400 t. and a quantity of grain which Antiochos III owed to Eumenes, and the historicity or otherwise of a Seleukid invasion of Pergamene territory in 197: but Walbank notes that the agreement made then was 'as a result of Roman intervention' [hence the Romans could raise it in 190/89], so it was not an endogenous arrangement between two wholly independent Hellenistic monarchies.

44. Chaniotis 1996.

45. Piccirilli 1973; Ager 1996; Magnetto 1997.

46. See notes 74–5 below.

47. The details and sources set out by Meißner 2008, 253–4 need not be repeated here.

48. Respectively, Plb. 21.14.7 (Livy 37.35.7 corresponds) and 21.17.2 (quotation tr. Paton), with Meißner 2008, 254, and Kay 2014, 38–42.

49. Livy 2.54.1, with Ogilvie ad loc., accepting it as historical and as contextualized by Hieron's victory over the Etruscans in 474.

50. *Staatsverträge* 2.227 (Livy 5.27.12–15; Diod. 14.98.5; Plut. *Camillus* 10.7); scepticism about its historicity in Harris 1971, 43. Ogilvie *ad loc.* notes on *pecunia* in 27.15 only that 'a Faliscan indemnity could have been recorded in the Annales'. The treaty with Falerii in 343 (Livy 7.38.1, mentioned in the commentary to *Staatsverträge* 3.462), is not entered specifically under that year in *Staatsverträge.*

51. That of 308 with Tarquinii (*Staatsverträge* 3.435; Livy 9.41.5–7; Diod. 20.44.9) may have built on the *foedus aequum* with Camerinum of (?)310 (*Staatsverträge* 3.430; Livy 9.36.7, etc; Harris 1971, 56, 99 challenges the Livian story but not the basic fact of the treaty) and is reasonably reliable, being followed two years later in 306 by a similar version with the Hernici, *Staatsverträge* 3.439 (Livy 9.43.5–7 and 23; Diod. 20.80.4); they were to pay for a two- or six-month *stipendium*, provide grain, and one tunic per man. A forty-year truce was concluded with Volsinii, Perusia and Arretium in 294 (*Staatsverträge* 3.461: Livy 10.37.4 (there is a ghost pre-echo under 310 or 309 [*Staatsverträge* 3.431] at Livy 9.37.12 and Diod.

20.35.5). Each city had to provide grain and clothing for soldiers straightaway, after which the formal truce specified a fine of 500,000 lb of *aes grave* from each city.

52. *Staatsverträge* 3.462 (Livy 10.46.12), its terms requiring a payment of 100,000 lb of *aes grave* and *stipendium* for that year to the soldiers. The battles recorded by Zonaras 8.1.10 for 292 are said by Schmitt in *Staatsverträge* to be a doublet.
53. The spectrum runs from Ogilvie 1965, 371 (on Livy 2.54.1: unquestioning acceptance) through Crawford 1985, 23 with n.31 (simple list, with one denial of historicity) to Oakley 2005, 539–41 (on Livy 9.41.6–7: deeply sceptical). Attempts to reconcile Varronian and non-Varronian dates help only in part.
54. Cornell 1995, 188, citing Livy 8.8.3.
55. The figure is widely cited (references in Angeli Bertinelli 1997, 370 on Plut. *Sulla* 25.4). Detailed survey in Magie 1950, 1.232–58, with brief summaries in Keaveney 1982, 110–15 and 230–3 and Hind 1994, 161–3.
56. Kay 2014, 39, Table 2.2.
57. *Staatsverträge* 2.205, with discussion by Knoepfler 2001, 81–2.
58. The two prime cases, Aitolia after 189 and the Asian cities after 83, are discussed below. To judge from the extant fragments, Antiphon's speech for the Samothrakians was about levels of tribute, not reparations.
59. Basic data and references in Meißner 2008, 246–7.
60. *Staatsverträge* 3.439 (Livy 9.43.5–7 and 23; Diod. 20.80.4).
61. Explanations may be either (a) ethnic, the Hernici being Italic and therefore 'one of us' as the Etruscans were not: or (b) economic, the Roman state edging towards the use of metal as currency; or (c) practical, derived from Roman awareness that the Hernici had little or no easy access to metals whereas the Etruscan cities did. Fortunately, all three possibilities are compatible with each other.
62. Cornell 1995, 364–8 (quotation at 366).
63. *Staatsverträge* 3.493. Given the length of the First Roman–Punic War and the scale of Roman losses of men and *matériel,* the figure of 2,200 t. stipulated by Catulus as the sum of required reparations (Plb. 1.62.9ff) looks more like a symbolic (100 t. for each of twenty-two years) than a real recompense: the nub of the matter lay rather in the twenty years over which repayment was to be spread.
64. Crawford 1985, 151; Kay 2014, 102–4.
65. The term 'wealth effects' is more usually used in a positive sense, to denote an increase in 'perceived wealth': but precisely because it applies to 'perceived' wealth (an investor or household 'feels' her/itself wealthier), its use in a negative sense, to denote an objective forced reduction in wealth, will not be symmetrical with the positive sense.
66. *Staatsverträge* 2.415.
67. Oliver 2007, 80–5, citing Baynham 2003.
68. Hansen and Nielsen 2004, 778–82 n.26 (G. Reger) at 782b; 1095–8 n.64 (L. Rubinstein) at 1097.
69. Le Rider 1993, with Livy 42.6.6–12 and Briscoe 2012, 173 for the delays.
70. ML 58 B, lines 12–17.
71. Derow 1989, 290 and 305; Grainger 1999, 511–20.
72. Its impact on antiquity urgently needs attention, at much closer range than was available for Graeber 2011.

73. The phrase is Grainger's (1999, 516).
74. Full survey in Magie 1950, 1.232–58, with Migeotte 1984, 339–43 nn.114–16.
75. An extreme case, that of Salamis on Cyprus, is known in detail from Cicero's Letters (*Ad Att.* 5.21, 10–13, whence Migeotte 1984, 254 n.5). Cf. also Migeotte 1984, 260 n.77 (Lampsakos *c.* 70), 314 n.100 (Tralleis in 62), 313 n.9 (Sardeis in 51/50), and 339–43 nn.114–16 (general).
76. Imprimis the Customs Law from Ephesos (Cottier et al. 2008).
77. Examples in Nafziger 2006, chapters 5 and 11. Dependency theory, though superficially an attractive possibility, also encounters objections (ibid. 144–8).
78. As also in antiquity: Douris of Samos, chronicling his island's history some 150 years after the Samian revolt of 441–439, claimed that Perikles as Athenian commander had had the Samian ship-commanders and marines first crucified in the market-place of Miletos and then battered to death (Douris, *FGrH* 76 F 67 ap. Plut. *Per.* 28.2–3). Whether the tale is true, garbled, exaggerated or an urban myth does not matter; what mattered for Douris was what it represented, namely a mood of bitter resentment that lived on for generations.
79. Summary version in Occhino et al. 2007; full version in their 2008 paper.
80. Kay 2014, 269–325.
81. Brief summary of relevant research by Devereux and Smith 2007, 2377–8.
82. White 2001.
83. Devereux and Smith 2007. These reparations are identified (ibid. 2379) as having been the largest in history, averaging 8.67 per cent of France's GNP annually for 1871–3.
84. Morrison 1992.
85. i.e. presumably devaluation, rises in taxation levels or debasement of currency.
86. Johnson 1956, 212–13.
87. Johnson 1956 provides a lucid summary of the theory, and the example of Iraqi oil exports is central to Morrison 1992.
88. Citing as potential sources 'the sacred treasuries at Olympia, Delphi, and Delos (to name only a few)', a referee challenges this statement. However, the tabus surrounding the use of a god's monies were substantial (Davies 2001; 2007), and the picture assembled by Migeotte 1984 of loans made by or to Greek cities is very largely one of *ad hoc* bilateral arrangements involving polities and individuals, not sanctuaries. The main exceptions were the various loans made over several centuries by Delian Apollo to various Aegean cities (Migeotte 1984, 141–66, n.45–7), but despite much debate the stresses which underlay them remain unidentified (Chankowski 2008, 367–9).
89. Devereux and Smith 2007, 2382.
90. In lieu, Kehne 2003 provides a summary survey for the whole of Graeco-Roman antiquity, but without commentary or reproduction of texts.
91. The same is true, regrettably, for the papers in Canfora et al. 1990.
92. For the detailed context, see Kitchen and Lawrence 2012, 2.47 and 3.93–7.
93. Luckenbill 1924, 55; more recent references and contextualization in Grayson 1991, 103–9.

BIBLIOGRAPHY

Acemoğlu, D., S. Johnson and J. A. Robinson (2005). 'Institutions as the fundamental cause of long-run growth', in *Handbook of Economic Growth*, edited by P. Aghion and S. Durlauf, 385–472. New York: Elsevier.

Acemoğlu, D., and J. A. Robinson (2016). 'Paths to Inclusive Political Institutions', in *Economic History of Warfare and State Formation*, edited by J. Eloranta, E. Golson, A. Markevich and N. Wolf, 3–50. Singapore: Springer.

Acton, P. (2014). *Poiesis: Manufacturing in Classical Athens*. New York: Oxford University Press.

Adcock, F. E. (1957). *The Greek and Macedonian Art of War*. Berkeley, CA: University of California Press.

Ager, S. L. (1996). *Interstate Arbitrations in the Greek World, 337–90 B.C.* Berkeley, CA: University of California Press.

Akrigg, B. (2007). 'The nature and implications of Athens' changed social structure and economy', in *Debating the Athenian Cultural Revolution: Art, Literature, Philosophy, and Politics 430–380 BC*, edited by R. Osborne, 27–43. Cambridge: Cambridge University Press.

Alcock, S. E. (1994). 'Breaking up the Hellenistic world: survey and society', in *Classical Greece: Ancient Histories and Modern Archaeologies*, edited by L. Morris, 171–90. Cambridge: Cambridge University Press.

Alonso Troncoso, V. (1987). *Neutralidad y Neutralismo en la Guerra del Peloponneso (431–404 a.C.)*. Madrid: Ediciones de la Universidad Autónoma de Madrid.

Amit, M. (1965). *Athens and the Sea: A Study in Athenian Sea-Power*. Brussels: Latomus.

Ampolo, C. (1987). 'I contributi alla prima spedizione Ateniese in Sicilia (427–404 A.C.)'. *Papers from the Institute of Archaeology* 42: 5–11.

Ampolo, C. (1979). 'Oikonomia: tre osservazioni sui rapporti tra la finanza el'economia greca', in *Annali del seminario di studi del mondo classico. Sezione di archeologia e storia antica* 1: 120–30.

Anderson, J. K. (1970). *Military Theory and Practice in the Age of Xenophon*. Berkeley, CA: University of California Press.

Andreades, A. M. (1933). *A History of Greek Public Finance*. (trans. C. N. Brown). Cambridge, MA: Harvard University Press.

Andreau, J., P. Briant and R. Descat, eds (2000). *Économie antique: La guerre dans les économies antiques*. Saint-Bertrand-de Comminges: Musée archéologique départemental.

Angeli Bertinelli, M. G., M. Manfredini, L. Piccirilli and G. Pisani, eds (1997). *Plutarco: Le Vite di Lisandro e di Silla*. Milan: Fondazione Lorenzo Valla/Mondadori.

Archibald, Z. H. (2013) *Ancient Economies of the Northern Aegean: Fifth to First Centuries BC*. Oxford: Oxford University Press.

Archibald, Z. H., J. K. Davies and V. Gabrielsen, eds (2011). *The Economies of Hellenistic Societies, Third to First Centuries BC*. Oxford: Oxford University Press.

Armstrong, J. (2016). *Circum Mare: Themes in Ancient Warfare*. Leiden: Brill.

Asmonti, L. (2015). *Conon the Athenian: Warfare and Politics in the Aegean 414–386 BC*. Stuttgart: Steiner.

Aubet Semmler, M. E. (2001). *The Phoenicians and the West: Politics, Colonies and Trade*. 2nd edn. Cambridge: Cambridge University Press.

Austin, M. M. (1994). 'Society and economy', in *CAH* VI^2, 527–64.

Austin, M. M., and P. Vidal-Naquet (1977). *Economic and Social History of Ancient Greece: An Introduction*. Berkeley, CA: University of California Press.

Austin, M. M., and P. Vidal-Naquet (1980). *Economic and Social History of Ancient Greece: An Introduction*. 2nd edn. Berkeley, CA: University of California Press.

Azzoni, A., and E. Dusinberre (2014). 'Persepolis Fortification Aramaic Tablet Seal 0002 and the keeping of horses', in Kozuh, Henkelman and Jones (2014), 1–16.

Baloglou, C. (1998). 'Hellenistic Economic Thought', in *Ancient and Medieval Economic Ideas and Concepts of Social Justice*, edited by S. T. Lowry and B. Gordon, 105–46. Leiden: Brill.

Barat, C. (2012). 'Relations et solidarités entre les cités grecques de la côte sud de la Mer Noire (VIIIe-IIIe s. av. J.-C.)', in *Les diasporas grecques du VIIIe à la fin du IIIe siècle av. J-C.*, *Pallas* 89, edited by L. Martinez-Sève, 217–44. Toulouse: Presses Universitaires du Mirail.

Barrandon, N. (2018). *Les massacres de la République romaine*. Paris: Fayard.

Bauer, A. (1893). *Die griechischen Kriegsaltertümer.* Munich: C. H. Beck.

Bauslaugh, R. A. (1991). *The Concept of Neutrality in Classical Greece*. Berkeley, CA: University of California Press.

Baynham, E. (2003). 'Antipater and Athens', in *The Macedonians in Athens, 322–229 B.C.*, edited by O. Palagia and S. V. Tracy, 23–9. Oxford: Oxbow.

Bengtson, H., and R. Werner (1962). *Die Verträge der griechisch-römischen Welt von 700 bis 338 v. Chr.*, II. München: C. H. Beck.

Beloch, J. (1886). *Die Bevölkerung der griechisch-römischen Welt*. Leipzig: Duncker & Humblot.

Beloch, J. (1893). *Griechische Geschichte* I. Strasbourg: K.J. Trübner.

Beresford, J. (2013). *The Ancient Sailing Season*. Leiden: Brill.

Bertosa, B. (2005). 'The Social Status and Ethnic Origin of the Rowers of Spartan Triremes'. *War and Society* 23: 1–20.

Bettalli, M. (1990). *Enea Tattico, La Difesa di una Città Assediata (Poliorketika)*. Pisa: ETS Editrice.

Bettalli, M. (2013). *Mercenari: Il Mestiere delle Armi nel Mondo Greco Antico*. Rome: Carocci.

Bielman, A. (1994) *Retour à la liberté. Libération et sauvetage des prisonniers en Grèce ancienne. Recueil d'inscriptions honorant des sauveteurs et analyse critique*. Lausanne: Ecole Francaise d'Athenes.

Bintliff, J. (2008). 'Considerations on Agricultural Scale-Economies in the Greco-Roman world', in *Feeding the Ancient Greek City*, edited by R. Alston and O. van Nijf, 17–31. Leuven: Peeters.

Bissa, E. (2009). *Governmental Intervention in Foreign Trade in Archaic and Classical Greece*. Leiden: Brill.

Blackman, D. (1969). 'The Athenian Navy and Allied Naval Contributions in the Pentecontaetia'. *GRBS* 10.3: 179–216.

Blackman, D. (2013). 'Classical and Hellenistic sheds', in Blackman and Rankov (2013), 16–29.

Blackman, D., and B. Rankov, eds (2013). *Shipsheds of the Ancient Mediterranean*. Cambridge: Cambridge University Press.

Blaineau, A. (2015). *Le Cheval de Guerre en Grèce Ancienne*. Rennes: Presses Universitaires de Rennes.

Blamire, A. (2001). 'Athenian Finance, 454–404 B.C.' *Hesperia* 70: 99–126.

Böckh, A. (1817). *Die Staatshaushaltung der Athener*. Berlin: Realschulbuchhandlung.

Böckh, A. (1828). *The Public Economy of Athens* (trans. G. C. Lewis). London: J.W Parker.

Böckh, A. (1842). *The Public Economy of Athens: To Which is Added, A Dissertation on the Silver Mines of Laurion* (trans. G. C. Lewis). 2nd edn. London: J. Murray.

Böckh, A. (1857). *The Public Economy of the Athenians, With Notes and a Copious Index*. Boston: Little, Brown and Company.

Boehringer, E. (1978). *Die Münzen von Syrakus*. Bologna: A. Forni.

Boix, C. (2003). *Democracy and Redistribution*. Cambridge: Cambridge University Press.

Bresson, A. (2000). *La cité marchande*. Paris: De Boccard.

Bresson, A. (2011). 'Grain from Cyrene', in *The Economies of Hellenistic Societies, Third to First Centuries* BC, edited by Z. Archibald, J. K. Davies and V. Gabrielsen, 66–95. Oxford: Oxford University Press.
Bresson, A. (2015). 'The cost of getting money in Early Ptolemaic Egypt', in *Law and Transaction Costs in the Ancient Economy*, edited by D. M. Ratzan and U. Yiftzh, 118–44. Ann Arbor: University of Michigan Press.
Bresson, A. (2016). *The Making of the Greek Economy: Institutions, Markets and Growth in the City-States.* Princeton, NJ: Princeton University Press (translation and revision of Bresson, A. (2008). *L'économie de la Grèce des cites,* 2 vols. Paris: Armand Colin.)
Bresson, A. (2020). 'Silverization, prices and tribute in the Achaemenid Empire', in Tuplin and Ma (2020), 3.209–48.
Bresson, A. (2022). 'Markets', in *The Cambridge Companion to the Ancient Greek Economy*, edited by S. von Reden, 221–36. Cambridge: Cambridge University Press.
Brewer, J. (1989). *The Sinews of Power: War, Money, and the English State, 1688–1783.* London: Unwin Hyman.
Briant, P. (1996). *Histoire de l'empire perse, de Cyrus à Alexandre*. Paris: Fayard.
Briant, P. (2002). *From Cyrus to Alexander: A History of the Persian Empire* (trans. of Briant (1996) by P. T. Daniels). Winona Lake, IN: Eisenbrauns.
Briant, P. (2018). 'The debate about the spread of Alexander's coinage and its economic impact: engaging with historiographical longue durée', in *Alexander the Great: A Linked Open World,* edited by S. Glenn, F. Duyrat and A. Meadows, 235–47. Bordeaux: Ausonius.
Brice, L. L., ed. (2020). *New Approaches to Greek and Roman Warfare.* Hoboken, NJ: Wiley & Sons.
Briscoe, J. (2012). *A Commentary on Livy Books 41–45.* Oxford: Oxford University Press.
Brodersen, K. (2008). 'Nützliche Forschung: Ps.-Aristoteles' Oikonomika II and die Haushalte griechischer Poleis', in Burrer and Müller (2008), 106–27.
Brosius, M. (1996). *Women in Ancient Persia, 559–331* BC. Oxford: Clarendon Press.
Brosius, M. (2021). *A History of Ancient Persia: The Achaemenid Empire.* Hoboken, NJ: Wiley & Sons.
Brun, P. (1983). *Eisphora – Syntaxis – Stratiotika: Recherches sur le Financement de la Guerre à Athènes au IVe Siècle av. J.-C.* Paris: Les Belles Lettres.
Brun, P., and Bielman, A., eds (1999). *Questions d'Histoire: Guerres et Sociétés dans les Mondes Grecs, de 490 à 322 avant J.-C.* Paris: Editions du Temps.
Brun, P., and Descat, R. (2000). 'Le profit de la guerre dans la Grèce des cités', in Andreau, Briant, and Descat (2000), 211–30.
Bruneau, P. (1968). 'Contribution à l'histoire urbaine de Délos', *BCH* 92.2: 633–709.
Bryant, J. M. (1990). 'Military technology and socio-cultural change in the ancient Greek city', *Sociological Review* 38.3: 484–516
Buck, R. J. (1998). *Thrasybulus and the Athenian Democracy.* Stuttgart: Steiner.
Buckler, J. (2003). *Aegean Greece in the Fourth Century* BC. Leiden: Brill.
Bugh, G. (1988). *The Horsemen of Athens.* Princeton, NJ: Princeton University Press.
Bullock, C. J. (1930). 'Dionysius of Syracuse. Financier'. *CJ* 25: 260–76.
Burke, E. M. (1978). 'The Greeks at war in the fifth and fourth centuries BC'. *Military Affairs* 42: 142–3.
Burrer, F. (2008). 'Sold und Verpflegungsgeld in klassischer und hellenisticher Zeit', in Burrer and Muller (2008), 74–90.
Burrer, F., and Müller, H., eds (2008). *Kriegskosten und Kriegsfinanzierung in der Antike.* Darmstadt: Wissenschaftliche Buchgesellschaft.
Bury, J. B. (1951). *A History of Greece to the Death of Alexander the Great.* 3rd revised edn. London: Macmillan.
Butler, M. (2010). 'The logic of opportunity: Philip II, Demosthenes, and the charismatic imagination'. *Syllecta Classica* 21: 1–33.

Buttrey, T. V. (1980). 'Seldom what they seem: the case of the Athenian tetradrachm', in *Ancient Coins of the Greco-Roman World. The Nickle Numismatic Papers*. Waterloo, ON: Wildred Laurier University Press.
Buttrey, T. V. (1982). 'Pharaonic imitations of Athenian tetradrachms', in *Proceedings of the 9th International Congress of Numismatics, Berne*, edited by T. Hackens, 137–40. Luxembourg: Association internationale des numismatistes professionnels.
Cahill, N. (2002). *Household and City Organization at Olynthus*. New Haven, CT: Yale University Press.
Cairns, F. (1984). '*Chrêmata Dokima*: IG XII, 9, 1273 and 1274 and the Early Coinage of Eretria'. *ZPE* 54: 145–55.
Campbell, B., and L. A. Tritle, eds (2013). *The Oxford Handbook of Warfare in the Classical World*. Oxford: Oxford University Press.
Canevaro, M. (2016). *Demostene,* Contro Leptine: *Introduzione, Traduzione e Commento Storico*. Berlin: De Gruyter.
Canfora, L., M. Liverani and C. Zaccagnini, eds (1990). *I trattati nel mondo antico. Forma, ideologia, funzione*. Roma: L'Erma di Bretschneider.
Capdetrey, L., and C. Hasenohr, eds (2012). *Agoranomes et édiles: institutions des marchés antiques*. Bordeaux and Paris: Ausonius/De Boccard.
Carney, E. (1996). 'Alexander and Persian Women'. *American Journal of Philology* 117.4: 563–83.
Carney, E. (2000). *Women and Monarchy in Macedonia*. Norman, OK: University of Oklahoma Press.
Cartledge, P. (1998). 'The economy (economies) of ancient Greece'. *Dialogos* 5: 4–24
Cartledge, P. (2001). 'The effects of the Peloponnesian (Athenian) War on Athenian and Spartan societies', in *War and Democracy: A Comparative Study of the Korean War and the Peloponnesian War*, edited by B. S. Strauss and D. R. McCann, 104–24. New York: Routledge.
Cartledge, P. (2002). 'The economy (economies) of ancient Greece' (= Cartledge 1998), reprinted in Scheidel and von Reden (2002), 11–32.
Cartledge, P., E. E. Cohen and L. Foxhall, eds (2002). *Money, Labour and Land: Approaches to the Economies of Ancient Greece*. London: Routledge.
Carugati, F. (2019). *Creating a Constitution: Law, Democracy, and Growth in Ancient Athens*. Princeton, NJ: Princeton University Press.
Casson. L. (1966). 'Galley Slaves'. *TAPA* 97: 35–44.
Casson, L. (1971). *Ships and Seamanship in the Ancient World*. Princeton, NJ: Princeton University Press.
Casson, L. (1995). 'The Feeding of the Trireme Crews and an Entry in *IG* ii^2 1631'. *TAPA* 125: 261–9.
Castrizio, D. (2000). *La monetazione mercenariale in Sicilia: strategie economiche e territoriali fra Dione e Timoleonte*. Catanzaro: Rubbettino.
Caven, B. (1990). *Dionysius I: Warlord of Sicily*. New Haven, CT: Yale University Press.
Cawkwell, G. L. (1962). 'Demosthenes and the *stratiōtic* fund'. *Mnemosyne* 15: 377–83.
Cawkwell, G. L. (1976). 'The imperialism of Thrasybulus'. *CQ* 26: 270–7.
Cawkwell, G. L. (1982). 'Isocrates', in *Ancient Writers: Greece and Rome Vol. 1 Homer to Caesar*, edited by T. J. Luce. New York: Scribner.
Cawkwell, G. L. (1984). 'Athenian naval power in the fourth century'. *CQ* 34: 334–5.
Cecchet, L. (2015). *Poverty in Athenian Public Discourse*. Stuttgart: Steiner.
Centre National de la Recherche Scientifique, ed. (1977). *Armées et Fiscalité dans le Monde Antique*. Paris: Éditions du Centre national de la Recherche scientifique.
Chandezon, C. (1999). 'L'économie rurale et la guerre', in Prost (1999), 195–208.
Chandezon, C. (2000). 'Guerre, agriculture et crises d'après les inscriptions hellénistiques', in Andreau, Briant and Descat (2000), 231–52.

Chaniotis, A. (1996). *Die Verträge zwischen kretischen Poleis in der hellenistischen Zeit*. Stuttgart: Steiner.
Chaniotis, A. (2005a). *War in the Hellenistic World: A Social and Cultural History*. Malden, MA: Blackwell.
Chaniotis, A. (2005b). 'Inscribed Instrumenta Domestica and the Economy', in *Making, Moving, and Managing: The New World of Ancient Economies, 323–31 BC*, edited by Z. H. Archibald, J. K. Davies and V. Gabrielsen, eds, 233–66. Oxford: Oxford University Press.
Chaniotis, A. (2011). 'The impact of war on the economy of Hellenistic *Poleis*: demand creation, short-term influences, long-term impacts', in Archibald, Davies, and Gabrielsen (2011), 122–41.
Chankowski, A. S. (2010). *L'éphébie hellénistique: Étude d'une institution dans les cités grecques des îles de la Mer Égée et de l'Asie Mineure*. Paris: De Boccard.
Chankowski, V. (2008). *Athènes et Délos à l'époque Classique. Recherches sur l'administration du sanctuaire d'Apollon délien*. Athens: École française d'Athènes.
Chankowski, V., and P. Karvonis, eds (2012). *Tout vendre, tout acheter: Structures et équipements des marchés antiques: Actes du colloque d'Athènes, 16–19 juin 2009*. Pessac: Ausonius.
Chodorow, A. (2015). 'Even ISIS Needs to Collect Taxes'. *Slate*. Accessed 2 March 2024: https://slate.com/business/2015/12/isis-collects-taxes-and-its-effort-exposes-some-big-weaknesses.html
Christ, M. (2007). 'The evolution of the *Eisphora* in Classical Athens'. *CQ* 57: 53–69.
Clark, M. (1990). 'The date of *IG* ii^2 1604'. *ABSA* 85: 7–67.
Clark, C., K. Jackson, P. Johnston, E. Robinson and H. Shatz (2017). *Financial Futures of the Islamic State of Iraq and the Levant Findings from a RAND Corporation Workshop*. Santa Monica, CA: RAND Corporation.
Clerc, M. (1893). *Les méteques athéniens*. Paris: Thorin & fils.
Cloche, F. (1934). *La Politique étrangere d'Athenes de 404 à 338 av. J.C.* Paris: F. Alcan.
Cohen, E. E. (1992). *Athenian Economy and Society: A Banking Perspective*. Princeton, NJ: Princeton University Press.
Coleman, J. E., K. O'Neill, M. Pomeroy, K. E. Carr and A. Heafitz (1992). 'Excavations at Halai'. *Hesperia* 61.3: 265–89.
Connor, W. R. (1988). 'Early Greek land warfare as symbolic expression'. *Past and Present* 119: 3–29
Cook, M. L. (1990). 'Timokrates' 50 Talents and the Cost of Ancient Warfare'. *Eranos* 88: 69–97.
Cornell, T. J. (1995), *The Beginnings of Rome. Italy and Rome from the Bronze Age to the Punic Wars (c. 1000–264 BC)*. London: Routledge.
Cottier, M. et al., eds (2008). *The Customs Law of Asia*. Oxford: Oxford University Press.
Crawford, M. H. (1985). *Coinage and Money under the Roman Republic*. London: Methuen.
Croiset, M. (1973). *Aristophanes and the Political Parties at Athens* (trans. J. Loeb). New York: Arno.
Cruickshank, W. W. (1954). *Topography, Movement and Supply in the Warfare of Ancient Greece south of Thessaly and Epirus*. Diss. University of London.
Cuomo, S. (2007). *Technology and Culture in Greek and Roman Antiquity*. Cambridge: Cambridge University Press.
Dal Borgo, M. (2015). *Thucydides, Father of Game Theory*. Diss. University College London.
Dal Borgo, M. (2022). 'Inequality in the Peloponnesian War', in *Capital in Classical Antiquity*, edited by M. Koedijk and N. Morley, 47–102. Cham, Switzerland: Palgrave Macmillan.
Dalby, A. (1992). 'Greeks Abroad: Social Organisation and Food Among the Ten Thousand'. *JHS* 112: 16–30.
Davidson, J. (1997). *Courtesans and Fishcakes: The Consuming Passions of Classical Athens*. Chicago: University of Chicago Press.
Davidson, J. (2011). 'Bodymaps: sexing space and zoning gender in ancient Athens'. *Gender & History* 23.3: 597–614.

Davies, J. K. (1971). *Athenian Propertied Families, 600–300 B.C.* Oxford: Clarendon Press.
Davies, J. K. (1978). *Democracy and Classical Greece.* Brighton: Humanities Press.
Davies, J. K. (1983). *Democracy and Classical Greece.* 2nd edn. Standford, CA: Stanford University Press.
Davies, J. K. (1995). 'The fourth-century crisis: what crisis?' in *Die Athenische Demokratie Im 4. Jahrhundert v. Chr.: Vollendung Oder Verfall Einer Verfassungsform?,* edited by W. Eder and C. Auffarth, 29–39. Stuttgart: Steiner.
Davies, J. K. (2001). 'Temples, credit, and the circulation of money', in *Money and Its Uses in the Greek world*, edited by A. Meadows and K. Shipton, 117–28. Oxford: Oxford University Press.
Davies, J. K. (2004). 'Athenian fiscal expertise and its influence'. *Mediterraneo Antico* 7: 491–512.
Davies, J. K. (2007). 'The Phokian hierosylia at Delphi: quantities and consequences', in *Corolla Cosmo Rodewald*, edited by N. Sekunda, 75–96. Gdansk: Akanthina.
Dawson, D. (1996). *The Origins of Western Warfare: Militarism and Morality in the Ancient World.* Boulder, CO: Westview Press.
de Angelis, F. (2016). *Archaic and Classical Greek Sicily: A Social and Economic History.* Oxford: Oxford University Press.
Dearden, C. W. (1976). *The Stage of Aristophanes.* London: Athlone Press.
Debidour, M. (2002). *Les Grecs et la Guerre, Ve–IVe Siècles: de la Guerre Rituelle à la Guerre Totale.* Monaco: Rocher.
de Callataÿ, F. (2000a). 'Les monnayages ciliciens du premier quart du IVe s.av.J.-C.', in *Mécanismes et innovations monetaires dans l'Anatolie achéménide*, edited by O. Casabonne, 93–128. Paris: De Boccard.
de Callataÿ, F. (2000b). 'Guerres et monnayages à l'époque hellénistique. Essai de mise en perspective suivi d'une annexe sur le monnayage de Mithridate VI Eupator', in Andreau, Briant, Descat (2000), 337–64.
de Callataÿ, F. (2003). *Recueil quantitatif des émissions monétaires archaïques et classiques.* Wetteren: Bibliothèque royale de Belgique.
de Callataÿ, F. (2023). 'Pseudo-civic, not civic: the abundant double sigloi struck by Cilician and Pamphylian cities (*c.* 460–333 B.C.E.)', in Meadows and Bodzek (2023), 45–69.
Delbrück, H. (1900). *Geschichte der Kriegskunst im Rahmen der politischen Geschichte.* Berlin: G. Stilke.
De Odorico, M. (1995). *The Use of Numbers and Quantifications in the Assyrian Royal Inscriptions.* Helsinki: University of Helsinki.
Derow, P. (1989). 'Rome, the fall of Macedon and the sack of Corinth', in *CAH* VIII^2, 290–323.
Descat, R. (1993). 'La loi de Solon sur l'interdiction d'exporter les produits attiques', in *L'emporion*, edited by A. Bresson and P. Rouillard, 145–61. Paris: De Boccard.
Descat, R. (1995). 'Marché et tribut: l'approvisionnement des Dix-Mille', in *Dans les pas des Dix-Mille, Pallas,* edited by P. Briant, 43, 99–108. Toulouse: Presses Universitaires du Mirail.
Descat, R. (2020). 'Le Pseudo-Aristote et les finances achéménides: un point sur la question', in *Achemenet. Vingt ans après. Études offertes à Pierre Briant à l'occasion des vingt ans du Programme Achemenet*, edited by D. Agut-Labordère, R. Boucharlat, F. Joannès, A. Kuhrt and M. W. Stolper, 79–93. Leuven: Peeters.
de Souza, P. (2017). 'Raiders from the Sea: The Maritime Context of the *Poliorketika*', in *Brill's Companion to Aineias Tacticus*, edited by N. Barley and M. Pretzler, 214–28. Leiden: Brill.
de Ste. Croix, G. E. M. (1953). 'Demosthenes' *Timhma* and the Athenian *Eisphora* in the Fourth Century B.C.'. *C&M* 14: 30–70.
de Ste. Croix, G. E. M. (1954). 'The Character of the Athenian Empire'. *Historia* 3: 1–41.
de Ste Croix, G. E. M. (1956a). 'Greek and Roman accounting', in *Studies in the History of Accounting*, edited by A. C. Littleton and B. S. Yamey, 14–74. London: Sweet & Maxwell.
de Ste. Croix, G. E. M. (1956b). 'The Constitution of the Five Thousand'. *Historia* 5: 1–23.
de Ste. Croix, G. E. M. (1972). *Origins of the Peloponnesian War.* London: Duckworth.

de Ste. Croix, G. E. M. (1981). *The Class Struggle in the Ancient Greek World from the Archaic Age to the Arab Conquests*. London: Duckworth.
Devereux, M. B., and G. W. Smith (2007). 'Transfer problem dynamics: Macroeconomics of the Franco-Prussian war indemnity'. *Journal of Monetary Economics* 54: 2375–98.
Devillers, O. (1998). 'Un portrait "césarien" de Gélon de Sicile (Diod. XI. 20–26)'. *L'Antiquité Classique* 67: 149–67.
Droysen, H. (1889). *Heerwesen und Kriegführung der Griechen*. Freiburg: J.C.B. Mohr.
Ducrey, P. (1985). *Guerre et Guerrier dans la Grèce Antique*. Paris: Payot.
Dziubiński, M., S. Goyal and D. E. N. Minarsch (2021). 'The strategy of conquest'. *Journal of Economic Theory* 191: 105–14.
Economou, E. M. L., and N. Kyriazis (2017). 'The Emergence and the Evolution of Property Rights in Ancient Greece'. *Journal of Institutional Economics* 13.1: 53–77.
Edwards, M. (2007). *Isaeus*. Austin, TX: University of Texas Press.
Ehrenberg, V. (1943). *The People of Aristophanes: A Sociology of Old Attic Comedy*. Oxford: Blackwell.
Ehrenberg, V. (1962). *The People of Aristophanes: A Sociology of Old Attic Comedy*. New York: Schocken Press.
Ehrhardt, N. (2003). 'Milet nach den Perserkrieg: Ein Neu Beginn?' in *Stadt und Stadtentwicklung in Kleinasien*, edited by E. Schwertheim and E. Winter, 1–19. Bonn: R. Habelt.
Eich, A. (2006). *Die politische Ökonomie des antiken Griechenland (6.-3. Jahrhundert v. Chr.)*. Cologne: Böhlau.
Ellis, S. (2021). 'Greek conceptualization of Persian traditions: gift-giving and friendship in the Persian empire'. *CQ* 71: 77–88.
Engels, D. (1978). *Alexander the Great and the Logistics of the Macedonian Army*. Berkeley, CA: University of California Press.
Erbse, H. (2010). 'Xenophon's Anabasis', in *Oxford Readings in Classical Studies: Xenophon*, edited by V. J. Grey, 476–501. Oxford: Oxford University Press.
Erdkamp, P. (1998). *Hunger and the Sword: Warfare and Food Supply in Roman Republican Wars (264–30 B.C.)*. Amsterdam: J. C. Gieben.
Erdkamp, P. (2005). *The Grain Market in the Roman Empire: A Social, Political and Economic Study*. Cambridge: Cambridge University Press.
Erdkamp, P. (2019). 'The Local Grain Market in the Roman World'. Accessed 20 March 2023: https://www.academia.edu/75211867/The_Local_Grain_Market_in_the_Roman_World
Fabre-Serris, J., and A. Keith, eds (2015). *Women and War in Antiquity*. Baltimore: Johns Hopkins University Press.
Fachard, S. (2012). *La defense du territoire: Étude de la* chora *érétrienne et de ses fortifications*. Gollion: Infolio.
Fachard, S., and E. M. Harris, eds (2021). *Destruction, Survival, and Recovery in Ancient Greece*. Cambridge: Cambridge University Press.
Fagan, G. G., and M. Trundle, eds (2010). *New Perspectives on Ancient Warfare*. Leiden: Brill.
Faraguna, M. (1998). 'Aspetti amministrativi e finanziari della monarchia macedone tra IV et III secolo a. C.'. *Athenaeum* 86: 349–95.
Faraguna, M. (2000). 'A proposito degli archivi nel mondo greco: terre e registrazioni fondiarie'. *Chiron* 30: 65–115.
Fawcett, P. (2016). '"When I squeeze you with *eisphorai*": taxes and tax policy in Classical Athens'. *Hesperia* 85.1: 153–99.
Fernández Nieto, F. J. (1989). 'Zur Problematik der Kriegskostenentschädigung in der Alten Welt (mit besonderer Berücksichtigung der griechischen Verhältnisse)', in *Symposion 1985: Vorträge zur griechischen und hellenistischen Rechtsgeschichte*, edited by G. Thür, 375–88. Cologne: Böhlau.

Feyel, C. (1999). 'Aperçu sur le financement de la guerre dans la cité classique', in Prost (1999), 209–21.
Fields, N. (2001). 'Et in Arcadia Ego'. *AHB* 15: 102–38.
Fields, N. (2006). *Ancient Greek Fortifications*. Oxford: Osprey Publishing.
Figueira, T. J. (1981). *Aegina: Society and Politics*. Salem, NH: Ayer.
Finley, M. I. (1963). *The Ancient Greeks*. London: Chatto & Windus.
Finley, M. I. (1965). 'Classical Greece', in *Second International Conference of Economic History, Aix-en-Provence, 1962: Trade and Politics in the Ancient World*, 12–35. Paris: Mouton.
Finley, M. I. (1970a). 'Aristotle and Economic Analysis'. *Past & Present* 47: 3–25.
Finley, M. I. (1970b). Review of B. A. van Groningen and A. Wartelle, *Aristote,* Économique (1968). *CR* 20: 315–19.
Finley, M. I. (1973). *The Ancient Economy.* Berkeley, CA: University of California Press.
Finley, M. I. (1975). *The Ancient Greeks.* Revised edn. Harmondsworth: Penguin.
Finley, M. I. (1985). *Ancient History: Evidence and Models*. London: Chatto & Windus.
Finley, M. I. (1987). *The Use and Abuse of History*. Revised edn. New York: Penguin Books.
Finley, M. I. (1999). *The Ancient Economy*. Updated edn. Berkeley, CA: University of California Press.
Finley, M. I. (2008). 'The Fifth Century Athenian Empire: A Balance Sheet', in *The Athenian Empire*, edited by P. Low, 14–40. Edinburgh: Edinburgh University Press.
Fischer-Bovet, C. (2013). 'Egyptian warriors: the *machimoi* of Herodotus and the Ptolemaic army'. *CQ* 63: 209–36.
Fischer-Hansen, T., T. H. Nielsen and C. Ampolo (2004). 'Italia and Kampania', in Hansen and Nielsen (2004), 249–320.
Flament, C. (2007). *Une économie monétarisée: Athenes a l'époque Classique (440–338).* Leuven: Peeters.
Flower, M. (1994). *Theopompus of Chios: history and rhetoric in the fourth century B.C.* Oxford: Clarendon Press.
Foldvari, P., and B. van Leeuwen (2015). 'Market Performance in Early Economies: Concepts and empirics, with an application to Babylon', in Van der Spek, Van Leeuwen and Van Zanden (2015a), 19–44
Folmer, M. (2022). *Elephantine Revisited: New Insights into the Judean Community and its Neighbors*. University Park, PA: Penn State University Press.
Ford, A. (2011). *Aristotle as Poet: The Song for Hermias and Its Contexts*. Oxford: Oxford University Press.
Forsdyke, S. (2012). *Slaves Tell Tales And Other Episodes in the Politics of Popular Culture in Ancient Greece.* Princeton, NJ: Princeton University Press.
Forster, R. S. (1927). *Isaeus*. Cambridge, MA: Harvard University Press.
Foxhall, L. (1993). 'Farming and fighting in early Greece', in Rich and Shipley (1993), 134–45.
France, J. (2006). 'Logistics and the Second Crusade', in Pryor (2006a), 77–93.
Frederiksen, R. (2011). *Greek City Walls of the Archaic Period, 900–480 BC*. Oxford: Oxford University Press.
Freitag, K. (2009). 'Achaea and the Peloponnese in the Late Fifth-Early Fourth Centuries', in *The Politics of Ethnicity and the Crisis of the Peloponnesian League*, edited by P. Funke and N. Luraghi, 47–102. Washington, DC: Center for Hellenic Studies.
French, A. (1991). 'Economic Conditions in Fourth Century Athens'. *G&R* 38: 24–40.
Futo Kennedy, R. (2015). 'Elite Citizen Women and the Origins of the *Hetaira* in Classical Athens'. *Helios* 42.1: 61–79.
Gabrielsen, V. (1985). 'The *naukrariai* and the Athenian navy'. *C&M* 36: 21–51.
Gabrielsen, V. (1994). *Financing the Athenian Fleet: Public Taxation and Social Relations.* Baltimore: Johns Hopkins University Press.

Gabrielsen, V. (2001). 'Economic activity, maritime trade, and piracy in the Hellenistic Aegean'. *Revue des Études Anciennes* 103: 209–40.

Gabrielsen, V. (2007). 'Warfare and the state', in Sabin, Van Wees and Whitby (2007), 248–72.

Gabrielsen, V. (2013). 'Warfare, statehood and piracy in the Greek world', in *Seeraub Im Mittelmeerraum*, edited by N. Jaspert and S. Kolditz, 133–53. Paderborn: Ferdinand Schöningh.

Gabrielsen, V. (2017). 'Financial, human, material and economic resources required to build and operate navies in Classical Greece', in *The Sea in History – The Ancient World*, edited by P. de Souza, P. Arnaud and C. Buchet, 426–42. Woodbridge: Boydell Press.

Gaca, K. L. (2010). 'The Andrapodizing of War Captives in Greek Historical Memory'. *TAPA* 140.1: 117–61.

Gallant, T. W. (1991). *Risk and Survival in Ancient Greece: Reconstructing the Rural Domestic Economy.* Stanford, CA: Stanford University Press.

Gallo, L. (2015). 'The Black Sea Area in Xenophon's Anabasis', in *The Danubian Lands between the Black, Aegean and Adriatic Seas (7th Century BC–10th Century AD)*, edited by G. R. Tsetskhladze, A. Avram and J. Hargrave, 49–52. Oxford: Archaeopress.

Garfinkel, M. R., and S. Skaperdas, eds (2007). 'Economics of Conflict: An Overview', in *Handbook of Defense Economics* II, edited by T. Sandler and K. Hartley, 649–709. Amsterdam: Elsevier.

Garrison, M. B., and W. F. M. Henkelman, eds (2023). *The Persian World and Beyond: Achaemenid and Arsacid Studies in honour of Bruno Jacobs.* Münster: Zaphon.

Garlan, Y. (1974). *Recherches de Poliorcétique Grecque*. Athens: École française d'Athènes.

Garlan, Y. (1977). 'La partage entre alliés des dépenses et des profits de guerre', in *Armées et Fiscalité dans le Monde Antique*, 149–64. Paris: Éditions du CNRS.

Garlan, Y. (1989). *Guerre et Économie en Grèce Ancienne.* Paris: La Découverte.

Garnsey, P. (1988). *Famine and Food Supply in the Graeco-Roman World: Responses to Risk and Crisis*. Cambridge: Cambridge University Press.

Garnsey, P., T. Gallant and D. Rathbone (1984). 'Thessaly and the Grain Supply of Rome during the Second Century BC'. *JRS* 74: 30–44

Gauthier, P. (1979). 'ΕΞΑΓΩΓΗ ΣΙΤΟΥ: Samothrace, Hippomédon et les Lagides'. *Historia* 28: 76–89.

Gauthier, P. (1987). 'Nouvelles récoltes et grain nouveau: à propos d'une inscription de Gazôros'. *BCH* 111: 413–18.

Glotz, G. (1931). *Histoire grecque,* II. Paris: Presses universitaires de France.

Goldman, M. L. (2015). 'Associating the *aulêtris*: flute girls and prostitutes in the Classical Greek symposium'. *Helios* 42.1: 29–60.

Gômez-Castro, D. (2018). 'Ancient Greek Mercenaries: Facts, Theories, and New Perspectives'. *War and Society* 38: 2–18.

Gomme, A. W. (1933). 'A Forgotten Factor of Greek Naval Strategy'. *JHS* 53: 16–24.

Gomme, A. W. (1945). *A Historical Commentary on Thucydides* I. Oxford: Clarendon Press.

Gomme, A. W. (1950). *A Historical Commentary on Thucydides* I. Oxford: Clarendon Press.

Gomme, A. W. (1956). *A Historical Commentary on Thucydides* II. Oxford: Oxford University Press.

Gomme, A. W. (1974). *A Historical Commentary on Thucydides* III. Oxford: Oxford University Press.

Gomme, A. W. (1962). 'The Old Oligarch', in *More Essays in Greek History and Literature*, edited by D. A. Campbell, 38–69. Oxford: Basil Blackwell.

González Almenara G. (2005). 'El precio de la mujer: la mujer como botín de guerra en la obra de Jenofonte'. *Fortunatae* 16: 73–80.

Goody, J. (2006). *The Theft of History*. Cambridge: Cambridge University Press.

Gorman, R. J., and V. B. Gorman (2014). *Corrupting Luxury in Ancient Greek Literature*. Michigan: University of Michigan Press.
Graeber, D. (2014). *Debt: The First 5000 Years*. 2nd edn. London: Melville House.
Graham, A. J. (1992). 'Thucydides 7.13.2 and the Crews of Athenian Triremes'. *TAPA* 122: 257–70.
Graham, A. J. (1998). 'Thucydides 7.13.2 and the Crews of Athenian Triremes: An Addendum'. *TAPA* 128: 89–114.
Grainger, J. D. (1999). *The League of the Aitolians*. Leiden: Brill.
Grainger, J. D. (2000). *Aitolian prosopographical studies*. Leiden: Brill.
Grandjean, Y. (2011). *Le rempart de Thasos*. Athens: École française d'Athènes.
Grayson, A. K. (1991). 'Assyria: Sennacherib and Esarhaddon', in *CAH* III^2 2.103–41.
Green, P. (2006). *Diodorus Siculus, Books 11 – 12.37.1. Greek history 480–431 BC: The alternative version*. Austin, TX: University of Texas Press.
Grenfell, B. P., and A. Hunt (1906). *The Hibeh Papyri I*. London: Egypt Exploration Fund.
Griffith, G. T. (1935). *The Mercenaries of the Hellenistic World*. Cambridge: Cambridge University Press.
Griffith, G. T. (1979). *A History of Macedonia* II. Oxford: Clarendon Press.
Grigoropoulos, D. (2016). 'The Piraeus from 86 BC to Late Antiquity: continuity and change in the landscape, function and economy of the port of Roman Athens'. *ABSA* 111.1: 239–68.
Gruen, E. S. (1984). *The Hellenistic world and the coming of Rome*, I–II. Berkeley, CA: University of California Press.
Grundy, G. B. (1911). *Thucydides and the History of his Age*. London: J. Murray.
Haas, C. (1985). 'Athenian Naval Power Before Themistocles'. *Historia* 34: 29–46.
Hale, J. (2009). *Lords of the Sea: The Epic Story of the Athenian Navy and the Birth of Democracy*. London: Gibson Square.
Hamel, D. (1996). *Athenian* Strategoi*: The Extent and Exercise of Authority in the Military Sphere, 501/0–322/1*. Diss. Yale.
Hamilton, C. D. (1979). *Sparta's Bitter Victories*. Ithaca, NY: Cornell University Press.
Hammond, N. G. L. (1967). 'The Origins and Nature of the Athenian Alliance of 478/7 BC'. *JHS* 86: 41–61.
Hammond, N. G. L. (1983). 'Army transport in the fifth and fourth centuries'. *GRBS* 24.1: 27–31.
Hansen, M. H. (1991). *The Athenian Democracy in the Age of Demosthenes: Structure, Principles and Ideology* (trans. J. A. Crook). Oxford: Blackwell.
Hansen, M. H. (2004). 'Introduction', in Hansen and Nielsen (2004), 3–153.
Hansen, M. H. (2006a). *Studies in the Population of Aegina, Athens and Eretria*. Copenhagen: Det Kongelinge Danske Videnskabernes Selslab.
Hansen, M. H. (2006b). *The Shotgun Method: The Demography of the Ancient Greek City-State Culture*. Columbia, MO: University of Missouri Press.
Hansen, M. H., and T. H. Nielsen, eds (2004). *An Inventory of Archaic and Classical Greek Poleis*. Oxford: Oxford University Press.
Hanson, V. D. (1983). *Warfare and Agriculture in Classical Greece*. Pisa: Giardini.
Hanson, V. D. (1991). 'The Ideology of Hoplite Battle, Ancient and Modern', in *Hoplites: The Classical Greek Battle Experience*, edited by V. D. Hanson, 3–11. Abingdon: Routledge.
Hanson, V. D. (1995). *The Other Greeks: The Family Farm and the Agrarian Roots of Western Civilization*. New York: Free Press.
Hanson, V. D. (1998). *Warfare and Agriculture in Classical Greece*. Revised edn. Berkeley, CA: University of California Press.
Hanson, V. D. (1999). *The Wars of the Ancient Greeks*. London: Cassell.
Harding, P. (1995). 'Athenian foreign policy in the fourth century'. *Klio* 77: 105–25.
Harris, E. M. (2002). 'Workshop, Household and Marketplace: The Nature of Technical Specialization in Classical Athens and Its Influence on Economy and Society', in Cartledge, Cohen and Foxhall (2002), 67–99.

Harris, E. M. (2016). 'The Legal Foundations of Economic Growth', in Harris, Lewis and Woolmer (2016), 116–46.
Harris, E. M. (2022). 'Law and economic growth in ancient Athens: review-article of F. Carugati, *Creating a Constitution: Law, Democracy, and Growth in Ancient Athens*'. *Polis* 39: 203–12.
Harris, E. M., and D. M. Lewis (2016). 'Introduction: Markets in Classical and Hellenistic Greece', in Harris, Lewis and Woolmer (2016), 1–38.
Harris, E. M., D. M. Lewis and M. W. Woolmer, eds (2016). *The Ancient Greek Economy: Markets, Households and City-States*. Cambridge: Cambridge University Press.
Harris, W. V. (1971). *Rome in Etruria and Umbria*. Oxford: Clarendon Press.
Harvey, P. (1986). 'New harvests reappear: the impact of war on agriculture'. *Athenaeum* 64: 205–18.
Hastings, M. (1979). *Bomber Command*. London: M. Joseph.
Heckel, W., F. S. Naiden, E. E. Garvin and J. Vanderspoel, eds (2021). *A Companion to Greek Warfare*. Hoboken, NJ: Wiley & Sons.
Henkelman, W. F. M. (2002). 'Exit der Posaunenbläser: on lance-guards and lance-bearers in the Persepolis Fortification archive'. *ARTA* 2002.007.
Henkelman, W. F. M. (2010). 'Consumed before the King', in *Der Achämenidenhof*, edited by B. Jacobs and R. Rollinger, eds, 667–776. Wiesbaden: Harrassowitz.
Henkelman, W. F. M. (2011). 'Parnakka's feat: *šip* in Parsa and Elam', in *Elam and Persia*, edited by J. Álvarez-Mon and M. B. Garrison, 89–166. Winona Lake, IN: Eisenbrauns.
Henkelman, W. F. M. (2017). 'Imperial signature and imperial paradigm: Achaemenid administrative structure and system across and beyond the Iranian plateau', in *Administration in the Achaemenid Empire: Tracing the Imperial Signature*, edited by B. Jacobs, W. F. M. Henkelman and M. W. Stolper, 45–256. Wiesbaden: Harrassowitz.
Henkelman, W. F. M. (2018a). 'Precarious gifts: Achaemenid estates and domains in times of war and peace', in *Guerre et paix en monde iranien: Revisiter les lieux de rencontre*, edited by F. Jullien, 13–66. Paris: Association pour l'avancement des études iraniennes.
Henkelman, W. F. M. (2018b). 'Bactrians in Persepolis – Persians in Bactria', in *A Millennium of History: The Iron Age in Southern Central Asia (Second and First Millennia BC)*, edited by J. Lhuillier and N. Boroffka, 223–55. Berlin: Dietrich Reimer.
Henkelman, W. F. M. (2020). 'Nakhtḥor in Persepolis', in Tuplin and Ma (2020), 2.193–223.
Henkelman, W. F. M. (2021). 'Local administration: Persia', in Jacobs and Rollinger (2021), 881–904.
Henkelman, W. F. M. (2023). 'Irdumartiya and the chiliarchies: the contemporaneity of the Persepolis Fortification and Treasury archives and its implications', in Garrison and Henkelman (2023), 235–300.
Henry, M. M. (2012) 'Hetairai', in *Oxford Classical Dictionary*, edited by S. Hornblower and A. Spawforth. 4th edn. Oxford: Oxford University Press. Accessed 4 March 2024: https://oxfordre-com.ezproxy-prd.bodleian.ox.ac.uk/classics/view/10.1093/acrefore/9780199381135.001.0001/acrefore-9780199381135-e-3080/version/1
Herda, A. (2019). 'Copy and Paste? Miletos before and after the Persian Wars', in *Réconstruire les villes: Modes, motifs, et récits*, edited by E. Capet, C. Dogniez, M. Gorea, R. Koch Piettre, F. Massa and H. Rouillard-Bonraisin, 91–120. Turnhout: Brepols.
Herman, G. (1987). *Ritualized Friendship and the Greek City*. Cambridge: Cambridge University Press.
Hignett, C. (1952). *A History of the Athenian Constitution*. Oxford: Clarendon Press.
Hind, J. G. F. (1994). 'Mithridates', in *CAH* IX^2, 129–64.
Hirshleifer, J. (1991). 'The paradox of power'. *Economics and Politics* 3.3: 177–200.
Hodkinson, S. (2000). *Property and Wealth in Classical Sparta*. Swansea: Classical Press of Wales.
Hoepfner, W., and L. Lehmann, eds (2007). *Die griechische Agora*. Mainz: Philipp von Zabern.
Hoff, M. (1997). 'Laceratae Athenae: Sulla's siege of Athens in 87/6 B. C. and its aftermath', in *The Romanization of Athens*, edited by M. Hoff and S. I. Rotroff, 33–51. Oxford: Oxbow.

Holloway, R. (2007). 'The Kainon coinage', in *Liber amicorum Tony Hackens*, edited by G. Moucharte, 223–7. Louvain-la-Neuve: Association de Numismatique Professeur Marcel Hoc.
Holmes, B. (2007). 'The *Iliad*'s economy of pain'. *TAPA* 137: 45–84.
Holt, F. L. (2016). *The Treasures of Alexander the Great: How One Man's Wealth Shaped the World.* Oxford: Oxford University Press.
Hoover, O. D., W. Fischer-Bossert, D. S. VanHorn and B. R. Nelson (2012). *Handbook of Coins of Sicily (including Lipara): Civic, Royal, Siculo-Punic, and Romano-Sicilian Issues: Sixth to First Centuries BC.* Lancaster, PA: Classical Numismatic Group.
Hopkins, K. (1978). 'Economic Growth and Towns in Classical Antiquity', in *Towns and Societies*, edited by P. Abrams and E. A. Wrigley, 35–77. Cambridge: Cambridge University Press.
Hopkins, K. (1983). 'Models, Ships and Staples', in *Trade and Famine in Classical Antiquity*, edited by P. Garnsey and C. R. Whittaker, 84–109. Cambridge: Cambridge University Press.
Hopper, R. J. (1979). *Trade and Industry in Classical Greece.* London: Thames and Hudson.
Horden, P., and N. Purcell (2000). *The Corrupting Sea: A Study of Mediterranean History.* Oxford: Oxford University Press.
Hornblower, S. (1991). *A Commentary on Thucydides* I. Oxford: Clarendon Press.
Hornblower, S. (2008). *A Commentary on Thucydides* III. Oxford: Oxford University Press.
How, W. W., and J. Wells (1912). *A Commentary on Herodotus: With Introduction and Appendixes. in two Vol. II, Books V–IX.* Oxford: Clarendon Press.
Hülden, O. (2020). *Das griechische Befestigungswesen der archaischen Zeit: Entwicklungen – Formen – Funktionen.* Vienna: Holzhausen.
Humphreys, S. C. (1978). *Anthropology and the Greeks.* London: Routledge.
Hunger, H., and R. J. van der Spek (2006). 'An astronomical diary concerning Artaxerxes II (year 42 = 363/2): military operations in Babylonia'. *ARTA* 2006.002.
Hunt, P. (1998). *Slaves, Warfare, and Ideology in the Greek Historians.* Cambridge: Cambridge University Press.
Hunt, P. (2010). *War, Peace and Alliance in Demosthenes' Athens.* Cambridge: Cambridge University Press.
Hunter, L. W. (1927). *Aineiou Poliorketika (Aeneas on Siegecraft), 'revised, with some additions' by S. A. Handford.* Oxford: Clarendon Press. (=Hunter and Handford (1927))
Hyland, J. O. (2013). 'Vishtaspa *krny*: an Achaemenid military official in 4th-century Bactria'. *ARTA* 2013.002.
Hyland, J. O. (2014). 'The casualty figures in Darius' Bisitun inscription'. *JANEH* 1: 173–99.
Hyland, J. O. (2020). 'Aršāma, Egyptian trade and the Peloponnesian War', in Tuplin and Ma (2020), 3.249–59.
Hyland, J. O. (2022). 'Persia's Lycian workforce and the satrap of Sardis'. *ARTA* 2022.002.
Jacobs, B., and R. Rollinger, eds (2021). *A Companion to the Achaemenid Empire.* Hoboken, NJ: Wiley & Sons.
Jameson, M. H. (1960). 'A decree of Themistokles from Troizen'. *Hesperia* 29.2: 198–223.
Johnson, H. G. (1956). 'The transfer problem and exchange stability'. *Journal of Political Economy* 64.3: 212–25.
Jordan, B. (1972). *The Athenian Navy in the Classical Period: A Study of Athenian Naval Administration and Military Organization in the Fifth and Fourth Centuries B.C.* Berkeley, CA: University of California Press.
Jordan, B. (2000). 'The crews of Athenian triremes'. *L'Antiquité Classique* 69: 81–101.
Jordan, B. (2003). 'Slaves among the Frogs'. *L'Antiquité Classique* 72: 41–53.
Jursa, M. (2009). 'On aspects of taxation in Achaemenid Babylonia', in *Organisation des pouvoirs et contactes culturels dans les pays de l'empire achéménide*, edited by P. Briant and M. Chauveau, 237–70. Paris: De Boccard.

Jursa, M. (2011). 'Taxation and service obligations in Babylonia from Nebuchadnezzar to Darius and the evidence for Darius' tax-reform', in *Herodotus and the Persian Empire*, edited by R. Rollinger, B. Truschnegg and R. Bichler, 431–48. Wiesbaden: Harrassowitz.

Jursa, M., and J. Hackl (2010). *Aspects of the Economic History of Babylonia in the First Millennium BC*. Münster: Ugarit-Verlag.

Kagan, D. (1961). 'The economic origins of the Corinthain War'. *La Parola del Passato* 80: 321–41.

Kagan, D. (1995). *On the Origins of War and the Preservation of Peace*. New York: Anchor Books.

Kagan, D., and G. F. Viggiano (2013). 'The hoplite debate', in *Men of Bronze: Hoplite Warfare in Ancient Greece,* edited by D. Kagan and G. F. Viggiano, 1–56. Princeton, NJ: Princeton University Press.

Kallet-Marx, L. (1993). *Money, Expense, and Naval Power in Thucydides' History, 1–5.24*. Berkeley, CA: University of California Press.

Kallet-Marx, L. (1994). 'Money talks: rhetor, demos and resources', in *Ritual, Finance, Politics: Athenian Democratic Accounts presented to David Lewis,* edited by R. Osborne and S. Hornblower, 227–52. Oxford: Clarendon Press.

Kallet, L. (1999). 'The diseased body politic, Athenian public finance, and the massacre at Mykalessos (Thucydides 7.27–29)'. *AJPh* 120: 223–44.

Kallet, L. (2001). *Money and the Corrosion of Power in Thucydides: The Sicilian Expedition and its Aftermath.* Berkeley, CA: University of California Press.

Kallet, L., and J. H. Kroll (2020). *The Athenian Empire: Using Coins as Sources*. Oxford: Oxford University Press.

Kalliontzis, Y., and N. Papazarkadas (2019). 'The contributors to the refoundation of Thebes: a new epigraphic and historical analysis'. *ABSA* 114: 293–315.

Kapparis, K. A. (2011). 'The Terminology of Prostitution in the Ancient Greek World', in *Greek Prostitutes in the Ancient Mediterranean, 800 BC–200 CE*, edited by A. Glazebrook and M. M. Henry, 222–55. Madison, WI: The University of Wisconsin Press.

Kapparis, K. A. (2017). *Prostitution in the Ancient Greek World*. Berlin: De Gruyter.

Kay. P. (2014). *Rome's Economic Revolution*. Oxford: Oxford University Press.

Keaveney, A. (1982). *Sulla, the Last Republican*. London: Croom Helm.

Kehne, P. (2003). 'Staatsverträge III: 1000 ausgewählte Internationalverträge (Staatsverträge) der griechisch-römischen Antike'. *Der Neue Pauly* 16: 338–437.

Kehne, P. (2008). 'In republikanischen Staats- und Kriegsverträgen festgesetzte Kontributionen und Sachleistungen an den römischen Staat: Kriegsaufwandskosten, Logistikbeiträge, Kriegsentschädigungen, Tribute oder Strafen?', in Burrer & Müller (2008), 260–80.

Kellogg, D. L. (2013). *Marathon Fighters and Men of Maple: Ancient Acharnai.* Oxford: Oxford University Press.

Kennedy, G. A. (1959). 'The earliest rhetorical handbooks'. *AJPh* 80: 169–78.

Kestemont, G. (1983). 'Tyr et les Assyriens', in *Redt Tyrus / Sauvons Tyr: Histoire phénicienne / Fenicische geschiedenis*, edited by E. Gruebel, E. Lepiński and B. Servais-Soyez, 53–78. Leuven: Leuven University Press.

Kienast, D. (1996). 'Der Wagen des Ahuramazda und der Ausmarsch des Xerxes'. *Chiron* 26: 285–313.

Kirsten, E. (1964). 'Aegina'. *Der Kleine Pauly* 1:160. Stuttgart: A. Druckenmüller.

Kitchen, K. A., and P. J. N. Lawrence (2012). *Treaty, Law, and Covenant in the Ancient Near East,* I-III. Wiesbaden: Harrassowitz

Klinkott, H. (2016). '"Dem König Erde und Wasser bringen." Persisches Unterwerfungsritual oder herodoteisches Konstrukt?', in *Diwan: Studies in the History and Culture of the Ancient Near East and the Eastern Mediterranean*, edited by C. Binder, H. Börm and A. Luther, 133–82. Duisburg: Wellem.

Klinkott, H. (2022). 'Söldner, Siedler und Soldate? Zum Status con und Umgang mit multiethnischen Streitkräften im Achaimenidenreich', in Sänger and Scheuble-Reiter (2022), 257–87.

Klotz, D. (2015). 'Darius and the Sabaeans: ancient partners in Red Sea navigation'. *JNES* 74: 267–80.

Knoepfler, D. (2001). *Éretria: Fouilles et recherches XI. Décrets érétriens de proxénie et de citoyenneté*. Lausanne: Payot.

Kolbe, W. (1899). 'De Atheniensium re navali quaestiones selectae'. *Philologus* 29: 503–52.

Konijnendijk, R. (2023). *Between Miltiades and Moltke: Early German Studies in Greek Military History*. Leiden: Brill.

Kozuh, M., W. F. M. Henkelman and C. E. Jones, eds (2014). *Extraction and Control: Studies in Honor of Matthew W. Stolper*. Chicago: Oriental Institute.

Krasilnikoff, J. A. (1992). 'Aegean mercenaries in the fourth to second centruies BC: a study in payment, plunder and logistics of ancient Greek armies'. *Classica et Mediaevalia* 43: 23–36.

Kratz, R. G., and B. U. Schipper (2022). *Elephantine in Context: Studies on the History, Religion and Literature of the Judeans in Persian period Egypt*. Tübingen: Mohr Siebeck.

Krentz, P. (1982). *The Thirty at Athens*. Ithaca, NY: Cornell University Press.

Krentz, P. (1997). 'The strategic culture of Periclean Athens', in *Polis and Polemos: Essays on Politics, War, and History in Ancient Greece in Honor of Donald Kagan*, edited by C. D. Hamilton and P. Krentz, 55–72. Claremont, CA: Regina Books.

Krentz, P. (2000). 'Deception in Archaic and Classical Greek warfare', in Van Wees (2000), 167–200.

Krentz, P. (2002). 'Fighting by the rules: the invention of the hoplite *agon*'. *Hesperia* 71: 23–39.

Krentz, P. (2007). 'War', in *The Cambridge History of Greek and Roman Warfare, Vol. I: Greece, the Hellenistic World and the Rise of Rome*, edited by P. Sabin, H. van Wees and M. Whitby, 147–85. Cambridge: Cambridge University Press.

Kroll, J. H. (1977). 'An archive of the Athenian cavalry'. *Hesperia* 46.2: 83–140.

Kroll, J. H. (2011). 'The reminting of Athenian silver coinage, 353 B.C.'. *Hesperia* 80: 229–59.

Kromayer, J., and G. Veith (1928). *Heerwesen und Kriegführung der Griechen und Römer*. Munich: C.H. Beck.

Kuhrt, A. T. (2007). *The Persian Empire: A Corpus of Sources from the Achaemenid Period*. London: Routledge.

Lambert, S. D. (2000). 'The Erechtheum workers of "IG" 2^2 1654'. *ZPE* 132: 157–60.

Langton, J. (1998). 'The Historical Geography of European Peasantries, 1400–1800', in *The Peasantries of Europe from the 14th to the 18th Centuries*, edited by T. Scott, 372–400. London: Longman.

Larsen, J. A. O. (1940). 'The constitution and original purpose of the Delian League'. *Harvard Studies in Classical Philology* 51: 175–213.

Launaro, A. (2016). 'Finley and the Ancient Economy', in *M. I. Finley: An Ancient Historian and His Impact*, edited by D. Jew, R. Osborne and M. Scott, 227–49. Cambridge: Cambridge University Press.

Laurenti, R. (1968). *Studi sull'economico attribuito ad Aristotele*. Milan: Marzorati.

Lawall, M. L. (2016). 'Transport Amphoras and Market Practice', in Harris, Lewis and Woolmer (2016), 254–73.

Lawrence, A. W. (1979). *Greek Aims in Fortification*. Oxford: Clarendon Press.

Lazenby, J. F. (1989). 'Hoplite warfare', in *Warfare in the Ancient World*, edited by J. Hackett, 54–81. London: Sidgwick & Jackson.

Lazenby, J. F. (1994). 'Logistics in Classical Greek Warfare'. *War in History* 1: 3–18.

Lee, J. W. I. (2004). 'For there were many *hetairai* in the army: women in Xenophon's *Anabasis*'. *The Ancient World* 35.2: 145–65.

Lee, J. W. I. (2007). *A Greek Army on the March: Soldiers and Survival in Xenophon's* Anabasis. Cambridge: Cambridge University Press.

Lenfant, D. (2007). 'On Persian *tryphê* in Athenaeus', in Tuplin (2007), 51–66.
Lenfant, D. (2009). *Les Histoires perses de Dinon et d'Héraclide*. Paris: De Boccard.
Le Rider, G. (1993). 'Les resources financières de Sèleukos IV et le paiement de l'indemnité aux Romains', in *Essays in honour of Robert Carson and Kenneth Jenkins,* edited by M. Price, A. Burnett and R. Bland, 49–67. London: Spink.
Lewis, D. M. (1989). 'Persian gold in Greek international relations'. *REA* 91: 227–34.
Lewis, D. M. (2021). 'Labour specialization in the Athenian economy: occupational hazards', in *Skilled Labour and Professionalism in Ancient Greece and Rome,* edited by E. Stewart, E. M. Harris and D. M. Lewis, 129–74. Cambridge: Cambridge University Press.
Liers, H. (1895). *Das Kriegswesen der Alten, mit besonderer Berücksichtigung der Strategie*. Breslau: W. Koebner.
Lintott, A. (1982). *Violence, Civil Strife and Revolution in the Classical City 750–330 BC*. London: Croom Helm.
Littman, R. J. (1988). 'Greek Taxation', in *Civilizations of the Ancient Mediterranean. Vol. II: Greece and Rome*, edited by M. Grant and R. Kitzinger, 795–808. New York: Charles Scribner's Sons.
Llewellyn-Jones, L. (2021). *Persians: The Age of the Great Kings*. London: Wildfire.
Lloyd, A. B. (2007). 'Darius in Egypt: Suez and Hibis', in Tuplin (2007), 99–115.
Loman, P. (2004). 'No Woman No War: Women's Participation in Ancient Greek Warfare'. *G&R* 51.1: 34–54.
Loomis, W. T. (1995). 'Pay differentials and class warfare in Lysias' Against Theozotides: Two obols or two drachmas'. *ZPE* 107: 230–6.
Loomis, W. T. (1998). *Wages, Welfare Costs and Inflation in Classical Athens*. Ann Arbor, IL: University of Michigan Press.
Loraux, N. (1986). 'Thucydide et la sédition dans les mots'. *Quaderni di storia* 12: 95–134.
Lozachmeur, H. (2006). *La collection Clermont-Ganneau*. Paris: De Boccard.
Luckenbill, D. D. (1924). *The Annals of Sennacherib*. Chicago: University of Chicago Press.
Luraghi, N. (2006). 'Traders, Pirates, Warriors: The Proto-History of Greek Mercenary Soldiers in the Eastern Mediterranean'. *Phoenix* 60: 21–47
Luther, A. (2021). 'Der *karanos* Hystaspes (*wšt'sp krny*): eine Hypothese', in *Beiträge zur Geschichte und Kultur des alten Iran und benachbarter Gebiete*, edited by H. Klinott, A. Luther and J. Wiesehöfer, 111–36. Stuttgart: Steiner.
Lutz, H. F. (1928). 'An agreement between a Babylonian feudal lord and his retainer in the reign of Darius II'. *University of California Publications in Semitic Philology* 9.3: 269–77.
Lyttkens, C. H. (1994). 'A Predatory Democracy? An Essay on Taxation in Classical Athens'. *Explorations in Economic History* 31: 62–90.
Ma, J. (2000). 'The fighting *poleis* of the Hellenistic world', in Van Wees (2000), 337–76.
Ma, J. (2020). 'Aršāma the vampire', in Tuplin and Ma (2020), 3.189–208.
MacDonald, B. R. (1982). 'The Import of Attic Pottery to Corinth and the Question of Trade during the Peloponnesian War'. *JHS* 102: 113–23.
Mackil, E. (2015). 'The Greek *polis* and koinon', in *Fiscal Regimes and the Political Economy of Premodern States*, Scheidel, W. and Monson, A., eds, 469–91. Cambridge: Cambridge University Press.
Macve, R. H. (1985). 'Some glosses on Greek and Roman accounting', in *Crux: Essays Presented to G. E. M. de Ste. Croix on His 75th Birthday*, edited by P. Cartledge and F. D. Harvey, 233–64. Exeter: Imprint Academic.
Magie, D. (1950). *Roman Rule in Asia Minor* I–II. Princeton, NJ: Princeton University Press.
Magnetto, A. (1997). *Gli arbitrati interstatali greci: introduzione, testo critico, traduzione, commento e indici, II: dal 337 al 196 a.C.* Pisa: Scuola Normale Superiore di Pisa.
Maier, F. G. (1961). *Griechische Mauerbauinschriften*. Heidelberg: Quelle & Meyer.
Manfredi, L.-I. (1995). *Monete puniche: repertorio epigrafico e numismatico delle leggende puniche*. Roma: Libreria dello Stato.

Mann, M. (1986). *The Sources of Social Power*. Cambridge: Cambridge University Press.
Manning, J. G., and G. J. Oliver (2017). Review of Ober (2015a). *The Journal of Economic History* 77.2: 599–601.
Manning, S. (2021). *Armed Forces in the Teispid-Achaemenid Empire: Past Approaches, Future Prospects*. Stuttgart: Steiner.
Mantoux, É. (1946). *The Carthaginian Peace, or the Economic Consequences of Mr Keynes*. London: Oxford University Press.
Marcoe, G. E. (2000). *Phoenicians*. London: British Museum Press.
Marsden, E. W. (1969). *Greek and Roman Artillery: Historical Development*. Oxford: Clarendon Press.
Marsh, F. B. (1943). *Modern Problems in the Ancient World*. Austin, TX: University of Texas Press.
Martinez Morales, J. (2015). *Women and War in Classical Greece*. Diss. University of Liverpool.
Martinez Morales, J. (2019). 'Women on the walls? The role and impact of women in Classical Greek sieges', in *Brill's Companion to Sieges in the Ancient Mediterranean*, edited by J. Armstrong and M. Trundle, 150–68. Leiden: Brill.
Martinez Morales, J. (2021). 'Women, diversity, and war off the battlefield in Classical Greece', in *Brill's Companion to Greek Land Warfare Beyond the Phalanx*, edited by R. Konijnendijk, C. Kucewicz and M. Lloyd, 122–44. Leiden: Brill.
Matarese, C. (2021). *Deportationen im Perserreich in teispidisch-achaimenidischer Zeit*. Wiesbaden: Harrassowitz.
Matthaiou, A. (2009). 'Τρια Ἀττικά ψηφίσματα', in *Attika Epigraphika: Studies in Honour of Christian Habicht*, edited by A. A. Themos and N. Papazarkadas, 83–7. Athens: Hellenikes Epigraphike Hetaireia.
Mattingly, H. B. (1968). 'Athenian Finance in the Peloponnesian War'. *Bulletin de Correspondence Hellenique* 92: 450–85.
Mattingly, H. B. (1997). 'The date and purpose of the Ps. Xenophon *Constitution of the Athenians*'. *CQ* 47: 352–7.
McClure, L. (2006). 'Introduction', in *Prostitutes and Courtesans in the Ancient World*, edited by C. A. Faraone and L. McClure, 3–18. Madison, WI: The University of Wisconsin Press.
McInerney, J. (1999). *The Folds of Parnassos: Land and Ethnicity in Ancient Phokis*. Austin, TX: University of Texas Press.
Meadows, A. (2023). 'Coinage in imperial space: Pseudo-Aristotle *Oikonomia* and the place of monetary production', in Meadows and Bodzek (2023), 3–31.
Meadows, A., and Bodzek, J., eds (2023). *Coinage in Imperial Space: Coins in the Economy of The Achaemenid and Early Hellenistic World* (= *Phoenix* 76: 1-305). Toronto: Classical Association of Canada.
Meier, F. G. (1994). 'Cyprus and Phoenicia', in *CAH* VI^2, 297–336.
Meiggs, R. (1972). *The Athenian Empire*. Oxford: Clarendon Press.
Meiggs, R. (1982). *Trees and Timbers in the Ancient Mediterranean World*. Oxford: Clarendon Press.
Meiggs, R., and D. M. Lewis, eds (1969). *A Selection of Greek Historical Inscriptions to the End of the Fifth Century* BC. Oxford: Clarendon Press.
Meiggs, R., and D. M. Lewis, eds (1988). *A Selection of Greek Historical Inscriptions to the End of the Fifth Century* BC. Revised edn. Oxford: Clarendon Press.
Meikle, S. (1979). 'Aristotle and the Political Economy of the *Polis*'. *JHS* 99: 57–73.
Meister, K. (1967). *Die Sizelische Geschichte bei Diodor von den Anfängen bis zum Tod des Agathokles*. Diss. Munich.
Meißner, B. (2008). 'Reparationen in der klassischen griechischen Welt und in hellenistischer Zeit', in Burrer and Müller (2008), 246–59.
Menut, A. D. (1957). 'Maistre Nicole Oresme: le livre de yconomique d'Aristote'. *Transactions of the American Philosophical Society* 47: 783–853.

Meritt, B. D., H. T. Wade-Gery and M. F. McGregor, eds (1939–53). *The Athenian Tribute Lists.* 4 vols. Princeton, NJ: ASCSA.
Meyer, E. (1901). *Geschichte des Alterthums* III. Stuttgart: J.G. Cotta.
Migeotte, L. (1983). 'Souscriptions athéniennes de la période classique'. *Historia 32.2*: 129–48.
Migeotte, L. (1984). *L'emprunt public dans les cités grecques. Recueil des documents et analyse critique.* Québec and Paris: Le Sphinx/Les Belles Lettres.
Migeotte, L. (1992). *Les souscriptions publiques cans les cités grecques.* Quebec: Le Sphinx.
Migeotte, L. (2000). 'Les dépenses militaires des cités grecques: essai de typologie'. *Entretiens d'archéologie et d'histoire. Économie antique. La guerre dans les économies antiques,* St-Bertrand-de-Comminges, 145–76.
Migeotte, L. (2014). *Les finances des cités grecques: Aux périodes classique et hellénistique.* Paris: Les Belles Lettres.
Millett, P. (1993). 'Warfare, economy, and democracy in Classical Athens', in Rich and Shipley (1993), 177–96.
Millett, P. (2001). 'Productive to Some Purpose? The Problem of Ancient Economic Growth', in *Economies beyond Agriculture in the Classical World*, edited by D. J. Mattingly and J. Salmon, 17–48. London: Routledge.
Mitchell, S. (1996). 'Hoplite warfare in ancient Greece', in *Battle in Antiquity*, edited by A. Lloyd, 87–105. London: Duckworth/Classical Press of Wales.
Monson, A. (2015). 'Egyptian fiscal history'. *JEH* 8: 1–36.
Monson, A., and Scheidel, W., eds (2015). *Fiscal Regimes and the Political Economy of Premodern States.* Cambridge: Cambridge University Press.
Moreno, A. (2007). *Feeding the Democracy: The Athenian Grain Supply in the Fifth and Fourth Centuries BC.* Oxford: Oxford University Press.
Morris, I. (2004). 'Economic Growth in Ancient Greece'. *Journal of Institutional and Theoretical Economics* 160: 709–42.
Morris, I. (2007). 'Early Iron Age Greece', in Scheidel, Morris and Saller (2007), 211–41.
Morris, I. (2009). 'The greater Athenian state', in *The Dynamics of Ancient Empires*, edited by I. Morris and W. Scheidel, 99–177. Oxford: Oxford University Press.
Morris, I. (2013). *The Measure of Civilization: How Social Development Decides the Fate of Nations.* New edn. Princeton: Princeton University Press.
Morris, I. (2014). *War: what is it good for? The Role of Conflict in Civilisation, from Primates to Robots.* London: Profile Books.
Morris, S., and J. Papadopoulos, eds (2023). *Ancient Methone, 2003–2013: Excavations by Matthaios Bessios, Athena Athanassiadou, and Konstantinos Noulas.* Los Angeles: Cotsen Institute of Archaeology.
Morrison, J. S. (1984). '*Hyperesia* in Naval Contexts in the Fifth and Fourth centuries BC'. *JHS* 104: 48–59.
Morrison, J. S., J. F. Coates and N. B. Rankov (2000). *The Athenian Trireme: The History and Reconstruction of an Ancient Greek Warship.* 2nd edn. Cambridge: Cambridge University Press.
Morrison, J. S., and R. T. Williams (1968). *Greek Oared Ships 900–322 BC.* Cambridge: Cambridge University Press.
Morrison, R. J. (1992). 'Gulf War reparations, Iraq, OPEC, and the transfer problem'. *American Journal of Economics and Sociology* 51.4: 385–99.
Mosley, D. J. (1973). 'Crossing Greek Frontiers Under Arms'. *RIDA* 20: 161–9.
Mossé, C. (1973). *Athens in Decline 404–86 B.C.* (trans. J. Stewart). London: Routledge.
Müller, H. (2008). 'Zur Erschließung antiker Kriegskosten'. *MBAH* 26: 185–207.
Müller, H. (2009). 'Reparationszahlungen an Rom zur Zeit der römischen Republik'. *Tyche* 24: 77–95.
Murray, A. V. (2006). 'Money and Logistics in the Forces of the First Crusade: Coinage, Bullion, Service, and Supply', in Pryor (2006a), 209–28.

Myers, S. L., and Kulish, N. (2016). '"Broken System" Allows ISIS to Profit From Looted Antiquities'. *The New York Times* (9 Jan. 2016).
Mynott, J., ed. and trans. (2013). *Thucydides: The War of the Peloponnesians and the Athenians*. Cambridge: Cambridge University Press.
Nadali, D. (2020). 'Numbers matter: On the nature and function of counting in warfare in the Neo-Assyrian period', in *Societies at War*, edited by K. Ruffing, K. Dross-Krüpe, S. Fink and R. Rollinger, 21–37. Vienna: Austrian Academy of Sciences Press.
Nafziger, E. W. (2006). *Economic Development*. 4th edn. Cambridge: Cambridge University Press.
Natali, C. (1995). 'Oikonomia in Hellenistic Political Thought', in *Justice and Generosity: Studies in Hellenistic Social and Political Philosophy*, edited by A. Laks and M. Schofield, 95–128. Cambridge: Cambridge University Press.
Naveh, J. (1981). 'The Aramaic ostraka from Tell-Arad', in *Arad Inscriptions*, edited by Y. Aharoni, 153–76. Jerusalem: Israel Exploration Society.
Naveh, J., and S. Shaked (2012). *Aramaic Documents from Ancient Bactria*. London: Khalili Family Trust.
Nestor, C., ed. (2009). *War-Booty: A common European cultural heritage*. Stockholm: Livrustkammaren.
Nippel, W. (2023). Review of Carugati (2019). *Klio* 105.2: 703–5.
North, D. C. (1990). *Institutions, Institutional Change and Economic Performance*. New York, NY: Cambridge University Press.
North, D. C., and R. P. Thomas. (1973). *The Rise of the Western World: A New Economic History*. Cambridge: Cambridge University Press.
North, D. C., J. Wallis and B. Weingast. (2009). *Violence and Social Orders*. Cambridge: Cambridge University Press.
Oakley, S. P. (2005). *A commentary on Livy* III: *Book IX*. Oxford: Clarendon Press.
Ober, J. (1978). 'Views of sea power in the fourth-century Attic orators'. *AncW* 1: 119–30.
Ober, J. (1985). *Fortress Attica: Defense of the Athenian Land Frontier, 404–322 B.C.* Leiden: Brill.
Ober, J. (1994). 'Classical Greek times', in *The Laws of War: Constraints on Warfare in the Western World*, edited by M. Howard, G. J. Andreopoulos and M. R. Shulman, 12–26 and 227–30. New York: Vintage Books.
Ober, J. (2008). *Democracy and Knowledge: Innovation and Learning in Classical Athens*. Princeton, NJ: Princeton University Press.
Ober, J. (2011a). 'Wealthy Hellas'. *The Journal of Economic Asymmetries* 8: 1–38
Ober, J. (2011b). *Political Dissent in Democratic Athens*. Princeton, NJ: Princeton University Press.
Ober, J. (2015a). *The Rise and Fall of Classical Greece*. Princeton, NJ: Princeton University Press.
Ober, J. (2015b). 'Classical Athens', in *Fiscal Regimes and the Political Economy of Premodern States*, edited by A. Monson and W. Scheidel, 492–522. Cambridge: Cambridge University Press..
Ober, J. (2015c). 'Classical Athens', in Monson and Scheidel (2015), 492–522.
Ober, J. (2022). *The Greeks and the Rational*. Berkeley, CA: University of California Press.
O'Brien, S., and D. Boatright (2013). *Warfare and Society in the Ancient Eastern Mediterranean*. Oxford: Archeopress.
Occhino, F., K. Oosterlinck and E. G. White (2007). 'How occupied France financed its own exploitation in World War II'. *American Economic Review* 97.2: 295–9.
Occhino, F., K. Oosterlinck and E. G. White (2008), 'How much can the victor force the vanquished to pay? France under the Nazi boot'. *Journal of Economic History* 68.1: 1–45.
O'Connor, S. (2013). 'The Daily Grain Consumption of Classical Greek Sailors and Soldiers'. *Chiron* 43: 327–56.
O'Connor, S. (2015). 'Private Traders and the Food Supply of Classical Greek Armies'. *JAH* 3: 173–219.

O'Connor, S. (2016a). 'The Agoranomoi at Cotyora (Xen. *An.* 5.7.21–9): Cerasuntians or Cyreans?' *CQ* 66: 84–99.

O'Connor, S. (2016b). 'Logistics (Greek)', in *Conflict in Ancient Greece and Rome: The Definitive Political, Social, and Military Encyclopedia, Volume One*, edited by S. e. Phang, D. Kelly, P. Londey and I. G. Spence, 338–42. Santa Barbara, CA: ABC-CLIO.

O'Connor, S. (2021a). 'Logistics', in Heckel et al. (2021), 227–40.

O'Connor, S. (2021b). 'Sailors, Soldiers, and Classical Greek Markets: The Constraints on Opportunism'. *CP* 116: 515–36.

O'Connor, S. (2022). 'Why Markets? The Provisioning of Classical Greek Military Forces on the Move through Friendly, Allied, and Neutral Territory'. *Klio* 104: 487–516.

Ogilvie, R. M. (1965). *A Commentary on Livy, Books 1–5.* Oxford: Clarendon Press.

O'Halloran, B. (2019). *The Political Economy of Classical Athens: A Naval Perspective.* Leiden: Brill.

Oliver, G. J. (2007). *War, Food and Politics in Early Hellenistic Athens.* Oxford: Oxford University Press.

Olson, S.D. (2006). *Athenaeus: The Learned Banqueters* Books III.106e-V. Cambridge, MA: Loeb.

Oosterlinck, K. (2008). 'Reparations', in *The New Palgrave Dictionary of Economics*, edited by M. Vernengo, E. Perez Caldentey and B. J. Rosser Jr. London: Palgrave Macmillan.

Osborne, R. (1987). *Classical Landscape with Figures: the Ancient Greek City and its Countryside.* London: George Philip.

Osborne, R. (1996a). '*Classical landscape* revisited'. *Topoi* 6: 49–64.

Osborne, R. (1996b). 'Pots, trade and the archaic Greek economy'. *Antiquity* 70, 31–44.

Osborne, R. (1998). 'Early Greek colonisation? The nature of Greek settlement in the West', in *Archaic Greece: New Approaches and New Evidence,* edited by N. Fisher and H. van Wees, 251–69. London: Duckworth/Classical Press of Wales.

Osborne, R. (2000). *The Athenian Empire* (LACTOR 1). The London Association of Classical Teachers.

Osborne, R. (2004). *Greek History.* London: Routledge.

Osborne, R. (2007a). 'Tracing cultural revolution in classical Athens', in *Debating the Athenian Cultural Revolution: Art, Literature, Philosophy, and Politics 430–380 BC*, edited by R. Osborne, 1–26. Cambridge: Cambridge University Press.

Osborne, R. (2007b). 'Archaic Greece', in Scheidel, Morris and Saller (2007), 277–301.

Osborne, R. (2009). *Greece in the Making 1200–479 B.C.* 2nd edn. London: Routledge.

Osborne, R., and P. J. Rhodes, eds (2017). *Greek Historical Inscriptions, 478–404 BC*. 1st edn. Oxford: Oxford University Press.

Osborne, R. (2023). *Athens and Attica: The Oxford History of the Archaic Greek World, Vol. 2.* Oxford: Oxford University Press.

Otto, W. G. A. (1928). *Beiträge zur Seleukidengeschichte des 3. Jahrhunderts v. Chr.* Munich: Bayerische Akademie der Wissenschaften.

Pakkanen, J. (2006). 'The Erechtheion construction work inventory (IG 1^3 474) and the Dörpfeld Temple'. *American Journal of Archaeology* 110.2: 275–81.

Pakkanen, J. (2013). 'The economics of shipshed complexes, Zea: a case study', in Blackman and Rankov (2013), 55–75.

Panagou, T. (2010). 'Η σφράγιση των αρχαίων ελληνικών εμπορικών αμφορέων. Κέντρα παραγωγής και συνθετική αξιολόγιση. Diss. National and Capodistrian University of Athens.

Panagou, T. (2016). 'Patterns of Amphora Stamp Distribution: Tracking Down Export Tendencies', in Harris, Lewis and Woolmer (2016), 207–29.

Parigi, C. (2019). *Atene e il sacco di Silla: Evidenze archeologiche et topographiche fra l'86 e il 27 a.C.* Wiesbaden: Reichert.

Parke, H. W. (1933). *Greek Mercenary Soldiers.* Oxford: Clarendon Press.

Parker, G. (1996). *The Military Revolution: Military Innovation and the Rise of the West, 1500–1800.* 2nd edn. Cambridge: Cambridge University Press.
Parker, G. (2004). *The Army of Flanders and the Spanish Road: the Logistics of Spanish Victory and Defeat, 1567–1659.* 2nd ed. Cambridge: Cambridge University Press.
Péré-Noguès, S. (2000). *Mercenaires et mercenariat en Occident de la fin du Ve siècle au IIe siècle avant J.-C.* Diss. Toulouse II-Mirail
Persson, K. G. (2015). 'Market performance and welfare: Why price instability hurts', in Van der Spek, Van Leeuwen and Van Zanden (2015a), 68–80.
Piccirilli, L. (1973). *Gli arbitrati interstatali greci, I: Dalle origini al 338 a.C.* Pisa: Marlin.
Piketty, T. (2014). *Capital in the Twenty-First Century. Translated by Arthur Goldhammer.* Cambridge, MA: Harvard University Press, first published 2013.
Pleket, H. W. (2008). 'Epilogue', in *Feeding the Ancient Greek City*, edited by R. Alston and O. van Nijf, 181–96. Leuven: Peeters.
Polanyi, K. (1957). 'Aristotle Discovers the Economy', in *Trade and Market in the Early Empires: Economies in History and Theory*, edited by K. Polanyi, C. M. Arensberg and H. W. Pearson, 64–94. Glencoe, IL: Free Press.
Polanyi, K. (1968). *Primitive, Archaic and Modern Economies.* Garden City, NY: Anchor Books.
Porten, B., and A. Yardeni (1986–99). *Textbook of Aramaic Documents from Ancient Egypt* I–IV. Winona Lake, IN: Eisenbrauns.
Porten, B., and A. Yardeni (2014–23). *Textbook of Ostraca from Idumaea* I–V. Winona Lake, IN: Eisenbrauns (2014–16) and University Park, PA: Penn State University Press (2018–23).
Pretzler, M. (2007). 'Arcadia: Ethnicity and Politics in the Fifth and Fourth Centuries BCE', in *International Trade from Solon to Socrates*, edited by P. Bang and C. Tuplin, 147–74. Rahden: Verlag Marie Leidorf.
Price, J. J. (2004). *Thucydides and Internal War.* 2nd edn. Cambridge: Cambridge University Press.
Pritchard, D. M. (2012). 'Costing festivals and war: The spending priorities of the Athenian democracy'. *Historia* 61.1: 18–65.
Pritchard, D. M. (2013). *Sport, Democracy and War in Classical Athens.* Cambridge: Cambridge University Press.
Pritchard, D. M. (2014). 'The public payment of magistrates in fourth-century Athens'. *GRBS* 54: 1–16.
Pritchard, D. M. (2015a). 'Public finance and war in ancient Greece'. *Greece & Rome* 61: 48–59
Pritchard, D. M. (2015b). *Public Spending and Democracy in Classical Athens.* Austin, TX: University of Texas Press.
Pritchard, D. M. (2018). 'The Horsemen of Classical Athens: Some Considerations on Their Recruitment and Social Background'. *Athenaeum* 106.2: 405–19.
Pritchard, D. M. (2019). *Athenian Democracy at War.* Cambridge: Cambridge University Press.
Pritchett, W. K. (1971–91). *The Greek State at War* I-V. Berkeley, CA: University of California Press.
Pritchett, W. K. (1971). *Ancient Greek Military Practices, Part 1.* Berkeley, CA: University of California Press (=*The Greek State at War* I).
Pritchett, W. K. (1974). *The Greek State at War* II. Berkeley, CA: University of California Press.
Pritchett, W. K. (1991). *The Greek State at War* V. Berkeley, CA: University of California Press.
Prost, F., ed. (1999). *Armées et Sociétés de la Grèce Classique: Aspects Sociaux et Politiques de la Guerre aux Ve et IVe s. av. J.-C.* Paris: Errance.
Pryor, J. H. ed. (2006a). *Logistics of Warfare in the Age of the Crusades*, 275–92. Aldershot: Ashgate.
Pryor, J. H. (2006b). 'Digest', in Pryor (2006a), 275–92.
Psoma, S. (2001). *Olynthe et les Chalcidiens de Thrace: Études de numismatique et d'histoire.* Stuttgart: Steiner.

Psoma, S. (2015). 'Athenian owls and the royal Macedonian monopoly on timber'. *Mediterranean Historical Review* 30.1: 1–18.
Quinn, J. (2018). *In Search of the Phoenicians*. Princeton, NJ: Princeton University Press.
Raaflaub, K. (1979). 'Beute, Vergeltung, Freiheit? Zur Zielsetzung des Delisch-Attischen Seebundes'. *Chiron* 9: 1–22.
Raaflaub, K. A. (1998). 'A Historian's Headache: How to Read 'Homeric Society', in *Archaic Greece: New Approaches and New Evidence*, edited by N. Fisher and H. van Wees, 169–93. London: Duckworth.
Raaflaub, K. (2009). 'Learning from the enemy: Athenian and Persian "Instruments of Empire"', in *Interpreting the Athenian Empire,* edited by J. Ma, N. Papazarkadas and R. Parker, 89–124. London: Bristol Classical Press
Randall, Jr., R. H. (1953). 'The Erechtheum workmen'. *AJA* 57.3: 199–210.
Rankov, B. (2013). 'Piraeus', in Blackman and Rankov (2013), 420–88.
Rawlings, L. (2007). *The Ancient Greeks at War*. Manchester: Manchester University Press.
Reger, G. (1994). *Regionalism and Change in the Economy of Independent Delos, 314–167 B.C.* Berkeley, CA: University of California Press.
Reumann, J. H. P. (1957). *The use of* oikonomia *and related terms in Greek sources to about A.D. 100, as a background for patristic applications*. Diss. University of Pennsylvania.
Rhodes, P. J. (1972a). *The Athenian Boule*. Oxford: Clarendon Press.
Rhodes, P. J. (1972b). 'The Five Thousand in the Athenian revolutions of 411 BC'. *JHS* 92: 115–27.
Rhodes, P. J. A. (1981). *Commentary on the Aristotelian Athenaion Politeia*. Oxford: Oxford University Press.
Rhodes, P. J. (1993a). *A Commentary on the Aristotelian Athenaion Politeia.* Oxford: Clarendon Press.
Rhodes, P. J. (1993b). *The Athenian Empire: with Addenda.* Oxford: Oxford University Press.
Rhodes, P. J. (2006). *A History of the Classical Greek World.* Oxford: Blackwell.
Rhodes, P. J. (2012). 'The Alleged Failure of Athens in the Fourth Century'. *Electrum* 19: 111–29.
Rhodes, P. J. (2013). 'The Organization of Athenian Public Finance'. *G&R* 60: 203–31.
Rhodes, P. J., and Osborne, R., eds (2003). *Greek Historical Inscriptions: 404–323 BC*. Oxford: Oxford University Press.
Rich, J., and G. Shipley, eds (1993). *War and Society in the Greek World.* London: Routledge.
Roberts, J. T. (1980). 'The impeachment trials of the Corinthian War'. *Hermes* 108: 100–14.
Roberts, J. T. (2017). *The Plague of War: Athens, Sparta and the Struggle for Ancient Greece.* Oxford: Oxford University Press.
Roberts, M. (1956). *The Military Revolution 1560–1660.* Belfast: Boyd.
Rollinger, R. (2018). 'Between deportation and recruitment. Craftsmen and specialists from the west in Ancient Near Eastern empires (from Neo-Assyrian times through Alexander III)', in *Infrastructure and Distribution in Ancient Economies*, edited by B. Woytek, 425–44. Vienna: Austrian Academy of Sciences Press.
Romilly, J. (1947). *De Thucydide et l'imperialisme athénien: la pensée de l'hisorien at la genese de l'oeuvre*. Paris: Les Belles Lettres.
Roochnik, D. (1996). *Of Art and Wisdom: Plato's Understanding of Techne.* University Park, PN: Penn State Press.
Rostovtzeff, M. (1941). *The Social & Economic History of the Hellenistic World.* Oxford: Oxford University Press.
Roth, J. P. (1999). *The Logistics of the Roman Army at War (264 B.C. – A.D. 235).* Leiden: Brill.
Rotroff, S. (2015). Review of Acton (2014). *BMCR*. Accessed 3 March 2024: https://bmcr.brynmawr.edu/2015/2015.04.23/
Rousseau, J.-J. (1984). *A Discourse on Inequality. Translated by Maurice Cranston.* New York, NY: Penguin Books.

Roy, J. (1967). 'The Mercenaries of Cyrus'. *Historia* 16: 287–323.
Roy, J. (1999). 'The economies of Arkadia', in *Defining Ancient Arcadia*, edited by T. Nielsen and J. Roy, 320–81. Copenhagen: Munksgaard.
Runciman, W. G. (1998). 'Greek hoplites, warrior culture, and indirect bias'. *Journal of the Royal Anthropological Institute* 4.4: 731–51.
Rung, E. V. (2015). 'The language of Achaemenid imperial diplomacy towards the Greeks: the meaning of earth and water'. *Klio* 97: 503–15.
Rüstow, W., and H. Köchly (1852). *Geschichte des Griechischen Kriegswesens von der Ältesten Zeit bis auf Pyrrhos*. Aarau: Verlags-Comptoir.
Sabin, P., H. van Wees and M. Whitby, eds (2007). *The Cambridge History of Greek and Roman Warfare I: Greece, the Hellenistic World and the Rise of Rome*. Cambridge: Cambridge University Press.
Sage, M. M. (1996). *Warfare in Ancient Greece: A Sourcebook*. London: Routledge.
Sallares, R. (1991). *The Ecology of the Ancient Greek World*. London: Duckworth.
Saller, R. P. (2005). 'Framing the Debate Over Growth in the Ancient Economy', in *The Ancient Economy: Evidence and Models*, edited by I. Morris and J. G. Manning, 223–38. Stanford, CA: Stanford University Press.
Samons, L. J. (1993). 'Athenian finance and the treasury of Athena'. *Historia* 42: 129–38.
Samons, L. J. (2000). *Empire of the Owl: Athenian Imperial Finance*. Stuttgart: Steiner.
Sänger, P., and S. Scheuble-Reiter, eds (2022). *Söldner und Berufssoldaten in der griechischen Welt: Soziale und politische Gestaltungsräume*. Stuttgart: Steiner.
Sargent, R. (1927). 'The use of slaves by Athens in warfare (II)'. *Classical Philology* 22: 264–79.
Schachter, A. (1981–94). *Cults of Boiotia*. London: Institute of Classical Studies.
Schaps, D. (1982). 'The women of Greece in wartime'. *Classical Philology* 77.3: 193–213.
Scheidel, W. (2004). 'Demographic and Economic Development in the Ancient Mediterranean World'. *Journal of Institutional and Theoretical Economics* 160: 743–57.
Scheidel, W. (2005). 'Military Commitments and Political Bargaining in Classical Greece'. *Princeton/Stanford Working Papers in Classics*.
Scheidel, W. (2017). *The Great Leveler: Violence and the History of Inequality From the Stone Age to the Twenty-First Century*. Princeton, NJ: Princeton University Press.
Scheidel, W., I. Morris and R. Saller, eds (2007). *The Cambridge Economic History of the Greco-Roman World*. Cambridge: Cambridge University Press.
Scheidel, W., and S. von Reden, eds (2002). *The Ancient Economy*. Edinburgh: Edinburgh University Press.
Schmalz, G. C. R. (2009). *Augustan and Julio-Claudian Athens. A New Epigraphy and Prosopography*. Leiden: Brill.
Schmid, S. G. (1999). 'Decline or prosperity at Roman Eretria? Industry purple dye works, public buildings, and related material'. *JRA* 12: 273–93.
Schmid, S. G. (2000). 'Sullan Debris from Eritrea (Greece)'. *Rei cretariae fautorum acta* 36: 169–80.
Schmitt, H. H. (1969). *Die Verträge der griechisch-römischen Welt von 338 bis 200 v. Chr.* Munich: C. H. Beck.
Scott, J. C. (1998). *Seeing like a State: How Certain Schemes to Improve the Human Condition Have Failed*. New Haven: Yale University Press.
Seager, R. (1967). 'Thrasybulus, Conon and Athenian Imperialism'. *JHS* 87: 95–115.
Seager, R. (1994). 'The Corinthian War', in *CAH* VI^2, 97–119.
Sekunda, N. V. (1985). 'Achaemenid colonization in Lydia'. *REA* 87: 7–30.
Sekunda, N. V. (1988). 'Persian settlement in Hellespontine Phrygia', in *Achaemenid History III: Method and Theory*, edited by A. Kuhrt and H. Sancisi-Weerdenburg, 175–96. Leiden: NINO.

Sekunda, N. V. (1991). 'Achaemenid settlement in Caria, Lycia and Greater Phrygia', in *Achaemenid History VI. Asia Minor and Egypt: Old Cultures in a New Empire,* edited by H. Sancisi-Weerdenburg and A. Kuhrt, 83–143. Leiden: NINO.
Serrati, J. (2007). 'Warfare and the state', in Sabin, Van Wees and Whitby (2007), 461–97.
Shear, J. (2001). *Polis and Panathenaia: The History and Development of Athena's Festival.* Diss. University of Pennsylvania.
Shear, T. L., Jr. (1993). 'The Persian destruction of Athens: evidence from the agora deposits'. *Hesperia* 62: 383–482.
Shipley, G. (1987). *A History of Samos 800–166 BC.* Oxford: Clarendon Press.
Shipley, G. (1993). 'Introduction: the limits of war', in Rich and Shipley (1993), 1–24.
Shipley, G. (2017). 'Aineias Tacticus in his Intellectual Context', in *Brill's Companion to Aineias Tacticus,* edited by N. Barley and M. Pretzler, 49–67. Leiden: Brill.
Skyrms, B. (2001). 'The stag hunt', *Presidential Address, Pacific Division of the American Philosophical Association.*
Smith, H. S., and C. Martin (2009). 'Demotic papyri from the Sacred Animal Necropolis of North Saqqara', in *Organisation des pouvoirs et contacts culturels dans les pays de l'empire achéménide,* edited by P. Briant and M. Chauveau, 23–78. Paris: De Boccard.
Snodgrass, A. (2016). 'Thespiai and the fourth-century climax in Boiotia', in *Boiotia in the Fourth Century B.C.,* edited by S. D. Gartland, 9–31. Philadelphia, PA: University of Pennsylvania Press.
Sommerstein, A. (1998). *Ecclesiazusae.* Oxford: Oxford University Press.
Spence, I. G. (1993). *The Cavalry of Classical Greece.* Oxford: Clarendon Press.
Spruyt, H. (1994). *The Sovereign State and Its Competitors.* Princeton, NJ: Princeton University Press.
Stahl, H.-P. (2003). *Thucydides: Man's Place in History.* Swansea: The Classical Press of Wales.
Stanley, P. V. (1976). *Ancient Greek Market Regulations and Controls.* Diss. University of California, Berkeley.
Stolper, M. W. (1985). *Entrepreneurs and Empire.* Leiden: NINO.
Stolper, M. W. (1998). 'Inscribed in Egyptian', in *Studies in Persian History: Essays in memory of David M. Lewis,* edited by M. Brosius and A. Kuhrt, 133–43. Leiden: NINO.
Strassler, R. B. (2009). *The Landmark Xenophon's Hellenika.* New York: Anchor Books.
Strauss, B. S. (1986). *Athens After the Peloponnesian War: Class, Faction and Policy 403–386 BC.* London: Croom Helm.
Stroud, R. (1971). 'Theozotides and the Athenian orphans'. *Hesperia* 40: 280–301.
Stroud, R. (1998). 'The Athenian Grain-Tax Law of 374/3 B.C.' *Hesperia Suppl.* 29: 1–140.
Stylianou, P. J. (1998). *A Historical Commentary on Diodorus Siculus Book 15.* Oxford: Clarendon Press.
Sullo, P., and J. Wyatt (2013). 'War reparations', in *Oxford Public International Law.* Oxford: Oxford University Press. (Updated version (2014) in *Max Planck Encyclopedia of Public International Law.*)
Szaivert, W., and R. Wolters (2005). *Löhne, Preise, Werte: Quellen zur römischen Geldwirtschaft.* Darmstadt: WBG.
Szirmai, A. (2015). *Socio-Economic Development.* 2nd edn. Cambridge: Cambridge University Press.
Tänzer, K. (1912). *Das Verpflegungswesen der griechischen Heere bis auf Alexander d. Gr.* Jena: Frommann.
Taylor, M. C. (2002). 'Implicating the *Demos*: a reading of Thucydides on the rise of the Four Hundred'. *JHS* 122: 91–108.
Temin, P. (2001). 'A Market Economy in the Early Roman Empire'. *JRS* 91: 169–81.
Thompson, W. E. (1981). 'Athenian leadership: expertise or charisma', in *Classical Contributions: Studies in Honour of M.F. McGregor,* edited by G. S. Shrimpton and D. J. McCargar, 153–9. Locust Valley, NY: J.J. Augustin.

Thomsen, R. (1964). *Eisphora*. Copenhagen: Gyldendalske Bokhandel.
Thorne, J. A. (2001). 'Warfare and agriculture: the economic impact of devastation in Classical Greece'. *GRBS* 42: 225–53.
Tilly, C. (1990). *Coercion, Capital, and the European States, AD 990–1990*. Oxford: Blackwell.
Toalster, D. (2011). *Unzeitgemäße Feldherren: Der Hipparch als Prototyp des erfolgreichen Feldherrn in Xenophons Hellenika*. Gutenberg: Computus.
Todd, S. C. (2000). *Lysias, with Translation and Commentary*. Austin, TX: University of Texas Press.
Tracy, S. V. (2003). 'A Major Athenian Letter-Cutter of the Late 5th and Early 4th Centuries BC: The Cutter of *IG* II^2 17', in *Gestures: Essays in Ancient History, Literature, and Philosophy presented to Alan L. Boegehold*, edited by G. W. Bakewell and J. P. Sickinger, 351–63. Oxford: Oxbow.
Tréziny, H. (2001). 'Le prix des murailles', in *Techniques et sociétés en Méditerranée*, edited by J.-P. Brun and P. Jockey, 367–80. Paris: Maison méditerranéenne des sciences de l'homme.
Trundle, M. (2004). *Greek Mercenaries from the Late Archaic Period to Alexander*. London: Routledge.
Trundle, M. (2006). 'Money and the Great Man in the 4th Century', in *Ancient Tyranny*, edited by S. Lewis, 65–76. Edinburgh: Edinburgh University Press.
Trundle, M. (2010a). 'Coinage and the transformation of Greek warfare', in Fagan and Trundle (2010), 227–52.
Trundle, M. (2010b). 'Light Troops in Classical Athens', in *War, Democracy and Culture in Classical Athens*, edited by D. M. Pritchard, 139–60. Cambridge: Cambridge University Press.
Trundle, M. (2020). 'Wealth and the Logistics of Greek Warfare: Food, Pay, and Plunder', in *New Approaches to Greek and Roman Warfare*, edited by L. L. Brice, 17–27. Hoboken, NJ: Wiley.
Tsigarida, B. (2011). 'Chalcidice', in *Brill's Companion to Ancient Macedonia*, edited by R, Lane Fox, 137–58. Leiden: Brill.
Tsingarida, A., and D. Viviers, eds (2013). *Pottery Markets in the Ancient Greek World (8th–1st centuries B.C.* Brussels: CReA-Patrimoine.
Tuplin, C. J. (1987). 'Xenophon and the garrisons of the Achaemenid Empire'. *AMI* 20: 167–245.
Tuplin, C. J. (1991). 'Darius and the Suez Canal', in *Achaemenid History VI. Asia Minor and Egypt: Old Cultures in a New Empire*, edited by H. Sancisi-Weerdenburg and A. Kuhrt, 237–83. Leiden: NINO.
Tuplin, C. J. (1996). *Achaemenid Studies*. Stuttgart: Steiner.
Tuplin, C. J. (1997). 'Achaemenid arithmetic: numerical problems in Persian history'. *Topoi* Suppl. 1: 365–421.
Tuplin, C. J. (1999). 'On the track of the Ten Thousand'. *REA* 101: 331–6.
Tuplin, C. J., ed. (2007). *Persian Reponses: Political and Cultural Interaction with(in) the Achaemenid Empire*. Swansea: Classical Press of Wales.
Tuplin, C. J. (2014). 'From Arshama to Alexander: Reflections on Persian responses to attack', in *From Source to History: Studies on Ancient Near Eastern Worlds and Beyond*, edited by S. Gaspa, A. Greco, D. Morandi Bonacossi, S. Ponchia and R. Rollinger, 668–96. Münster: Ugarit-Verlag.
Tuplin, C. J. (2016). 'The Persian military establishment in western Anatolia: a context for Celaenae', in *Kelainai-Apameia Kibotos: une métropole achéménide, hellénistique et romaine*, edited by A. Ivantchik, L. Summerer and A. von Kienlin, 15–27. Bordeaux: Ausonius.
Tuplin, C. J. (2017). 'War and peace in Achaemenid imperial ideology'. *Electrum* 24: 31–54.
Tuplin, C. J. (2018). 'Xenophon, Isocrates and the Achaemenid Empire: history, pedagogy and the Persian solution to Greek problems', in *Xenophon and Isocrates: Political Affinities and Literary Interactions* (= *Trends in Classics* 10.1), edited by M. Tamiolaki, 13–55. Berlin: De Gruyter.
Tuplin, C. J. (2019). 'Paradise revisited', in *L'Orient est son jardin: hommage à Rémy Boucharlat*, edited by S. Gondet and E. Haerinck, 477–501. Leuven: Peeters.

Tuplin, C. J. (2020a). 'Sigillography and soldiers: cataloguing military activity on Achaemenid period seals', in *The Art of Empire in Achaemenid Persia,* edited by E. Dusinberre, M. Garrison and W. F. M. Henkelman, 329–459. Leiden: NINO/Leuven: Peeters.

Tuplin, C. J. (2020b). 'The Bodleian Letters: Commentary', in Tuplin and Ma (2020), 1.61–283.

Tuplin, C. J. (2020c). 'The military environment of Achaemenid Egypt', in Tuplin and Ma (2020), 3.291–328.

Tuplin, C. J. (2020d). 'Aršāma, prince and satrap', in Tuplin and Ma (2020), 3.3–72.

Tuplin, C. J. (2021). 'Royal p(a)laces: lexical reflections on Achaemenid residences', in *Achemenet: Vingt ans après,* edited by R. Boucharlat and D. Agut-Labordère, 403–14. Leuven: Peeters.

Tuplin, C. J. (2022). 'Mercenaries in the Greek world: a Persian perspective', in Sänger and Scheuble-Reiter (2022), 235–55.

Tuplin, C. J. (2023). 'A jewel in the crown: reflections on the place of *Cyropaedia* in Xenophon's *oeuvre*', in Garrison and Henkelman (2023), 449–85.

Tuplin, C. J. in press. 'Markets, mercenaries and the Achaemenid Empire', forthcoming in *Aegean Mercenaries,* edited by M. Trundle, T. Fuji, D. Gomez and L. L. Brice. Leiden: Brill.

Tuplin, C. J., and J. Ma, eds (2020). *Aršāma and his World: The Bodleian Letters in Context* I–III. Oxford: Oxford University Press.

Ussher, R. G. (1973). *Aristophanes: Ecclesiazusae*. Oxford: Clarendon Press.

Van der Spek, R. J. (2011). 'The "silverization' of the economy of the Achaemenid and Seleukid Empires and Early modern China', in Archibald, Davies and Gabrielsen (2011), 402–20.

Van der Spek, R. J. (2017). Review of Bresson 2016. *Journal of Economic History* 77: 601–04.

Van der Spek, R. J., B. van Leeuwen and J. L. van Zanden, eds (2015a). *A History of Market Performance: From Ancient Babylonia to the Modern World.* London: Routledge

Van der Spek, R. J., B. van Leeuwen and J. L. van Zanden (2015b). 'Markets from Ancient Babylonia to the Modern World: An Introduction', in Van der Spek, Van Leeuwen and Van Zanden (2015a), 1–16.

Van der Spek, R. J., B. van Leeuwen and J. L. van Zanden (2015c). 'Markets from Babylon to Belfast: Some concluding remarks', in Van der Spek, Van Leeuwen and Van Zanden (2015a), 529–44.

Van Groningen, B. A. (1933). *Aristote: Le second livre de l'Économique*. Leiden: A.W. Sijthoff,

Van Wees, H. (2004). *Greek Warfare: Myths and Realities*. London: Duckworth.

Van Wees, H. (2007). 'War and society', in Sabin, Van Wees and Whitby (2007), 273–99.

Van Wees, H. (2010). 'Those who sail are to receive a wage: naval warfare and finance in Archaic Eretria', in Fagan and Trundle (2010), 205–26.

Van Wees, H. (2013a). *Ships and Silver, Taxes and Tribute: A Fiscal History of Archaic Athens.* London: I.B. Tauris.

Van Wees, H. (2013b). 'Farmers and hoplites: models of historical development', in *Men of Bronze: Hoplite Warfare in Ancient Greece,* edited by D. Kagan and G. F. Viggiano, 222–55. Princeton, NJ: Princeton University Press.

Van Wees, H., ed. (2000). *War and Violence in the Greek World.* London: Duckworth/Classical Press of Wales.

Vassallo, S. (2011). 'Le battaglie di Himera alla luce degli scavi nella necropolis occidentale e alle fortificazioni. I luoghi, I protagonisti'. *Sicilia Antiqua* 7: 17–38.

Vassallo, S. (2016). 'Guerre et mort à Himère: les tombes de soldats grecs tués dans les batailles de 480 et 409 avant notre ère', in *Violences de guerre, violences de masses: une approche archéologique*, edited by J. Guilaine and J. Sémelin, 51–60. Paris: La Découverte,

Vaughn, P. (1991). 'The Identification and Retrieval of the Hoplite Battle-Dead', in *Hoplites: The Classical Greek Battle Experience*, edited by V. D. Hanson, 38–62. Abingdon: Routledge

Vial, C. (1984). *Délos Indépendante.* Athens: École Française d'Athènes.

Vidal-Naquet, P. (1968). 'The Black Hunter and the origin of the Athenian *ephebeia*'. *Proceedings of the Cambridge Philological Society* 14: 49–64.

Villaronga, L. (1973). *Las monedas hispano-cartaginesas*. Barcelona: Patrocinado por la Sección Numismático del Circulo Filatélico y Numismático.
Visonà, P. (1998). 'Carthaginian Coinage in Perspective'. *American Journal of Numismatics* 10: 1–27.
Vlassopoulos, K. (2016). Review of Ober (2015a). *BMCR*. Accessed 3 March 2024: https://bmcr.brynmawr.edu/2016/2016.03.04/
Vleeming, S. P. (1991). *The Gooseherds of Hou*. Leuven: Peeters.
Waerzeggers, C. (2006). 'The Carians of Borsippa'. *Iraq* 68: 1–22.
Walbank, F. W. (1979). *A Historical commentary on Polybius* III. Oxford: Clarendon Press.
Walcot, P. (1979). 'Cattle Raiding, Heroic Tradition, and Ritual: The Greek Evidence'. *History of Religions* 18.4: 326–51.
Wallinga, H. T. (1993). *Ships and Sea-Power Before the Great Persian War*. Leiden: Brill.
Warry, J. (1980). *Warfare in the Classical World*. London: Salamander Books.
Waters, M. (2014). *Ancient Persia: A Concise History of the Achaemenid Empire*. Cambridge: Cambridge University Press.
Waters, M. (2014b). 'Earth, water and friendship with the king: Argos and Persia in the mid-fifth century', in Kozuh, Henkelman and Jones (2014), 331–6.
Wheeler, E. L. (2007). 'Introduction', in *The Armies of Classical Greece*, edited by E. L. Wheeler, xi–lxiv. Aldershot: Ashgate.
Wheeler, E. L. (2011). 'Greece: Mad Hatters and March Hares', in *Recent Directions in the Military History of the Ancient World*, edited by L. L. Brice and J. T. Roberts, 53–104. Claremont, CA: Regina Books.
White, E. N. (2001). 'Making the French pay: The costs and consequences of the Napoleonic reparations'. *European Review of Economic History* 5: 337–65.
Whitehead, D. (1990). *Aineias the Tactician: How to Survive Under Siege*. Oxford: Clarendon Press.
Wiesehöfer, J. (2021a). 'Persian *paradeisoi*. Parts of an imperial landscape and gardens "full of trees and wild animals"', in *Palaeopersepolis: Environment, Landscape and Society in Ancient Fars*, edited by S. Balatti, H. Klinkott and J. Wiesehöfer, 79–94. Stuttgart: Steiner.
Wiesehöfer, J. (2021b). 'Deportations', in Jacobs and Rollinger (2021), 871–8.
Will, E. (1960). 'Chabrias et les finances de Tachôs'. *Revue des études anciennes* 62: 254–75.
Will, E. (1975). 'La territoire, la ville et la poliorcétique grecque'. *Revue Historique* 253.2: 297–318.
Will, E. (1979). *Histoire politique du monde Hellénistique* I. 2nd edn. Nancy: Presses Universitaires de Nancy.
Wilson, E., trans. (2023). *The Iliad* by Homer. New York: W. W. Norton & Company.
Winterling, A. (1991). 'Polisbegriff und Stasistheorie des Aeneas Tacticus. Zur Frage der Grenzen der griechischen Polisgesellschaften im 4. Jahrhundert v. Chr.'. *Historia* 40: 193–229.
Wintjes, J. (2010). '"Keep the women out of the camp!" Women and military institutions in the Classical world', in *A Companion to Women's Military History*, edited by B. Hacker and M. Vining, 15–59. Leiden: Brill.
Wormell, D. E. W. (1935). 'The Literary Tradition Concerning Hermias of Atarneus'. *Yale Classical Studies* 8: 57–92.
Wrenhaven, K. L. (2012). *Reconstructing the Slave: The Image of the Slave in Ancient Greece*. London: Bloomsbury.
Zoepffel, R. (2006). *Aristoteles: Oikonomika, schriften zu Hauswirthschaft und Finanzwesen*. Berlin: Akademie-Verlag.

INDEX LOCORUM

The letter *t* following an entry indicates a page with a table.

Biblical References

Greek and Latin Texts

Miscellaneous Inscriptions, Papyri, Tablets and Texts

GENERAL INDEX

www.ingramcontent.com/pod-product-compliance
Ingram Content Group UK Ltd.
Pitfield, Milton Keynes, MK11 3LW, UK
UKHW020249290926
15470UKWH00002B/821

9 781350 471788